To My Lovely Ma...
Becouse ...

INSIDE MUSIC 2005

INSIDE MUSIC 2005

THE INSIDER'S GUIDE TO THE INDUSTRY

Kevin Harris & Stephen Colegrave

EBURY PRESS

First published in Great Britain in 2004

10 9 8 7 6 5 4 3 2 1

First published by
Ebury Press
Random House, 20 Vauxhall Bridge Road, London SW1V 2SA

Random House Australia (Pty) Limited
20 Alfred Street, Milsons Point, Sydney, New South Wales 2061, Australia

Random House New Zealand Limited
18 Poland Road, Glenfield, Auckland 10, New Zealand

Random House South Africa (Pty) Limited
Endulini, 5A Jubilee Road, Parktown 2193, South Africa

The Random House Group Limited Reg. No. 954009

www.randomhouse.co.uk

A CIP catalogue record for this book is available from the British Library.

Cover Design by Dave Breen
Interior by seagulls

ISBN 0 09189 5391

Printed and bound in Great Britain by Mackays of Chatham plc

Papers used by Ebury Press are natural, recyclable products made from wood grown in sustainable forests.

ACKNOWLEDGEMENTS

We would like to thank all the interviewees: Muff Winwood, Lucian Grange, Eddie Pillar, Darcus Beese, Saul Galpen, Jon Fowler, Jazz Summers, Martin Deller, Tony English, Jay Kay, Jazzie B, Bobby Gillespie, Judge Jules, Sam O' Riorden, Wayne Hector, Charlise Rookwood, Woolfie, Guy Moot, Mark Richardson, Neil Ferris, Howie B, Sly and Robbie, Stephen Budd, Barry Dickins, Simon Moran, Jeremy Joseph, Alex Jones Donelly, Paul Rees, Rap Saunders, Dave Picconi, Steve Knott, Ian Dutt, Charlie Beuthin, Jodie Dalmeda, Phil Mount, Brad Lazarus and Jamie Caring

A big thank you to Remi Harris at AIM, Jamie Binns, AGR, Prue at ITB Manufacturing, Alchemy, Native Management, Sony Music and Kwami Kwaten, Colin Lester, Wayne Clark, Benjamin Moor, the team at Z Management, Bluey, Dick Leahy and Marilene, Azeez and Tungi

Special thanks to everyone at Longlost Brother Management and a Big Brother thank you to Kevin Simpson – the man in the background who makes it all happen

Our publishers, Jake Lingwood and Claire Kingston (how did you put up with us!) – thank you for your patience and guidance…

We would like to dedicate the book to everyone who has inspired us and helped us

From Stephen: To my Wife and inspiration, Hilary, for putting up with my obsession and of course my children Oliver, Rupert and Lucy.

From Kevin: To Cleo, my Love, my friend and my partner who walked this journey with me and together we did it

To my family (Elizabeth Mahon and Caroline, etc) and most importantly God for his guidance.

CONTENTS

PREFACE

The music business can drive you mad. There is too much manufactured crap and not enough people doing it for themselves. The best bits of this book are about people having a go, not sitting in offices expecting everything to be done for them.

2005 is a crucial time for music. It must decide whether it is going to have the courage of its convictions and rise above supermarket mediocrity and over-packaged material. The future is not about online, or digital, or mergers, or indies. It's about whether artists are going to be supported and encouraged to break boundaries and make music great again.

Whether you sit behind a desk, hang out in clubs, in a studio or on the stage, that's why you should be in the business and that's why you should read on …

INTRODUCTION

Inside Music is more than just another book on the music business. Its aim is to encourage you to look at the business through fresh eyes. It's our belief that success comes from having the right attitude, not encyclopaedic knowledge.

In writing this book, we have spoken to those people who have the courage, vision, passion and talent to make music inspiring and exciting. People who believe that the business is more than a balance sheet and who strive continually beyond the expected to make a difference.

We hope this book will give you simple but powerful insights and encourage you to push yourself further to break through the barriers of mediocrity and cynicism that hold so many back from creating the brilliance that the music business needs to hold its rightful place in our hearts.

WHY GO INSIDE THE MUSIC INDUSTRY?

It is fashionable to write off the music industry. Journalists like writing cynical articles about the rise in piracy or the death of the single. The big record companies don't exactly help as they seem, more than ever, to be putting size and profit before promoting originality and creativity.

The reality is different. The music business isn't about corporate agendas: it's really a collection of thousands of talented individuals who are defining popular culture for millions of people. It might have only been going in its current form for less than fifty years, but its impact reaches far beyond its physical size. For most of us music defines much of our life. Great songs can uniquely inspire us; they can instantly evoke events and relationships for us; and get under our skin in a way that even books and films will never do.

Our enthusiasm doesn't mean that we aren't critical. If we had our way we would get rid of the majority of executives in major labels, especially the middle ranks, and we'd make do with far fewer lawyers, accountants, pluggers, managers and so-called celebrity DJs. Similarly we would like lots more white labels, indies, good artists, live venues and real record shops – but nothing is perfect.

As a key element in popular culture, music is continually evolving and refuses to stand still. This book can only give you a snapshot of what's happening. Some aspects are improving, others are getting worse.

Yes, it's true that downloading and file sharing is damaging CD sales, so all those trendy forecasters were right: the Internet is becoming very important for music. Still they weren't completely right – who would have thought that sales of vinyl would be booming and, instead of being tied to their computers, more people were getting out there and experiencing live music? Don't expect the music business to behave predictably. It's far too creative to do any such thing.

WHY WE WROTE THIS BOOK

It's simple. We read all the other books about music and thought they were missing the point. Too many are either out of date or too academic and superficial.

It's not meant to be an encyclopaedia or a dictionary of music. We don't want it to appeal to anoraks. The whole point is to give you a flavour of what it's really like to be in the thick of the music world and to give you some useful tips and contact information.

We've had lots of support from people involved in all aspects of music. The interviews conducted especially for this book are a far better barometer of the business than any amount of statistical analysis. Hopefully, you will also get a sense that many of the interviews were lots of fun.

Between us we've done many different things in the music business – many of them badly enough for us to have learned something from our mistakes. Our involvement stretches from performing to recording, songwriting, A&R, plugging, marketing, managing, promoting, releasing a compilation, DJ-ing and writing about it. Between us we span punk to hip hop, but most of all we still get a rush when we hear a new artist or song, and that's what music is all about.

The format of the book is a mixture of comment, analysis, interviews, tips and listings. In each section we have put together an overview which represents our own personal views. This is then followed by interviews selected to show contrasting views and positions. The tips are based on personal experience from ourselves and the people we trust. We hope that reading all the sections will give you an all-round view of how the music world works and is changing.

Our intention is to update the book every year: we are already starting on the next edition.

WHAT WE REALLY THINK ABOUT THE BUSINESS

There are many different music businesses and scenes. All work to different visions, rules, levels of passion and artistic integrity. They often end up in the same record shop and conform to the same legal and compliance frameworks, but their originators and their audiences can be completely different. Overall though, **we feel the business has often fallen into the trap of believing its own PR and has tried too hard to turn a creative business into a bland corporate mass**. This has nothing to do with music and everything to do with egos.

In this book we are keen to differentiate between artists and entertainers, just as we see clear differences between those who are part of the corporate machine and those who are independent and take advantage of the new opportunities to do it for themselves.

INTRODUCTION

It's not easy to be an artist in 2005. The major labels are not particularly interested in discovering and breaking you, unless you have developed your act and material to a level where they just have to push a button to send out your first three hit singles. Then when they finally agree to give you a deal, they will want to repackage you so you look more like another band that's been successful for a rival label. Then unless you are an instant success, they won't want to take up their option for a second album.

Even if you are a success, it's hard to keep your integrity and independence once you are a part of the major label treadmill. **The irony of being an artist in 2005 is that you need more artistic integrity and business smartness than ever before.** Traditionally these two things were meant to conflict, but now one cannot be protected without the other. Never is this more important than when you start out. This book will give you tips about how to work the business and the music scene to get your artistic break. More importantly, if you understand the legal side and other business procedures, you are less likely to fail at the beginning of your brilliant career.

Of course the business itself is undergoing huge structural change. Supermarkets have managed to do what defeated the Monopolies and Mergers Commission, by reducing CDs by four or five pounds. It may seem great for the consumer, but it's not so great for anyone who wants to buy or sell any music outside the Top 40 charts. *Top of the Pops'* audience has declined from 20 million to about 5 million and is likely to be consigned to a digital channel. As if that were not enough, 100 million people around the world are registered with legal and illegal download sites.

All this change may be giving many well-fed record executives sleepless nights but it is inevitable, because the music business is an important part of popular culture and as such is more exposed to change than any other business.

UNDERSTANDING AND TAKING ADVANTAGE OF THE CHANGING BUSINESS

Whenever change happens, opportunities are created. Many of those to whom we have talked welcome change and are making it work for them. Take

Channel U. A couple of guys spotted that the growing British urban music scene was fed up with the over-packaged American urban product being pumped out by the existing media. This gave them the idea of setting up a digital TV station that encouraged kids on the street to send in their videos and text to screen their comments. Nobody was more surprised than they were when, within three months of their launch in February 2003, they were reaching audiences of up to one million. Not bad for a small independent outfit.

The biggest change in the business is the opportunity to do more for yourself, whether it's to set up your own magazine, radio or TV station, or produce and sell your own records. Of course technology has played its part in this, but it's mainly a question of having the balls to go out there and do it.

Make sure you read the interview with Eddie Pillar from Acid Jazz Records. He didn't need the latest technical equipment, he just chanced his arm, had a thousand records made, sold them and did the same again and again, until he built up a successful indie label. And he's not alone. AIM (Association of Independent Music) represents over 450 indie labels, many set up in the last few years in just the same way.

It's just as well that there are enough people out there who have the guts to do it for themselves, because otherwise this would be an incredibly boring book. If the business was left up to the major labels – as much as we respect some of their artists – we might as well give up on music and stay at home and play computer games.

If it wasn't for the indies and enterprising managers and producers, many of the best artists of the future would never get the breaks they deserve and we'd still be consuming over-packaged and marketed media.

IT'S STILL ABOUT GETTING A HIT

As always 2004 has seen relatively new acts come through to become part of the public's consciousness. The Darkness and The Snow Patrol are two recent examples. As this book shows, this isn't just a lottery. The efforts of a team of smart and creative people, from lawyers to managers, producers, pluggers, A&R, marketing executives, publishers and songwriters, all have to be harnessed and an artist's ability to achieve hits consistently will determine whether they are successful and are given the money and power to develop and build their careers.

We have purposely talked to people who have a good track record for being responsible for hits, whether they be Wayne Hector who has been responsible for writing Westlife's biggest hits or Robbie and Sly who produced Bob Marley's legendary hits in Studio One. What they have in common is an instinct for what makes a hit, even if it's difficult to define, and the determination to succeed.

EVERYTHING CHANGES AND NOTHING CHANGES

No business changes as fast as the music business. New artists continually burst on the scene. Labels merge and change management, and people shift. In many ways the last two years have seen the biggest change, from the invention of the iPod, to a supermarket price war, the decline in dance music, the technology available to 'do it yourself' and the increasing dominance of Clear Channel in the live area.

However, some things don't change, such as the ability to get a hit. It doesn't matter whether music is delivered online, in a supermarket, on digital radio or even by telepathy, it's still only relevant if it inspires and means something to its audience. Making money from these different access points is just a logistical, business problem, it's of no concern to real people who just want to listen to as much good music as possible.

The real test of the health of the music business is a personal one. Are you excited about today's acts? **When did you last hear a song that you found yourself singing when you were alone?**

Of course something has been lost. In the Producers' section we talk about the move away from an organic sound that has made the production of many of today's acts seem thin and predictable. There is more pressure on new acts not to take risks and a trend to over-package even the most creative artists. Yes, the viewing figures for *Top of the Pops* are miserable, but the media has changed. In many ways the business is better. Live performances are stunningly produced and venues so much better. Musical tastes are more eclectic, with the middle-aged baby-boomer generation still interested and buying contemporary music. Music itself is more portable, and accessible, and there has never been a better time to try to make your own.

Perhaps the real test will be when you can walk into an elevator and hear good music. Something that's so good that you have to ask reception for the name of the artist. Then you'll know that the music business is really pumping. Meanwhile it continues to inspire, excite, frustrate and confound. And as always, it's more than just a business – it's part of all our lives.

1

2

3

4

5

6

7

8

9

10

11

12

13

14

15

RECORD LABELS

WHAT IS THE ROLE OF THE RECORD LABEL?

Love them or hate them, the five major labels, EMI, Sony, Universal, BMG and Warner, dominate and control a huge amount of the music business. Soon there are likely to be just three majors controlling 75% of the world's record sales. But they are not having it all their own way. 2002 was the first year that sales of computer games in the UK outstripped sales of CDs. In 2003 mobile ring tunes outsold the whole singles market.

So why are computer games outselling records? Is it the free downloads or the legacy of years of sterile dance music? Why are teenagers keener to buy phonecards than CDs? One thing is unquestionable – the business is under extreme pressure, which is substantially changing the approach and demeanour of the majors and giving the independents new opportunities.

It may not be easy for the big record labels to satisfy the armies of shareholders and city analysts, but sometimes they don't make life easy for themselves.

The original record company business model was very smart. In essence, a large proportion of its costs are paid by the artist. Although the artist gets an advance, it's really just a loan, paid back from their royalties or points. A recording artist pays all production costs and the company insists on outright ownership of the copyright. Even the publishing and film businesses don't expect the creator to do this.

It doesn't stop there. Even the packaging costs are charged to artists at such a high rate that they cover physical production. Then there is every taxi, and meal with executives, and on and on.

Although passing over 100% of copyright is slowly breaking down for the most successful acts, the concept that 'You pay and we own' is still the norm. So with such an attractive business model why are the majors finding it so hard to make money?

Probably the labels' greatest business weakness is optimism. Too many CDs are marketed in the UK. More than 25,000 new singles and albums are released each year. This creates huge competition for retail space. The only way to get good shelf space is to be in the charts and the only way to get in the charts is to spend heavily on marketing.

It doesn't help that the majors spend more each year launching an album. If you took the average cost of launching a Top 20 single, indexed it against inflation and divided it by the relative sales today and twenty years ago, you would get out of the business. Even if the majors' strike rate of hits remains constant over time, the huge increase in the costs of launching records is bleeding much-needed profits.

Instead record labels seek to increase profits in two ways: increased exploitation of back catalogue, and more outsourcing of A&R and development.

Whether it's compilation catalogues, advertisements, or ring-tones, the labels are keen to exploit every last piece of copyright. One major made up its total loss in singles income over the past three years in mobile ring-tones alone. There's nothing wrong with this businesslike approach to back catalogue, except that it is increasingly taking management time away from the lifeblood of the business, creating new bands and new material.

Nearly as sterile as back catalogue is the nostalgia business of reissuing back catalogue of 'super bands' who are creatively dead or increasingly really dead. Who would have thought when The Beatles split up that thirty years later they would have a No. 1 hit album in 26 countries, or that two years later Paul McCartney would be the highest-grossing touring artist, pulling in over $60 million from his middle-aged fans?

When the sales of the majors are analysed, and once-aging super bands and back catalogue are discounted, a declining remainder is dedicated to the high-risk business of recording new material – the original reason for record labels' existence.

A new breed of smart record executives has found a way to manage risk in this area. A quick analysis shows that the development of new bands is the highest-risk activity, as well as consuming vast amounts of valuable management time.

Meanwhile there are many independent labels concentrating on breaking and developing contemporary acts. Their ability to develop and market artists more cost effectively is not surprising: they have lower overheads and the focus that comes from risking their own, rather than a corporation's, money. Of course many independents have the advantage of specialising in a single genre, which means they can focus on a narrower target audience for their marketing, and a smaller number of specialist retailers in terms of distribution. However, there are lessons to be learned by the majors.

Determined to do anything other than adapt their core business, the major labels have taken over 'cool' independents or entered distribution deals with them. There's a long list of once-famous independents that have been bought up in this way including Island, London, A&M, Chrysalis, and Motown. The majors have effectively taken the competition from long-standing, mid-tiered independents out of the markets.

Even so, the independent sector is alive and kicking. A new generation of independent labels has been set up; more than 450 are paid-up members of AIM. Not all are run out of back bedrooms. Some like Sanctuary and Independiente are becoming medium-sized.

New technology and new attitudes to promotion and marketing, as well as enthusiasm for new technology development, fuels the sector. 2003 saw the introduction of the iPod and Apple's 62p a track downloads on the iTunes site. Microsoft, not wanting to be left out, has launched OD2 in joint venture with Tiscali, the Italian Internet provider, and Peter Gabriel. This offers legal downloads for a monthly subscription. MP3.com has tens of thousands of bands available for download worldwide. Many are unsigned, but they are finding an audience. Some, like Avril Lavigne, go on to succeed and sign with majors.

And that's just the legal part of downloading. New file-sharing sites are making it harder for the majors, but are getting music into more hands. A typical site is Earth Station 5, whose mission statement is: 'The next generation in P2P (peer-to-peer) file sharing is here. Resistance is futile.'

This independent spirit means that some of the relatively new independents are giving the majors a hard time and breaking out of the small time to achieve significant sales success.

THE FUTURE OF THE MAJORS

It's difficult to predict the future for record labels. The sale of Warner Music has shaken the majors and it seems likely that there will soon be only three worldwide major labels, causing even more of a stranglehold on old-fashioned distribution. These majors will try to grab a slice of the buoyant live market and its associated merchandising business.

To pursue sales volume, these majors have developed a new retail sector, namely supermarkets. At first this seemed a great sales opportunity. They could benefit from huge efficiencies by delivering straight into their central warehouses. But currently, and even more so in the future, this policy is sucking out profit from the majors. As they have grown their market share, supermarkets have treated music like any other category, forcing down the average price of CDs in their stores from £14.99 to £9.99. It's not just the supermarkets that are commoditising music: over the past eighteen months the London *Evening Standard* has been giving away free compilation CDs as promotions with their ES magazine.

In the short term there has been a positive sales volume effect. According to the BPI newsletter (20 February 2004), album sales volume increased by 4.9% in 2003 and total revenue by 2.1% compared with a decline in both in 2002. In fact there were 234 million albums shipped in the UK.

However, there are serious implications for the future. The increasing dominance of the major supermarkets is putting pressure on the rest of the retail trade. This threatens the one monopoly the majors still have: distribution to thousands of record shops.

The dominance of the supermarkets also pushes consumers to the Internet, because they will only stock a few of the 25,000 single and albums produced every year. If the other retailers disappear, the Net will be the place to find music not stocked in supermarkets.

The majors won't disappear, but they are going to have to change and, even more importantly, there are huge opportunities for the independent sector.

THE FUTURE OF THE INDEPENDENTS

The independent sector is already healthier than for twenty-five years. It will keep growing for three reasons:

- the market context, i.e. all the above;
- music genres that encourage do it yourself, from dance to urban;
- a heady mix of new technology and new creative entrepreneurs; artists in all areas are understanding that to have control and be successful they have to do it for themselves.

OTHER OPPORTUNITIES

The major labels have understood that there is a growing business in back catalogue, compilations and licensing existing material. However, this does not have to be limited to the majors: there are opportunities for independents to make money in this area.

Anyone can produce compilations, as long as they have a good concept and the patience to clear all the rights. Sony Music demonstrated how creative compilation concepts could be when they developed the School Disco.com franchise. This is a perfect hook to reformat a wide range of back catalogue and has the added advantage of associating itself with specific club nights. The result has been more than 200,000 sales per compilation, and a nice earner for Sony.

There's no reason why an independent couldn't have done the same and many do. There are many opportunities to exploit in licensing music from other countries. Some regional music can appeal to large communities in the UK as well as interested fans, such as the Latin community which numbers hundreds of thousands of potential customers.

TIPS FOR NEWCOMERS

- Think beyond the major labels – there are many different opportunities in indies, management company labels, and with producers who are developing young bands. These will give you a great start if you want to run your own label.
- If you decide to work for a major, be careful to work with the right team. Make sure you work with many different bands, and experience marketing and plugging as well as seeing A&R at work, but be careful not to get sucked into the corporate lifestyle and culture, if your ambition is to do it for yourself.
- Even if you are determined to work for a major, think of a 'boutique' like Parlophone which is part of EMI, or a smaller corporate like Sanctuary, as these will be more entrepreneurial and forward-looking.
- Remember, getting into a record company is just as hard as it has always been. Unless you have a specific skill, like a top-flight law degree or the typing skills of a robot, you will need to pull any contacts you have to get a work placement in a label. To work in the business you have to impress. It's not enough to know about the music scene and the business, you have to know what you like and why.
- If you want to have your own label, working for a major might just reinforce 'old world' thinking. Majors rely on 'lazy marketing'. You are going to have to do your own plugging on the strength of your personality and product, not because of a corporate track record and wallet. You can't afford a large, paid-for marketing programme, so you have to create your own buzz. Nor can you rely on a huge distribution network to ensure that your product is stocked and merchandised nationwide.

  If you can't work for an indie, we recommend you work with other related music services such as music management firms, concert agents or any part of the business involved in making financial decisions around the artist. Additionally attend a business seminar/course or seek a marketing placement with another street-type product, such as a skateboard or extreme sports clothing company or some other cool, youth-targeted product. This will teach you viral marketing, experiential communication, online promotion and guerrilla PR – all of which are concepts that marketing departments of the major labels are only just beginning to find out about but are everyday business practices for the best small labels.

Note: Viral marketing can be compared to word of mouth, but it operates over the Internet and is a cost-effective way of reaching millions of people through their computers. Most viral campaigns start off small and then spread through people passing on the information to other Internet users. Record labels use viral marketing to target music fans by sending them previews of music and video tracks.

THE VIEW FROM WITHIN

MUFF WINWOOD – SENIOR VP, SONY A&R UK

Originally bass player and writer with The Spencer Davis Group, Muff had three No. 1 singles in the sixties. In 1967 he joined Island Records at its inception. In 1978 he joined CBS as director of A&R. Here he signed the best bands of the Eighties including Adam & The Ants, Wham! and The Clash. In 1991 he moved to Sony, where he helped build the careers of Jamiroquai, Des'ree, Toploader and Reef.

What do you think of the music business today?

Basically the record companies have run out of money. There's more than one reason. Sure, we've been profligate, but there's free downloads on the Internet and the supermarkets have driven down the cost of CDs. Five years ago a CD selling for £9.99 in Tesco could not be bought for less than £14.99. That's £5 that's been taken out of the business. Other areas of the business are doing well. Live has never been better. People are spending money on music. They can spend £150 for a ticket to Glastonbury, but are just not spending on CDs.

What do you think is going to happen to the major labels?

The lack of CD sales could see the end of record companies as we know them. The way they are going, there won't be any A&R people, but just buyers like at Marks & Spencer. Music buyers will be like underwear buyers. I think music companies will be like music banks – places you come to with a music idea you want people to invest in. It's already rare for someone to say, 'Listen to my demo, develop my act and after two years will you put out my record?' Management companies and publishers will develop acts as never before. Publishers are already very active, putting together writers and artists. The world's changed, our guys are getting material that's ready to go. Instead of saying we'll 'develop it', we're now saying we'll 'buy it'.

What do you look for in an act?

I always say to my A&R guys before they sign an act, they need to know what the first single is and where do they want the first review to be, in *Smash Hits* or *Kerrang*. They should know what type of producer they want, you have to have it all worked out. Signing an act is like gambling on the horses. You have to study the form. Does the artist have a good voice? Does he look good? Does he look fashionably good? He must look cool, not like he works in a bank and changes his clothes at six o'clock. Is their music fashionable – does it look like it sounds? Are they under 25 or over 25? If they are 19 they have time. The graph of talent shows you tend to peak at 25. Your creative energies and life experiences tend to cross at 25. If a guy hasn't written a great song by 25, he's probably not likely to – the same goes for singing a great song.

Can't a good band be styled? Why is the look so important?
People have to have it to begin with. I saw a band the other day that just looked wrong. They played well, but they looked like four different students on four different courses. They were about 23, but one looked like he was on a science course, one on an arts course who looked cool, but the others didn't. They all had different hairstyles, that always throws me. Groups should have a collective look.

You know what you want from a band, but what do you look for in a good A&R man?
I don't know, I just get a hunch. It seems to work, the ones I feel good about usually work out. There's something about the way people talk about music that marks them out as having potential. You have to be sympathetic towards A&R people because I say to myself, 'Shit, I remember what a struggle it was when I did that.' You might not always be able to help people but you can give them time and listen. When they start out, the most important thing to me is that every gig they invite me to is good. I want to know if people really believe in the band. If they do I usually go with it.

So in the future, with all the pressures on the business, how will Sony change? Will they be as arrogant as they have in the past?

No, we're learning humility. We don't feel so powerful as money is tighter. We have to be fitter, and more businesslike, but we must always be music led. I wouldn't take anyone on if they weren't music led.

How much does it cost to make a record?
The costs have been pretty standard over the last five years. It costs about £10,000 a track. Sometimes people spend £15,000. Anything over that and you've lost the plot. So an album of 12 tracks costs between £100,000 and £150,000. Then there's the video. If you're a small indie band then your first video will cost about £5,000; if you're a pop or R&B band, then if you don't spend £100,000 you're not competing. Look at the MOBO or Brits awards – I'll bet you every video you see there cost more than £100,000. So for many young bands you're talking about £250,000 of costs before you even start looking at marketing or promotion.

So what's the answer? Can't Sony set up a special development company, and invest £300,000 and help young acts get started?
We already do. We have three indie labels that do just that, but we don't talk about it. The last thing we want is to make it look as though we are involved. Sometimes we will use an indie to put out a band to take the pressure off and give them time to get it right. We did that with Jamiroquai – Acid Jazz missed out on securing their deal to us, but we let them put out their first album; it gave them room to breathe. In the seventies and eighties we did lots of this. After that there was so much money we got out of the habit, but now we're starting again. Launching bands in this way gives us a chance to get it right later and not to have blown too much money.

What plans do you have for Sony now you've got a bigger role?
Over the last year I've tried to make sure Sony is A&R led, but it takes time to turn an Elephant around.

Rumour has it that Richard Branson takes you out for dinner every year to try to persuade you to work for him. Is it true?

Yes, it's true. He's very clever. If he meets someone and offers them a job, if they say no, he marks it in his diary and a year later he gives them a ring and takes them out to dinner to try to persuade them again. He did it to me for four or five years. I didn't take up his offer, because even though he is brilliant, he's involved in too many businesses. It's too easy for him to get rid of his music businesses if they were not doing well. He has certainly come a long way since I first met him when his office was a barge at Swiss Cottage. I remember I asked him if I could use the toilet, he said he would show me the way and there were none – we had to go behind the bushes on the tow path. He seems to have improved his accommodation since then!

EDDIE PILLAR – FOUNDER, ACID JAZZ RECORDS

Eddie still runs Acid Jazz. His success has been impressive. He has signed Jamiroquai, Brand New Heavies, D-Influence, Galliano, Young Disciples and has been instrumental in developing a unique British sound. Eddie's a leader and not a follower. He hates the majors and isn't afraid to have a go at the corporate music business which he thinks is bad for music.

How did you make your first record?

I saw an advert in the back of the *NME*. It said, 'Records made for £200 for a thousand singles.' I called and they asked for artwork, a master tape and a cheque. So I found a studio, made the records and then had 1,000 vinyls made for me. Then I sold them to record shops for a profit and thought, 'This shit works,' so I made another record.

Can you really make a great record in your bedroom?

I've heard brilliant records that have never seen the light of day because there's been no marketing. You have to put the package together to make a success, but of course you need to start off with a good record.

How do you feel about the corporate labels?

I'm always excited when I hear young kids saying, 'Fuck the corporate

record labels.' I am going to do it my way and release my own records. So Solid Crew is a brilliant example. The only problem with them is I don't understand why they adopted American gangster violence – it's not a true reflection of the richness of West Indian black culture.

What advice would you give to anyone who wanted to start their own label?
Do it step by step and put your own product out. I tell kids studying on a music and media course, if you want to get into this business, then you must get off your arse and go and do it. Make your own white labels, get work experience, make mistakes, because that's the only way you're going to learn.

Don't A&R people have a tough time? Aren't they always taking a risk?
A&R people at a big label don't make any real decisions or take any real risks. The real decision is made three levels below by the young entrepreneur who makes a decision whether he pays the mortgage or spends £1,500 to make a record. The A&R guy or the label boss at the major label are just risking corporate money not their own – where's the bollocks in that? There are too many executives with no understanding of the business. There is no filtering down of knowledge. No teaching kids how the stuff really works. When they are ripped off, they are booted out before they have a chance to speak.

So what advice would you offer when selecting a manager? Do you go for the creative manager or the deal maker?
A creative manager will do all the hard work on your single, your performance, image and the real things that help you create great material and get a deal. Creative managers always get sacked because artists don't want to pay real money to someone who grew up with them. A manager finds an artist and develops them. They earn £10 and pay the manager £2. Then they earn £100 and pay £20. Then the band get paid £1,000 and are happy to pay the manager £100. Now they earn £100,000 and feel great and say, 'Why are we paying you £20,000?' Then they become really big time and earn a million and then tell you to fuck off when you ask for £200,000. That's people in the music business.

Surely, the major labels must do something right?

I think some are good at what they do, but I don't like the way they treat music. They pretend they care, when in fact they could be selling widgets or soap powder. Music is at its healthiest when there is a surge of independence. Like in the eighties and nineties when people got off their arse and just did it. So what did the majors do in the nineties? They just bought out all the indies, keeping the three best-selling artists and chucking out anyone creative and the guy who set it up. Look at Creation Records. McGee is one of the geniuses of the music business. Sony bought Creation and then ousted him. This was mad. They just wanted to kill the competition and buy their success in the charts. They failed to realise that buying indies, and then sacking the founder, was getting rid of the key source of creativity in the music business, or perhaps they just didn't care.

LUCIAN GRANGE – CHAIRMAN, UNIVERSAL

Lucian Grange is one of the most powerful men in the record company sector, with a fearsome reputation, but as he says:

If you had a one-year-old puppy sitting behind a door with a big title on the door like 'Chairman' some people would still be nervous. [*Smiles*] Perception is very different from reality. Too many people see confidence and character as being arrogant.

How did you get started in the business?

I used to get the sandwiches for someone who ran an artist management company and DJ agency in 1978. I just hung with people because they liked the same music as me. All I wanted to do was be around music and people who made music.

What is your business philosophy?

It's about investing in new artists and re-energising your company every twelve months, because if you don't do these things you quickly start to slide backwards.

Is that the secret of your success?
I have always been able to say no, if no is the correct response.

How do you manage the heads of your labels?
I advise them or, if I need to, I give them constructive criticism. If that doesn't work I *tell* them. If there's a problem I try to go through a logical or rational way to fix it. But like a pilot, if they can't fix it, you don't let the plane crash, you quickly put someone else in their place to save it.

Are you satisfied with Universal's current performance?
No, I'll never be happy. I could have No. 1 or 2 positions in every chart and I still wouldn't be happy.

So is it profit or creativity that motivates you?
Listening to something that I like and seeing it become a success is the greatest buzz. When I open the paper and see it's made No. 1 it's only because hundreds of thousands of people agree with me.

In your position don't you have to be worried about profit?
Sure, if the bottom line is not healthy you just have to hire someone else. That makes the job fascinating. I love what I do. I trust my judgement and love people with flavour, ego attitude and opinions. That's why I love Jazz Summers and Alan McGee. They are repeaters, they keep coming back with hits that make money.

Are you proud of what you've achieved at Universal?
I'm proud of a dozen artists we've signed across different labels. The ones that are unique and bring a class and quality of their own. I'm proud of what we've achieved as a group. I know we're signing acts that will take us somewhere in the next two, three, four years. It's about looking forward.

So what are your biggest challenges?
Signing and breaking the right artists. The ones who are important and shifting attitude.

What do you think of downloading music?

Serial uploaders who share hundreds of files with each other are wrong. It's having a drastic impact on the business. Thousands and thousands of jobs are being lost because it's robbing the industry of revenue. But used properly these new channels give us the opportunity to get music to the public on many different levels. Piracy is a short-term problem: making music even more accessible and portable is an opportunity.

Returning to the talent you've signed at Universal, which artist do you regret not signing?

The Darkness. [*Looks pained*] It really pisses me off. Every one of our labels passed on it. Did it proudly. They got it wrong on every level from MD to talent scout.

How do you see your role in terms of the company? Is it all about giving everyone a hard time?

It's the ability to assess who's got potential. It's not just about whether they're getting the ball in the net, but are they worth sticking with? Football is littered with people that had a dodgy two or three seasons, but all of a sudden they turn it round. So the person who can encourage the right person is the manager. He's the one with talent.

It seems the Lucian school of man management is very unforgiving. We want to know more and he gives us a football analogy.

Football is about people with a natural talent, who want to make a lot of money. Remember, competition breeds champions. If you have three players competing for one position, the two that don't get it will try even harder than the one that does. It's the same here. He doesn't want the other two taking his gigs. Every time one of our companies does well with an artist, the first people I tell are the other companies. I ring them up and ask them how they feel about it, then I put the phone down.

THE VIEW FROM WITHIN

If you could take three records to a desert island, what would they be?
Is there anyone else on this desert island that I could swap them with?

No, just you. Just three albums.
The Sex Pistols' *Never Mind the Bollocks*, Elvis Presley's *Greatest Hits* and Stevie Wonder's *Greatest Hits*.

Enough said.

1
2
3
4
5
6
7
8
9
10
11
12
13
14
15

RECORD LABELS

THE 5 MAJORS

BMG INTERNATIONAL - EUROPE

Bedford House, 69-79 Fulham High Street, London SW6 3JW

T: 020 7384 7500 F: 020 7973 0345

Website: bmg.com

EMI GROUP PLC

27 Wrights Lane, London W8 5SW

T: 020 7795 7000 F: 020 7795 7755

Website: emigroup.com

SONY MUSIC ENTERTAINMENT REGIONAL OFFICE

10 Great Marlborough Street, London W1F 7LP

T: 020 7911 8400 F: 020 7911 8600

Website: sonymusiceurope.com

UNIVERSAL MUSIC INTERNATIONAL

8 St James Square, London SW1Y 4JU

T: 020 7747 4000 F: 020 7747 4499

Website: umusic.com

WARNER MUSIC EUROPE

83 Baker Street, London W1M 2LA

T: 020 7535 9000 F: 020 7535 9450

Website: wmg.com

RECORD LABELS

ANGEL AIR RECORDS
Unicorn House, Station Road West,
Stowmarket, Suffolk IP14 1ES
T: 01449 770138 F: 01449 770133
Website: angelair.co.uk

AUTOMATIC RECORDS
Unit 5 Waldo Works, Waldo Road,
London NW10 6AW
T: 020 8964 9020 F: 020 8960 5741
Website: automatic.uk.com

AZULI RECORDS
25 D'Arblay Street, London W1V 3FH
T: 020 7287 1932 F: 020 7439 2490
Website: azuli.com

BEGGARS GROUP
17-19 Alma Road, Wandsworth,
London SW18 1AA
T: 020 8870 9912 F: 020 8871 1766
Website: beggars.com

BLOOD AND FIRE
Room 105, Ducie House, 37 Ducie
Street, Manchester M1 2JW
T: 0161 228 3034 F: 0161 228 3036
Website: bloodandfire.co.uk

BLOW UP RECORDS
Unit 127, Stratford Workshops,
Burford Rd, London E15 2SP
T: 020 8534 7700 F: 020 8534 7722
Website: blowup.co.uk

BUCKS MUSIC GROUP
Onward House, 11 Uxbridge Street,
London W8 7TQ
T: 020 7221 4275 F: 020 7229 6893
Website: bucksmusicgroup.co.uk

CHERRY RED RECORDS
Unit 17, 1st Floor, Elysium Gate West,
126-128 New King's Rd, London
SW6 4LZ
T: 020 7371 5844 F: 020 7384 1854
Website: cherryred.co.uk

CIRCUS ARGO HOUSE
Kilburn Park Road, London NW6 5LS
T: 020 8960 2013 F: 020 8969 1948
Website: circusrecords.net

COOKING VINYL
10 Allied Way, London W3 0RQ
T: 020 8600 9200 F: 020 8743 7448
Website: cookingvinyl.com

CURB RECORDS
45 Great Guilford Street,
London SE1 0ES
T: 020 7401 8877 F: 020 7928 8590
Website: curb.com

DEMON MUSIC GROUP
4th Floor, Holden House, 57 Rathbone
Place, London W1T 1JU
T: 020 7396 8899 F: 020 7470 6655
Website: vci.co.uk

DOME RECORDS
59 Glenthorne Road, Hammersmith,
London W6 0LJ
T: 020 8748 4499 F: 020 8748 6699
Website: domerecords.co.uk

DOMINO RECORDING CO
PO Box 4029, London SW15 2XR
T: 020 8875 1390 F: 020 8875 1390
Website: dominorecordco.com

THE DRILL HALL
3 Heathfield Terrace, London, W4 4JE
T: 020 8747 8111 F: 020 8747 8113
Website: independiente.co.uk

EAGLE HOUSE
22 Armoury Way,
Wandsworth, London SW18 1EZ
T: 020 8870 5670 F: 020 8875 0050

ECHO LABEL LTD
The Chrysalis Building,
13 Bramley Road, London W10 6SP
T: 020 7465 6169 F: 020 7229 4498
Website: chrysalis.co.uk/echo_link_frame.html

EDEL RECORDS
12 Oval Rd, London NW1 7DH
T: 020 7482 4848 F: 020 7482 4846
Website: edel.com

END RECORDINGS
18 West Central Street, London
WC1A 1JJ
T: 020 7419 9199 F: 020 7419 9099
Website: the-end.co.uk

FAITH AND HOPE RECORDS
23 New Mount Street, Manchester
M4 4DE
T: 0161 839 4445 F: 0161 839 1060
Website: faith-and-hope.co.uk

GLASGOW UNDERGROUND
Argyle House, 1103 Argyle Street,
Glasgow G3 8ND
T: 0141 564 5251 F: 0141 357 6688
Website: glasgowunderground.com

GLO RECORDS
84 Queens Road, Watford, Hertfordshire
WD1 2LA
T: 01923 690700 F: 01923 249495
Website: glo.uk.com

GRAND CENTRAL RECORDS
3rd Floor, Habib House, 9 Stevenson
Square, Manchester M1 1DB
T: 0161 245 2002 F: 0161 245 2003
Website: grandcentralrecords.com

GREENSLEEVES RECORDS
Unit 14, Metro Centre, St. John's Road,
Isleworth, Middlesex TW7 6NJ
T: 020 8758 0564 F: 020 8758 0811
Website: greensleeves.net

GUT RECORDS
Byron House, 112a Shirland Road,
London W9 2EQ
T: 020 7266 0777 F: 020 7266 7734
Website: gutrecords.com

HOPE RECORDINGS
Loft 5, The Tobacco Factory, Raleigh
Road, Southville, Bristol BS3 1TF
T: 0117 953 5566 F: 0117 953 7733
Website: hoperecordings.com

HOSPITAL RECORDS
Red Corner Door, 17 Barons Court Rd,
London W14 9DP
T: 020 7386 8760 F: 020 7381 8014
Website: hospitalrecords.com

JAZZ FM/HED KANDI
26/27 Castlereagh Street, London
W1H 5DL
T: 0207 706 4100 F: 0207 723 9742
Website: hedkandi.com

RECORD LABELS

KICKIN MUSIC
Unit 8, Acklam Workshops
10 Acklam Road, London W10 5QZ
T: 020 8964 3300 F: 020 8964 4400
Website: kickinmusic.com

LEAF LABEL
Suite 219, Bon Marche Building,
241 Ferndale Rd, London SW9 8BJ
T: 020 7733 1818 F: 020 7733 5818
Website: posteverything.com/leaf

MARKET SQUARE MUSIC
Market House, Market Square, Winslow,
Buckinghamshire MK18 3AF
T: 01296 715228 F: 01296 715486
Website: marketsquarerecords.co.uk

MINISTRY OF SOUND
103 Gaunt Street, London SE1 6DP
T: 020 7378 6528 F: 020 7403 5348
Website: ministryofsound.com

NINJA TUNE
90 Kennington Lane,
London SE11 4BX
T: 020 7820 3535 F: 020 7820 3434
Website: ninjatune.net

NUKLEUZ RECORDS
1 Pepys Court, 84-86 The Chase,
London SW4 0NF
T: 020 7720 7266 F: 020 7720 7255
Website: nukleuz.co.uk

ONE LITTLE INDIAN RECORDS
34 Trinity Crescent, London SW17 7AC
T: 020 8772 7600 F: 020 8772 7601
Website: indian.co.uk

PIAS RECORDINGS UK
338B Ladbroke Grove, London
W10 5AH
T: 020 8324 2500 F: 020 8324 0040
Website: pias.com

REACT MUSIC
138b West Hill, Putney, London
SW15 2UE
T: 020 8780 0305 F: 020 8788 2889
Website: react-music.co.uk

ROADRUNNER RECORDS
Tech West House, Warple Way,
London W3 0UL
T: 020 8749 2984 F: 020 8749 2523
Website: roadrunnerrecords.co.uk

ROUGH TRADE RECORDS
66 Golborne Road, London W10 5PS
T: 020 8960 9888 F: 020 8968 6715
Website: roughtraderecords.com

RYKODISC LTD
329 Latimer Road, London W10 6RA
T: 020 8960 3311
Website: rykodisc.com

SANCTUARY GROUP
45-53 Sinclair Rd, London W14 0NS
T: 020 7602 6351 F: 020 7300 6593
Website: sanctuarygroup.co.uk

SKINT RECORDS
Shipwrights Yard, 73A Middle Street,
Brighton BN1 1AL
T: 01273 738527 F: 01273 739323
Website: skint.net

SNAPPER MUSIC
Unit 3, The Coda Centre, 189 Munster
Road, Fulham, London SW6 6AW

T: 020 7610 0330 F: 020 7386 7006
Website: snappermusic.com

SOMA
2nd Floor, 342 Argyle Street,
Glasgow G2 8LA
T: 0141 229 6220 F: 0141 226 4383
Website: somarecords.com

TELSTAR ENTERTAINMENT GROUP
107 Mortlake High Street, London
SW14 8HQ
T: 020 8878 7888 F: 020 8392 6847
Website: telstar.co.uk

UNION SQUARE MUSIC
Unit 2, The Grand Union Office Park,
Packet Boat Lane, Cowley, Uxbridge
UB8 2GH
T: 01895 458515 F: 01895 458 516
Website: unionsquaremusic.co.uk

V2 MUSIC
131-133 Holland Park Avenue, London
W11 4UT
T: 020 7471 3000 F: 020 7603 4796
Website: v2music.com

WAGRAM MUSIC UK
Unit 203, Westbourne Studios,
242 Acklam Road, London W10 5YG
T: 020 8968 8800 F: 020 8968 8877
Website: wagram.fr

WALL OF SOUND RECORDINGS
Office 3, 9 Thorpe Close, London
W10 5XL
T: 020 8969 1144 F: 020 8969 1155
Website: wallofsound.net

WARP RECORDS
Spectrum House, 32-34 Gordon House
Road, London NW5 1LP
T: 020 7284 8350 F: 020 7284 8360
Website: warprecords.com

XL RECORDINGS
1 Codrington Mews, London W11 2EH
T: 020 8875 6255 F: 020 8871 4178
Website: xl-recordings.com

ZTT RECORDS
The Blue Building, 42-46 St. Luke's
Mews, London W11 1DH
T: 020 7221 5101 F: 020 7221 3374
Website: ztt.com

1

2

3

4

5

6

7

8

9

10

11

12

13

14

15

A&R

WHAT IS THE ROLE OF A&R?

A&R is the music business. Without new artists the business is nothing. If A&R didn't break new artists we'd only have middle-aged stadium bands and back catalogue. Who wants that?

A&R remains the most important part of a major record label, but its scope and risk profile has changed significantly over the past twenty years. Of course we have to be careful not to slip into nostalgia, to a golden age of A&R. Too much has always been expected of A&R men, but today's expectations are higher, and the back-up given to A&R considerably less.

Majors are under more short-term pressure to deliver results than ever before. A £500,000 development cost to break a band needs to start making a quick return or it soon starts to ruin a major's quarterly figures. Backing too many of the wrong bands can certainly end a career, and increasingly can endanger the survival of a label.

This results in A&R increasingly playing it safe and getting involved later in the development process to lower the risk and shorten the payback. Which is serious. It's freezing out young talent that could have made it a generation ago.

A&R IS KILLING BANDS

It's not just the initial break that is more difficult. The chances of getting through to your second album is harder these days as A&R are reluctant to stick their neck out and support you in the way they used to. This is because the corporate philosophy dictates that good management knows when to 'cut their losses'. To artists this seems mad. They've spent all this money so why are they giving up now? It doesn't make sense unless you're looking at a balance sheet.

If a label passes on their option for a second album, it kills a band. It's terminal. Once you are seen as a failure by other labels there is no going back. It's rare to survive once you have lost momentum in this business.

The sad truth is that your first album failing to meet expectations might just be bad luck. It might not have sold well because there were too many other launches competing with it, or you had a bad plugger or PR. Or you could have flopped because the label made you play safe in the studio. Too many artists with talent and potential don't make it past this point.

A&R AT MAJOR LABELS ISN'T A&R ANY MORE

In many ways A&R in the majors behaves more like a purchasing or buying department. They want to buy ready-developed and packaged product from people they know. Some might as well be buyers at Top Shop.

Why has A&R abdicated the responsibility of nurturing and developing new talent? At first sight it's a mystery when you consider that many people at the top of major labels have been legendary A&Rs. They must be under such short-term pressures that they forget the past. Also there seems to be a new breed of record executive more concerned about the size of their offices and holding on to their jobs than putting their neck on the line and backing raw talent. Somehow paying a mortgage on a Shoreditch flat beats risking it on a band that gets under your skin but hasn't polished its act yet.

And what about so-called great A&R directors? Too many are 'associated' with great hits rather than actually responsible for them. If these are the directors, how can you expect them to recruit anyone better? That's why too many A&R managers are ex-DJs or seemingly connected trendsetters, who talk the talk but couldn't spot the next big thing even if it was handed to them on a plate.

The guys at the top aren't stupid. That's why they bought indie labels to provide an in house solution to the A&R gap. The problem is that over time their unique A&R culture has been eroded by their new masters. Whatever anyone says, Island today cannot nurture and scout talent like it could in Chris Blackwell's day. One glaring exception is Parlophone. We're not sure what they're on, but they seem to be able to maintain an indie integrity even though they are owned by EMI. Having Coldplay and Radiohead on your roster isn't bad.

Daniel Miller is a great example of someone prepared to stand by an artist, to give them time to come good. He put the weight of his indie label, Mute, behind Moby, even though for a long time people didn't get it. He just stuck at it until they did.

IT'S NOT EASY BEING IN A&R

Although we're critical about A&R in major labels, that doesn't mean we don't understand that it's a tough job. The successful A&R is a bit like a superstar. But the pressure is always on. Everyone is asking you what you have done and who you have signed.

The A&R conundrum is: if you sign something big and it doesn't work you can be out of a job, but if you don't sign anything for too long you could be out of a job. If you over-think it, you will not survive. You have to use your gut, as you have to do with most things in the music business.

WHY ARE SO MANY A&R MANAGERS FAILING TO SIGN GOOD NEW TALENT?

It all stems from the fact that they aren't able to trust their own judgement and gut instinct. They follow each other around like sheep. As soon as one A&R

guy finds one band, seven more are chasing the same band. This makes a label feel confident about bidding for them, otherwise there's little urgency. It's as if a label will trust everyone else except themselves. The culture of risk analysis has seeped into the A&R culture of major labels and is apparently irreversible.

Another trend is for more importance to be placed in the person bringing the band to the label than the talent of the band itself. So if Simon Fuller or Jazz Summers brings a band, it's going to be looked at very differently, because their track record seems to minimise the risk.

HOW TO BE GOOD AT A&R

The best advice is simple: have the courage of your convictions. The crucial time to be strong is when you bring your first act to the A&R meeting. You've probably been working hard, finding and getting the confidence of the artist for at least six months to get to this stage. This meeting will be stuffed with senior executives, because you're asking to spend a significant amount of company money.

Don't get phased. Remember, everyone will come up with reasons why you shouldn't sign. The worst is when you walk in with an artist that breaks the mould. You'll have to face a barrage of accepted truths all based on the past and with no relevance for the future. 'Girl bands don't sell, garage doesn't sell, electronic music doesn't sell.' If you took them literally no record would ever sell – so don't.

You have to fight for what you want. More often than not the meeting will say no, but don't give up. Take your boss to the studio or to see the band gig. If you push hard enough it will come down to one thing. Perhaps it's the fact that although he loves track 1, he's not sure the third is a hit, or it might be simply that he doesn't like the guitarist's hairstyle. Whatever it is you have to push and push and get them signed. The more we talk to people at the top of A&R the more we realise that strength and confidence is the most valued attribute for success.

YOU'VE MANAGED TO GET YOUR BAND SIGNED, NOW WHAT?

Signing the band is just the chance. If you're ever going to be taken seriously you have to make them a success. Major labels are huge machines, and unless you kick them and get them behind the artist you have signed, you'll never make it. You must get everyone behind the band from marketing to the producer. It's your job to make sure everyone in the company understands the band's vision. There will be conflicts. In a sense you should be the person who is most on the band's side within the company.

Once the act is signed, you are the main contact and relationship holder for the band within the label. You are responsible for them as long as they remain at the label. In many ways you operate as a mini MD of your own label. It's like being a film producer.

You have to pick the team, from the producer and mixer in the studio to the in-house PR. Of course different acts require different levels of service. An inexperienced pop artist needs lots of attention, while a more experienced artist with a strong sense of direction will need less. Remember, signing a band is good, but is nothing unless you can break them successfully, and after that to be really great you need to break them internationally. To be in the club, you need to have a No. 1 hit. When you have done this you have arrived.

TIPS FOR NEWCOMERS

- Find great new bands in your area and tip labels and managers about them. This will eventually establish your name to those who could offer you a job.
- Many people start off as scouts; they may have been part of the college circuit, worked for a record shop or as a DJ, or in a management company.
- Use your gut to make decision, but learn everything you can about hit songs and how records are made.
- To succeed as an A&R scout you have to find something hot and convince the A&R manager. If he doesn't like it, then pitch the A&R director.
- Spend lots of time round the A&R manager and the studio to learn as much as you can about the business.
- Follow your gut.

THE VIEW FROM WITHIN

DARCUS BEESE – ISLAND RECORDS

In the business more than 15 years, Darcus has been at Island through turbulent times, changing from a leading indie into a corporate. MDs have gone, heads have been chopped, artists dropped, even the building interior has changed, but Darcus goes on. We want to find out how he has survived and flourished. But first we ask him how, as a young A&R guy, you get the label to listen to your ideas and go with what you're saying.

You have to work for it to earn respect and to get people to listen to you. I was a larger than life character, but that worked against me. I had to turn around from being a scout to being an A&R executive. Why should they listen to me? You know they were thinking. 'Who is this little upstart, earning loads of money, as A&R people do?' You've got to turn that around.

So what has made the biggest difference to the way you operate?

The Sugababes. This success came just as the new management came in. It was amazing how people who had asked 'What's Darcus been doing?' changed their mind. Of course they still thought I was a cocky little bugger, but now they gave me respect. You have to change perception about you and the only way you can do that is to change every day a little bit about you.

What does it really feel like to put the company's money where your mouth is? To persuade a label to lay out £150,000 to release a single?

You wake up on Tuesday morning before the mid-week's figures come in feeling like a bag of nerves. You know that all the time you spent on that artist hangs on that one day. It's when you get an early indication on what the sales are going to be in the charts. By Friday you get a sense of where you're going to be in the charts. With the Sugababes I knew it was going to be a No. 1 single and less than a No. 1 would have been failure.

But surely you don't always get it right?

Sure, you can be working with a band for a long time and nothing happens, everybody thinking it's shit and all that energy and emotion's been wasted. It's tough. But sometimes you can turn it around. It just takes a tipping point to change everything. Sugababes were signed to London Records and everybody was saying you're crazy for signing them. The tipping point was the 'Freak Like Me' bootleg that caught people's imagination.

The backing of your label has obviously been key to giving you the support to make these sort of moves. How important is it to work with the right label?
Island is good because at least here people care about music and we work together as a team. Communication is everything. Once I've signed an act, everybody here knows what they must do. Of course it's my responsibility to make sure they understand the plot. People must understand why you signed your act.

But sometimes it must go wrong?
Yeah, when you take your eye off the ball. But I try to learn from my mistakes. I make sure I speak to everybody every day about all my acts. The responsibility always comes back to the A&R man if there are any fuck ups. I'm the axis everything spins around within the label.

In a creative business there must be conflicts?
You try to avoid conflicts before they happen. It's about talking to people at the early stage. It's all about understanding people and where they are coming from. I learnt that with the very first act I signed: Hinda Hicks. She was a good-looking Tunisian girl, but nobody at the label cared at the start. Jazz Black, the producer-manager, and I were very involved in developing her, from creative to marketing. We worked hard to make it work, even managed to get the album made for £60,000. She had a Top 20 album, a Top 10 single and the other two singles were Top 20. She had three MOBO nominations and two Brits.

You would have thought at that point she would have gone from strength to strength. Come the second album she fell out with her manager, and then I realised how difficult she was to manage and appreciated how good the first manager was. I should have kept the management team together. Her new manager became her boyfriend – to my mind disaster. Although I was part of the creative process I wasn't steering it. Her boyfriend persuaded her to make the wrong record.

I sat down with Lucian Grange to discuss which artists to keep and which to drop. I said I want to keep Hinda Hicks because she's good, and Lucian asked whether I thought she was good or brilliant. I paused and looked at him. I said, 'I don't think she has got what it takes to go all the way.' To be successful you must know exactly what you want and have that resilience that comes from self-belief. She didn't seem to have it, the conviction, so she couldn't make a decision.

The Sugababes have put you on the map. How do you get to the next level?
Over the last five years I've gone from being an A&R manager with no hits, to having hits, to understanding Europe and now onto America. To get to the next level of success you need to play on a bigger stage – that's why America's important. Now I've got Motown putting out Amy Winehouse, it's moving. Next year I'll know what the Yanks are all about.

How does it really feel to be staring success in the face?
I feel under even more pressure. Once you start having success your head's above the parapet. You can't say you're just learning or hiding behind people's coat tails. I proved to myself that I can do it and to other people that matter to me, but I've still got a long way to go in the business. I know I can get more hits because my taste is good. What really gets to me is when you see an act being badly positioned, but somehow the labels use their muscle to push it through. Sometimes it can work the other way around. There can be a public perception that an artist is not doing well, like Beverly Knight on Parlophone, but internally there's enough belief and traction to make sure she gets to do another album. You know eventually that she's going to be a huge success.

So positioning a band properly from the start is important?
The hardest thing is to know where you start. Unless you pick up an act that

1 2 3 4 5 6 7 8 9 10 11 12 13 14 15

already has heat it's hard to know where to start from. It's not until the middle of the campaign or the end that with the benefit of hindsight you realise you should have done it better. For example, with Amy Winehouse I think I should have released an album instead of a single.

What advice would you give to someone thinking about working in A&R?
The only thing you have got as an A&R man is your opinion and your taste.

SAUL GALPEN – NUDE RECORDS

Saul was a very successful A&R man turned record label owner when he set up Nude Records. He has a calm and humble manner for someone whose career has seen such success as signing Suede as his label's first act.

How did you start the label?
I worked for the majors and signed a few big acts including Simply Red, but I got bored of record label politics and thought, I'm going to start up my own record label and run. So I did – from my bedroom in West Hampstead. A few months later Sony Records approached me to work with them because of my track record, so I ended up doing a licence deal with them. Suede was one of the biggest-selling acts.

How did you manage to sign them?
It was at a gig in New Cross. There were eight other A&R guys at the venue, because *NME* had tipped them off that there would be three hot acts on that night. Interestingly, Suede was not one of the three, but they gave such a fresh and outstanding performance that it blew me away. Even so they were ignored by every single A&R there that night.

Saul goes on to tell us how at 9.00 the next morning he called Suede and the rest is history. How did the eight A&R guys miss the opportunity?
Many A&R guys don't have the balls to think outside the tested formula of what the industry thinks the public wants. What they sign is predictable and ends

up being very expensive to market because they just compete with other acts of a similar nature. Much of the recent decline in music sales is because the industry just isn't signing exciting new acts that can push the boundaries. There are one or two that have done well such as Coldplay and The Darkness, but on the whole what the public are given to buy is pretty crap.

What do you look for in a band?
I look for a band that leaves me thinking I must, must sign them. The hairs need to stand up on the back of my neck. I need to feel 100% confident that if I get behind them they will become a success. They need to have a leading edge not just musically, but also socially. They have to be like no other act, so they can carve out their own identity. In a way Suede manifested this. They had a distinction and a style that made many people in the industry see them as one of the most important bands of the Nineties, because they kick-started Britpop.

So how did running a label compare to being an A&R man?
I have loads more fun running Nude. [*Laughs*] Now I can release my own music how and when I want. The biggest buzz is the creative side from hearing great songs, to finding the right producer for a particular track.

And how early on do you know if you have a success or failure?
You know pretty early on if a record is not going to break by the reactions of your own staff. If they aren't hyped up by the record, you've a problem. If you believe in it you just have to try to carry on and pull something back.

So what is it like working in a major with the pressure to break a band?
It's at its worst when the initial launch strategy does not go to plan, especially when the first single does not even get into the Top 20. Three to six months and even more goes into planning the release, and the whole record company machine has been put into motion. But a label will probably give a new act two or three singles before they start counting the costs. Then it will depend on the power of persuasion of the artist's management and the track

record of the A&R to keep the project afloat and to keep everyone else in the label motivated.

If they are still behind the act success will depend on them finding a tipping point that will change everything. It might be radio, especially Radio 1, combined with the support of television and the press. Working at majors I have witnessed the panic and fear that everyone goes through while they wait for the results from the radio playlist. It's like kids waiting for their A-level results. Forget about a *Pop Idol* contestant crying because Simon Cowell has rejected them on TV, a label not getting their new act on the playlist is far worse.

What do you do to reduce this pressure?

It's about signing albums at a low level, and recording them on a small budget. You must plan carefully and work out the best way you can break a band without putting yourself into a situation where you have no financial room to move and respond to opportunities. If you build the base slowly you are giving yourself and them a bigger chance of survival. Also you have to find other ways of promoting and selling the act without being at the mercy of the media.

In this business you never know when you are minutes away from winning the lottery. You might have been down for ages, but what keeps you going is the excitement that one day you might see the next big band of the future and be part of it. You wait and you wait for the buzz, and when it happens nothing can compare.

THE A&R PEOPLE WHO ARE MAKING A DIFFERENCE

Daniel Miller	Mute Records
Keith Wozencroft	Emi Music UK and Ireland
Lincoln Elias	Sony Music
Eddie Pillar	Acid Jazz
Martin Mills	The Beggers Group
Dan Keeling	Parlophone
Chris Briggs	Emi Music UK and Ireland
Richard Russell	Xl Records
Darcus Beese	Island Records Group
David Bates	Db Records
Kevin Robinson	Illustrious
Andy Mcdonald	Independiente
Saul Galpen	Founder of Nude
Nathan Thompson	Parlophone

1

2

3

4

5

6

7

8

9

10

11

12

13

14

15

MANAGERS

WHAT IS THE ROLE OF THE MANAGER?

Virtually all managers started their careers by taking a risk on a young band because they knew that if they didn't, they would never be able to live with themselves. The managers interviewed in this book talk with a religious intensity about the first time they heard their band as if it was a life-changing revelation.

Successful managers' belief in their bands is matched by an incredibly strong belief in themselves. This is not a job for the faint-hearted. Since the earliest rock bands, great managers have relied on a mixture of guts and ability to get things done.

The simplest definition of management came from Nils Stevenson, ex-road manager of the Sex Pistols and manager of Siouxsie and the Banshees: 'They sing, and I do all the rest and when they can't sing, I tell them to take some bloody rest ...'

When Nils first met Siouxsie and the Banshees he knew barely anything about the complexities of management, but he succeeded in breaking the band and getting a major record deal. Every year hundreds of new managers are trying to break new bands, and breathing life into an ageing music business.

New managers remain the lifeblood of the business because many established managers realise that maintaining successful bands is far more profitable and less risky than breaking new bands. This is why even the best new acts find it difficult to find an established manager unless they have a personal connection.

For the majority of bands, good management is probably the single most important factor in breaking into the business. Conversely, **bad management has probably been responsible for consigning many bands with potential to obscurity**. In the crucial early period of a band's life the manager's ability to showcase his band, pull favours to produce a great demo tape and strike a good record deal are essential.

MANAGING SUCCESS

Managers' status, survival and success depend solely on their bands. Breaking a new band requires showmanship and timing. It's all about making the band seem successful before they have even started. Take too long to break a band and they'll lose momentum. Big labels don't want to buy old news or someone that everybody else has passed on.

Breaking a band is just the start. Good managers think three steps ahead and know where they want to place the band. It's too easy for the band to be so focused on getting signed that they are prepared to take any deal. The manager needs to be more detached, to work with the lawyer to ensure the terms are the very best that can be secured.

The choice of label, the priority given to the band in that label, and the recording and publishing deal are going to shape the band's whole future. They are going to dictate whether the band is going to be a one-album wonder or a major act.

Increasingly, record labels expect managers to bring them finished product. As the cost of launching a band continues to increase, labels are unlikely to take a risk on a rough demo tape. They are now looking for at least three highly produced tracks, and a clear idea of the band's look and positioning.

Too many young managers expect the labels to have a major input into the material and look of the act, when really they just want to buy a developed package.

IT'S ALL ABOUT RELATIONSHIPS

Aspiring managers, who know how to bully venue owners, record labels and roadies, also need to know how to build relationships to make it to the big time. All the successful managers we know combine inner strength with an ability to charm and motivate everyone around them. That's because they realise that their existence relies on the support and confidence, not just of the band, but its label and all its other advisers.

As bands become successful they often resent the amount of money their manager is taking. This is usually 15% or 20%, and is taken off the top after any expenses. That means if there are five members of the band, their manager takes £200,000 out of the first million and the five of them share the remaining £800,000 leaving them only £160,000 each. It's even worse when tour revenues are split because often managers take their commission off before tour expenses, which means they might end up earning more than their total band's take.

It doesn't matter that a manager has let the group use their van free, paid the petrol, put up the money for their demo tape and bought the drinks and the drugs. This is now. This is the big money and, flushed with success, the band will only keep their manager if they have a good relationship and he or she delivers. Good managers manage to absorb huge amounts of pressure and act as a barrier between the band and the increasing demands on them, whether from partners, record execs or fans. In the end, it's managers' ability to do this seemingly effortlessly that will be worth more than any contracts they sign.

After the band, the next most important relationship they develop will be with the record company. Managers who do not keep their confidence invariably get replaced. That doesn't mean that a good manager does everything a record company wants. It's easy for a new band to get lost in a large label. The manager needs to fight continually for attention, marketing spend and information. However, none of this will achieve anything if there isn't mutual respect and agreement to the strategy behind marketing the band.

Many relationships between bands and their original managers end badly, and in court. There is often fault on both sides, but the demands that record companies make on managers change as the band develops. Why should the gutsy, streetwise fixer who managed with sheer will-power and a sense of showmanship to get the band noticed understand a sophisticated global marketing campaign for an established supergroup? Some do, but many don't.

If you're a young manager of a successful young band, there are classic warning signs. The most common is that the band is taking meetings with the record company without you. One record executive is spending lots of time socially with the band. They are about to pull the 'If you want to get to the next stage you are going to need a professional manager' stunt on you.

When we interviewed the record labels for this book, everyone had pulled this stunt at some time. Usually it was not part of some sinister plan, but just a frustration that the manager didn't talk their language. Interestingly the newly appointed 'professional' manager usually got a better deal from the record label, even though they chose him. With huge advances and acts with less potential, the big labels have to have managers that are team players.

Whether it's because of a breakdown of relationship with the band or the record company, when the relationship has gone – it's gone. Very occasionally the new manager will take them on in a junior role, perhaps as tour manager, but usually egos on both sides make this impossible. Many young managers can be faced with little to show financially from beating the odds and breaking a successful band. If they are on a 30- or 60-day notice period, and the band is still to launch its first album, they will end up with virtually nothing.

THE SUPER LEAGUE MANAGERS

Many big managers are famous in their own right. Increasingly their wealth rivals their most successful clients. However, most started the same way as new managers breaking bands today. Few had any formal training about the business and most made terrible mistakes when they started.

The success of the best managers in the business is based on an ability to understand the business and find a way to get the best out of record labels, but never to lose self-belief and the love of music.

MANAGERS

It's too easy to dismiss successful managers as at worst sharks or at best fixers, but they are not. The creative contribution of many managers to the business is often under-estimated. As the most trusted but most detached member of the band, the manager is uniquely placed to advise the band on everything including choice of song, the arrangement, and how they look.

Loving the music business is one thing, understanding it is far harder. Great managers understand how the business is changing and how to enable their clients to benefit from these changes. Many successful managers are far more open and interested in the possibilities opened up by the Internet than most record executives.

The great benefit of being perceived as a successful manager is the ability to be able to operate on a completely different level in the business. Big labels hungry for successful acts will start coming to managers. It becomes a question of which label to pitch clients to, rather than to anyone who will take a meeting. Powerful managers can manage their clients' careers strategically and plan how to develop them across three or more albums. The relationship with a record company that has had to fight against its competitors for an artist is very different. The manager is much more in the driving seat.

Nothing demonstrates the power of successful managers more than their ability to renegotiate an existing record deal. Often managers will inherit a very poor deal with a new client. Persuading the record company that this is not in anyone's interests is one of the toughest negotiations they will have to make. Good managers know how to convince record companies that there is something in it for them to improve the terms, perhaps the opportunity to extend the contract to more albums.

Another sign of a good manager is their understanding that the deal they strike with the record company has to be properly balanced. There is no point in single-mindedly going for a huge advance without looking at the points or even understanding how the expenses are accumulated. There's always a danger that a deal focused on an advance might raise the cost of a second album to a level where the record label passes, wrecking the long-term plan for the band.

Increasingly established managers are becoming international, as the business becomes more global. In the past managers used separate American management. Today many managers of supergroups realise they have a global product and make sure marketing, touring and merchandising are all integrated. Bowie and the Stones started the trend of branding individual tours, with logos and looks, which became recognised in their own right. These create perfect vehicles for sponsorship, literally in Pink Floyd's case when VW launched a limited edition of their cars with the tour logo.

MANAGERS WHO MANUFACTURE BANDS

Arguably the most creative managers in entrepreneurial terms are managers like Simon Fuller who literally create their bands from nothing. Of course there is nothing new in this business. In the Sixties, The Monkeys were a manufactured band and managed to achieve a level of TV exposure that even Simon would have envied.

The pop genre lends itself to this type of management, which literally creates its own product. In retrospect, creating these bands seems deceptively simple. However, this is probably the most competitive part of the business. The core target audience may be nine-year-old girls, their mums and grans, but they are inundated by marketing messages about girl and boy brands. To create a marketing programme which cuts through this noise requires exceptional marketing and promotional ideas.

The beauty of manufacturing your own band as a manager is that you have far more control. Often you can hire and fire band members. You can have more control over naming, styling the band and picking their material. Sponsorship and merchandising can be embedded into the band's planning, whether it is expressed in Spice Girl dolls or the *Spice World* movie.

TIPS FOR NEWCOMERS

- ***Find a great act*:** Sounds obvious but you must find a great act to manage. You have to really get on with both them and their music because you're going to be living and breathing it, 24/7.
- ***Understand the labels*:** The odds are against you, but the best way to beat them is to understand the part of the business that has the greatest impact on your potential clients' success – the record label. If you can find a mutual interest between your act and the label, everyone is happy.
- ***Learn the business*:** Today managers have to understand the music business inside out. Join a label, or a management company, to make connections and find out how everything works.
- ***Be a one-man record label*:** Record labels are increasingly expecting you to do their job for them. Ideally you develop your act to a point where a smug record executive just has to sign a contract and everything is ready to go. That means three convincingly promising hit singles already brilliantly produced and mastered. So you need to know how to do a development deal with a producer to have a chance of 'going past go'.
- ***Be a creative entrepreneur*:** You need to make decisions both on creativity and business at the same time, e.g. to persuade the band to use the right material at the same time as you're negotiating their first indie label record deal.
- ***Think about the future today*:** The best managers are visionaries, seeing past the next tour and album. They know where they want to take the band. Unless you drive the band forward, it's never going to make it.
- ***Keep the pressure on*:** From the moment you sign with a label, time is against you. If you don't make an impression with the first single, you won't get real commitment behind the first album. If the first album doesn't meet

expectations, the label could well pass on the second. Then you have a band with a bad track record on your hands and no deal.

- ***Manage expectations*:** Both the band and labels need to know what is expected of each other. Labels have to believe you have a clear plan for their long-term success, but you must get them to focus on the resources you need to make your band a success, while keeping the band focused on the next album can get them past the last bad venue or broken-down tour bus. You have to keep the band moving and give them a sense of purpose.
- ***Be a control freak or die*:** Trusting managers don't survive any longer than lazy ones. If you're going to survive as a manager you have to read and check every invoice and always ask for back-up. It's not that labels set out to rip clients off, but in tough financial times every expense has to be billed. So if an executive's taken his new PA out to lunch he has to find a client to charge for his taxi, her flowers, their meal and sometimes, who knows, even a hotel room. If you don't have back-up you'll never know. Watch out for 'phantom items': you check the invoices against the marketing plan and everything seems to be charged as agreed, but did they actually happen? Did the plugging happen? Were the CDs actually sent to the radio station? Did 2,000 flysheets really get posted? You need to know. When you know they didn't, you must chase it and you mustn't pay.
- ***Confronting a label*:** If you think you have been wrongly invoiced, don't make it personal. Don't get all moral and offended. Do refuse to accept the financial statements. Do stand firm. Dealing with a label is like dealing with any other large organisation. If you want to maximise your share of attention and ensure extra costs are not lost on your account, you must show you're on top of everything.
- ***Find out more*:** Contact the Music Manager's Forum and get hold of its guide, *The MMF Guide to Professional Music Management*, available to non-members – a brilliant information source.

THE VIEW FROM WITHIN

JON FOWLER – SENIOR PARTNER, ASM

As an associate at ASM, a management company looking after major artists such as George Michael, Holly Valance and Bond, Jon seems to be very much at ease with himself. In the calm atmosphere of his offices – dominated by a grand piano – we ask whether he thinks major labels are changing: are there fewer 'players' and real characters?

Current financial restraints means labels are starved of any level of 'risk' artists or indeed executives. Senior Executives are too expensive to fire and junior levels are cheap enough to resource but the 'engine room', the middle level which used to be full of wonderfully talented and gregarious characters, is certainly no more.

What was it like when you were an executive at Sony?

I was an international marketing executive at Sony for eight years, responsible for UK signed artists' overseas sales. To realise these goals my function was to work closely with artist management and the labels marketing department to provide a global marketing strategy ensuring that all the Sony Music affiliates around the world had the right marketing information to sell the artist in their territory.

When I 'swapped sides' I felt hugely empowered moving from one culture to another and was excited to be acting on behalf of the artist. It confirmed my theory that the business should be about the artist and the music. Too many major companies consider their senior executives more important than the artist. In recent years label heads have become all powerful, especially in the US. If they don't like your artist you've no chance. Power is vested in very few people there. No matter how good your music is, if your face doesn't fit you're not going to sell in America.

From the label's perspective it's all about meeting financial criteria. Much depends on chart position and sales – that's what releases the marketing funds. The better the act performs in the charts, the more money is released.

Which is completely understandable. With international it's about getting the nod from the senior execs: getting on thier 'radar' so to speak.

So how do you get the best for your artist with these sort of people?

Don't give them any reason to take their foot off the pedal or move on to another record. Something as simple as cancelling a day of press and PR for no reason will do significant damage to the artist–label relationship – it demotivates the local label which simply means your artist slips down the list of 'To Dos' for that day!

Be prepared to adapt your product – if you want to enjoy sales in SE Asia but your video contains nudity or violence then edit the clip to suit the local market. Whatever you do, do not give the label a reason not to promote your record. There is always another record to promote from the label, there certainly isn't always another single from your band to promote.

What about Jazz Summers' theory that you go for mid-America first with touring and promotions and then hit the other territories?

I can see the logic, especially as the States have such large venues that you can reach a large audience. But you have to work really hard and be prepared to invest a considerable amount of time to break an artist there. Yes, it's about getting in front of the audience and the American promotional team to build up your profile, but you'll need a big budget as well. Remember it takes a lot of time, money and commitment to tour in America, and it can eat into any profit you have made from your success in Europe.

Do you manage unsigned talent?

No, for ASM they have to have a record deal in place and are usually established artists. We look for artists that are successful but need an experienced and trusted management team who can deal with their label and all the other aspects of their career.

What do you hate about the business?

The way it treats artists who almost made it big, but not quite. Life after being in a band can be very miserable. It's great while you're being looked after by your label's promotional machine, but the bubble soon bursts when you realise you've been dropped by the label and you're skint. People in the street still see you as a star, but you're struggling to make ends meet. Some have managed it better, like Andrew Ridgeley, the other half of Wham! He is a close friend of mine and I've watched how brilliantly he has coped with life after fame.

The marketing campaign for Holly Valance's debut single caught people's attention.
Yeah, the public think she's very successful. She sold over a million records on the strength of one single, but she really needs two or three hits. She's at a critical stage of her career – three and a half minutes from total obscurity or four minutes from a great career if she gets another hit out.

So what do you think creates a hit record?
Three appearances on *CD:UK* have a lot to do with it. However good the song is, if you don't promote it, you will flop.

JAZZ SUMMERS – INDEPENDENT MANAGER

Jazz's clients have included Wham!, Lisa Stanfield, The Verve, Badly Drawn Boy, and the Snow Patrol. Our interview takes place around the kitchen table of his West London house. Jazz is full of energy and enthusiasm. He is very welcoming, but you wouldn't want to get on the wrong side of him or let him down in any way. Interviewing him is easy, as he is a great talker and passionate about the business. We ask him how he started out.
Managing Richard Digance. I did everything for him – I did his books, drove him to gigs. He lived in my house. I mortgaged it to buy him a van. My girlfriend at the time, Tracy Lea, cooked for him and washed his clothes. He even expected me to chat up his women for him. But then, I got fired. Rule number one – one day you will get fired, it's a real emotional thing. When Richard Digance rang up and said he didn't think it was working and he wanted this

bloke Joe Lusting as his new manager, it was like a divorce. I had given him my life for three years.

Do you feel as emotionally involved with your artists today? How do you decide who to work with?
I only manage an artist if I love the music and really love the people. An artist has got to have something special. If someone asked me to manage Iron Maiden, I wouldn't, even if I could make a million pounds a year. It's nothing personal, I just don't like them. My motto is that if you get the music right the money comes. Once I've made the decision to represent you, I represent you 100%. My interest is your interest. I am not in any record company pocket, nor in any publishing company or agent's pocket.

At times I have been really annoyed to find that some people are in other people's pockets. As a member of the Manager's Forum, I am pushing it to bring in a code of conduct for managers. There are too many managers out there ripping bands off. But I'm just as annoyed when I see managers who are just incompetent. Even when a band is massive you can lose it by making one mistake; playing the wrong gig, the wrong festival and at the wrong time. The worst is to over-expose a band at the wrong time.

Was this why you've taken a slower approach to building Badly Drawn Boy's profile?
Yes. When he started there was so much hype that fourteen record companies wanted to sign him. What we had to do was play down the hype, because it could have ruined him. If we hadn't, the press might have turned on him and buried him before he had even started. We wanted to give him space to develop as an artist. I didn't want to do a deal that was too big for him. We did a very structured deal with Excel. It was a three-album deal with fantastic points. It really wasn't hundreds of thousands of pounds. It was just a solid deal that enabled the record company to breathe and him to develop long term. They didn't have to flog him to death from the beginning. Everyone thinks I do massive deals. I don't. I do what is sensible for the artist.

You have a reputation for going to extreme lengths to break an artist and probably your most famous success was breaking Wham! in the States. How did you do it?

When we finally broke Wham! in America, it became obvious to me that it was the only pop band that you could take from practically nowhere to stadiums. This was because of the enormous push MTV, a new medium, gave them. The way to break America is to actually go there, play gigs and do PR. George decided he only wanted to do eight gigs, that's why we had to play stadiums. I remember the meeting with the label well. 'Look, Jazz,' they said, 'we think you're making a mistake on these stadiums and you could kill the band.' They all had a go at me, even Simon Napier Bell, my partner, who was meant to be on my side ...

I went home that night, with every last bit of my energy sapped. I was ready to give up when I listened to my answerphone and found a message saying that ticket sales for the stadium in Miami had gone mad. There were 8,000 kids outside the box office trying to buy tickets. I knew it would work. I rang the guy immediately in Miami and told him to say to everybody he had sold 30,000 tickets. It did the trick: all the other stadiums came in. George and Andy were convinced and sure enough by the end of the weekend he had sold 35,000 tickets; then we did 40 or 50,000 in San Francisco and two nights in Chicago at 20,000 each and 45,000 in Toronto. I was proved right. I learnt then that if twenty people in the room are against you, but you know you're right, you have to go with your instinct. I always have.

What's it like dealing with the major labels now?

What happens is the myth of 'Jazz' walks into the room. I don't take any bull-shit. I am tough, but not unreasonable. Some people might think I am trying to get something I shouldn't. Recently I went to talk to a couple of bosses of a record company about an artist they really wanted. I said I want this deal, and they asked how they could convince me to accept a little bit less. I said, 'You can't.' They said, 'What is this new negotiation tactic to say no?' I said that I was not asking for something unreasonable and they gave in.

What do you think is most important, points or an advance?

Yes. Of course a band needs something to live on. Record companies aren't stupid. They're only lending you money, so you want good points as well. The problem with lots of young managers is they don't understand. They have laid out five or six grand and they're skint. They just want to get a 150 grand advance so they have 30 grand in the bank. They don't know about points. They are offered 14 or 15, sometimes as low as 12, when they should get at least 20.

So what's the secret to working with record companies successfully?

You have to work with record companies as partners. I ran a record company for ten years and I saw some pretty bad managers. We're at a turning point in the business. Everybody's realising there are too many excesses and it's time to get back to basics. People are going to have to make albums for £50,000 or £70,000, not £250,000 or more. We have just made a fantastic album by Terra Diablo for £16,000.

When I took over The Verve they were £1.2 million in debt, because the record companies had allowed them to run up huge expenses. They were going to end up paying for it out of their royalties. It couldn't go on, it had to be sorted out.

How do you 'sort it out'?

First I sit down with the artist and their management, lawyer and accountant team and tell them they have to back me 100%. Even if you are stuck in a watertight contract, you can use the artist, as long as they are successful, to get your pound of flesh. If your artist is successful you need to look at two things: what the deal is about and how bad it really is. Then you have to see what your room to manoeuvre is – how many albums are left in the deal, can you up the points to extend the deal? Can you do a new deal on back catalogue? Usually if they see you have the artist with you and selling well, you can get somewhere.

What do you think about recoupment?

Recoupment is a joke ... it's illusionary. Say you get a £200,000 advance at 20 points; it's going to take you forever to recoup. The average record costs £8.20. Twenty points leaves you with £1.60. Then you have to take off the ridiculous packaging deduction of 25%. Ridiculous because for 40p you can make a CD, booklet and everything. You're really paying a manufacturing deduction, which makes you wonder what the record company is paying for. So you are left with £1.40 and you have to pay the producer out of that. You've probably got to sell 250,000 records to recoup. That means you have to go platinum first.

The labels are laughing. At £8 they've already made the artist pay all their manufacturing costs. So they give £1.60 to the artist. Then they have to pay 60p for the copyright. Most major record companies own their own distribution. If they don't, it will cost no more than 4% to buy it in. They give 10% to most stores, but to be on the safe side, let's say 14%. They are still making more than 50% margin. After 75,000 records they have recouped the advance and everything, but the artist has another 175,000 sales to go until they recoup.

We begin discussing the future of record companies and agree they are like the dinosaurs – never more powerful and arrogant than just before they were extinct. Jazz sums it up like this:

Record companies must think more about the future. Kids today are not asking for a new stereo. They want bigger speakers for their computer. Music's made and played on computers. Then in the middle we've got record companies controlling an outdated, cumbersome means of distribution. Personally, I'm not scared about the Internet. Anything that gets more music into more people's hands is great. It's the record companies that have to work out what they're going to do in the future. It has to be something more than distribution. There are lots of bright kids in record companies that get it. It's the ones at the top in their ivory towers who don't.

LAST THOUGHT ...

The future of management is exciting. Controlling talent in other creative industries such as TV and film and where personalities are key, such as sport, is where the power is moving. Just as Hollywood talent agencies 'package' movies, so there are huge opportunities for future managers to exploit the development vacuum left by the cost-cutting programmes at major labels, by packaging, promoting and exploiting all possible output from their clients from publishing, recording, live, online, merchandising and even TV. Their ability to bring the artist closer to all potential distribution points will enable them to give their clients more creative control and be more efficient and flexible.

Perhaps, 'manager' is too narrow a definition for this role, but managers are best placed to become these players. The most creative and entrepreneurial have no limits to their future.

If you're considering management as a career, it's worth thinking about the future. We have emphasised the importance of understanding how to package artists prior to a label deal. Perhaps we should push it further and encourage you not to do the label deal, but do it yourself. Remember as a manager you are in a unique position, as only you and the artist are involved in everything. Labels may be important but they have little control over tours, merchandising or online fan clubs. This 360° vision positions you perfectly to exploit new technologies and trends.

So happy hunting – for that special act. The one you cannot live without managing. Remember, the future is limitless ...

1 2 3 4 5 6 7 8 9 10 11 12 13 14 15

ARTIST MANAGEMENT

STEVE ALLEN ENTERTAINMENTS
60 Broadway, Peterborough, Cambs
PE1 1SU
T: 01733 569589 F: 01733 561854
Email: steve@sallenent.co.uk
Website: sallenent.co.uk
Director: Steve Allen

BEST PR
3rd Floor, 29–31 Cowper Street, London
EC2A 4AT
T: 020 7608 4590 F: 020 7608 4599

CA MANAGEMENT
Air Studios, Lyndhurst Road, London
NW3 5NG
T: 020 7794 0660 F: 020 7916 2784
Email: adam@camanagement.co.uk
MD: Adam Sharp

HAL CARTER ORGANISATION
101 Hazelwood Lane, Palmers Green,
London N13 5HQ
T: 020 8886 2801 F: 020 8882 7380
Email: artistes@halcarterorg.com
Website: halcarterorg.co.uk
Managing Director: Hal Carter

CHOIR CONNEXION & LONDON COMMUNITY GOSPEL CHOIR
9 Greenwood Drive, London E4 9HL
T: 020 8531 5562 F: 020 8523 4159
Email: groovking@aol.com
Website: lcgc.org.uk
Principal: Bazil Meade

CLASSIC PICTURES ENTERTAINMENT
Shepperton Studios, Studios Rd,
Shepperton, Middx TW17 0QD
T: 01932 592016 F: 01932 592046
Email: ben.williams@classicpictures.co.uk
Website: rwcc.com
Marketing Mgr: Ben Williams

COALITION MANAGEMENT
Devonshire House, 12 Barley Mow
Passage, London W4 4PH
T: 020 8987 0123 F: 020 8987 0345
Email: management@coalitiongroup.co.uk
Tim Vigon/Tony Perrin

COURTYARD MANAGEMENT
22 The Nursery, Sutton Courtenay,
Oxon OX14 4UA
T: 01235 845800 F: 01235 847692
Email: mail@cyard.com
Partner: Chris Hufford

CRAZEL TOWN
Unit 20 Montpelier Court, Station Road,
Bristol BS6 5EE
T: 0117 942 6677 F: 0117 942 6677
Email: matt@crazeltown.com
Website: crazeltown.com
Manager: Matt Booth

CREATION MANAGEMENT LTD
2 Berkley Grove, Primrose Hill, London
NW1 8XY
T: 020 7483 2541 F: 020 7722 8412
Email: Creation.management@dial.pipex.com
MD: Stephen King

CRIMSON MUSIC MANAGEMENT
Red Bus Studios, 34 Salisbury Street,
London NW8 8QE
T: 020 7724 2243 F: 020 7724 2871
MD: Catherine Crawley

MANAGERS

CRISPY MUSIC LTD
15 Barley Hills, Thorley Park, Bishops Stortford, Herts CM23 4DS
T: 01279 865070 F: 01279 834268
Email: simon@ozrics.com
Website: ozrics.com
MD: Simon Baker

PAUL CROCKFORD MANAGEMENT (PCM)
Latimer House, 272 Latimer Rd, London W10 6QY
T: 020 8962 8272 F: 020 8962 8243
Email: pcm.assistant@virgin.net
MD: Paul Crockford

STEVE CROSBY MANAGEMENT LTD
Bentley Lodge, Brighton Road, Banstead, Surrey SM7 1AN
T: 01737 271503 F: 01737 355443
Email: scm@bootscoot.demon.co.uk
Director: Steve Crosby

CRUISIN' MUSIC
Charlton Farm Studios, Hemington, Bath BA3 5XS
T: 01373 834161 F: 01373 834164
Email: sil@cruisin.co.uk
Website: cruisin.co.uk
MD: Sil Willcox

CULTURAL FOUNDATION
Hollin Bush, Dalehead, Rosedale, North Yorkshire YO18 8RL
T: 01751 417147 F: 01751 417804
Email: cultfound@supanet.com
MD: Peter Bell

DAVID CURTIS MANAGEMENT
Priors Hall, Tye Green, Elsenham, Bishop Stortford, Hertfordshire CM22 6DY
T: 01279 813240 F: 01279 815895
Email: procentral@aol.com
Website: pasadena.co.uk
Director: David Curtis

D2MM (DIRECT2 MUSIC MANAGEMENT)
3, 6 Belsize Crescent, Belsize Park, London NW3 5QU
T: 020 7431 1609 F: 020 7431 1609
Email: david@d2mm.com
Website: d2mm.com
Director: David Otzen

DADDY MANAGEMENT
15 Holywell Row, London EC2A 4JB
T: 020 7684 5229 F: 020 7684 5230
Email: nicky.demuth@virgin.net; paul.benney@virgin.net
Management Asst: Nicky Demuth

DARA MANAGEMENT
Unit 4, Great Ship Street, Dublin 8, Ireland
T: +353 1 478 3455
F: +353 1 478 2143
Email: irishmus@ioe.ie
Website: irelandcd.com
MD: Joe O'Reilly

DARK BLUES MANAGEMENT
Puddephats, Markyate, Herts AL3 8AZ
T: 01582 842226 F: 01582 840010
Email: info@darkblues.co.uk
Website: darkblues.co.uk
Office Mgr: Fiona Hewetson

JACKIE DAVIDSON MANAGEMENT
The Business Village, 3 Broomhill Rd, London SW18 4JQ
T: 020 8870 8744 F: 020 8874 1578
Email: jackie@jdmanagement.co.uk
Website: jdmanagement.co.uk
MD: Jackie Davidson

LENA DAVIS JOHN BISHOP ASSOCIATES
Cotton's Farmhouse, Whiston Road, Cogenhoe, Northamptonshire NN7 1NL
T: 01604 891487 F: 01604 890405
Lena Davis

DAYTIME ENTERTAINMENTS
28 Harvist Rd, Queens Park, London NW6 6SH
T: 07973 479 191
Email: diane@daytime-ent.com
Website: daytime-ent.com
MD: Diane Young

DCM INTERNATIONAL
Suite 3, 294-296 Nether Street, Finchley, London N3 1RJ
T: 020 8343 0848 F: 020 8343 0747
Email: dancecm@aol.com
Website: dancecrazy.co.uk
MD: Kelly Isaacs

DD PRODUCTIONS
38 Johnston Terrace, London NW2 6QJ
T: 020 8450 0069 F: 020 8450 0079
Email: ddproductions@easynet.co.uk
Website: duranduran.com
Office Manager: Emma Anderson

DOGMA MANAGEMENT
Bank Chambers, Market Place, Stockport SK1 1UN
T: 0161 480 4281 F: 0161 480 0904
Email: zhian@dogma.uk.com
Manager: Zhian Hopwood

DOMAIN MUSIC
Unit 9, TGEC, Town Hall Approach Road, London N15 4RX
T: 020 8375 3608 F: 020 8375 3487
Email: info@domainmusic.co.uk
Website: domainmusic.co.uk
Dir: Michael Lowe

DAVID DORRELL MANAGEMENT
25 Duncan Terrace, London N1 8BS
T: 020 7689 8858 F: 020 7278 0768
Email: dorrell@dircon.co.uk
Shane Egan

STEVE DRAPER ENTERTAINMENTS
2 The Coppice, Beardwood Manor, Blackburn, Lancashire BB2 7BQ
T: 01254 679005 F: 01254 679005
Email: steve@stevedraperents.fsbusiness.co.uk
Website: stevedraper.co.uk
Owner: Steve Draper

DREADED SUNNY DAY MUSIC LTD
5 St. John's Lane, London EC1M 4BH
T: 020 7549 2807
Email: info@dreadedsunnyday.com
Website: dreadedsunnyday.com
MD: Mark Jackson
or: Barry Dye

EAR FOR MUSIC MANAGEMENT
Studio 52, Canalot Studios, 222 Kensal Road, London W10 5BN
T: 020 8960 7449 F: 020 8960 7524
Email: info@earformusic.tv
Partner: Steve Crosby

EARTH MUSIC
50 Hadley Rd, Barnet, Herts EN5 5QR
T: 020 8441 3247

MANAGERS

ECLIPSE-PJM
PO Box 3059, South Croydon, Surrey
CR2 8TL
T: 020 8657 2627 F: 020 8657 2627
Email: eclipsepjm@btinternet.com
MD: Paul Johnson

EG MANAGEMENT LTD
PO Box 4397, London W1A 7RZ
T: 020 8540 9935
A&R: Chris Kettle

EGO 3M1
Cooper House, 2 Michael House,
London SW6 2AD
T: 020 7731 8899 F: 020 7384 9666
Email: info@justegoit.com;
info@egopr.com
Director: Dylan Watkins

ELITE SQUAD MANAGEMENT
Valtony, Loxwood Road, Plaistow,
W Sussex RH14 0NY
T: 01403 871200 F: 01403 871334
Email: tony@elitesquad.freeserve.co.uk
MD: Tony Nunn

EMKAY ENTERTAINMENTS
Nobel House, Regent Centre, Blackness
Road, Linlithgow, Lothian EH49 7HU
T: 01506 845555 F: 01506 845566
Email: emkay@cwcom.net
Proprietor: Mike Kean

EMPEROR MANAGEMENT
2 Brayburne Ave, London SW4 6AA
T: 020 7720 0826 F: 020 7720 1869
Email: john.empson@btopenworld.com
MD: John Empson

ENTERTAINMENT AGENCY
Little Haven, Elmore Lane, Quedgeley,
Gloucestershire GL2 3NW
T: 01452 721966 F: 01452 722489
MD: Norman R Broady

EPM
Unit 204, The Saga Centre, 326 Kensal
Rd, London W10 5BZ
T: 020 8964 4900 F: 020 8964 9752
Email: jonas@electronicpm.co.uk
Website: electronicpm.co.uk
Partner: Jonas Stone

ESCAPE MUSIC MANAGEMENT
45 Endymion Road, London SW2 2BU
T: 020 8244 0915 F: 0870 458 0272
Email: mail@escapeman.com

EUROPEAN ARTS & MEDIA
11-12 Warrington Place, Dublin 2,
Ireland
T: +353 1 664 4700
F: +353 1 664 4747
Email: info@euroartsmedia.com
Website: euroartsmedia.com
Dir: Nigel Tebay

EXTREME MUSIC
4-7 Forewoods Common, Holt, Wilts
BA14 6PJ
T: 01225 782984
Email: george@xtrememusic.co.uk
Website: xtrememusic.co.uk
MD: George Allen

FBI
Routenburn House, Routenburn Road,
Largs, Strathclyde KA30 8SQ
T: 01475 673392 F: 01475 674075
Email: wbrown8152@aol.com
Owner: Willie Brown

FEEDBACK COMMUNICATIONS
The Court, Long Sutton, Hook,
Hampshire RG29 1TA
T: 01256 862865 F: 01256 862182
Email: feedback@crapola.com
Website: crapola.com
Management: Keir Jens-Smith

MALCOLM FELD AGENCY
Malina House, Sandforth Road,
Liverpool,
Merseyside L12 1JY
T: 0151 259 6565 F: 0151 259 5006
Email: malcolm@malcolmfeld.co.uk
Website: malcolmfeld.co.uk
Agent/Manager/Promoter: Malcolm Feld

FIRST COLUMN MANAGEMENT LTD
The Metway, 55 Canning St, Brighton,
East Sussex BN2 0EF
T: 01273 688359 F: 01273 689445
Email: fcm@firstcolumn.co.uk
Director: Phil Nelson

FIRST MOVE MANAGEMENT LTD
137 Shooters Hill Rd, Blackheath,
London SE3 8UQ
T: 020 8305 2077 F: 020 8305 2077
Email: firstmoves@aol.com
Website: firstmove.biz
Creative Director: Janis MacIlwaine

FIRST STEP MANAGEMENT
96 George St, Mansfield,
Nottinghamshire
NG19 6SB
T: 01623 642778 F: 01623 642778
Email: first.step@Tesco.net
Website: theearlofsound.co.uk
MD: David Butcher

FIVEMILESHIGH
17 Maidavale Crescent, Styvechale,
Coventry CV3 6FZ
T: 07811 469888
Email: dave@fivemileshigh.com
MD: Dave Robinson

FLAMECRACKER MANAGEMENT
PO Box 394, Hemel Hempstead
HP3 9WL
T: 01442 403445 F: 01442 403445
Email: kdavis@aol.com
Website: frantik.org
Manager: Karen Davis

FLAMINGO RECORD MANAGEMENT
Thornhurst Place, Rowplatt Lane,
Felbridge,
East Grinstead RH19 2PA
T: 01342 317943 F: 01342 317943
Email: ed@badgerflamingoanimation.co.uk
Website: badgerflamingoanimation.co.uk
MD: Ed Palmieri

FLICK PRODUCTIONS
PO Box 888, Penzance, Cornwall
TR20 8ZP
T: 01736 788798 F: 01736 787898
Email: info@flickpro.demon.co.uk

FLUENT MUSIC
PO Box 8840, Solihull, Birmingham
B91 3DW
T: 0121 764 5078 F: 0121 764 5080
Email: fluent@kingadora.com
Website: fluentmusic.com
Manager: Mark Chester

FLUKE
Pan West, 326 Kensal Road, London
W10 5BZ

T: 020 8960 2252 F: 07968 404 374
Email: julian@fluke.demon.co.uk
Manager: Julian Nugent

THE FLYING MUSIC CO LTD
FM House, 110 Clarendon Road,
London W11 2HR
T: 020 7221 7799 F: 020 7221 5016
Email: info@flyingmusic.co.uk
Website: flyingmusic.com
Derek Nicol, Paul Walden

FORMIDABLE MANAGEMENT
4th Floor, 40 Langham Street, London
W1W 7AS
T: 020 7323 4410 F: 020 7323 4180
Email: info@formidable-mgmt.com
Website: formidable-mgmt.com
Directors: Carl Marcantonio, Nik
Jameson

ROGER FORRESTER MANAGEMENT
18 Harley House, London NW1 5HE
T: 020 7486 8056 F: 020 7487 5663
MD: Roger Forrester

FRESHWATER HUGHES MANAGEMENT
PO Box 54, Northaw, Herts EN6 4PY
T: 01707 661431 F: 01707 664141
Email: hughesee@tiscali.co.uk
fresh@btconnect.com
Jackie Hughes/Brian Freshwater

FRIARS MANAGEMENT LTD
33 Alexander Road, Aylesbury,
Buckinghamshire HP20 2NR
T: 01296 434731 F: 01296 422530
Email: fmluk@aol.com
Website: fmlmusic.com
MD: David Stopps

FUNKY STAR
4 Moray Place, Glasgow G41 2AQ
T: 0141 423 0149 F: 0141 423 0149
Email: info@funkystar.org.uk
Website: funkystar.org.uk
Director: Alan McCusker-Thompson

FURTIVE MASS TRANSIT SYSTEMS LLP
First floor, 7-13 Cotton's Gardens,
Shoreditch, London E2 8DN
T: 020 7613 5666 F: 020 7739 6872
Email: mail@furtive-mts.com
Website: furtive-mts.com

FUTURE MANAGEMENT
PO Box 183, Chelmsford, Essex
CM2 9XN
T: 01245 601910 F: 01245 601048
Email: Futuremgt@aol.com
Website: futuremanagement.co.uk
MD: Joe Ferrari

PATRICK GARVEY MANAGEMENT LTD
Top Floor, 59 Lansdowne Place, Hove,
East Sussex BN3 1FL
T: 01273 206623 F: 01273 208484
Email: patrick@patrickgarvey.com
Website: patrickgarvey.com
Director: Andrea McDermott

GEMS
Firs Cottage, 5 Firs Close, Forest Hill,
London SE23 1BB
T: 020 8291 7052 F: 020 8699 2279
Email: genica.pigfish@virgin.net
Website: dreamcatcher-
records.enta.com
MD: Gem Howard-Kemp

KIM GLOVER MANAGEMENT
PO Box 468, Maidstone, Kent
ME14 1HQ
T: 01622 759444 F: 01622 754749
Email: kimglovermgmt@aol.com
MD: Kim Glover

GOLA ENTERTAINMENT
7 Crofton Terrace, Dun Laoghaire,
Co.Dublin, Ireland
T: +353 1 202 0909
F: +353 1 280 1229
Email: gola@iol.ie
Website: moyabrennan.com
Managers: Tim Jarvis & Leon Brennan

GOLDPUSH LTD
38 Langham Street, London W1N 5RH
T: 020 7323 9522 F: 020 7323 9526
Email: razgold@goldpush.com
MD: Raz Gold

GR MANAGEMENT
974 Pollokshaws Rd, Shawlands,
Glasgow, Strathclyde G41 2HA
T: 0141 632 1111 F: 0141 649 0042
Email: g.r@dial.pipex.com
MDs: Rab Andrew/Gerry McElhone

GRANT & FORESIGHT
192D Brooklands Road, Weybridge,
Surrey KT13 0RJ
T: 01932 855337 F: 01932 851245
Email: davidmanagement@aol.com
MD: David Morgan

JAMES GRANT MANAGEMENT
Syon Lodge, London Road, Isleworth,
Middlesex TW7 5BH
T: 020 8232 4100 F: 020 8232 4101
Email: paul@jamesgrant.co.uk
Website: jamesgrant.co.uk
Joint MD: Paul Worsley

GRAPEDIME MUSIC
28 Hurst Crescent, Barrowby, Grantham,
Lincolnshire NG32 1TE
T: 01476 560241 F: 01476 560241
Email: grapedime@pjbray.globalnet.co.uk
A&R Manager: Phil Bray

STAN GREEN MANAGEMENT
PO Box 4, Dartmouth, Devon TQ6 0YD
T: 01803 770046 F: 01803 770075
Email: sgm@clara.co.uk
Website: keithfloyd.co.uk
MD: Stan Green

GRINNING RAT MUSIC MANAGEMENT
19a High Street, Midsomer Norton,
Bath BA3 2DR
T: 01761 419333
Email: info@grinningrat.co.uk
Website: helenaonline.com
MD: Ian Softley

PETER HAINES MANAGEMENT
Montfort, The Avenue, Kingston,
Lewes, East Sussex BN7 3LL
T: 01273 475846
Email: peter@uktourist.freeserve.co.uk
Manager: Peter Haines

TONY HALL GROUP OF COMPANIES
16-17 Grafton House, 2-3 Golden Sq,
London W1F 9HR
T: 020 7437 1958 F: 020 7437 3852
Email: tony@tonyhallgroup.com
MD: Tony Hall

KEITH HARRIS MUSIC
204 Courthouse Road, Maidenhead,
Berkshire SL6 6HU
T: 01628 674422 F: 01628 631379
Email: keithharris1@compuserve.com
MD: Keith Harris

LES HART (SOUTHAMPTON ENTERTAINMENTS)
6 Crookhorn Lane, Purbrook,
Waterlooville, Hants PO7 5QE
T: 023 9225 8373 F: 023 9225 8369
Email: rod@leshart.co.uk
Website: leshart.co.uk
Proprietor: Rod Watts

THE HEADLINE AGENCY
32 Beechmount Drive, Clonskeagh,
Dublin 14, Ireland
T: +353 1 296 6041
F: +353 1 296 6042
Email: info@musicheadline.com
Website: musicheadline.com
MD: Madeleine Seiler

HEADQUARTERS PUBLICITY
Tir na Nog, The Hamlet, The Bank,
Marlcliff, Bidford on Avon,Warwickshire
B50 4BU
T: 01789 772955 F: 01789 772955
Email: johntully@thehamlet6.freeserve.co.uk
Proprietor: John Tully

HEADSTONE MANAGEMENT
46 Tintagel Way, Woking, Surrey
GU22 7DG
T: 01483 856 760
Email: colinfwspencer@hotmail.com
Website: sub-5.com
MD: Colin Spencer

DENNIS HEANEY PROMOTIONS
Whitehall, Ashgrove Road, Newry,
Co Down BT34 1QN
T: 028 3026 8658 F: 028 3026 6673
Email: dennis_heaney@hotmail.com
Website: susanmccann.com
Director: Dennis Heaney

HEAVENLY MANAGEMENT
47 Frith Street, London W1D 4SE
T: 020 7494 2998 F: 020 7437 3317
Email: info@heavenlymanagement.com
Dirs: Martin Kelly, Andrew Walsh

HEAVYWEIGHT MANAGEMENT
33 Sunnymead Road, London
SW15 5HY
T: 020 8878 0800 F: 020 8878 3080
Email: info@heavyweight.com
Website: heavyweightman.com
MD: Simon Goffe/Emily Moxon

HUG MANAGEMENT
51-55 Highfield Street, Liverpool L3 6AA
T: 0151 737 2381 F: 0151 288 9450
Email: mail@hugmanagement.com
Website: hugmanagement.com
MD: Mark Cowley

HUTT RUSSELL ORGANISATION
PO Box 64, Cirencester, Gloucestershire
GL7 5YD
T: 01285 644622 F: 01285 642291
Email: shows@huttrussell.co.uk

IE MUSIC LTD
111 Frithville Gardens, London W12 7JG
T: 020 8600 3400 F: 020 8600 3401
Email: info@iemusic.co.uk
Website: iemusic.co.uk
David Enthoven

IMPRO MANAGEMENT
35 Britannia Row, London N1 8QH
T: 020 7704 8080 F: 020 7704 1616
Email: guy@impromanagement.com
Director: Guy Trezise

IN DEMAND MANAGEMENT
25 Cambridge Gardens, Edinburgh
EH6 5DH
T: 07967 361 146 F: 0131 467 5882
Email: info@indemand.co.uk

INDUCTIVE MANAGEMENT
PO Box 20503, London NW8 0WY
T: 020 7586 5427 F: 020 7483 2164
Email: Inductrec@aol.com
Director: Colin Peel

INFLUENTIAL
PO Box 306, Manchester M14 6GX
T: 07050 395 708
Email: info@influential.net
Website: influential.net
MD: Mike Swindells

INS-YNC
74 Harberton Rd, London N19 3JP
T: 020 7263 5299 F: 020 7263 5299
Email: charlie@ins-ync.co.uk
Website: ins-ync.co.uk
MD: Charlie Inskip

INTELLIGENT MUSIC MANAGEMENT LTD
42A Malden Road, London NW5 3HG
T: 020 7284 1955 F: 020 7424 9876
Email: info@glatmanent.com
MD: Daniel Glatman

INTERCEPTOR ENTERPRISES
98 White Lion Street, London N1 9PF
T: 020 7278 8001 F: 020 7713 6298
Email: info@interceptor.co.uk
Manager: Charlie Charlton

INTERZONE MANAGEMENT
Interzone House, 74-77 Magdalen Road, Oxford OX4 1RE
T: 01865 205600 F: 01865 205700
Email: interzone@rotator.co.uk
Website: rotator.co.uk
MD: Richard Cotton

INTUITION MUSIC LTD
1 Devonport Mews, London W12 8NG
T: 020 7565 4750 F: 020 7565 4751
Email: berni@intuitionmusic.com
Website: MewsMedia.com
MD: Bernie Griffiths

IRC2 LONDON LTD
2nd Floor, 12 Mercer Street, London
WC2H 9QD
T: 020 7240 8848 F: 020 7240 8864
Email: irc2london@aol.com
MD: Lenny Zakatek

JAM X MANAGEMENT
22A Lambolle Place, London NW3 4PG
T: 020 7813 0833 F: 020 7209 0019
Email: jamx@easynet.co.uk
Dir: Julian Able

JAMDOWN LTD
Stanley House Studios, 39 Stanley Gardens, London W3 7SY
T: 020 8735 0280 F: 020 8930 1073
Email: othman@jamdown-music.com
Website: jamdown-music.com
MD: Othman Mukhlis

1 2 3 4 5 6 7 8 9 10 11 12 13 14 15

MANAGERS

JBM MANAGEMENT
317 Portway, Woodhouse Park,
Manchester M22 0DL
T: 0161 610 1856 F: 0161 610 1856
Email: JBMManagement@aol.com
MD: Jason Brierley

JESTER MUSIC
PO Box 903, Sutton, Surrey SM2 6BY
T: 020 8642 1679 F: 020 8642 5203
Email: info@jestermusic.co.uk
Website: jestermusic.co.uk
MD: Andy Cook

JFD MANAGEMENT
310 King Street, London W6 0RR
T: 020 8748 9488 F: 020 8748 9489
Email: jfdmanagement@pavilion.co.uk
MD: Jasmine Daines

JIVE ENTERTAINMENTS
PO Box 5865, Corby, Northamptonshire
NN17 5ZT
T: 01536 406406 F: 01536 400082
Email: hojive@aol.com
MD: Dave Bartram

JKM MANAGEMENT
3 Robb Road, Stanmore, Middlesex
HA7 3SQ
T: 020 8954 1064 F: 020 7253 8480
Email: jmartin@musicchoice.co.uk
Jason Martin

PHIL JONES LTD
826 Wilmslow Road, Manchester
M20 2RN
T: 0161 445 9904 F: 0161 445 9764
Email: philjones_presents@msn.com
Website: event-associates.co.uk
MD: Phil Jones

JPR MANAGEMENT
Unit 4 E & F, Westpoint, 33-34 Warple
Way, London W3 0RG
T: 020 8749 8874 F: 020 8749 8774
Email: info@jprmanagement.co.uk
Website: jprmanagement.co.uk
John Reid

PAT KANE/HUE & CRY
9 Crown Rd South, Glasgow G12 9DJ
T: 07718 588497
Email: patkane@theplayethic.com
Website: theplayethic.com
Singer/Writer: Pat Kane

KLUBDOCTORZ ARTIST MANAGEMENT
PO Box 4809, Bournemouth, Dorset
BH7 6WA
T: 0786 643 3936 F: 0870 706 4830
Email: paul@klubdoctorz.co.uk
Website: klubdoctorz.co.uk
Operations Director: Paul Woodgate

KRACK MUSIC MANAGEMENT
East Yorkshire
T: 01405 861124
Email: alan@krack.prestel.co.uk
MD: Alan Lacey

KSO RECORDS
PO Box 159, Chathan, Kent ME5 7AQ
T: 07956 120837
Email: ksorecords@hotmail.com
Website: ksorecords.pwp.blueyonder.co.uk
MD: Antonio Sloane

KTM
754 Fulham Road, London SW6 5SH
T: 020 7731 7074 F: 020 7736 8605
Email: KTM@dircon.co.uk

KUDOS MANAGEMENT
Crown Studios, 16-18 Crown Road, Twickenham, Middx TW1 3EE
T: 020 8891 4233 F: 020 8891 2339
Email: kudos@camino.co.uk
MD: Billy Budis

LEAP
33 Green Walk, London NW4 2AL
T: 020 8202 4120 F: 020 8202 4120
Email: leap@gideonbenaim.com
MD: Gideon Benaim

LEBOR ARTIST MANAGEMENT LTD
PO Box 366, Egham, Surrey TW20 8DN
T: 01784 740040 F: 01784 741549
Email: info@leborgroup.com
Website: leborgroup.com
Joint MDs: Matthew Atkinson/Jeremy Lebor

LET IT ROCK MANAGEMENT
PO Box 3, Newport NP20 3YB
T: 07973 715875 F: 01633 677672
Email: alan.jones@amserve.com
Principal: Alan Jones

LEVEL 22 MANAGEMENT
6 Hyldavale Ave, Gatley, Cheshire SK8 4DE
T: 0161 428 3150 F: 0161 428 3150
Email: level22uk@yahoo.co.uk
Director: Randolph Mike

LINE-UP PMC
9A Tankerville Place, Newcastle-upon-Tyne, Tyne and Wear NE2 3AT
T: 0191 281 6449 F: 0191 212 0913
Email: c.a.murtagh@btinternet.com
Website: on-line-records.co.uk
Owner: Christopher Murtagh

LONG TERM MANAGEMENT
Suite B, 2 Tunstall Road, London SW9 8DA
T: 020 7733 5400 F: 020 7733 4449
Email: paulette@longterm.freeserve.co.uk
MD: Paulette Long

LOOSE
PO Box 67, Runcorn, Cheshire WA7 4NL
T: 01928 566261
Email: jaki.florek@virgin.net
Manager: Jaki Florek

MAD MANAGEMENT LTD
7 The Chase, Rayleigh, Essex SS6 8QL
T: 01268 771113 F: 01268 774192
Email: madmanagementltd@aol.com
MD: Alex Rose

MADISON MANAGEMENT
6 Cinnamon Gardens, Guildford, Surrey GU2 9YZ
T: 01483 237603
Email: info@madisonmanagement.co.uk
Website: madisonmanagement.co.uk
Artist Manager: Paul Harvey

MADRIGAL MUSIC
Guy Hall, Awre, Glocs GL14 1EL
T: 01594 510512 F: 01594 510512
Email: artists@madrigalmusic.co.uk
Website: madrigalmusic.co.uk
MD/Head of A&R: Nick Ford

MAKO MUSIC LTD
Basement, 71 Netherwood Rd, London W14 0BP
T: 020 7602 0705 F: 020 7602 0705
Email: dombrownlow@makomusic.com
Website: makomusic.com
MD: Dominic Brownlow

THE MANAGEMENT COMPANY
PO Box 150, Chesterfield S40 0YT
T: 0870 746 8478
Email: mail@themanagementcompany.biz
Website: themanagementcompany.biz
MD: Tony Hedley

MAP MANAGEMENT
208 Huyton Lane, Huyton, Liverpool, Merseyside L36 1TQ
T: 0151 489 6142 F: 0151 449 3518
Email: mike@virgo-music.demon.co.uk
Mgr: Mike Walker

MARKO POLO (UK)
The Barn, Fordwater Lane, Chichester, West Sussex PO19 4PT
T: 01243 789786 F: 01243 789787
Email: markoPolo@compuserve.com
Website: markopolo.co.uk
Director: Mark Ringwood

MARSHALL ARTS MANAGEMENT
Leeder House, 6 Erskine Road, London NW3 3AJ
T: 020 7586 3831 F: 020 7586 1422
Email: info@marshall-arts.co.uk
Website: marshall-arts.co.uk
MD: Barrie Marshall

RICHARD MARTIN MANAGEMENT
18 Ambrose Place, Worthing, West Sussex BN11 1PZ
T: 01903 823456 F: 01903 823847
Email: ric@ricmartinagency.com
Website: hot-chocolate.co.uk
Manager: Richard Martin

NIGEL MARTIN-SMITH MANAGEMENT
54 Princess Street, Manchester M1 6HS
T: 0161 237 9237 F: 0161 236 7557
Director: Nigel Martin-Smith

MATRIX MANAGEMENT
91 Peterborough Road, London SW6 3BW
T: 020 7731 3053 F: 020 7371 8613
Email: matrixrecording@connectfree.co.uk
Manager: Sarah Partridge

MAXIMUM MUSIC
9 Heathmans Road, Parsons Green, London SW6 4TJ
T: 020 7731 1112 F: 020 7731 1113
Email: info@maximummusic.co.uk
MD: Nicky Graham, Deni Lew

MBL
1 Cowcross St, London EC1M 6DR
T: 020 7253 7755 F: 020 7251 8096
MD: Robert Linney

MICHAEL MCDONAGH MANAGEMENT
The Studio, R.O. 63 Station Road, Winchmore Hill, London N21 3NB
T: 020 8364 3121 F: 020 8364 3090
Email: caramusicltd@dial.pipex.com
Director: Michael McDonagh

MCLEOD HOLDEN ENTERPRISES LTD
Priory House, 1133 Hessle High Road, Hull, East Yorkshire HU4 6SB
T: 01482 565444 F: 01482 353635
Email: info@mcleod-holden.com
Website: mcleod-holden.com
Chairman: Peter McLeod

TONI MEDCALF MANAGEMENT
31 Grove Road, Barnes, London SW13 0HH

T: 020 8876 2421 F: 020 8876 6621
Email: TTMManagement@aol.com
Artist Manager: Toni Medcalf

METAMORPHOSIS MANAGEMENT
Crown House, 225 Kensington High St, London W8 6SA
T: 020 7361 1515 F: 020 7937 3867
Email: mark@crownmusic.co.uk
Manager: Mark Hargreaves

MIDI MANAGEMENT LTD
The Old Barn, Jenkins Lane, Great Hallingbury, Essex CM22 7QL
T: 01279 759067 F: 01279 759069

NAME MUSIC
Innovation Labs, Watford Rd, Harrow, Middx HA1 3TP
T: 020 8357 7305 F: 020 8357 7326
Email: sam@name-uk.net
MD: Sam Shemtob

NATIVE MANAGEMENT
Unit 32, Ransome's Dock, 35-37 Parkgate Rd, London SW11 4NP
T: 020 7801 1919 F: 020 7738 1819
Email: info@nativemanagement.com
Website: nativemanagement.com
MD: Peter

NEM PRODUCTIONS (UK)
Priory House, 55 Lawe Road, South Shields, Tyne and Wear NE33 2AL
T: 0191 427 6207 F: 0191 427 6323
Email: 100604.2015@compuserve.com
Website: nemproductions.com
Dave Smith

NETTWERK: ORNADEL MANAGEMENT
Clearwater Yard, 35 Inverness St, London NW1 7HB
T: 020 7424 7500 F: 020 7424 7501
Email: eleanor@nettwerk.com
Website: ornadel.com
Guy Ornadel

NO HALF MEASURES LTD
Studio 19, St. George's Studios, 93-97 St. George's Road, Glasgow G3 6JA
T: 0141 331 9888 F: 0141 331 9889
Email: info@nohalfmeasures.com
Website: nohalfmeasures.com
MD: Dougie Souness

NO QUARTER MANAGEMENT
171 Tolcarne Drive, London HA5 2DN
T: 020 8868 0170
Email: info@noquartermanagement.com
Website: noquartermanagement.com
Director: Christian Miller

RICHARD OGDEN MANAGEMENT
7, Russell Gardens, London W14 8EZ
T: 020 7751 1300 F: 020 7348 0831
Email: mail@richardogdenmanagement.com
Website: richardogdenmanagement.com
MD: Richard Ogden

PARK PROMOTIONS
PO Box 651, Oxford 0X2 9AZ
T: 01865 241717 F: 01865 204556
Email: info@parkrecords.com
Website: parkrecords.com
MD: John Dagnell

PARLIAMENT MANAGEMENT
PO Box 6328, London N2 0UN
T: 020 8444 9841 F: 020 8442 0983
Email: woolfmanw@cs.com
A&R: Damian Baetens

MANAGERS

PART ROCK MANAGEMENT LTD
Level 2, 65 Newman St, London
W1T 3EG
T: 020 7224 1992 F: 020 7224 0111
Email: stewartyoung@mindspring.com
MD: Stewart Young

JUSTIN PERRY MANAGEMENT
PO Box 20242, London NW1 7FL
T: 020 7485 1113
Email: info@proofsongs.co.uk

PEZ MANAGEMENT
15 Sutherland House, 137-139
Queenstown Road, London SW8 3RJ
T: 020 7978 1503 F: 020 7978 1502
Email: perryfmorgan@hotmail.com
Management: Perry Morgan

PILOT MANAGEMENT
222 Canalot Studios, 222 Kensal Road,
London W10 5BN
T: 020 7565 2227 F: 020 7565 2228
Email: dayo.pilotcreativeagency.com
Manager: Amanda Fairhurst

PJ MUSIC
156A High Street, London Colney,
Hertfordshire AL2 1QF
T: 01727 827017 F: 01727 827017
Email: pjmusic@ukonline.co.uk
Website: schmusicmusic.com
Dir: Paul J Bowrey

PLATINUM MANAGEMENT
42 Cheriton Close, Queens Walk, Ealing,
London W5 1TR
T: 020 8997 8851 F: 020 8997 8851
Email: carolyn@platinum.fsnet.co.uk
MD: Carolyn Norman

THE PRECIOUS ORGANISATION
The Townhouse, 1 Park Gate, Glasgow
G3 6DL
T: 0141 353 2255 F: 0141 353 3545
Email: elliot@precioustoo.com
MD: Elliot Davis

PREMIERE SUITE
4, Delme Court, Maytree Road, Fareham,
Hampshire PO16 0HX
T: 01329 238449 F: 01329 233088
Email: premiere@agents-uk.com
Website: premiere.org.uk
Dir: Del Mitchell

PRESTIGE MANAGEMENT
8600 Wilbur Avenue, Northridge,
California, 91324 USA
T: +1 818 993 3030
F: +1 818 993 4151
Email: prestige@gte.net
MD: Richard Rashman

PRINCIPLE MANAGEMENT
30-32 Sir John Rogersons Quay,
Dublin 2, Ireland
T: +353 1 677 7330
F: +353 1 677 7276
Email: jenn@numb.ie
Website: u2.com
MD: Steve Matthews

PROBE PRODUCTIONS
Unit 1Y Cooper House, 2 Michael Road,
London SW6 2AD
T: 0207 371 8174 F: 0207 371 8754
Email: probeproductions@o-mix.co.uk
Website: o-mix.co.uk
MD: Alex Kerr-Wilson

PRODMIX DJ MANAGEMENT & PRODUCTION
61 Railway Arch, Cambridge Grove, London W6 0LD
T: 020 8742 6600 F: 020 8742 6677
Email: info@prodmix.com
Website: prodmix.com
Director: Karen Goldie-Sauve

PURE MANAGEMENT
18 Chilham Place, Macclesfield, Cheshire SK11 8TG
T: 07747 152 524
Email: pureinc@dircon.co.uk
Website: pureacts.com
MD: Michael G. Hatton

QARAJ' LTD
1 King's House, 396, King's Road, London SW10 0LL
T: 020 7352 2239 F: 020 7349 0249
Email: info@qaraj.com
Website: qaraj.com
MD: Michele Baldini

RAZZAMATAZZ MANAGEMENT
Crofters, East Park Lane, Newchapel, Surrey RH7 6HS
T: 01342 835359 F: 01342 835433
Email: mcgrogan@tinyworld.co.uk
Dir: Jill Shirley

RDPR MUSIC MANAGEMENT
155 Potton Road, Biggleswade, Bedfordshire SG18 0ED
T: 01453 832876 F: 01767 314551

RETALIATE FIRST MANAGEMENT
Unit 9, Darvells Works, Common Rd, Chorleywood, Herts WD3 5LP
T: 01923 286010 F: 01923 286070
Email: mgmt@retaliatefirst.co.uk
Website: ianbrown-online.co.uk
MD: Steve Lowes

MARLENE ROSS (MANAGEMENT) LTD
1 York Street, Aberdeen AB11 5DL
T: 01224 573100 F: 01224 572598
Email: enquiries@runrig.co.uk
Website: runrig.co.uk
Manager: Marlene Ross

ROUGH TRADE MANAGEMENT
66 Golborne Road, London W10 5PS
T: 020 8960 9888 F: 020 8968 6715
Email: kelly.kiley@roughtraderecords.com
Website: roughtraderecords.com
Artist Co-ordinator: Kelly Kiley

ROUTE ONE MANAGEMENT
24 Derby St, Edgeley, Stockport, Cheshire SK3 9HF
T: 0161 476 1172
Email: andylacallen@yahoo.co.uk
Website: spinning-fields.com
Director: Andy Callen

ROVAL/ACT MUSIC
PO Box 8, Pudsey, Leeds, West Yorks LS28 5XA
T: 01274 621272 F: 01274 621271
Email: val@cbsman.sagehost.co.uk
MD: Val Driver

SAFFA MUSIC LTD
Arena House, 12-15 Plough and Harrow Road, Edgbaston, Birmingham B16 8UR
T: 0121 694 5135 F: 0121 248 6007
Email: info@safa.co.uk
Website: rubyturner.com
MD: Geoff Pearce

SAFI SOUNDS MANAGEMENT & PROMOTION
PO Box 572, Huddersfield HD3 4ZD
T: 01484 340975
Email: info@safisounds.co.uk
Website: safisounds.co.uk
Mgr: Sarah Hutton

CHARLES SALT MANAGEMENT
Leacroft, Cheriton Cross, Cheriton Bishop, Exeter, Devon EX6 6JH
T: 01647 24502 F: 01647 24052
Email: charlie35@supanet.com
Website: lizardsun-music.co.uk
MD: Charles Salt

ALBERT SAMUEL MANAGEMENT
42 City Business Centre, Lower Road, London SE16 2XB
T: 020 7740 1600 F: 020 7740 1700
Email: asm@mission-control.co.uk
Website: asmanagement.co.uk
Director: Albert & David Samuel

SANCTUARY MUSIC MANAGEMENT LTD
Sanctuary House, 45-53 Sinclair Road, London W14 0NS
T: 020 7602 6351 F: 020 7603 5941
Email: info@sanctuarygroup.com
Website: sanctuarygroup.com
Rod Smallwood

SAPHRON MANAGEMENT
c/o 36 Belgrave Road, London E17 8QE
T: 020 8521 7764
Email: saphron@msn.com
Artist Manager: Annette Bennett MMF

SATELLITE ARTISTS
Studio House, 34 Salisbury St, London NW8 8QE
T: 020 7402 9111 F: 020 7723 3064
Email: satellite_artists@hotmail.com
MD: Eliot Cohen

SCHOOLHOUSE MANAGEMENT LTD
42 York Place, Edinburgh EH1 3HU
T: 0131 557 4242
Email: bruce@schoolhousemanagement.co.uk
Website: schoolhousemanagement.co.uk
MD: Bruce Findlay

DAVE SEAMER ENTERTAINMENTS
46 Magdalen Road, Oxford, Oxfordshire OX4 1RB
T: 01865 240054 F: 01865 240054
Email: dave@daveseamer.co.uk
Website: daveseamer.co.uk
MD: Dave Seamer

SEVEN MUSIC PROMOTIONS
PO Box 2042, Luton, Beds LU3 2EP
T: 01582 595944 F: 01582 612752
Email: j.waller@7mps.co.uk
Website: 7mps.co.uk
Dir/A&R: Jonathan M Waller

SIREN PRODUCTIONS
5 Cavalry Gardens, London SW15 2QQ
T: 020 8871 3761 F: 0709 200 4055
Email: ellise@sirenproductions.freeserve.co.uk
Dance Artist/Label Mgr: Ellise Theuma

SIZE: MUSIC
PO Box 798, London EN1 1ZP
T: 020 8350 1221

SLICE DJ & ARTIST MANAGEMENT
The Clockhouse, 220 Latimer Road, London W10 6QY
T: 020 8964 7623 F: 020 8964 0101
Email: suzanne@slice.co.uk
Website: slice.co.uk
Director: Simone Young

SMA TALENT
Birchlands, The Warren, Radlett, Herts
WD7 7DU
T: 01923 859933 F: 01923 859213
Email: carolynne@smatalent.com
MD: Carolynne Wyper

SMALL WORLD
18a Farm Lane Trading Centre, 101
Farm Lane, London SW6 1QJ
T: 020 7385 3233 F: 020 7386 0473
Email: tina@smallworldmanagement.com
Manager: Tina Matthews

SMI/EVERYDAY PRODUCTIONS
33 Mandarin Place, Grove, Oxon
OX12 0QH
T: 01235 771577 F: 01235 767171
Email: smi_everyday_productions@yahoo.com
VP Special Projects: Dave Wareham

SOLEMUSIC INDUSTRIES
Unit B1, Glenwood Business Park,
Glasgow G45 9UG
T: 0141 634 6300 F: 0141 634 6303
Email: info@solemusic.co.uk
Website: solemusic.co.uk
MD: Stevie Middleton

SOLID SENDERS
93 Ronald Park Avenue, Westcliff On
Sea, Essex SS0 9QP
T: 01702 341983
Email: irene@solidsenders.freeserve.co.uk
Website: wilkojohnson.co.uk
Manager/Agent: Irene Knight

SOUND IMAGE UNIT
2B, Banquay Trading Estate, Slutchers
Lane, Warrington, Cheshire WA1 1PJ
T: 01925 445742 F: 01925 445742
Email: info@frogstudios.co.uk
Website: frogstudios.co.uk
MD: Steve Millington

SOUND PETS
PO Box 158, Twickenham, Middlesex
TW2 6UP
T: 0976 577773 F: 0870 1684068
Email: robinhill@soundpets.freeserve.co.uk
Director: Robin Hill

SOUNDS LIKE A HIT LTD
Studio 222, Canalot Production Studios,
222 Kensal Rd, London W10 5BN
T: 020 8962 0000 F: 020 8962 0011
Email: steve@soundslikeahit.com
Website: soundslikeahit.com
Director: Steve Crosby

SPEED MANAGEMENT LTD
PO Box 2500, Croydon, Surrey
CR4 2WR
T: 0845 125 9447 F: 0845 125 9448
Email: enquiries@speedmanagement.co.uk
Website: speedmanagement.co.uk
MD: Giles Baxendale

MAL SPENCE MANAGEMENT
Cherry Tree Lodge, Copmanthorpe,
York, North Yorks YO23 3SH
T: 01904 703764 F: 01904 702312
Email: malspence@thedandys.demon.co.uk
Website: thedandys.demon.co.uk
MD: Mal Spence

SPHINX MANAGEMENT
2 Unity Place, West Gate, Rotherham,
South Yorkshire S60 1AR
T: 01709 820379 F: 01709 369990
Email: tributebands@btconnect.com
Website: tribute-entertainment.co.uk

SPLIT MUSIC
13 Sandys Rd, Worcester WR1 3HE
T: 01905 29809 F: 01905 613023
Email: split.music@virgin.net
Website: splitmusic.com
MD: Chris Warren

SPRINT MUSIC LTD
High Jarmany Farm, Jarmany Hill,
Barton St David, Somerton, Somerset
TA11 6DA
T: 01458 851010 F: 01458 851029
Email: info@sprintmusic.co.uk
Website: sprintmusic.co.uk
Consultant: John Ratcliff

STRIKE BACK MANAGEMENT
271 Royal College St, Camden Town,
London NW1 9LU
T: 020 7482 0115 F: 020 7267 1169
Email: maurice@baconempire.com
MD: Maurice Bacon

STRONGROOM MANAGEMENT
120-124 Curtain Road, London
EC2A 3SQ
T: 020 7426 5132 F: 020 7426 5102
Email: coral@strongroom.com
Website: strongroom.com/management
GM: Coral Worman

SWAMP MUSIC
PO Box 94, Derby, Derbyshire
DE22 1XA
T: 01332 332336 F: 01332 332336
Email: chrishall@swampmusic.co.uk
Website: swampmusic.co.uk
MD: Chris Hall

SYLVANTONE PROMOTIONS
17 Allerton Grange Way, Leeds, West
Yorkshire LS17

JOHN TAYLOR MANAGEMENT
PO Box 272, London N20 0BY
T: 020 8368 0340 F: 020 8361 3370
Email: john@jt-management.demon.co.uk
MD: John Taylor

PAUL ANTHONY TAYLOR PRODUCTIONS LTD
63 Langholm Crescent, Darlington, Co.
Durham DL3 7SX T: 01325 353898
Email: bruce@patpl.co.uk
Website: patpl.co.uk
MD: Paul Anthony Taylor

TFF MANAGEMENT
Lovat House,
Gavell Road, Kilsyth, Glasgow G65 9BS
T: 01236 826555 F: 01236 825560
Email: tessa@tffpr.com
MD: Tessa Hartmann

TK1 MANAGEMENT LTD
6 Greenland Quay, Surrey Quays,
London SE16 7RN
T: 020 7740 3119 F: 020 7740 3119
Email: info@tk1management.com
Website: tk1management.com
Dirs: Trina Torpey & Kathryn Nash

TOTAL CONCEPT MANAGEMENT (TCM)
PO Box 128, Dewsbury, West Yorkshire

TSUNAMI SOUNDS
The Gables, Avenue Road, Cranleigh,
Surrey GU6 7LE
T: 01483 506114 F: 01483 506113
Email: info@tsunami-sounds.com
Website: tsunami-sounds.com
Director: Ken Easter

TWOPOINTNINE LTD
PO Box 44607, London N16 0YP
T: 020 7241 6544 F: 020 7241 6544
Email: info@2point9.com
Website: 2point9.com
Dirs: Billy Grant, Rob Stuart

UNIQUE CORP LTD
15 Shaftesbury Centre, 85 Barlby Road, London W10 6BN
T: 020 8964 9333 F: 020 8964 9888
Email: info@uniquecorp.co.uk
Website: uniquecorp.co.uk
MD: Alan Bellman

UNITED COLOURS OF SOUND (MANAGEMENT) LTD
PO Box 54, Northaw, Hertfordshire EN6 4DA
T: 01707 661431 F: 01707 664141
Email: information@unitedcoloursofsound.com
Website: unitedcoloursofsound.com
Brian Freshwater

UP MANAGEMENT
PO Box 630, Bushey, Bushey Heath, Herts WD23 3YS

VALUE ADDED TALENT MANAGEMENT (VAT)
1 Purley Place, London N1 1QA
T: 020 7704 9720 F: 020 7226 6135
Email: vat@vathq.co.uk
Website: vathq.co.uk
MD: Dan Silver

VASHTI
PO Box 1400, Maidenhead, Berkshire SL6 1GU
T: 01628 620082 F: 01628 637066
Email: info@sheilaferguson.com
Website: sheilaferguson.com
MD: Sheila Ferguson

VERGE MANAGEMENT LTD
Henry A Crosbie, Business Centre, Ossory Road, Dublin 3, Ireland
T: +353 1 856 0526
F: +353 1 856 0527
Email: lorcan.ennis@verge.ie
Website: verge.ie
MD: Lorcan Ennis

VEX MANAGEMENT
21c Tressillian Rd, London SE4 1YG
T: 020 8469 0800 F: 020 8469 0800
Email: paul@vexmgmt.demon.co.uk
Website: vex-entertainment.com
MD: Paul Ablett

VINE GATE MUSIC
4 Vine Gate, Parsonage Lane, Farnham Common, Bucks SL2 3NX
T: 01753 643696 F: 01753 642259
Email: vinegate@clara.net
Website: salenajones.co.uk
Partner: Tony Puxley

VIOLATION MANAGEMENT
26 Mill Street, Gamlingay, Sandy, Bedfordshire SG19 3JW
T: 01767 651552 F: 01767 651228
Email: dicky_boy@msn.com
Manager: Dick Meredith

VISION PROMOTIONS
10 Gottfried Mews, off Fortess Road, London NW5 2HN
T: 020 7482 6622 F: 020 7482 5599
Email: visionpromotions@madasafish.com
Head of Promotions: Rob Dallison

MANAGERS

VRUK MANAGEMENT
Top Floor, Voysey House, Barley Mow Passage, Chiswick, London W4 4GB
T: 020 8987 2456 F: 020 8987 2444
Email: vruk@volumerecords.co.uk
MD: Tony Vickers

W1 MUSIC MANAGEMENT
101a Wendover House, Chiltern Street, London W1U 7NR
T: 020 7486 7100 F: 020 7935 3669
Email: feeney@w1mm.com
Manager: Stewart Feeney

JOHN WALLER MANAGEMENT & MARKETING
The Old Truman Brewery, 91 Brick Lane, London E1 6QN
T: 020 7247 1057 F: 020 7377 0732
Email: john.waller@dial.pipex.com
MD: John Waller

LOUIS WALSH MANAGEMENT
24 Courtney House, Appian Way, Dublin 6, Ireland
T: +353 1 668 0309
F: +353 1 668 0721
Email: louiewalsh@eircom.net
MD: Louis Walsh

WAR ZONES AND ASSOCIATES
33 Kersley Road, London N16 0NT
T: 020 7249 2894 F: 020 7254 3729
Email: wz33@aol.com
Richard Hermitage

WEDGE MUSIC
63 Grosvenor Street, London W1X 9DA
T: 020 7493 7831 F: 020 7491 3028
Email: info@tonygordon.com
Manager: Tony Gordon

STEPHEN WELLS MANAGEMENT
9 Woodchurch Road, London NW6 3PL
T: 020 7372 5488 F: 020 7372 5488
Stephen Wells

STEVE WELTMAN MANAGEMENT
91 Manor Road South, Hinchley Wood, Esher, Surrey KT10 0QB
T: 020 8398 4144 F: 020 8398 4244
Email: sweltman@ukgateway.net
Proprietor: Steve Weltman

WHAT MANAGEMENT
3 Belfry Villas, Belfry Ave, Harefield, Uxbridge, Middlesex UB9 6HY
T: 01895 824674 F: 01895 822994
Email: whatmanagement@blueyonder.co.uk
Mick Cater/David Harper

WHITE TIGER MANAGEMENT
55 Fawcett Close, London SW16 2QJ
T: 020 8677 5199 F: 020 8769 5795
Email: whitetigermanagement@hotmail.com
MDs: Paul & Corinne White

ALAN WHITEHEAD MANAGEMENT
79 The Ryde, Hatfield, Hertfordshire AL9 5DN
T: 01707 267883 F: 01707 267247
Email: alan_whitehead_uk@yahoo.com
MD: Alan Whitehead

WHITEHOUSE MANAGEMENT
PO Box 43869, London NW6 1WN
T: 020 7209 2586 F: 020 7209 7187
Email: sue@whitehousemanagement.com
MD: Sue Whitehouse

WHITENOISE MANAGEMENT LTD
8 Southam St, London W10 5PH
T: 020 8964 1002 F: 020 8964 0021

Email: info@whitenoisemanagement.com
Website: whitenoisemanagement.com
MD: Chris Butler

WICKED WOLF MANAGEMENT
4 Meadow Walk, Wallington, Surrey
SM6 7EJ
T: 020 8669 1407
Email: seamus@wickedwolf.co.uk
Website: dnadoll.com
MD: Seamus Murphy

WILD HONEY MANAGEMENT
10 Lansdowne Road, Hove, East
Sussex BN3 3AU
T: 01273 738704 F: 01273 732112
Email: jimtracey@aol.com
Website: wildhoney.co.uk
Jim Tracey

WILDLIFE ENTERTAINMENT
Unit F, 21 Heathmans Road, London
SW6 4TJ
T: 020 7371 7008 F: 020 7371 7708
Email: info@wildlife-entertainment.com
Managing Directors: Ian McAndrew,
Colin Lester

MARTIN WYATT
21c Heathmans Road, Parsons Green,
London SW6 4TJ
T: 020 7751 9935 F: 020 7731 9314
Email: brightmusic@aol.com
MD: Martin Wyatt

1

2

3

4

5

6

7

8

9

10

11

12

13

14

15

LAWYERS

WHAT IS THE ROLE OF THE MUSIC INDUSTRY LAWYER?

Lawyers and the entertainment business seem to be inextricably linked. The music business is no exception. Everybody in the business knows someone who was screwed because they didn't get proper legal advice.

Some firms have large media practices that cover all areas of the entertainment business; others have a reputation for music much more than other entertainment areas. Of these some work mostly for record labels and publishing companies, while others concentrate on talent.

It's tempting to be negative about lawyers; to see them as an expensive luxury. Our experience is different. Of course there are some fat cat lawyers, but many music lawyers are keen to help talented young musicians. Often the firms specialising in talent give newcomers free introductory advice and keep early bills as low as possible. The best operate their own unofficial A&R programme, seeking out the best talent and deciding to invest time in exceptional cases.

Remember, though, we're talking about lawyers. Like all lawyers, they are expensive, and even if you have a 'soft' introductory deal they will soon expect to bill a minimum of £100 an hour and many two or three times as much. The biggest, big shot lawyers can top £500. So like all expensive habits it's important to use them wisely and for maximum effect.

CHOOSING THE RIGHT LAWYER

If your manager is experienced, he will probably recommend you a lawyer. There's nothing wrong with this as long as you avoid a conflict of interest by ensuring that you use someone else to advise you on your contract with your manager. But treat this as a recommendation, not a done deal. You must choose a lawyer that you trust and importantly someone with whom you can communicate.

Like humans generally, music lawyers come in all shapes and sizes. There are definitely some distinct types:

- *The Cool Cats* – these are the aspiring musicians who like to hang out at all the right gigs and award ceremonies; they're great from the point of view of understanding your music, but best at representing your interests.
- *The Power Players* – these really want to be agents and get off on the power trip; they talk big deals and promise the earth, but only a few deliver.
- *The Suit* – a conservative suit covers an old school lawyer; they pride themselves on being unimpressed by the glamour of the business and in the worst cases can revel in cynicism.
- *The Big Negotiator* – but remember, good negotiators are not necessarily good lawyers.

It sounds a bit naff, but the way to choose a lawyer is to think about the qualities you look for in a best friend. You need to trust them implicitly. Like friends, beware of those that tell you stories about their other clients. Pick the one that doesn't patronise but can explain the most complicated legal point in simple and clear terms. The best lawyer for you is not necessarily the right one for someone else.

GETTING THE BEST OUT OF YOUR LAWYER

First, ensure there is no ambiguity about fees. Exactly what are the fees? Retainers are rare, but can be negotiated. If not, look to agree a ceiling at which point you will be informed and your approval sought before more fees are accumulated. Make sure you know how often you will be billed and how soon you will be expected to pay.

As with all expensive advisers, remember the clock is always ticking. The biggest waste of time is giving unclear instructions. Building a relationship is important, but meetings without purpose or clearly defined outcomes are an unnecessary expense. You need to agree a simple plan of action at the beginning of the relationship.

What deal are you going for? What are the priorities? You should be aiming for a minimum and maximum estimation of fees for this plan.

You must decide how to use your lawyer from the outset. From an artist's perspective it is essential to work out how he fits into the team. You don't want to duplicate resources between your manager, accountant and lawyer.

Beware of lawyers who are only interested in taking on clients they think they can get a deal for. They are likely to act more like managers, and their enthusiasm for the deal could lead them to be impartial. Also, make sure your lawyer is acting for you and not deferring to or in constant sole communication with your manager.

While managers usually negotiate contracts the lawyer should be part of the negotiation planning. Often they will know the preferred contractual terms and negotiation tactics of individual labels and have invaluable strategic input.

MUSIC LAW MADE SIMPLE

This is a short overview of the key points of music law.

PUBLISHING AND COPYRIGHT

Although the record deal is popularly considered the most important thing in the music business, there is often much more long-term value in a publishing deal. It is usually the member of the band who writes the material who ends up with a prosperous old age.

Before a publishing deal can be done, copyright has to be established. This sounds straightforward, but is not always so. There are many famous court cases of claims and counter claims of disputed authorship and blurred areas where copyright is challenged, such as sampling.

Traditionally, aspiring writers and artists have used recorded delivery or registered post to send a copy of their work to themselves, a friend or even better a solicitor or bank. We recommend you only do this as a temporary first step. Real copyright protection is only gained through exploitation; anyway, if you don't exploit your copyright you're never going to generate any money.

As the copyright owner there are two types of exploitation rights which you can grant and for which you can obtain money. These are 'mechanical' and 'performance' rights.

Mechanical rights generate revenue from other people who use your material, and performance rights give you revenue when your song is performed, recorded or broadcast.

In this country, the Mechanical Copyright Protection Society Ltd (MCPS) protects mechanical rights for its members and the Performing Rights Society (PRS) for performance rights.

In a publishing deal, the copyright owner grants the publisher administrative rights to definitively establish his or her copyright and then to exploit it commercially on the copyright's behalf in return for a percentage of the revenue created. To maximise revenue the publisher will promote the material and then license it. The publisher's other duties are to collect and pass on royalties, after retaining their agreed share and to protect their client against copyright infringement.

In publishing contracts a percentage of revenue is retained by the publisher for a specified body of material for an agreed time period. As in a record deal an advance can and should be negotiated.

Negotiating the length of the deal is important, because successful material can have a very long exploitation life. Just think of the number of 30- or 40-year-old song tracks that feature in today's TV ads. The starting price for well-known tracks will be £70,000 per year.

Although the number of tracks and albums covered by the publishing contract will often mirror the record label deal, the crucial timescale can be the number of years the publisher continues to have the right to exploit the material after the contract for new material has expired. Typically for a new artist this will be at least ten years, but can often be for life unless negotiated.

Next check the number of territories covered. Just as publishers want perpetual exploitation rights, they will also want global rights. This might not be in your interest as their clout and contacts may vary by market and you may find a better publisher for an important market. This gets complicated if the publisher is subcontracting in a territory because this could alter the definition of net receipts and affect your revenue share.

It is difficult to tie a publishing company legally to deliver specific deals or revenue streams. They always want to cover themselves with that all-embracing legal phrase, 'to make best endeavours to promote their clients material and so raise revenue' – something like this will be in virtually every publishing contract and it doesn't give you any guarantees. The best reassurance you can get is to discuss in detail the publisher's plans to exploit your work, take references and look at their track record.

RECORD DEALS

From a new artist's point of view there is a sense of unreality about negotiating a record deal. It has probably been a dream since the first time they thought of being in a band. However, it's important to realise that getting a good deal can make a huge difference to your music career.

If a full-blown exclusive record deal is not on offer, you might go for a development deal. If a record company doesn't consider you to be ready to record and promote your first album, but still thinks you have potential they will offer you a modest personal advance and pay recording costs.

Be careful about the assignment of rights to ensure total flexibility for your next recording deal. There are two types of rights that can be assigned or handed over in any record deal. These are copyright in sound recording and performance rights. Copyright in sound recording is usually owned by whoever pays for the recording, while performance rights are owned by the performing artists. It is important to be able to get these rights back at the end of the deal, even if you have to repay some costs.

If you're lucky enough to get a full-blown exclusive record deal you'll find that some of this investment is 'recoupable' from the artist and must be paid back; the rest isn't and is 'unrecoupable'. Recoupable costs tend to be personal and recording items, and unrecoupable, promotional and marketing. An advance is paid against artist's royalties. The advance and all recoupable costs need to be paid back before royalty payments are paid.

Obviously, record companies need to protect their investment and will seek to tie in artists as much as they can.

FOUR KEY CONSIDERATIONS

There are four key considerations when looking at any deal:

- *Creative control:* Unless you are a superstar, total control will be difficult to negotiate, but you should be able to get reassurance that the record label has the same vision and check out their track record with other artists. Some labels will leave their artists alone and give them flexibility at the recording stage, while others won't.
- *Advances:* Securing the minimum advance is important. Often living expenses for 18 months, costs of professional advisers and associated expenses like transport, rehearsal space and personal equipment are budgeted. The record company will calculate in terms of projected sales. However, the advance is most likely to depend on how much a record company wants you and who else they are competing against. Take a long-term view. Negotiating an exceptionally high advance at the expense of everything else can mean making a bad deal.

  Big advances can lead to too high expectations. If your first album doesn't meet expectations it's more likely to be your last, especially if your advance has established an expensive precedent. If you make record labels pay above the odds they will be on your back all the way.
- *Recoupment:* Record companies are risking their money, so when they succeed they want to make serious money. Often new artists do not realise that they are paying for their own recording costs. Good managers keep a careful eye on these costs. Recoupment doesn't happen until all these costs are repaid from royalties. That's why recoupment costs need to be defined exactly.

- *Royalties:* Every record company calculates royalties differently. You need to check whether they are a percentage of retail or dealer price. Obviously you want it to be based on the retail price because it is considerably higher and outside the control of the record company.

  Another thing to watch out for is the packaging deduction, sometimes called 'container charges', of 20–25%. In our opinion they are just another way for the record company to reduce your royalty payments, as the cost of packaging is really only a fraction of this cost.

  It is difficult to be definitive about what is a good royalty deal; however, a minimum 18% of retail price with a minimum 20% packaging deduction is not bad.

OTHER CONSIDERATIONS

The release commitment is important. The contract should commit the record company to release the album within two or three months after delivery in each specified territory. If they don't, you need to be free to go elsewhere. The record company will probably want to take an override royalty until the recording costs are returned.

Defining territories is another consideration. Most deals are global, but split territory deals do exist. An artist may want to use a different label to break into America or another territory.

OTHER TYPES OF DEAL

Some artists have their own recording facilities and considerable production expertise. In this case the record label might agree a cost-inclusive advance. This will include a budget for recording costs and is called a 'record funding deal'.

Net profit deals are sometimes offered by small labels. There is no royalty, but the artist acts as a joint venture partner and nothing is paid to them until all costs are repaid. Then the artist has a profit share. Usually this is a 50/50 split or sometimes slightly in the artist's favour. If you have a big hit, this type of deal can be very profitable for the artist, but it can take a long time to move into profit to trigger payment and a moderate success may never see any profits.

Licence deals are where the rights owner licenses out the copyright for a period of time for a specified territory. The most common form of this is granting a non-exclusive licence for a single track for a compilation. Otherwise they are usually granted for specific territories. Sometimes artists who produce their own music and therefore own the copyright can do a larger licence deal to enable them to retain the underlying rights.

TONY ENGLISH: A MUSIC LAWYER'S PERSPECTIVE

Tony English is one of the music industry's elite lawyers, representing some of the most powerful key figures. His firm, Russells, started in 1974 and was one of the first firms to specialise in music law. His perspective of how music law works is a general overview rather than a detailed analysis.

THE ROLE OF A MUSIC LAWYER

We're at the interface between capital (the music business) and creativity (artist or entrepreneurs). They both have different interests and desires, but they need each other. The objective is to find a suitable marriage between both that is fruitful for each party. That's why a lawyer role is integral to the music business.

Intellectual property is the whole basis of the music industry. Without it there is no business. Intellectual property is largely based on rights granted by the creator of the rights to the various parties such as record labels and publishers, etc. The lawyers are involved in establishing what rights should be granted and the restrictions.

THINGS TO CONSIDER WHEN SECURING A LABEL DEAL

Before getting involved in the detail of any label deal, work out your desired strategy. Have a clear focus (mission statement) regarding what you want to achieve and your market position. If you are unfocused or unclear about your objectives your label might fail, so it's important that you get the strategy right.

● YOUR TEAM

Reputation in the industry is important because it's so small, particularly if you want to attract creative or business partners. Lack of reputation and experience means you'll find it difficult to build the right platforms allowing you to leverage what you have.

● PRODUCT COMMITMENT

Before focusing on the details of the deal, consider how many albums or singles you're looking to release per year. You will then know how much finance you're going to need.

● FINANCE

There are two ways of developing a record label:

(a) *Organic growth*: You use your own funds to grow the business.
Pros: You have ownership, control and all the profits.
Cons: There will be a lack of funding, and you need to work out where will you get this from to cover you over the long period in creating product, marketing and collect your income.

(b) *Joint venture*: You receive funding for your label. In my experience most joint venture deals are product led (on the power of the music/artist).
Pros: You're more than likely to be able to grow the company faster; it gives you the ability to sign more artists and invest more on your marketing campaign.
Cons: You're diluting your ownership and the control to share your profits; anyone investing in a label will want a clear exit; at some time that allows them to take some sort of capital gain or buy the partner out.

● WHAT PARTNERS SHOULD I CONSIDER FOR MY VENTURE?

You may find it easier to do partnership deals with trade partners.

(a) *Trade partners*: Major or independent record labels or those with a vested interest in the music business who understand your business needs and will be able to help you grow; for instance, you may be able to piggy back on certain arrangements such as pressing and distribution fees from a major.

(b) *Non-trade partners*: People outside the music industry who find it difficult to understand how the business works or how it makes a profit.

- DIFFERENT TYPES OF LABEL DEALS

(a) *Override royalty*: This comes from the difference between the royalty the label gets paid and what the artist gets. For example, if the label is paid a royalty of 25% and the artist is paid a royalty of 18% then the override royalty is 7%.

Pros: They are not traditional cross-collateralised deals; in other words, you get the royalty paid on record sales whether or not the other artists you're signing to the label are unsuccessful. You're not concerned with A&R or marketing spend which is an advantage because if you sign ten artists to the label and only one is successful then you're getting an override royalty on that artist. The major record company partner will try and bring some element of cross collateralisation into the deal.

Cons: Because you're getting a fixed override royalty there's a limited upside. You're very unlikely to be having any capital asset because you'll be paid this royalty for a limited time.

(b) *Profit share*: In this type of deal you build a capital asset (ownership). You will be a proper label in the UK, pressing and distributing your own records. Therefore on a 50/50 deal you'll be taking 50% of the UK profits if you are successful, which is more substantial and lucrative than a royalty override.

Pros: If you're establishing a capital gain on an exit you will realise that gain and make substantial capital payment to yourself. As legislation stands you'll get taper relief which will bring down your marginal tax rate on capital gain to 10%.

Cons: Cross-collateralisation if you go back to the example of signing ten acts and only one is a success. Those ten who have not been a success will be a burden on the one act because the cost will come off the top. It's important that the one act that is successful is enough to cover the ten that are not or you're going to make a loss.

● TYPES OF FUNDING AVAILABLE

It's unusual for anyone to do capital funding into a company. All funding will be loan or advance funding. Interest may be payable on the funding.

● EXCLUSIVITY

Many entrepreneurs who enter into partnership deals come from other areas of the business such as music management, publishing or agents, etc. Therefore they'll have to discuss with partners if this is acceptable. This will depend on salary: if it's low then s/he will have an argument that other interest provides extra income needed.

● LENGTH

These deals go on for a minimum of five years. However, you have to consider a disaster clause because anyone investing will want the right to pull out if the business is not going according to plan. If the financier pulls out early, should s/he still own shares in the joint venture? What happens to outstanding loans if the investors pulls out? Do they have to be repaid or are they written off?

● EXIT PROVISIONS

In the music business trade sales are the normal exit while flotations are the exception. The investor will generally want an exit provision allowing them either to force out the entrepreneur or realise the company value. The major record label on the whole will try and get a valuation based on a formula of some kind on the previous years' profits. The entrepreneur will try and resist that because such a formulaic approach does not give a true value for a record label. The only way you can test the value of the label is to take it out to the market and see what other record labels would be prepared to pay for it.

● DRAG AND TAG PROVISIONS

Drag provision: forces minority shareholders to sell their shares when majority shareholders sell theirs.

Tag provision: the right for minority shareholders to compel majority shareholders to sell and include minority shareholders' stake in any sales of shares by majority shareholders.

To realise the company's full value it's better for it to be sold 100% to a competitor.

CONSIDERATIONS RELATING TO RECORD DEALS

- PRIORITY ACT

Artist would ideally like to be a priority act when they sign to a label. There are a limited number of acts per year who actually get priority treatment internationally. This means for the act they will have considerably more marketing spent on them than other acts within the label. There are no contractual ways to ensure a large amount of money is spent on marketing. A strategy the artist adviser can take is securing large sums of money (advances) from the record label which puts them under financial exposure. It does not guarantee priority because we all know that major record labels, even if they've paid large advances, can write off an artist if the product is not right. However, it does encourage the major record companies to give priority if the advances are substantial.

- THE NEW ARTIST PREMIUM

With new artists you tend to get better deals than their position in the marketplace would warrant. This comes down to the A&R team involved who are going to want their name linked to a new artist rather than an established act, signed by someone else. For A&R it means longevity in the business because they were responsible for signing and breaking a new act.

- LOSS LEADER DEALS

When a major label is not having particular success in a certain area of music or does not have it developed, they'll sometimes offer better deals to an established artist than can be commercially justified because they want to buy into success and establish their position within the marketplace.

- STRIKE RATE

When looking at a record label you should assess what portion of their artists have gone on to become a success. It's a pretty obvious point but this should be considered when drawing up a list of potential labels.

- TYPES OF RECORD DEALS

(a) *Royalty deals*: These are the most common deals. Their advantage is the certainty of payments. You're getting paid a royalty based on a retail or dealer price which is difficult to manipulate. Major record labels tend to do these deals since they don't want artists looking at what profits they're making.
Disadvantage: Recording costs fully recouped.

(b) *Profit share deals*: The artist will share in, let's say, 50% profits of what the record label make. Larger profit margin for artists from record companies that do their own P&D in the UK as opposed to licensing the recording to a third party.
Disadvantage: You need to make a profit so if you're not selling albums no one gets paid. Also all costs including marketing costs come off the top.

RECORD CONTRACTS

Music industry contracts are quite complex. Many can go on for longer than five years. This raises the issues of enforceability of contracts in the courts and is a grey area under English law. Lawyers have to make judgements when preparing long-term contracts as to what they feel will be acceptable if challenged in the courts. The main issues to consider when preparing a contract are as follows:

- *Advances*: The personal advances to artists will depend upon how hot they are in the market place. To confuse the picture some record labels include recording costs with personal advances.
- *Terms/Product commitment*: How many albums will be released? If you're signing to a major record company they will want to have you committed to a minimum of one album with an option of at least four more, because of level of investment which can be £500,000 plus.

- *Recording cost*: These are fully recoupable except for profit share deals.
- *Territory*: Major record labels like to sign acts for the world, but I've noticed a trend with a lot of artists where they sign to different labels in different territories. However, if there is a major commitment from the label they will force you to sign for the world. When looking at territories ask, does the UK label have a track record in breaking acts in that territory? Especially when it comes to the States, where labels in this country don't have a history of success in breaking artists there. Certain issues arrive from doing multi-territory deals, e.g. no label is going to want to pay 100% recording cost without having the world. So if you're going to take away the US then the UK record company is going to want the American record label to share a portion of the recording cost, which also applies to video and artwork costs if the UK label don't have world rights.
- *Copyrights*: Major record labels will generally own the rights for the life of copyright, which is effectively for perpetuity.
- *Promotional aspect*: TV advertising spend; part of this is recoupable against the artist royalty. Music video costs will be recoupable 50% against record royalty and the remainder against any video income.
- *Long-form video*: Majors don't want to commit to long-form video but the artist will want to have the right to have long-form video made. The compromise situation is that if the artist wants to make the video then the label has the right of first refusal on a matching right basis.
- *Tour support*: The artist will want something inserted in the agreement to cover this but labels will not want to put a figure on this.

MUSIC PUBLISHING

There are three separate occasions when you can do the deal:

(a) *Early on*: before you get record company interest; this increases the risk to the music publisher so your advances and royalties will be lower. It's not the time I would recommend a writer to do the deal, unless they need the cash to tide them through.

(b) *Before release*: when the album's been recorded and just before the first single release. Based on the artist market position and profile built from press and industry attention.

(c) *After release*: this can lead to far bigger rewards if the single or album's been successful, putting you in the position for larger advances and royalty rates, since the publisher can project on the level of sales they expect.

PRINCIPAL DEAL ISSUES

- *Advances*: This comes down to the writer's value in the marketplace, which is a judgement issue. You often find the publisher would prefer the artist adviser to put forward a proposal on what they want. It's up to the experience of the adviser to know how far they can push advances. If you over-pitch, the publisher may walk from the deal without even getting back to you.
- *How royalties are paid*
  (a) *At source*: You get the royalty calculated around the world as if the UK publisher had been the publisher in each country.
  (b) *Receipts based*: In a receipts-based deal, a sub-publisher or licence in an overseas territory will deduct a fee from the gross receipts before remitting those monies back to the UK. For example, if you have $100 arising in America and you've got a 75/25 deal on at source bases the writer will get $75 credited to their account.

  If, however, in a receipts deal with a sub-publisher deduction of 25%, the UK publisher will receive $100 less 25% (being the sub-publisher share) and then 75% of that is going to be credited to the writer's account. In this example the writer will get $56.25 credited to their account rather than the $75 dollars in an at source deal.
- *Income streams*
  (a) *Mechanical royalties*: paid from the record company to the publisher arising from the sale of records.
  (a) *Performance rights*: collected by PRS; pays 50% of performance income direct to the writer and the other 50% to the music publisher.
  (c) *Sync rights*: the use of music on advertisement, films and TV production.
  (d) *Grant rights*: the right to use the songs in a dramatic context on stage. Some writers will want to exclude grant rights from their deal. If they're

considering using songs in this way as it's not common for publishers to obtain this type of usage. Usually it's the writer(s) who obtain the usage in a theatrical context.

- *Retention period:* How long is the music publisher going to have rights over the songs? Nowadays this is less than the life of copyright; this is a major negotiation point and lawyers will know how far they can take this. Usually publishers often want fifteen years' retention period and of course writers want the songs back as soon as possible.
- *Term*: Traditionally publishing contracts don't go on as long as record contracts because there is less financial commitment from publishers compared to record labels who take marketing into consideration.
- *Minimum commitment*: The publisher will want from the writer one album per year, meaning that they have a percentage of the songs on the album they control. This will determine for the publisher the level of advance given to the writer. If a writer/artist can guarantee that 90% of the songs they write will go on the album then it puts them in a better position.

THE ROLE OF MANAGERS

To my mind artists' careers are generally best served when they have a manager/lawyer team to represent them. Artists are up against the whole music industry (including record company and publishers) with all their expertise and experience, and need a strong team to protect their interests and further their careers, and do so in a manner with which they're happy as far as creative aspects are concerned. Having a manager and lawyer together as a team representing the artist is essential. The lawyer's role is generally over once deals are done. However, the manager's role generally begins at that stage; they are going to have to deal with day-to-day issues arising out of a record deal and ensure that the album is made satisfactorily; that the right producers and mixers are chosen and that the artist's career generally is looked after.

What artists must understand is that record companies are not geared towards looking after an artist's career. By definition they're only concerned with the recording aspect and don't have experience in dealing with an artist's overall career. Developing an artist's career involves much more than dealing with record releases: issues such as songwriting, press, touring and merchandising need to be coordinated. Record companies have limited if no expertise in these areas and if an artist leaves these issues to a record company the chances are they will not be looked after properly. A manager's expertise and experience will be based on coordinating the different threads of an artist's career to ensure that they work together as harmoniously as possible.

'You don't need a manager,' David Bowie once said, 'just a great lawyer.' Some established artists survive quite happily with *only* having a lawyer but whether the absence of a manager helps their careers is open to question. Some artists are simply not interested in delegating any responsibility to a manager and want total control over their careers. Obviously, just having a lawyer suits them fine. This, however, is the exception and not the rule.

When negotiating management contracts with managers and their representatives, the lawyer is placed in a slightly unusual position. With other contracts the artist is entering into, there is a clear distinction between the roles of the artist and the company the artist is contracting to. However, in the case of management, the artist is negotiating with someone on their own team, which clearly makes the negotiations far more sensitive than any other negotiations. There's no point in the lawyer trying to get the best possible deal for the artist if once the deal is signed the manager is demotivated. It's therefore essential on management deals that both artist and manager are happy that a fair compromise has been reached.

One needs to look at when management deals should be done as far as the manager is concerned. Most established managers are not really interested in concluding a management deal until the artist they are representing has a record deal on the table. There are various reasons for this. First, no manager is going to want to look too pushy at an early stage in developing their relationship with an artist. Secondly, although it's difficult to say what a manager's obligations are under a management agreement, managers will not want to take on obligations to an artist until they feel there is something they can do – namely, until there's a record deal on the table. This tends to coincide with the artist's perspective on doing management deals as, of course, artists don't want to commit themselves for a long period of time to someone they've perhaps only recently met; therefore most artists don't want to sign management deals until the record deal is on the table. Generally, therefore, the management deal tends to be done shortly before the record deal is concluded.

MANAGEMENT CONTRACTS

- *Term:* The first issue is how long the management contract is going to continue for, which largely depends on whether the artist is new developing or established. Obviously, a manager negotiating a record deal and committing resources to building a new developing artist's career will want a reasonably lengthy period of time, say up to five years. **The artist would like to be in a position where they can dismiss the manager at any time. However, it's unrealistic for the artist to expect a significant commitment from a manager if they put this forward as a negotiating position.** Managers will also be looking towards record cycles. The length of time of a management agreement is not as relevant as the album cycle. If it takes an artist three years to record and promote an album, then managers will have to wait three years to receive their commissions. In the circumstances, managers will often try to base the management agreement on album cycles.
- *Commission:* The other key issue in management contracts is commission. The starting point under UK practice is 20%. The manager's starting point is that he would like this commission on the artist's gross earnings but there are a number of commonly accepted exclusions, e.g. commission on record income will often exclude advances related to recording costs or video costs and often the producer's royalty (traditionally deducted from the artist's royalty) will not be subject to management commission. Commission payable on publishing and merchandising tends to be straightforward, based on artists' receipts, although some

artists do not want to pay commission on the writer's 50% share of performance income – the only income they receive directly.

One of the main areas of negotiation on management contracts traditionally is commission due on touring. The manager would ideally like to receive 20% of gross earnings on touring while the artist would like to have a commission of 20% of net profits on touring. A compromise is generally reached somewhere between the two positions. For instance, if a US tour generates gross earnings of $1 million and there are $900,000 expenses, profits on the tour are $100,000. If the manager gets commission on 20% of gross then s/he will receive $200,000 which means that the artist has a loss on tour of $100,000. If, however, the manager's commission is based on profits then s/he will receive $20,000 and the artist will have a profit of $80,000 from that tour.

- *Sunset provisions:* Traditionally, managers only receive commission on material made or services rendered during the term of their management agreement, e.g. records made and songs written during the term of the management agreement. The question is how long the manager keeps on receiving his commission after the end of term of the management agreement on these recordings and songs. The managers' starting point is that they would like to have continuing commission on these recordings and songs forever. Their position will be that the record company receive its profits forever and producers receive royalties forever so why should managers not receive a perpetual commission? Artists, on the other hand, would like the commission to drop off immediately after the end of the term of the management agreement. Their position will be that managers are no longer managing them and therefore should not be entitled to receive further commission. Again, a compromise needs to be reached between these two positions and traditionally a period of time at full-rate commission followed by a period of time at reduced commission is agreed between the parties.
- *Key-man provision:* Often managers will contract through a management company and in this arrangement individual managers will provide their services through that management company. The artists' representatives in

negotiating the deal will need to ensure that if for any reason individual managers don't provide their services, e.g. because of death or illness, then the artist should be entitled to terminate the management agreement. Without such a provision, the management agreement would continue even though the key person behind it was no longer providing their services.

P&D CONTRACTS

These contracts, regarding pressing and distributing records, are among the first that any newly formed label will have to deal with. The pressing or manufacturing side of the contract is straightforward as there will be a price per unit charged for the manufacture of the records. The distribution aspect is more complex. The record label and distributor first need to agree how long this contract will carry on for and what product is covered by the deal, e.g. are all records to be released by the label going to be put through this distribution contract or are some, e.g. vinyl records, to be distributed elsewhere? What services will the distributor provide? These must be so set out, e.g. is the distributor going to provide a sales service through a sales force? If so, how is this to be charged? Under distribution deals, distributors supply records to dealers and collect the earnings from the sales. Distributors take a fee based on a percentage of the earnings they receive for providing this service, although sometimes a charge on a per unit basis is made. Issues such as stock risk, faulty goods, returns, discounts, copyright clearances, credit control, bad debts, exports and accounting need to be resolved. The amount of the distribution fee will depend on the label's turnover: the greater the volume the lower the fee. If a label does a P&D deal in conjunction with a joint venture arrangement the label should piggy back on any P&D arrangements its joint venturer has. Often a joint venture partner will seek an uplift for providing this service.

FUTURE TRENDS

The majors' business model is under strain. It is predicated on paying substantial advances and spending substantial amounts of money on recording costs and marketing to develop artists, get them into the charts and achieve substantial sales. The traditional business model relies on the major success of a limited number of artists paying for the lack of success of the majority of artists. The continuing downward trajectory of global sales has led to the returns that the majors have been dependent on reducing in the past few years. This in return has led to majors wanting the artists to be fully developed when they sign them. On the whole, majors appear to have abdicated responsibility for developing artists as obviously signing a fully developed artist reduces risk to the record label as they know what they're getting when they sign the record deal.

The financial strain on the majors has therefore made them more risk averse and there are indications that they're looking at their model and considering moving into areas where they can take advantage of the income streams generated by artists outside the traditional sale of records. The major record companies have a threshold for sales under which it's simply not worth their while signing artists. **Unless a major record company believes they can sell at least a quarter of a million albums, they are not geared under their current business model to signing and developing that artist.** This has led, to my mind, to a significant opportunity for new start-up labels often based on management operations.

Because new labels don't have majors' large overheads and can use different ways of marketing, they can develop artists at a lower threshold, control initial costs better and make profit on lower record sales. When these labels have a major success on their hands, a major record company tends to buy them up as it's preferable to pay extra for something already successful than take a risk on signing developing artists. Many of the major international artists broken out of the UK in recent years have been developed on independent labels.

Branding is an important issue in this context. Artists historically, whether they like it or not, have been a brand. Possibly the biggest brand in the music industry was The Beatles who still generate a lot of money from their brand. **The majors have realised that when artists are developing their brand, the majors are financing this development but only receiving a profit participation on sales of records**, which is a limited part of the artist's income stream. The artist, meanwhile, having used record company funds to build up their brand, is able to do a large publishing deal and demand large fees for live work and merchandising. It's inevitable therefore that majors are looking at this branding issue, particularly as some of the smaller record companies have recognised this and are participating quite openly in the different income streams of the artists.

Obviously, the Internet has had a major impact on the record business and is blamed to a large extent by the majors for their recent financial problems. This may, however, be part of a more general problem that the public have got used to receiving music for free. They not only get music for free on the Internet but also there are many TV channels devoted to music and radio constantly pumping out music. It's impossible to walk through a shopping mall without being bombarded by music. Music is ubiquitous and therefore record companies need to establish a unique selling point to sell records to a jaded public. This is the main task record companies have ahead of them to secure their income stream. If the public now want a unique experience in relation to music they are as likely to go and see an act live as they are to buy a record. The live experience is extremely valid to the public and this explains why, despite the doom and gloom at the record company, artists have been cashing in.

TIPS FOR NEWCOMERS

- ***Qualifications*:** To become a solicitor in the UK, you need a law degree and must complete a one-year Legal Practice course and a two-year training contract. If your degree is not in law you will need to take the Common Professional Examination, a one-year conversion course. In house lawyers can be barristers. They have a legal degree and have been to bar school. After a minimum of one year's training they can practise as a barrister. Barristers cannot become partners in law firms. If you don't have a law degree you can get a qualification as a legal executive. This can be studied at evening classes or on day release. After many years you can become a fully qualified solicitor.
- ***Working in house or for a private firm*:** Working in house you will have to get used to corporate politics and culture, but have the opportunity of climbing the management ladder. Building your own private practice in a law firm is hard work as competition is intense, but the satisfaction of building up your own list of clients can be financially and personally rewarding.

THE VIEW FROM WITHIN

MARTIN DELLER – MUSIC LAWYER

Martin Deller sits below the obligatory gold and platinum discs. He is easy to talk to and enthusiastic about the business. His firm mostly represents artists, managers and producers, rather than record labels. We start by asking what advice he gives to new artists

The first agreement most artists will be asked to sign will be a management agreement. This is probably the most important agreement they'll ever sign, as it will govern all the money they earn in the future. Too many people don't get legal advice at this stage, because they don't think they can afford it and often the relationship with their manager starts on as much a friendly as a professional footing.

It's clear that for a lawyer, you have considerable sympathy for struggling musicians.

Most of our clients have no money when they start. We would rather they came to us with no money and we work something out, instead of signing a bad management agreement.

Surely you can't just take everyone off the street.

You only want to spend a lot of time with people for no money if you think there's a better than average chance of success. [*Smiles*]

How do you decide who to invest your time in?

We don't rely on our own judgement, we take advice from third parties who are in the know. They might be a trusted client who is a producer or an A&R man.

What is so bad about these agreements they bring you?

You would be amazed. I have seen some appalling management agreements. The worst thing is the length of time they're committed to a manager, because these agreements are usually exclusive. The problem is nobody knows how good a manager is until they actually manage you. By the time you find out they are no good you are committed. For as long as seven years in some cases.

Tell us more about the pitfalls of a manager's agreement.
The two main problems are the term of the agreement and limiting the manager's expenses. A good agreement in the UK will ensure that managers will only get commission on recordings that are recorded and released or songs that are written and exploited during the term of the management agreement. They will get their commission on these materials, but limited to a full rate of commission for five years and a half rate for the next five.

What about expenses?
You have to be very definite about how expenses are going to be calculated and what costs incurred by the artist may be permitted to be deducted from income prior to commission being calculated and paid. You have to decide what they can spend without approval and how expenses are going to be paid.

How does the lawyer work with the manager to put the deal together?
A good manager is quite capable of constructing what we call a deal memo. Normally this is done in conjunction with the lawyer. The lawyer will give his comments then the manager will try to negotiate the terms with any interested record companies. When the negotiations are complete, the record company will issue their contract.

Major labels all have their own standard contracts. What's your view on these?
They do all have their own standard contracts, although they have variations as well. Some major record companies long-form agreements are as much as eighty pages long. It takes a very long time to negotiate.

So how do you know which parts are up for negotiation and which aren't?
It depends on the client. How much the record company or companies want the band. If you're acting for a band that every major label is after at the same

time you can pick a label and try to drive a very hard bargain and see whether they will bite.

When it comes to negotiating the advance, biggest is always best, isn't it?
Of course it's important to get an adequate advance. It has to provide enough money to support the band until royalties are payable. In the music business you can never be sure how many records you're going to sell, so the advance is the only money you know you're going to get. There is a problem though, if you have a very high advance, because normally in exercising options for the second and subsequent albums they would expect to pay a higher advance for each album. If the first album doesn't work they'll start having cold feet about picking up the second album. The risk has just multiplied. The record label might come back and say: 'We're not going to pick it up for £300,000, we'll do it for £150,000, will you take it?' Often they might not even do that, and might just say: 'Well actually, no. Let's just leave it.'

Tell us about recoupable costs.
The problem with recording deals is there are so many costs that you have to recoup before you receive your royalties. So say you receive a £100,000 advance, you soon owe much more because the record company put you in a studio and you make an album. Let's say this costs £100,000, now you need to recoup £200,000. Then you need to make a video for another £50,000 and so on. Before you know it, you have to recoup £250,000 plus. That's an awful lot of records you have to sell before you see a cheque. There are an enormous number of bands that do not recoup. You'd be amazed at the number of bands, even successful ones.

How does this compare to recoupment on publishing deals?
The only thing you have to recoup in your publishing agreement is your advance, so you recoup quickly. For many bands, publishing royalties provide a regular source of income. The record contract is merely a vehicle for getting their music recorded; the real money comes from live work and publishing. The problem can be that if there is only one band member

writing the material he gets all the publishing money. It can leave a bitter taste in the mouth of the other band members. For example, it has been suggested in the press that Noel Gallagher has written most of the songs for Oasis and gets the lion's share of the publishing royalties. Not all bands work this way. Some bands may only have a couple of principal writers but all band members agree to share the publishing equally. I think this provides a sense of unity for a band and possibly will mean that a band stays together for longer than if one member was acquiring all of the songwriting royalties.

What about problems over band members falling out. How do you as a lawyer deal with this when they're all your clients?
If we are instructed by a band, there's a certain problem because we're advising all of them. So either they have to take individual representation to be advised on their agreement among themselves or do it themselves. Unfortunately, many bands do not contemplate their own internal agreements. Band members come and go. As they get older some might want to record and not tour. There are many issues about how income is divided.

So our band have done a deal, made a successful album with a small label. Now they want to do a deal with a major, but their current label has the option for four more albums. What would you do?
The small label has to be bought out. There might actually be a provision in the original agreement for this eventuality. It's becoming far more common for small labels to become development vehicles for the majors, especially as they've cut back on A&R.

You're talking about production agreements.
Typically these are offered by a producer, writer or manager who has access to studios, producers and recording facilities. The production agreement they will offer artists is essentially an exclusive recording contract. Under the terms of the contract they'll offer to make a certain number of recordings for you. You will then split the profits you earn from the recordings, normally 50/50. Just like a recording contract, there will be options for other albums as well. There

might be an express clause that says, 'This production company must secure a deal with a major third party record company within a period, say, twelve months, to release the recordings or you can terminate the agreement.'

There could be a problem of going into negotiations with a partner who potentially has a different agenda.
Yes, this can be a problem. The label or individual you've signed with will be driving and controlling negotiations with the third party. So if there's an agreement with say EMI, the agreement for the artist's recording services is going to be between the production company and EMI. The deal will be driven by the strength of relationships between the production company and certain majors.

How did you decide to become a music lawyer?
Music has always been part of my life. My grandfather and father were both professional musicians. Originally I wanted to be a zoologist but my careers adviser showed me the most employed and most unemployed people after university. Zoologists were in the bottom five and lawyers were in the top five. So I changed to law. Once I had decided on law, music law was an obvious choice. I saw my grandfather's recording agreements from the fifties. They were a page and a half long and sometimes without a royalty. Often they just had a fixed fee of ten or fifteen quid. It was absolutely appalling.

How did you come to specialise in music law?
At law college I took a specific media and entertainment option. The difficult thing then was to find a training contract with a firm that had a music practice. Most are too small to be in a position to take on 'trainees'. I had to go out to work for music lawyers for no money just to get relevant experience on my CV. I was lucky and after working for a specialist music firm, Searle's, I eventually got a training contract at Hamlins Solicitors. It's really difficult to get a training contract in a media practice and I'd advise anyone who is serious to do as many placements as possible to build up the right CV, because competition is fierce.

What do you think is important to make it?

You have to be committed, not just because it's difficult to get into, but because you have to expect to earn much less than your contemporaries. If I was a city lawyer my salary would be in another world. Everyone thinks it is the most glamorous part of law, but often it's just hard work. An eighty-page contract for a record deal is probably just as boring as an eighty-page contract for constructing an office block. Some things are exciting. For me the best is that someone goes from being unknown to being hugely successful and knowing you contributed to this in some small way, especially when they trusted you on the way and took your advice. To be good you have to be interested in the business. When I take on a new client I always try to go to see them play live. How many people's jobs would take them to a dingy pub in Camden to see a band play?

Martin Deller is a lawyer with Searle's Solicitors and can be contacted at martindeller@yahoo.co.uk

LAWYERS

BENEDICTS
Just House, Beavor Lane, London
W6 9UL
T: 020 8741 6020 F: 020 8741 8362
Email: john@@benedicts.biz
Website: benedicts.biz
Partner: John Benedict

BRABNERS CHAFFE STREET
1 Dale St, Liverpool L2 2ET
T: 0151 600 3000 F: 0151 600 3009
Email: francis.mcentegart@brabnerscs.com
Website: brabnerschaffestreet.com
Solicitor, Media: Francis McEntegart

BRAY AND KRAIS SOLICITORS
70-71 New Bond Street, London
W1S 1DE
T: 020 7493 8840 F: 020 7493 8841
Email: bandk@brayandkrais.com
Senior Partner: Richard Bray

BRENNAN & CO
Suites 5 & 6, Manchester House,
46 Manchester Street,
London W1U 7LS
T: 020 7486 6081 F: 020 7486 6082
Email: erika@brennanand.co.uk
Senior Partner: Erika Brennan

BURLEY & COMPANY
10 Gray's Inn Square, Gray's Inn,
London WC1R 5JD
T: 020 7404 4002 F: 020 7405 2429
Christopher Burley

JOHN BYRNE & CO
Sheraton House, Castle Park,
Cambridge CB3 0AX
T: 01223 370063 F: 01223 370065
Email: JB@johnbyrne.co.uk
Principal: John Byrne

CALVERT SOLICITORS
77 Weston Street, London Bridge,
London SE1 3RS
T: 020 7234 0707 F: 020 7234 0909
Email: mail@calvertsolicitors.co.uk

CLINTONS
55 Drury Lane, London WC2B 5RZ
T: 020 7379 6080 F: 020 7240 9310
Email: amm@clintons.co.uk
Website: clintons.co.uk
Partner: Andrew Myers

COLLINS LONG SOLICITORS
24 Pepper St, London SE1 0EB
T: 020 7401 9800 F: 020 7401 9850
Email: info@collinslong.com
Website: collinslong.com
Partners: James Collins & Simon Long

COLLYER-BRISTOW
4 Bedford Row, London WC1R 4DF
T: 020 7242 7363 F: 020 7405 0555
Email: cblaw@collyerbristow.com
Website: collyerbristow.com
Partner: Howard Ricklow

SIMON CONROY SOLICITORS
Second Floor,43-45 St John St,
London EC1M 4AN
T: 020 7490 1276 F: 020 7490 1298
Email: mail@simonconroy.com
Website: simonconroy.com
Simon Conroy

LAWYERS

JIM COOK
38 Grovelands Road, London N13 4RH
T: 020 8350 0613 F: 020 8350 0613
Email: jim@jcook21.freeserve.co.uk
Solicitor: Jim Cook

DAVENPORT LYONS
1 Old Burlington St, London W1S 3NL
T: 020 7468 2600 F: 020 7437 8216
Email: jware@davenportlyons.com
Website: davenportlyons.com
Partner: James Ware

DECHERT
2 Sergeants' Inn, London EC4Y 1LT
T: 020 7583 5353 F: 020 7353 3683
Email: marketing@dechertEU.com
Website: dechert.com
Chief Exec: Sir Peter Duffell

DENTON WILDE SAPTE
5 Chancery Lane, Clifford's Inn, London EC4A 1BU
T: 020 7320 6516 F: 020 7320 6571
Email: rwa@dentonwildesapte.com
Website: dentonwildesapte.com
Partner: Robert Allan

DLA (SOLICITORS)
3 Noble Street, London EC2V 7EE
T: 020 7796 6182 F: 020 7796 6113
Email: ian.penman@dla.com
Website: dla.net
Associate, Media etc.: Ian Penman

EDMONDS BOWEN
4 Old Park Lane, London W1K 1QW
T: 020 7629 8000 F: 020 7221 9334
Email: info@edmondsbowen.co.uk
Website: edmondsbowen.co.uk
Consultant: Nick Pedgrift

ENGEL MONJACK
16-18 Berners St, London W1T 3LN
T: 020 7291 3838 F: 020 7291 3839
Email: info@engelmonjack.com
Website: engelmonjack.com
Lawyer: Jonathan Monjack

FIELD FISHER WATERHOUSE
35 Vine Street, London EC3N 2AA
T: 020 7861 4000 F: 020 7488 0084
Email: info@ffwlaw.com
Website: ffwlaw.com

FINERS STEPHENS INNOCENT
179 Great Portland Street, London W1N 6LS
T: 020 7353 4000 F: 020 7580 7069
Email: marketing@fsilaw.co.uk
Website: fsilaw.com
Marketing Assistant: Katie Mackenzie

NIGEL DEWAR GIBB & CO SOLICITORS
43 St John St, London EC1M 4AN
T: 020 7608 1091 F: 020 7608 1092
Email: ndg@e-legaluk.co.uk
Website: e-legaluk.co.uk
Principal: Nigel Dewar Gibb

GRAY & CO
Habib House, 3rd Floor, 9 Stevenson Square, Manchester M1 1DB
T: 0161 237 3360 F: 0161 236 6717
Email: grayco@grayand.co.uk
Website: grayand.co.uk
Partner: Rudi Kidd

GSC SOLICITORS
31-32 Ely Place, London EC1N 6TD
T: 020 7822 2222 F: 020 7822 2211
Email: info@gscsolicitors.com
Website: gscsolicitors.com
Managing Partner: Saleem Sheikh

HAMLINS
Roxburghe House, 273-287 Regent Street, London W1B 2AD
T: 020 7355 6000 F: 020 7518 9100
Email: ent-law@hamlins.co.uk
Website: hamlins.co.uk
Managing Partner: Laurence Gilmore

HARBOTTLE AND LEWIS
Hanover House, 14 Hanover Square, London WIS 1HP
T: 020 7667 5000 F: 020 7667 5100
Email: info@harbottle.com
Website: harbottle.co.uk
Partner, Head of Music Gp: Ann Harrison

HART-JACKSON & HALL
3A Ridley Place, Newcastle upon Tyne, Tyne and Wear NE1 8JQ
T: 0191 232 1987 F: 0191 232 0429
Partner: Mr PA Hall

HENRY HEPWORTH
5 John Street, London WC1N 2HH
T: 020 7242 7999 F: 020 7539 7201
Email: leisure@h2o-law.com
Website: h2o-law.com

HOWARD LIVINGSTONE, SOLICITOR
37 Trinity Rd, E.Finchley, London N2 8JJ
T: 020 8365 2962 F: 020 8365 2484
Email: aooa76@dsl.pipex.com
Website: fsvo.com/musiclawyer
Music Lawyer: Howard Livingstone

HOWLETTS
60 Grays Inn Road, London WC1X 8LA
T: 020 7404 5612 F: 020 7831 0635
Email: howletts@zoom.co.uk
Partner: David Semmens

JAYES & PAGE
Universal House, 251 Tottenham Court Rd, London W1T 7JY
T: 020 7291 9111 F: 020 7291 9119
Email: enquiries@jayesandpage.com
Website: jayesandpage.com
Partners: Anthony Jayes, Bob Page

JENS HILLS & CO
Northburgh House, 10 Northburgh Street, London EC1V 0AT
T: 020 7490 8160 F: 020 7490 8140
Email: info@jenshills.com
Principal: Jens Hills

MC KIRTON & CO
83 St Albans Avenue, London W4 5JS
T: 020 8987 8880 F: 020 8932 7908
Email: michael@mckirton.com
Senior Partner: Michael Kirton

KLEGAL SOLICITORS
1-2 Dorset Rise, London EC4Y 8AE
T: 020 7694 2500 F: 020 7694 2501
Email: philip.daniels@kpmg.co.uk
Website: klegal.co.uk
Music Industry Solicitor: Philip Daniels

LEE & THOMPSON
Greengarden House, 15-22 St Christopher's Place, London W1U 1NL
T: 020 7935 4665 F: 020 7563 4949
Email: mail@leethompson.com
Website: leeandthompson.com
Senior Partner: Andrew Thompson

LEE CROWDER SOLICITORS
39 Newhall Street, Birmingham B3 3DY
T: 0121 236 4477 F: 0121 236 0774
Email: frances.anderson@leecrowder.co.uk
Website: leecrowder.co.uk
Partner: Frances Anderson

LOVELLS
Atlantic House, Holborn Viaduct,
London EC1A 2FG
T: 020 7296 2000 F: 020 7296 2001
Email: lindy.golding@lovells.com
Website: lovells.com
Partner: Lindy Golding

LEONARD LOWY & CO
500 Chiswick High Road, London
W4 5RG
T: 020 8956 2785 F: 020 8956 2786
Email: lowy@leonardlowy.co.uk
Website: leonardlowy.co.uk
Principal: Leonard Lowy

MACLAY, MURRAY & SPENS, LONDON
10 Foster Lane, London EC2V 6HR
T: 020 7606 6130 F: 020 7600 0992
Email: murray.buchanan@mms.co.uk
Website: mms.co.uk
Consultant: Murray J. Buchanan

MAGRATH & CO
52-54 Maddox Street, London W1S 1PA
T: 020 7495 3003 F: 020 7409 1745
Email: alexis.grower@magrath.co.uk
Website: magrath.co.uk
Consultant: Alexis Grower

MANCHES
Aldwych House, 81 Aldwych, London
WC2B 4RP
T: 020 7404 4433 F: 020 7430 1133
Email: manches@manches.co.uk
Website: manches.co.uk

MARRIOTT HARRISON
12 Great James St, London WC1N 3DR
T: 020 7209 2000 F: 020 7209 2001
Email: tony.morris@marriottharrison.co.uk
Website: marriottharrison.com
Partner and Head of Media: Tony Morris

MISHCON DE REYA
Summit House, 12, Red Lion Sq,
London WC1R 4QD
T: 020 7440 7000 F: 020 7404 5982
Email: feedback@mishcon.co.uk
Website: mishcon.co.uk
Partner: David Glick

ROBIN MORTON, SOLICITOR
22 Herbert St, Glasgow G20 6NB
T: 0141 337 1199 F: 0141 357 0655
Email: robinmorto@aol.com

MULTIPLAY MUSIC CONSULTANTS
Maple Farm, 56 High Street, Harrold,
Bedford MK43 7DA
T: 01234 720785 F: 01234 720664

OLSWANG
90 Long Acre, London WC2E 9TT
T: 020 7208 8888 F: 020 7208 8800
Email: olsmail@olswang.com
Website: olswang.com
Partner: John Enser

PINSENT CURTIS BIDDLE
1 Gresham Street, London EC2V 7BU
T: 020 7606 9301 F: 020 7606 3305
Email: martin.lane@pinsents.com
Website: pinsents.com
Managing Partner: Martin Lane

ROHAN & CO SOLICITORS
Aviation House, 1-7 Sussex Road,
Haywards Heath, West Sussex
RH16 1RX
T: 01444 450901 F: 01444 440437

Email: partners@rohansolicitors.co.uk
Website: rohansolicitors.co.uk
Rupert Rohan, Edward Glauser

ROSS & CRAIG
12A Upper Berkeley Street, London
W1H 7QE
T: 020 7262 3077 F: 020 7724 6427
Email: david.leadercramer@rosscraig.com
Website: rosscraig.com
Managing Director: David Leadercramer

RUSSELLS
Regency House, 1-4 Warwick Street,
London W1R 6LJ
T: 020 7439 8692 F: 020 7494 3582
Email: media@russells.co.uk
Mr R Page

SAMPLE CLEARANCE SERVICES LTD
PO Box 3367, Brighton, East Sussex
BN1 1WX
T: 01273 326999 F: 01273 328999
Email: saranne@sampleclearance.com
Website: sampleclearance.com
Managing Director: Saranne Reid

SCHILLINGS
Royalty House, 72-74 Dean Street,
London W1D 3TL
T: 020 7453 2500 F: 020 7453 2600
Email: legal@schillings.co.uk
Website: schillings.co.uk
Office Manager: Shelley Vincent

SEARLE'S SOLICITORS
The Chapel, 26A Munster Road, London
SW6 4EN
T: 020 7371 0555 F: 020 7371 7722
Email: searles@searles-solicitors.co.uk
Partner: Helen Searle

SEDDONS
5 Portman Square, London W1H 6NT
T: 020 7725 8000 F: 020 7935 5049
Email: davidk@seddons.co.uk
Website: seddons.co.uk
Partner: David Kent

SHERIDANS
14 Red Lion Square, London
WC1R 4QL
T: 020 7404 0444 F: 020 7831 1982
Email: entertainment@sheridans.co.uk
Partner: Stephen Luckman

THE SIMKINS PARTNERSHIP
45-51 Whitfield Street, London
W1T 4HB
T: 020 7907 3000 F: 020 7907 3111
Email: info@simkins.com
Website: simkins.com
Head of Music Group: Julian Turton

SPRAGGON STENNETT BRABYN
Crown House, 225 Kensington High St,
London W8 6SA
T: 020 7938 2223 F: 020 7938 2224
Email: legal@ssb.co.uk
Website: ssb.co.uk
Office Manager: Chris Weller

STEELE & CO
11 Guilford St, London WC1N 1DT
T: 020 7421 1720 F: 020 7421 1749
Email: WilkinsM@steele.co.uk
Website: steele.co.uk
Consultant: Mark FR Wilkins

TARLO LYONS
Watchmaker Court,
33 St John's Lane, London EC1M 4DB
T: 020 7405 2000 F: 020 7814 9421

Email: info@tarlolyons.com
Website: tarlolyons.com
Partners: Stanley Munson, D Michael Rose

TAYLOR JOYNSON GARRETT
Carmelite, 50 Victoria Embankment, London EC4Y 0DX
T: 020 7300 7000 F: 020 7300 7100
Email: pmitchell@tjg.co.uk
Website: tjg.co.uk
Partner: Paul Mitchell

TENON STATHAM GILL DAVIES
66 Chiltern St, London W1U 4JT
T: 020 7535 1400 F: 020 7535 1640
Email: john.statham@tenongroup.com
Solicitor/Partner: John Statham

DAVID WINEMAN SOLICITORS
Craven House, 121 Kingsway, London WC2B 6NX
T: 020 7400 7800 F: 020 7400 7890
Email: law@davidwineman.co.uk
Website: davidwineman.co.uk
Irving David

HIGHLY RECOMMENDED LEGAL

Russells

Bray And Krais

Clintons

Sheridans

Searles

Lee & Thompson

Addleshaw Goddard

Andrew Lewis

Simkins Partnership

1

2

3

4

5

6

7

8

9

10

11

12

13

14

15

ARTISTS

WHAT IS THE ROLE OF THE ARTIST?

Artists should lead the music business. They have the right to be bold, take risks and be larger than life. Since the teenager was invented in the 1950s, generations of kids have stuck posters of artists on their bedroom walls, played their records when nobody else seemed to understand them and lived their lives through them.

Artists have a huge responsibility to be true to themselves and create music that is daring, exciting and controversial. When people talk about the lack of excitement in the music business, they usually blame the labels, particularly the majors or the Internet, or supermarkets, or producers, but if there's no great music to record, or no great performers to produce, nothing else matters. Of course there are brilliant exceptions, but today artists are not what they used to be or what they should be.

That's why if you are an aspiring artist, we challenge you to ignore the artists of the last few years. Instead cast your mind back to when performers really kicked ass. When hip hop, house and rave culture was young and fresh it pushed boundaries and new experiences, as punk had done before. It was a time of new fashion trends, social issues, and creative expression – music mattered. Soul II Soul were a great example of this with the funky dread and their fashion label. Their global spirit and identity was soaked up by all nationalities, all of whom could relate to their lyrics celebrating struggle and keep on moving.

ARTISTS WITH ATTITUDE

Remember when Madonna burst on the scene. It's easy to forget, now that she's a member of the establishment, but in the eighties and nineties she was a mega artist with a creativity that left her audience gagging for more. Even the Spice Girls were great entertainers and performers. They were bold, brash and colourful. Sophisticated observers may have hated them, but they had spunk and connected with their audience in a way nobody does today. Millions of little girls screamed 'Girl Power'. They might have lacked creative coolness, but they had attitude, raw enough to push them forward. Virtually all the pop acts that have been put together since the Spice Girls are so neatly packaged that they are arid. Most acts today may as well have been created by parents or schoolteachers for all they challenge society.

CONTROVERSY IS GOOD

Check out the history of great artists and entertainers. You'll find they all broke boundaries, creating an establishment backlash. Rock 'n' roll was 'the music of the devil'. At the outset of his career Elvis was considered lewd and outrageous. **The revolutionary crossover between white country music and black R&B he pioneered in the Fifties was branded 'nigger music'.** In the decades following, parents who had themselves jived to rock 'n' roll feared the worst when their kids got into the Rolling Stones in the Sixties; punk and heavy metal in the Seventies; house, jungle, hip hop and rap in the Eighties and Nineties.

Even if you look at the music business as simply a business, and strip it of any emotion, today's business is in danger of suffering the same problems as Nike and Levi's had in the 1990s. Nobody wanted to wear the same trainers and jeans brands as their parents, and their market share dived. In the same way, kids today don't want music that is so bland and packaged that their parents understand it, and at worse listen to it – that's what today's business is doing. It's hitting the business harder than the Internet.

ARTISTS, ENTERTAINERS AND MANUFACTURED PERFORMERS

There are two types of performers – artists and entertainers. The music industry is structured to manage and process both.

Artists have musical integrity and are creatively led and more inner directed, because they are guided by their own unique attitude and voice. They often write their own songs and are easy to spot, from Bob Marley and Bob Dylan to U2 to Oasis to Coldplay and Amy Winehouse.

Entertainers develop their career through a more outward directed process. Usually they don't write their own songs. They are more like actors, performing songs as if they were scripts, and doing everything they can to give them personality and make them believable. Entertainers include: Robbie Williams, the Spice Girls, J-Lo, Westlife, Justin Timberlake, Destiny's Child and Liberty X. The natural skills of artists and entertainers often cross over. Whether you're an artist or an entertainer, unless you express yourself with sincerity and your own voice, you won't make it.

Many people are negative about *manufactured performers*. They fail to appreciate that some of our greatest performers were created by the manufacturing process – just check out the Motown acts. They were all products of a manufacturing system. The difference between them and artists today is not how they were manufactured, but the degree of talent they applied to their acts and careers. So why are manufactured acts not as good today? We believe it's because labels are lazier and less willing to take risks. They seem to think that if you can just find four good-looking artists who can sort of sing in key and dance in time together, all you need is enough radio and television coverage to make them a hit. No wonder independent labels are growing so fast. They know the majors can't be bothered to spot true talent, and they can. They have the time to develop talent, instead of kicking mediocrity into the big time.

1 2 3 4 5 6 7 8 9 10 11 12 13 14 15

ARTISTS

If you're a manager or an executive at a label, we hope this section has inspired you to throw out some of the old dried-up formulas that are killing the business. Hopefully you'll look a little further for talent that does not conform to the stereotype and remember why you went into the business in the first place.

TIPS FOR NEWCOMERS

- ***Live and breathe musical integrity:*** Like a politician, your integrity is all you have. This integrity needs to show itself in everything you do, whether it's a song, promo video, live performance or interviews in the press or on TV. When the public are first exposed to you they ask themselves, 'Do I believe that this artist or band is real, or are they pretending to be real?' What determines whether you are 'real' or 'cool' can come down to the smallest details. It could be that you look great, but your performance might just be a bit too eager.
- ***Find your voice and sound:*** As a vocalist, working with a vocal coach to find your unique voice can make all the difference. Be careful not to 'over-sing'. Under-singing is a great way to let your personality come out. Never let a producer or label impose a sound on you that isn't part of you. You need to collaborate with the right people to get what you want. Working with the right songwriter and producer is key, so don't sit back and leave it all to the label – take control and make your own connections,
- ***You're never 'off duty':*** Those around you expect you to have good taste, to know what's cool and not cool. If you don't they'll soon lose confidence in you. Being an artist is tough. Even at a first meeting when a label is listening to your demo, they want to get a real feeling for your unique spirit and attitude.
- ***Choosing your team:*** There is always pressure on an artist to sign the first deal they are offered. After all, it's usually taken long enough to get it, but resist it. The wrong deal and the wrong label can finish you before you even get started. Beware of record executives who talk the talk. Many hide behind a label's reputation. Work out early on whether they're looking to develop you as an entertainer or an artist. If you don't think they understand your artistic integrity, don't sign or they'll just package you to hell.

- ***Creative conflict:*** There will be many points in your career when serious creative decisions have to be made. There will be times when you don't agree with your label. If you refuse to go along with the label, they might withdraw their support, perhaps subtly at first. There's no straight answer about how to avoid these conflicts, but agreement upfront always helps. Before you sign a deal it's worth being very specific about your creative brief and getting the label to play back their understanding of that vision, as a check. Once signed, make sure your manager earns his or her money in managing expectations with the label.
- ***Don't give up:*** Keep improving your music and at the same time push to make it happen. Sell your CDs, build a fan base, turn your dream into reality and then get your deal. It sounds harsh, but remember you can always get better: keep pushing and get out there.
- ***Wanting it enough:*** It's a terrible cliché, but you have to want it badly enough. You must have bullet-proof self-belief, but never arrogance. People often confuse the two. Arrogance is the number one career killer in the music business, whereas self-belief is what keeps you going when more sensible people have given up and become accountants.
- ***'One-person record label':*** We've invented this term to demonstrate the importance of taking hold of your own destiny in the music business. You need to behave as if you're a record label and you are your most important client. Think about your own development, promotion and distribution. You need to hook up with a producer, or manager producer who can help you develop your own sound and produce at least three tracks that are potential hit singles and ready to go.
- ***Promoting yourself:*** Getting a crowd is increasingly important. It gives you financial power to get promoters and eventually labels. It starts right at the beginning. When you want to get your first gig in a local pub, getting another booking is more dependent on how many

of your friends you can get to come down to the pub than your musical ability.

- ***Know the local scene:*** Learn how to work it. Start with the local papers. There's usually a music page, written by a local journalist with a genuine interest and knowledge of the local scene. Its worth trying to get to know them. Check out the listing magazines. Go to the venues and meet the promoters. But remember this type of venue will want a demo and a press pack first. Colleges are also worth a try, especially if a friend goes there. Talking of friends, offer to support their bands and vice versa.
- ***Make every gig successful:*** Get your friends along, give them flyers and get them to bring their friends along too. Use your common sense, arrive early, try to do a proper sound check, ring ahead and check out the PA and what equipment you need.
- ***Avoid pay-to-play venues:*** Some venues charge you a non-refundable deposit for the PA, which is in effect charging you to play. GigRight UK produces a fair venue listing book circuit, which is a good source to find venues.
- ***Don't just gig, sell CDs too:*** Find someone with a CD writer. When you get some money get some labels and some proper artwork done. Then put a website together, start to make things tangible. Build that fan base; labels want to see a following before they sign these days.
- ***Find the tipping point to success:*** What's the one thing that will make the difference? It could be creating a strong local fan base, as the Stone Roses did in Manchester, and The Stereophonics in Wales. Both built a big live reputation before getting a deal. Or it could be that your tipping point is to hook up with a great songwriter, or do a joint venture deal with an independent label allowing you to produce your three hit tracks before you even walk through the door of a major label.
- ***A record deal isn't the only option:*** If you can't get a record deal, don't give up: you could push for a licensing deal. They're easier to get

because you don't get an advance, but if you can produce your own records cheaply it's a possibility. You can get the same promotion, distribution and royalty as in a normal deal, but without the advance, so you only license it for five or ten years. Or go for a distribution deal that allows you to bypass the record companies altogether. Most distributors will give you a small advance to cover printing and pressing costs and will do some advertising, although you'll have to do much of the promotion yourself. However, there are compensations: as you're virtually operating as a record company, you'll get the majority of the profits.

THE VIEW FROM WITHIN

JAZZIE B – SOUL II SOUL

With Soul II Soul, Jazzie B sold millions of albums around the world, creating a new musical sound. He's proved you can keep true to yourself and be a huge success. Jazzie is a man with a message and one of those rare people who has great ideas but also makes them happen brilliantly. From the beginning he understood that music is first a business and to survive you have to sell records. The big question is: how did he do it and hold on to his integrity as an artist?

It's all about self-empowerment. First you must focus on building your own power base, so that you have a position to apply leverage from. This can be through economic power, or working with like-minded people. You must lead by example, then you can dictate how things are done around you. Too many bands are so keen to get a record deal that they'll just sign up to whatever the label wants. Whereas if you prove yourself and have a strong base, the label will sign with you because they want what you are. When Virgin Records came to us we already had a massive following here and in America. We had a little empire making money from merchandising. You've got to set an example; don't talk about it – do it.

In many ways Soul II Soul has been seen as the voice of young black people. Doesn't this make you feel under pressure to help empower them?

You wouldn't believe the millions of requests I get from people. They believe I should give them all sorts of things. I try to work with those I can, but if I responded to everyone I'd be the Pope. If every black person had to walk with that on their shoulders they wouldn't survive.

Why was it so hard for another British black act to get their level of worldwide success?

[*Smiles*] Because there are no more Jazzie Bs or Don Taylors! No, seriously, this country has never recognised what it's got. It's a real shame. At one time I thought some of the younger executives at the labels would be more in tune with what our music stood for, and our culture. It's not about the labels employing black executives, it's about them employing the right ones regardless of race. Mick Clarke was a white A&R guy, he was great, he signed us and other great bands. However, I've not walked into a label in the UK and met a black executive who's got the power.

So have you found that many execs don't understand black music?
What amazes me is when people say it isn't a problem. If you walk into a record label and you can't relate to me because you can't understand my music, then that is a real problem, and it happens too often. **What's happened is that music executives have become bigger, fatter bastards and have tried to create music that they can control.** But you can't keep black music down, because technology gives kids the ability to do it themselves. As a result they're producing music that their audience wants. That's why urban is probably the biggest selling music worldwide.

But still you say that there is no other Jazzie B?
When I say there is no other Jazzie B, I mean that a lot of acts don't have a clear vision of where they are going. Sometimes they don't have a choice because they lead the industry and there is no support for them. That puts them in a corner because if they don't have an opinion, they have no option but to do a deal and do what the label wants. It was different for us. Before we even signed we paved our way, created our scene, music, identity and ways of earning income without needing the label.

What advice do you have for young black kids wanting to work for labels?
The future for black executives is not just about economics. It's about like-minded people coming together who share a similar vision that's deeper than bling and ego.

So where do you see the future of black music?
We're going to turn back to that sound system culture, where a posse was born. A time when stories were told and culture was expressed through

music. Now as a people we are smart enough to own what we create. God gives us a time to live in, so let's hope we use our time to our best ability.

JAY KAY – JAMIROQUAI

He's sold 30 million records. When we go down to his house to interview him, we expect Jay Kay to speak his mind. He doesn't let us down, especially when it comes to talking about his label, Sony. He isn't being vindictive, just honest. This might make uncomfortable reading for his label, but as he says:
How I'm talking in this interview is exactly how I talked to the label from day one. From my first day of dealing with the label I had to fight them. They wanted to change my logo right from the start and presented me with a paper that said: 'I will give away the rights to the Jamiroquai Buffalo Man registered trademark for the sum of one pound.' They said sign so we can use the logo on letterheads. They wanted me to give away the right to my logo and design for one pound. You've got to watch every move they take.

Why do you feel so strongly about this?
Labels think they know everything. They should listen more to the artist. If I'd listened to them my career would probably be over. Lincoln told me one of my albums had no singles then I sold 8.3 million albums. Then I had to fight to get the money to make the 'Virtual Insanity' video and then we won five MTV awards and one Grammy.

There's nothing worse as an artist than feeling you're being sold a line to meet a corporate agenda. Jay agrees and tells us the lengths the label went to in trying to convince him that he should make a Greatest Hits album.
A few weeks back Muff came down to my house and asked, 'What about if you get writer's block? If you did would you consider doing a Greatest Hits album?' Then he went away and a couple of weeks later Lincoln came down to my house as well. He sits there and says: 'Jay, man, why don't you do a Greatest Hits, man, the fans want it.' I tell him: 'I'm not putting out any greatest hits.' They're just using me as a sacrificial lamb because the Americans

are on their case for performing badly. I resent them using me for their interest, instead of building my career.

We move on to ask him about writing and creating music. He changes completely, anger replaced by passion.
It's better than any drugs, sex or fast cars. You have this melody in your head. Then to see it happen is such a buzz. I love the experience. I'm in this business to write songs that are memorable and classic. I don't want to write songs like some of the shit you hear in the charts.

What were your earliest musical influences?
I was brought up listening to jazz and other great artists. My ears became tuned into connecting with what works. A lot of today's songs are flat. When I write I want people to remember my songs. Try to think of a great catchy and well-arranged song, written over the last few years – there aren't many. Now sing a Stevie Wonder track or a Beatles song and it's easy to remember.

How do you approach writing a song?
The melody starts in my head and then I jam with the band. It's about building the track with many levels, a bit like making a sandwich. You fill it with layers and layers that are finely mixed with different flavours. That's why my melodies have movement and are catchy. It's the blend of the two elements. [*Sings to demonstrate.*] It's about building the track with melody parts that lift the song and then throwing in another one that lifts or takes it to another place. You play me a chord and I know what's going to work. So many songs use major chords, but that's shit and basic. For me it's about using loads of minor chords.

We start talking about the album he's working on.
I'm taking my time. In the past we had to record to very tight deadlines. To the point that I'd be singing the songs from the sheets of paper I'd just written them on. It worked then because that was the vibe, but now I need to approach it in a style that allows me to go deeper. So when I start recording

vocals I will be so part of the song that everything flows just how I want it to. I know that people say that what I recorded before was great, but you're only as good as your last album.

In view of your strong character, how do you work with producers?
Some idiots come into the studio and try to force their views on me. They try to get me using their songs, but that's not me. I write my songs because only I know what I want to say and how to express it. You have to be very careful when you work with producers, because they will always try to add their own stuff, that's not you and will cheapen it. It's about keeping a rein on them.

You now have a lot of power – how do you use it?
Having power, as you put it, is pointless if you're off your trolley all the time, but now I'm off that stuff. I'm operating on all cylinders and it's great because I'm buzzed up and this gets everyone going. I don't want to be like Michael Jackson, or Madonna, with nutters following me around, not allowing me to be myself. In this business loads of people want to be big stars, but they don't know what they're taking on. It's not about getting into the charts, it's about staying in the business your way. It's all you have. People will convince you that they know better. But when you're dropped, it's you that the public consider to be a failure, not the executive who didn't spend time understanding what you're about. Look what's happened to Daniel Bedingfield: he came out with this street vibe and now it's something else. What happened to the real guy? I'll tell you, he let go. He let someone else take control of his talent. Now he's doing those sloppy love songs, because they told him, sing this and we'll sell in America. If a label comes and tries to tell me what to do, I'll do it my way. What's important is that my friends and those close to me like my stuff. They grew up with me.

Jay might be a tough proposition for a label, but his determination to fight for his music must be worth any amount of corporate pain. He delivers, and will continue to deliver even better songs that move people, that will continue to play on the radio long after the label's shareholders have spent their precious dividends.

BOBBY GILLESPIE – PRIMAL SCREAM

In this short interview we concentrate on the attitude you need to make a great track.

There are no rules about how to make a great record. It can take three minutes or three years. When you're creating music it can feel like a matter of life or death. You can get that feeling that something else is taking you there. It's just like there is a spirit and your energy is coming through the music. As if it has to come out and it is beyond your control. When you listen to great tracks you pick up on this energy and it touches the listener's soul. It's what's happening between the notes that gives it the power. Jim Dickinson, the producer who also played with Aretha Franklin and the Rolling Stones, used to say there was a battle between good and evil.

What do you mean by a 'battle'?

I think what he means is that music can put a spell on you, because it dominates the atmosphere and the energy around you. I play my best stuff when I'm just like a vessel. I let the music come through without thinking about it or interfering with it.

So do you feel that music has a power that goes beyond anything rational?

Music is very powerful and can make you want to wreck the place. Kids used to do that when rock 'n' roll first came on to the scene. They were so suppressed that this music was able to give them a great release. They were wrecking cinema halls and dance halls because the music just got to them. That's how strong music is. It just wants to make you go crazy and get off your head.

It still seems strange that it is so difficult to put into words what makes music become great.

THE VIEW FROM WITHIN

You can't put it exactly into words, any more than you can describe why people fall into love with certain other individuals. Like music, the relationship might be good or destructive, but for some reason they're drawn to it and can't let it go. Just as you can't explain the emotion of love, you can't define the essence of what makes a great record.

Do you think the music that's been released recently is all becoming a bit bland?
Even if a lot of it doesn't do it for me, it's good that people can now make music from their homes. Everything can be done on a computer, so it's now so cheap to record your music. It's good for people to feel free to express themselves without using big expensive studios and owing record labels thousands of pounds. Now they can do it without labels and press their own records and release them. I guess if you have a strong voice your music will be heard eventually.

Like so many other creative people we've interviewed, Bobby is excited about the future and the possibility of more people being able to express themselves.

1
2
3
4
5
6
7
8
9
10
11
12
13
14
15

ARTIST MANAGEMENT

Alison Moyet	Sanctuary Management
Amy Winehouse	Brilliant 19 Ltd
Angie Brown	DCM International
Annie Lennox	19 Management
Ant & Dec	James Grant Management
Apache Indian	Boom Management
Ash	Out There Management
Atomic Kitten	Integral Management
Badly Drawn Boy	Big Life Management
Belle & Sebastion	Banchory Management
Beth Orton	Azoffmusic Management
Beverley Knight	Dave Woolf Ltd/Outside Management
Big Brova	Shalit Global Management
Billy Bragg	Sincere Management
Bjorn Again	BA Management
Blazin Squad	Albert Samuel Management
Blue	Intelligent Music Management Ltd
Blur	CMO Management (Int.) Ltd
B Movies Heroes	FiveMilesHigh
Brian Eno	Opal-Chant
Bob Geldof	Jukes Production Ltd
Bobby Womack	David Morgan Management
Boy George	Wedge Music
Carl Cox	Cosmack Management
Charlatans	Steve Harrison Management
Charlotte Church	Azoffmusic Management
Charlotte Day	Roger Boden Management
Chemical Brothers	MBL
Chris De Burgh	KTM

ARTISTS

CJ Mackintosh	Cosmack Management
Cliff Richard	Cliff Richard Organisation
Coldplay	Coldplay Management
Coral, The	Skeleton Key Management
Corrs	John Hughes
Craig David	Wildlife Entertainment
Culture Club	Wedge Music
Daniel Bedingfield	Empire Artist Management
Darius	Brilliant 19 Ltd
Darkness, The	Whitehouse Management
David Bowie	Outside Management
David Gray	Mondo Management
Depeche Mode	(Mute Records)
Des'ree	Outside Management
Dido	Nettwerk Management UK
Don Henley	Azoffmusic Management
Doves	Dave Rofe
Duran Duran	DD Productions
Eagle Eye Cherry	The Umbrella Group
Elaine Page	Sanctuary Music Management
Elbow	TRC Management
Elton John	21st Century
Embrace	Coalition Management
Estelle	Empire Artist Management
Everything But the Girl	JFD Management
Faithless	Faithless Live Ltd
Fatboy Slim	Anglo
Feeder	Riot Management

411	Street Side Records
Franz Ferdinand	Supervision
Gabrielle	J Management
Gareth Gates	19 Management
Gemma Fox	Jamie Mckenzie
George Michael	ASM Management
Gibson Brothers	Denis Vaughan Management
Gipsy Kings	Denis Vaughan Management
Girls Aloud	Louise Walsh
Goldfrapp	Midnight to Six Management
Gorillaz	CMO Management (Int.)
Groove Armada	Hall or Nothing Management
Guns n' Roses	Sanctuary Music Management
Heather Small	Bandana Management Ltd
Hot Chocolate	Richard Martin Management
Incognito	Creation Management Ltd
Iron Maiden	Sanctuary Music Management
Jamelia	Shalit Global Management
Jamie Cullum	Aire International
Jarvis Cocker	Rough Trade Management
Jimmy Page	Trinifold Management
Joss Stone	Fresh Water Hughes
Kylie Minogue	Terry Blamey Management
Kym Marsh	Safe Management
Lamb	Blue Sky Entertainment
Leftfield	Lisa Horan Management
Levellers, The	First Column Management Ltd

ARTISTS

Lighthouse Family	Independent Sound Management/ Kitchenware Management
Louis King	Lisa Horan Management
Lulu	Louis Walsh Management
Madness	Rudge
Manic Street Preachers	Hall or Nothing
Mark Knopfler	Paul Crockford Management
Massive Attack	West
Mercury Rev	Ignition Management
Misteeq	21st Artist
Moloko	Graham Peacock Management
Morcheeba	CMO Management International
Myleene Klass	Safe Management
Natasha Bedingfield	Empire Artist Management
Oasis	Ignition Management
Paul Carrack	Alan Wood Agency
Paul Oakenfold	Terra Firma Management
Paul Trouble Anderson	Prodmix DJ Management & Production
Paul Young	What Management
Pet Shop Boys	Sanctuary Music Management
Phats & Smalls	Deluxe Management
Placebo	Riverman Management
Polyphonic Spree, The	TRC Management
Prodigy	Midi Management Ltd
Pulp	Best PR
Radiohead	Courtyard Management
Ray Davies	Sanctuary Music Management
Reef	Furtive Management
Richard Ashcroft	Terra Ferma Management

Robbie Williams	IE Music Ltd
Rolling Stones, The	Rupert Loewenstein
Ronan Keating	Louis Walsh Management
Samantha Mumba	Louis Walsh Management
Sarah Balfour	The Yukon Management
Seal	Azoffmusic Management
Seb Fontaine	Represents Artist Management
Shaun Escoffery	Eclipse-PJM
Slade	Hal Carter Organisation
Snow Patrol	BigLife Management
So Solid Crew	Albert Samuel Management
Sons & Daughters	Banchory Management
Spiller	F&G Management
Starsailor	Heavenly Managment
Stereophonics, The	Marsupial Management
Suede	Interceptor Enterprises
Sugababes	Metamorphosis Management
Supergrass	Courtyard Management
Texas	GR Management
Thirteen senses	TRC Management
Tom Jones	Valey Music
Travis	Wildlife Entertainment
U2	Principle Management
UB40	Part Rock Management Ltd
Westlife	Louis Walsh Management
Who, The	Trinifold Management
Will Young	19 Management
Zero 7	Solar Management

1

2

3

4

5

6

7

8

9

10

11

12

13

14

15

DJs

WHAT IS THE ROLE OF THE DJ?

Great DJs are not created in bedrooms, they have to get out there and be part of the scene. You need plenty of character and personality, to hold a crowd. The top DJs today created their own nights and clubs, even if it meant breaking into warehouses to create their own venues.

Unlike other artists good DJs never perform the same set. They have to be able to capture the mood of the crowd, and know when to take it to another level. Dance music might have taken the role to new heights, but great DJs are not constrained by one music genre.

In many ways, DJs are far more plugged in and understand the scene much better than promoters and venue owners. They often produce and remix as well as collaborate with new artists. This enables them to broaden their output and to evolve their style continually.

For most people the rise of the DJ as celebrity and artist is forever associated with the Ministry of Sound and the island of Ibiza. Dance music has built its own fashion and drug culture, venues and lifestyle, but is associated with a generation who are now as likely to be planning a mortgage as their next trip to Ibiza.

Of course dance music is still a phenomenon, but twelve and thirteen year olds aren't listening to it any more, and this age group will drive the future shape of the business. Even Ibiza is becoming passé, as the clubs are reluctant to play hip hop or R&B and even Space finds it hard to fill its terraces. Top DJs continue to command thousands of pounds, but increasingly the real money is abroad.

THE FUTURE FOR DJs AND DANCE MUSIC

Many of the best-known DJs are over forty. Norman Cook, Carl Cox, Paul Oakenfold and Pete Tong are all in this club, but with enough resilience to outlast the decline of dance music. Their versatility and capacity for hard work is amazing. They've become famous musicians in their own right and will continue to be an important part of the music scene over the next few years like other established artists. Norman Cook is a good example. Anyone who can draw 250,000 people to a beach party in Brighton, sell five million copies of one album, is hardly going to slip into retirement.

Dance music doesn't have the monopoly of celebrity DJs. Take Tim Westwood, pioneer of hip hop and rap. His Radio 1 *Rap Show* has been so popular it has been extended to two nights a week and his last compilation album went platinum. DJs are poised to be successful players in the future.

TIPS FOR NEWCOMERS

- ***Be multi-skilled:*** You need the technical ability, the music knowledge and preparation of someone who spends too much time in their bedroom, but you also need to be social, be able to promote yourself and entertain a crowd.
- ***Just start – anywhere:*** A friend's birthday, a village hall, a pub – anywhere you can learn on the job without mistakes being too serious. It's best to start with a crowd who you know are more likely to be on your side.
- ***Plug into the scene:*** Get a part-time job at your local record shop or run a club night. The more contacts, the more chances of a gig.
- ***Get hold of the best tunes:*** Check out white labels, use promo tapes and unfinished mixes. Blag about your profile to labels and promotion companies to get their latest material.
- ***Be a performer:*** Know what type of crowd you're playing to and their musical taste. Learn to read them and anticipate where to take them in terms of mood. Be confident but not too confident.
- ***Prepare:*** Work out your options before you gig; make sure you know your material inside out, and have enough back-up to change the mood and style if needed.

THE VIEW FROM WITHIN

JUDGE JULES – DJ

Was it tough starting out as a DJ?

The biggest struggle I had in the early years was not money but creating records that got a reaction. I must have made a hundred records before anything became a success. It was really gutting. When I listen back to those early tunes, they sound really bad, but I put just as much love and passion into them as my successful ones nine years later. It's all part of a learning curve. You have to make mistakes before you find out what works and what doesn't. You just have to keep going and learning as you go.

When did you realise you had made your name?

Probably about 1995 and 1996, when every gig I did was rammed. I was successful because I played the tunes I really loved, which were house and trance. I started off playing funk and hip hop which I adore, but I always thought house was the missing jigsaw piece.

What do you have to do to make it big as a DJ?

You must go out there and create your own parties. If you really want to be good you have to put out your own records. Almost every DJ that has made it big over the last five years has done so by putting out their own tracks. Then people want to come to see you play your own records on your own set.

What keeps you working so hard now you're successful enough to take it easy?

It's the excitement of standing in front of a crowd and playing great tunes. As long as the music is great I love my job, but great tunes are like number 19 buses, when one comes along it's brilliant. I get a buzz from sitting at home on Friday sorting out my set for each gig. Then an even bigger buzz standing in front of the crowd and playing the records I've chosen. I have a schoolboy enthusiasm about it, even today.

Name top five tips for what makes a good DJ?

- You must have technical ability.
- You must be able to read a crowd.
- You must know the music directions the club is looking for.
- Performance behind the decks is key. There's a big difference between a head-up and a head-down DJ. You can be brilliant at the technical side but if you're a head-down DJ you won't carry the crowd. It's important to interact and perform to the crowd as long as it doesn't detract from the music. Remember, the music is king.
- Don't do the expected. Don't listen to music journalists. It's about dipping in and out of things and trying things out.

What is it like to be you, Judge Jules, on a daily basis. What's your schedule for next week?

- Come back from Helsinki.
- Gym.
- Mix new album for Ministry.
- Dinner to discuss A&R consultancy with label.
- Organise moving to new home.
- DJ for three nights in America.
- Fly back; spend night at home.
- Next day fly to China and DJ the same night.

This is a typical week. Over the following weeks Judge Jules is committed to playing in India, Singapore, back to America for four nights, then on to Malaysia, Russia and a few more gigs in Europe. We next ask him how different it is in a studio from playing live.

I remember when I first started out playing on pirate radio, I was so nervous I'd wait for the record to end before switching it. Then I went to Kiss pirate radio. That helped me grow. It took me seven years to learn from my mistakes, but it was very amateur in those days.

How much would it cost us to book you for a party. Could we get you for £5000?
It depends where, the size of the venue and day of the week. It's hard to give you exact figures. I'm not the most expensive DJ out there, it's not all about big bucks, it's about relationships.

You reportedly earned £1200 per minute for a New Year's Eve party.
Yes, but believe me, that doesn't happen often.

SAM O'RIORDEN – MD, SERIOUS ARTISTS MANAGEMENT

Sam runs Serious, the biggest, most respected DJ artist management agency in the country. Norman Jay and Judge Jules are clients. He's turned Serious into one of dance music's most famous businesses. We ask him what makes a good DJ.
Everyone has a good promo CD, but I'm looking for someone who has that something extra. It's no different than looking for any other artist. They must look right and be able to hold a crowd. It's more than just spinning a tune. One year Jules performed to more people than U2. He has to know how to work the crowd, how to give them a good night.

Who's your favourite DJ?
Eddie Halliwell is one of the best. We look after him and he's spectacular because he manages to blend incredible scratching with really good mixing. The only other person who can do that is Carl Cox. When I first saw Eddie play, I knew I had to work with him.

What makes a successful DJ?
What you must realise is that many of today's successful DJs didn't start out because they wanted to be successful but for the love and buzz of playing records. They got off on introducing new tunes to the crowd and that buzz is what keeps them going, not success and money. It's not about fame, or being in demand, it's about being able to do what they love; the ones that don't, don't make it.

What can a successful DJ expect to earn?

Anywhere from £150 to £15,000 per gig, depending on experience. It can be more. For one of my clients I've charged more than £1000 per minute for a 120 minute set, but it isn't always in your interest to be too greedy. It's more important to build long-term relationships with promoters.

Finally, what are your do's and don'ts for aspiring DJs?

Do's

- Have a desire and will to succeed at all costs.
- Use your initiative and make it happen. (Even the best DJs like Norman Jay and Judge Jules had to find their own venues and promote their own nights and do anything that enabled them to play the music they wanted.
- Get out there and see what people are reacting to and what excites them.
- Know your records.
- Be able to select tunes.
- Be prepared to work hard.
- Get on to all the record labels' mailing lists so you're sent all the good tunes upfront.

Don'ts

- Don't be too demanding especially when you haven't yet built up any credibility.
- Don't fall into the drug culture – some DJs do it and are successful, but you need to be focused on the job.
- Don't ever turn up late for a gig.
- Don't forget you have to be a performer and entertain.
- Don't confuse personality and ego.
- Don't try to go against the music policy of the venue.

1
2
3
4
5
6
7
8
9
10
11
12
13
14
15

DJ EQUIPMENT RETAILERS

CONNECT RECORDS
18 Badger Rd, Binley, Coventry,
West Midlands CV3 2PU
T: 024 7626 5400

DJ GEAR
P.O Box 135, Manchester, Lancashire
M23 0XD
T: 0870 0260044

DJ MEGADEALS
Freepost Mid 30975, Atherstone,
Warwickshire CV9 2BR
T: 0870 7606412

DJ SUPERSTORE
Unit 5, Airborne Ind Est, Arterial Rd,
Leigh-On-Sea, Essex SS9 4EX

GUILDFORD SOUND & LIGHT LTD
Moorfield Rd, Guildford, Surrey
GU1 1RB
T: 01483 502121

RS 100
56 Park Rd, Glasgow, Lanarkshire
G4 9JF
T: 0141 337 1100

SAPPHIRES SOUND & LIGHT LTD
4/6 Burlington Parade, London
NW2 6QG
T: 020 8960 8989

SMART SOUND DIRECT
Unit 5-7, 38-40 Town End, Caterham,
Surrey CR3 5UG
T: 01833-340-647

SOUND DIVISION
Montague House, 389 Liverpool Rd,
Islington, London N1 1NP
T: 020 7609 3999

WEST END DJ LTD
10-12 Hanway St, London W1T 1UB
T: 020 7637 3293

SELECTION OF THE COUNTRY'S BEST CLUBBING VENUES

LONDON

CAFE DE PARIS
3, Coventry St, London W1D 6BL
T: 020 7734 7700

FABRIC LONDON LTD
77a Charterhouse St, London EC1M 6HJ
T: 020 7336 8898

KABARET
70 New Bond St, London W1S 1DE
T: 020 7629 3844

MEDICINE BAR (SHOREDITCH)
89 Great Eastern St, London EC2A 3HX
T: 020 7739 5173

MINISTRY OF SOUND
103, Gaunt St, London SE1 6DP
T: 0870 0600010

PO NA NA SOUK BAR
82 The Broadway, London SW19 1RH
T: 020 8540 1616

SCALA
275 Pentonville Rd, London N1 9NL
T: 020 7833 2022

SCHOOLDISCO.COM
25 Cowper St, London EC2A 4AP
T: 0871 8721234

WALKABOUT AT THE LIMELIGHT
136 Shaftesbury Avenue, London
W1D 5EZ
T: 020 7255 8620

BLACKPOOL

THE SYNDICATE
Church St, Blackpool, Lancashire
FY1 3PR
T: 01253 753222

BRIGHTON

THE ARK
159 Kings Rd Arches,
Brighton, East Sussex BN1 1NB
T: 01273 770505

AUDIO
10 Marine Parade, Brighton,
East Sussex BN2 1TL
T: 01273 606906

THE BEACH
171-181, Kings Rd Arches
Brighton, East Sussex BN1 1NB
T: 01273 722272

CONCORDE
2 Madeira Drive, Brighton, East Sussex
BN2 1EN
T: 01273 207241

THE FUNKY BUDDAH LOUNGE
169-170 Kings Rd Arches,
Brighton, East Sussex BN1 1NB
T: 01273 725541

ZAP CLUB
189-192, Kings Rd Arches, Brighton,
East Sussex
T: 01273 202407

KENT

THE BASEMENT
22 High St Lenham, Maidstone, Kent
ME17 2QD
T: 01622 753041

LEEDS

THE ELBOW ROOM
64 Call Lane, Leeds, West Yorkshire
LS1 6DT
T: 0113 245 7011

MINT CLUB
8 Harrison St, Leeds, West Yorkshire
LS1 6PA
T: 0113 244 3168

LIVERPOOL

CREAM LIVERPOOL LTD
40-42 Slater St, Liverpool, Merseyside
L1 4BW
T: 0151 709 1693

FUDGE
10-16, Wood St, Liverpool, Merseyside
L1 4AQ
T: 0151 708 9992

MANCHESTER

CRUZ 101
101 Princess St, Manchester, Lancashire
M1 6DD
T: 0161 950 0101

THE LATE ROOM
23 Peter St, Manchester, Lancashire
M2 5QR
T: 0161 833 3000

ONE CENTRAL STREET LTD
1 Central St, Manchester, Lancashire
M2 5WR
T: 0161 211 9000

SUGAR LOUNGE BAR
Arch 12, Deans Gate Locks, Manchester
M1 5LH
T: 0161.834 1600

NEWCASTLE

FOUNDATION NIGHT CLUB
57 Melbourne St, Newcastle Upon Tyne,
Tyne And Wear NE1 2JQ
T: 0191 2618985

SHEFFIELD

GATECRASHER ONE
121 Eyre St, Sheffield, South Yorkshire
S1 4QW
T: 0114 276 6777

THE SKOOL DISCO
Unit 201, J C Albyn Complex, Burton
Rd, Sheffield, South Yorkshire S3 8BZ
T: 0114 221 3033

SCOTLAND

ROOM AT THE TOP
2-6 Jarvey St, Bathgate, West Lothian
EH48 4EZ
T: 01506 635123

EDINBURGH

THE BONGO CLUB
37 Holyrood Rd,
Edinburgh, Midlothian EH8 8BA
T: 0131 558 8844

THE LIQUID ROOM
9c Victoria St, Edinburgh, Midlothian
EH1 2HE
T: 0131 225 2564

THE VENUE
15-21 Calton Rd,
Edinburgh, Midlothian EH8 8DL
T: 0131 557 3073

GLASGOW

ARCHAOS & YANG
25-37 Queen St,
Glasgow, Lanarkshire G1 3EF
T: 0141 204 3189

THE ARCHES
253 Argyle St,
Glasgow, Lanarkshire G2 8DL
T: 0141 565 1023

ABERDEEN

BABYLON
Alford Place, Aberdeen, Aberdeenshire
AB10 1YD
T: 01224 595001

DRUM
40-42 Windmill Brae,
Aberdeen, Aberdeenshire AB11 6HU
T: 01224 210174

ESPIONAGE
120 Union St, Aberdeen, Aberdeenshire
AB10 1JJ
T: 01224 561006

1

2

3

4

5

6

7

8

9

10

11

12

13

14

15

SONGWRITING

WHAT IS THE ROLE OF THE SONGWRITER?

THE MOST POWERFUL PEOPLE IN THE MUSIC BUSINESS

Let us introduce you to the most important force in the music industry. They control everyone from artist, record label, publisher, manager, radio, TV to the public. Labels have been crushed because they didn't listen. Artists have lost deals and been consigned to history because they lacked respect. Chairmen and executives have been sacked because of them.

If you're in the business, you will have experienced the power of the song-writer at every turn, in the studio, at every A&R meeting, presenting a new band to an MD, and on the agenda at every radio and TV station. Yes, we're talking about the hit single people – without them you're nothing in this business. They control you and you must obey.

GET OFF YOUR HIGH HORSE

If you're an artist and your label says to you: 'We need a hit single', you'd better take it seriously – they do. Your life and their lives depend on coming up with the goods. Once the label have committed to spending £150,000 to record and market it, you'd better not give them something average.

Why are hit singles so important? In their own right they're not. In 2003 more money was generated for record labels by ring-tones, than singles, but

1 2 3 4 5 6 7 8 9 10 11 12 13 14 15

that isn't the point. This is because the public respond to great songs. A hit single puts you on the map and gets you into the public consciousness. That's why millions of pounds each year are spent in promoting singles. So there is huge competition to produce the coolest, catchiest tune to get that hit.

It's weird. In many ways a single is an amazing creative form, requiring a high level of creativity, integrity and style to pull it off, but still many artists look down at them and feel they're 'selling out'. Perhaps it's because A&R are all over you when you're making a single. They throw around phrases like 'hooks' as if they're bits of techno babble, rather than a creative opportunity.

A successful hit single is like a business plan for a label. Your demo might interest them, but if your first single is a hit, then you're in the game and you'll get what you want.

Fortunately there are many writers and songwriters who understand the importance of great songs and how to write them. Some enjoy fantastic success.

In songwriting there are no exact rules or formulae to guarantee a great song; however, there are some songwriting principles that make a hit much more likely.

OTHER WAYS TO EARN MONEY WRITING SONGS AND MUSIC

ADVERTISING

Advertising uses music as an important part of its ability to get impact with its audience and to increase brand recognition and personality. This is a long tradition from the Hovis and Hamlet music in the 1970s to the Levi's campaign in the '80s and '90s.

While advertising is a voracious user of back catalogue, there's a demand for specially commissioned music for 30 second ads or less. If you find composing a 3 minute single is tight then try 1 minute.

With advertising it's all about working to a brief and at speed. The money can be good and it's not as difficult to get to work for an advertising agency as you think, definitely not as difficult as getting to work for a major. But you have to listen to what they want and hit the deadline, otherwise you may as well not bother.

The reason it's easier to get a commission from an ad agency is all about numbers. There are more of them and fewer songwriters or composers hitting on them. Every creative team has a say in who they use, their TV production team just advises. Creatives are susceptible to meeting songwriters, because they love the idea of meeting people from the business.

Get a good demo and go for it. Buy the advertising trade magazine *Campaign* and track the creative teams that are winning all the awards, then send them the demo and meet them. You will get the job as much on your personality as your demo. Advertising is all about front and appearances. The Darkness is a good example of a band that started working for advertising. They wrote the music for Ikea ads.

DOING A DEAL WITH A MUSIC LIBRARY

Library music companies are good sources of income for new and experienced writers and composers. Generally you work with the company to produce complete albums and they then make these available to advertising agencies, video production companies, film and TV production companies. They have to pay when they use anything from the library, and you usually get a 50% cut of the usage fees.

To get a deal with a music library you need to put together a demo. This demo has to be put together with the end usage in mind. Advertising agencies are only going to want very short segments, but they're going to want those segments to have some shape and drama. Film and TV are going to want some moody instrumental, so don't make it all lyric based. It's best to think of the demo as a music source, rather than a piece in itself. It needs to have a variety of styles, textures and moods, but it must not be derivative because the library will already have too much average music. The lottery for any writer who has a deal with a music library is whether their music becomes a popular theme tune. It can happen: the music for ITV's long-running police drama *The Bill* was originally a piece of library music and must still be producing good usage fees for its writers.

WRITING FOR TV AND FILM

TV and film production companies directly commission composers and writers. They are chosen by the director with the approval of the producer. Certain producers like working with certain people. The music soundtrack is particularly important to film. In fact the depth of the soundtrack and surround-sound projection are among the key elements that lift a film into a different type of entertainment experience from a made-for-TV movie.

Getting to work in films is all about making connections. Most films spend a long time in development. The trick is spotting one with potential and attaching yourself to it. Get to know the producer and director, ask to read the script and produce a demo for a scene. Before you know it you'll be part of the team, but remember there are no guarantees. The madness of films is that after two years of drinking and talking, the money will come, it will be green lighted and then it's a mad rush to shoot it. At least you will have some time because music is usually the last thing on anyone's mind until the shoot is over. It can work out incredibly well for an artist, such as Gary Jules who had a Christmas No. 1 with 'Mad World' because of *Donnie Darko*, after struggling for years.

COMPUTER GAMES

Computer games need good music on their soundtrack to add drama and excitement. Originally happy to use library music or back catalogue, computer companies are now beginning to commission original music. Current consoles are DVD-based, and have the capacity for much more music, and there is definitely a trend towards more lyric-based soundtracks.

This is still a young medium in terms of commissioning music and there are still no set deals. In many ways they have had to over-pay for library music and back catalogue. They are beginning to learn that for not much more they can have soundtracks specially written to work with their visuals.

It's a medium worth getting into. For the last few years it has outsold CDs and in some ways has a closer connection to the male youth audience than music. The scale of the industry can be seen by the fact that there are over a hundred car games released a year.

TIPS FOR NEWCOMERS

- ***Attitude:*** You have to go for it. If you want to be a songwriter you must get a demo together that is hit quality. Limit it to two or three songs that really work. Invest in good production and a singer who can do justice to your work.
- ***Collaborate:*** Great songwriters collaborate with each other, artists and producers. They know the business and are known. Often it's not as simple as someone does the words, someone else the music or the production; great songs come from a team, from different people reaching the same point from different angles. If you're starting out, hook up with a band, work with them. Hang around studios and help them develop artists.
- ***Should artists write their own material?*** There are significant commercial benefits from writing your own material, but the record labels know that not all artists can write a hit single and all mainstream artists need one if they're going to be a success. What's the point of having the publishing rights if they're worthless?
- ***Be commercially aware but not commercially obsessed:*** Trends come and go in the music business. Record labels try to sign the latest trend, but songwriters who write to the latest trend tend not to be successful. Great songs are based on a combination of universal truths and integrity. They have to resonate with their audience and be believable.
- ***Keep it simple:*** Good songwriters know that their ideas need time and space to grow. One or two ideas that are developed will work better than flooding the song with too many ideas. It's the way you develop and evolve simple ideas that give a song interest and make it catchy.
- ***Find your voice:*** Just as producers need to find their sound, songwriters need to find their voice. It can be adapted for different musical styles but you need to find your voice by having an opinion about what you like and don't like, and experimenting until you find it.

- ***Be truthful:*** It's an irony that in the artificial packaged world of hit songs, truth is an incredibly powerful weapon. Being true to your feelings and intent is essential as the public sees through any hint of artificiality immediately. This is why collaboration with the artist and performer is essential to ensure the song is true to them as well; otherwise their performance will fail to live up to your vision.
- ***Don't work in a vacuum:*** To be a successful writer you have to live and breathe music. Listening to music stimulates thoughts and listening to the greats inspires. Sometimes you want to listen just to experience the feeling it evokes, sometimes you want to pull it apart and see how it works, like a first-year medical student with a body. It doesn't matter – it's all learning, even though it's often by osmosis.
- ***Be a control freak:*** If you're truly collaborating as part of a team, then you should have an opinion about the song as a whole, from production to performance to packaging. If you don't know the producer, get to know them. Get their confidence, explain your vision. The same goes for the artist. Begin to learn how your work is translated, live or recorded. See how you can hear and see the finished product as you write it, go to the gig and see if the response is as you expected, listen to the radio and see how it plays away from a studio with perfect reproduction.
- ***Don't be afraid to be a perfectionist:*** The hit single relies on nanoseconds of timing and the most precise emotional shades and shape to succeed. If it's 99% truthful it fails. The amount of emotion and consideration invested in 3 minutes is beyond any other medium and requires perfection; nothing else will do.

THE VIEW FROM WITHIN

WAYNE HECTOR – SONGWRITER

Wayne is a very successful songwriter who takes his art seriously. He has had nine No.1 hits. We want to know what it feels like to produce a hit. How much is it process and construction, how much instinct and emotion?

There are some people out there who are very calculated and into process and it works for them. But I have to have a spiritual investment in a song for it to work. You know when you have written something complete. When I sing a line, I feel my chest swell because I know there is something beautiful about it. There's no point in finishing a song unless you get that magical feeling, because who wants to produce average music?

How does Wayne prepare himself to write a hit song?

If I'm writing for a rock band like Def Leppard, I'll soak myself in that type of music for months. I don't listen to anything else. It's about changing your mindset so that you understand the emotions and context of the specific type of music and get into the heads of the audience. It's all about experimenting. Sometimes I'll try dozens of melodies before I find one acceptable.

How important is the title?

They're really important. You should know what to expect from the song just from the title. It's like the backdrop for a play. As soon as the curtain rises and you see a woman crying, you immediately understand the emotion of the scene.

Writing for many different artists, how important is it to understand and relate to their different personalities?

Very important, because the song has to be believable for the artist. There must be a part of them and their personality coming out of the song. It might be an attitude, or singing style. That's why it's important for me to meet and spend time with the artist, before I work with them. The public can see a mile off when the artist is doing something that isn't them. You can actually feel it in the record if the artist doesn't truly feel what they are singing.

I get sent loads of tapes, and it's always the first impression that counts. If I get the vibe I respond to it. That's how [producer] Steve [Mac] and I work together. We get a vibe in the studio, then the melody and the words just flow. I'm sure every hit Steve and I have written has happened in the first few minutes of working on the song. When it works, and I sing back the song and it sounds as if it could be on the radio, then cool.

So what is the magic formula, is there a right way to write a song?
You never find one way to write a song. There are millions of ways to write it, you just have to find out what works for you. The artist singing it can make or break it too. Sometimes it comes across how you want it, sometimes it doesn't. You could have the best song in the world, but if you've got the wrong producer on it, then it's never going to go the way you want. I have worked closely with the producer Steve Mac for many years. We have the same attitude about songwriting. We're perfectionists. We're always proud of what we put out. Steve and I take our time, we often take a week or two just to write a song. We've started a song one year and not finished it until the next, because it took that long to find the right meaning and chord structure.

What did it feel like to get your first No. 1 hit?
Amazing! Your first No. 1 is great, but when you start getting your fourth, fifth and seventh, it's strange because anything below a No. 1 starts to feel like a failure. It's almost as if I'm competing with myself to go one better.

But after nine No. 1s, there must be a formula?
There really isn't. A song can come from almost anywhere. It's as if they were waiting in the sky for you. You can be writing for an hour trying different melodies and hooks and then it comes. The real trick is recognising it when it does.

How important is trusting your judgement in the music business?
It's the hardest thing to trust your judgement against a thousand opinions. Look at Simon Cowell. He's successful because he's completely honest with

himself. Simon knows what Simon likes and that's why he's so big. He has the same ears as the man on the street. If you play Simon something he'll tell you within five minutes whether he likes it or not. Usually by the time he's heard the first verse and the chorus. He doesn't um and ah about it like other A&R men. They'll tell you how much they love it and how brilliant it is, and then you'll never hear from them again. Not Simon, he knows what he wants, and says it like it is.

It all sounds perfect, but it can't always be. Do you ever get writer's block?
Oh yeah, every few months. The first time I got it, I tried to fight it. I put myself in a worse position for at least four months. I just couldn't think of anything. My manager told me to stop and rest. I did for at least two months. Then one day I was walking in the street and a song idea popped into my head.

How do you find your ideas and make a hook line stand out?
Everything has been written before, or sung before, so the art of songwriting is about finding a new way to say it. You might forget the rest of the lyrics, but when it comes to this song you get the power of the emotion just from the hook line. It's that power that you're looking for from a chorus line. Once you've heard the line, 'Love lifts us up where we belong, where eagles fly', you don't need to hear the rest of the song because you get a sense of hope within seconds. That's when a song is powerful and when it connects with people. It taps into our animal emotion. **We're all the same. We hate, love, dream, but more than anything we hope.** We don't even love as much as we hope. Most of the time, 'We hope to love.' With songwriting you're trying to find the points where everybody meets. The best songs and the most simple songs find this and mean a lot to most people. We all dream and aspire to the same things, we probably all dislike the same things.

'Flying Without Wings', which you wrote for Westlife, is a great example of this at its best.
They did a really good job with it. They love to sing. They like singing and

having fun, more than any other band I've worked with. I think you hear the sincerity in their vocals, that's why they are great guys and that's why it went to No. 1.

What's your advice for aspiring songwriters?
My best advice is to keep going, don't give up. I'm sure there are loads of people out there who can write songs as good as me. The main difference between success and failure is probably opportunity; so if you can't find one way in, look for another. When I first started in the business, I was a singer. It didn't work out, but I could write a song and that gave me another way in. You must keep looking for openings, and when you've found one make something of it. I'm glad of my success, because it provides me with more opportunities. The crazy thing is that now people are offering me record deals, when they never would have before my success. But now I like what I do. It allows me to pursue my love of all types of music. As a songwriter I get the opportunity to write for pop, R&B, rock, country & western and hip hop. Who wants more than that?

CHARLISE ROOKWOOD – SONGWRITER

She is signed to Universal. She has written for Atomic Kitten, Blue, Murder Inc. and Kylie, and is one of the most in-demand writers on the scene

How did you get your first break?
I packed my bags and went to America, even though I only knew one person there. I took my last £400 and went for it. I went to parties and networked like mad. You don't get anywhere as a writer by sitting around. I hooked up with the guys from Murder Inc. one night in a club and they invited me to their studio at four o'clock in the morning. They played me some of their stuff and I rewrote a hook for them. I ended doing three tracks on their *Irve Dotti Presents Inc*. album.

Then one day I was walking past Tower Records in Times Square and heard my voice singing a track on the album. I went inside and found it. I wasn't even credited on the cover. I didn't receive any points or royalties. Still even though I didn't get a penny, it opened doors.

What's your latest project?
My biggest project is working with Killa Kella, who was a beatbox champion a few years ago. I met him a couple of years ago, and I've worked with him for about a year, whenever I can grab the time between projects. At first I had no idea where it was going. Then he got signed with BMG, and I've written half his album. **A mutual friend hooked us up with 50 cents and his producer Wookid, who produces all the top American urban acts.** We had a brilliant meeting and played him all our stuff. Wookid really liked it and wanted to work with us, and agreed to produce six or seven tracks. He doesn't often do that.

How versatile do you have to be to get on?
To survive as a writer you have to be open-minded and work on projects that might not be your first option. I would like to write for artists like Coldplay, Alanis Morissette or U2. That's my natural style. I like to write songs organically with just guitar or piano. **For me if a song sounds great without production then I know I'm on to something special.**

How important is working with a good producer?
Working with good producers is extremely important. You don't want to write a great song and then put naff production behind it. But it takes time to find the right producers you can gel with. I tend to feel comfortable with the ones who want to push the musical boundaries, but still understand how to make a song sound big.

How do you get on with your publisher?
He thinks I'm more suited to indie artists than the pop thing. He wants to find more indie artists to take my songs, but most of these sort of bands write their own stuff. I'm working on the new Incognito album. It's really good. It's real music.

What advice would you give to a new writer?

Go out and do it for yourself, because if you wait for others you will end up being frustrated. Find producers, experiment and try to be versatile in your writing.

KEY SONG WRITERS

WINDSWEPT MUSIC (LONDON) LTD

CHRIS BALLARD/ANDY MURRAY (Producer/Writers)

Wrote and produced 'Love On The Line' (No.4) 'We Dreamin' (No.3) 'Flip Reverse' (No.2) and 'Here For One' (No.6) for Blazin' Squad. Wrote and produced entire 'Clea' album for Warners. Currently working with Lisa Mafia, Jay Sean and Gemma Fox.

CIARON BELL (Producer/Writer)

Wrote and produced 'The Way That You Are' on Atomic Kitten's 2nd album. Written and produced 'Someone Like Me' on current Atomic Kitten album and Greatest Hits. Written song 'Cast The First Stone' on Michelle (Pop Idol) album. Currently working with both Liz and Jenny from Atomic Kitten on solo albums.

LEE BENNETT (Melody/Lyric)

Co-wrote Sonique single 'Alive'. Co-written 2 songs for boy band Phixx. Previously had singles with Jamie Benson, Allstars, Frou Frou and Big Ben. Currently working on songs for Tina Turner and Mark and Sam with John McLaughlin on Island Records boy band V.

DEBBIE FFRENCH (Melody/Lyric)

Wrote 'Naughty Girl' for Holly Vallance. Written and co-produced 1st & 2nd singles for the new Sony Australia artist Tammin Sursok (*Home & Away*).

DAVE JAMES (Producer/Writer/ Melody/Lyric)

Wrote and produced Sonique single 'Alive'. Written and produced 3 songs for Michelle Lawson. Written and produced 'Hold On Me' (No.10) for Phixx plus 4 other tracks for the Phixx album. Written second single 'Betcha Neva' for Lava Records artist Cherie Amore. Written and produced 'Don't Know Why' for Bellefire album on East West. Co-written and produced 1st single 'Public Enemy #1' for Hypo Psycho.

STUART KERSHAW (Producer/Writer)

Co-wrote & produced 11 songs on 1st Atomic Kitten album including 'Right Now', 'See Ya' & 'Whole Again'. Co-wrote & produced 3 songs on 2nd Atomic Kitten album. Currently working on new girl group Geenie Queen.

JOHN MCLAUGHLIN – (Melody/Lyric)

Co-wrote and produced 7 songs on Busted's album including 'What I Go To School For' and No.1 'You Said No'. Co-wrote and produced 'You Make Me Wanna' for Blue and co-wrote and produced 'Where You Want Me' on the current Blue album. Written and produced for 'Hypo Psycho' album on Snapper Records. Currently working on new project for Simon Cowell. Written and produced all songs for Boyband Phixx.

QUIZ/LAROSSI (Producer/Writers)
Written & produced 5 Westlife songs including 'When A Woman Loves A Man' on the current album. Written & produced 2 songs on current Gareth Gates album. Written & Produced 'Damn' on Bellefire album for East West. Currently working on Simon Cowells Tenors act plus new Scottish boy band signed to Simon Cowell.

ROGER RUSSELL (DOUBLE R) (Producer/Writer)
Wrote & produced 'Romeo' album for Relentless. Currently working with Blue (Virgin), Maxi Priest (Relentless/ Virgin) and Louise Setara (BMG).

LLOYD SCOTT (Producer/Writer/Melody/Lyric)
New songwriter just signed to Windswept. Currently working with Layla (Blues Mgmt) and various songwriters.

ANDY WRIGHT (Producer/Writer)
Co-wrote and produced 'Leave Me Alone' on first Natalie Imbruglia album. Has co-written and produced the last two Jeff Beck albums for Sony, which have spawned numerous TV ads and film soundtracks. Produced & mixed numerous singles including "Reach" S Club 7 & "Eternal Flame" Atomic Kitten. Currently working on tracks with Maxi Priest.

SONY/ATV MUSIC PUBLISHING (UK) LIMITED

DON BLACK (OBE) (Songwriter/Lyricist)
Michael Jackson – single "Ben" – Lyrics, Lulu – single "To Sir With Love" – Lyrics, Olivia Newton John – "Sam" – Lyrics, Barbra Streisand – "With One Look" – Lyrics, Matt Monroe – "Walk Away" – Lyrics, Jose Carreras & Sarah Brightman – "Amigos Para Siempre" – Lyrics, Glen Campbell – "True Grit" – Lyrics, Barbra Streisand – "As If We Never Said Goodbye" – Lyrics, George Benson & Patti Austin – "I'll Keep Your Dreams Alive" – Lyrics, Hot Chocolate – "I'll Put You Together Again" – Lyrics
MUSIC IN FILMS:
James Bond Theme Songs
"The World Is Not Enough" – Lyrics,
"Tomorrow Never Dies" – Lyrics
"The Man with the Golden Gun" – Lyrics
"Diamonds Are Forever" – Lyrics
Thunderball" – Lyrics, The Pink Panther Strikes Again, The Italian Job and Born Free – single "Born Free" – Lyrics
PLAYS – all lyrics for the following West End/Broadway shows: *Dracula*, *Bombay Dreams*, *Tell Me on a Sunday*, *Sunset Boulevard*, *Aspects of Love*, *Billy*

GARY BARLOW & ELIOT KENNEY (TRUENORTH) (Songwriters/producers)
Atomic Kitten – album tracks 'Always Be My Baby' and 'I Won't Be There' on album 'Ladies Night' – Written/Produced
Blue – single 'Guilty' and one album track on album of the same title 'Guilty' – Written/Production

Delta Goodrem – single 'Not Me Not I' and 5 other album tracks on album 'Innocent Eyes' – Writers

Mark Owen – single '4 Minute Warning' & 3 album tracks on 'In Your Own Time' – Written/Produced

Blue – album track 'Supersexual' on album 'One Love'

Amy Studt – album track 'Testify' on album 'False Smiles – Writer/Producer

Donny Osmond – album 'Somewhere In Time' – Production

David Charvet (France) – album track 'If I Don't Tell You Soon' on album 'Leap Of Faith'

TOMMY D
(Songwriter – track/Producer)

Joss Stone – "Secret Love" – Writer

Janet Jackso – album track "Slo Love" – Writer

Kylie Minogue – album track "You Make Me Feel" – Writer

Joss Stone – album track "Don't Break My Heart" on album "Standing Tall" – Writer

Gareth Gates – album track "Downtown" on album " What My Heart Wants To Say" – Writer

Kylie Minogue – album track "More More More" on album "Fever" – Writer

Sophie Ellis Bextor – album track "I Believe" on album "Read My Lips" – Writer

Eagle Eye Cherry/Neneh Cherry – single "Long Way Round – Writer

Toploader – single "Just Hold On" – Production

Tom Jones & Cerys Matthews – single "Baby It's Cold Outside" – Production

Catatonia – album "International Velvet"– Production

Right Said Fred – singles "I'm Too Sexy/Deeply Dippy & Don't Talk Just Kiss" – Production

JOHN REID (Songwriter – topline)

Juliet Schoppman (Germany) – "I Still Believe" – German Idol Winners' single – Writer

Guy Sebastian (Australia) – single "Angels Brought Me Here" – Australian Idol Winners' single – Writer

Kym Marsh – album track "Don't Break My Heart" on album "Standing Tall" – Writer

H and Claire – album track "All I Want Is You" on album "Another You Another Me" – Writer

Westlife – single "Unbreakable" – Writer

Nick Lechey (US) – single "This I Swear" – Writer

Kelly Clarkson (US) – single "A Moment Like This" – American Idol Winners' single – Writer

Tina Turner – single "When The Heartache Is Over" – Writer

Andrea Bocelli (Italy) – single "Questo Vi Prometto" – Writer

Garux (France) – album track "Say It Out Loud" – Writer

Nightcrawlers – single "Push The Feeling On" – Writer

Rod Stewart – album track "Into Your Arms" on album "Human" – Writer

JONY ROCKSTAR
(Songwriter – track/producer)

Sugababes –album tracks 'Caught In A Moment', 'Conversation's Over' and 'Sometimes' on album 'Three' – Writer/Producer

Sugababes – single 'Stronger' and one album track on album 'Angels With Dirty Faces' – Written/Production
Sugababes – singles 'Overload', 'New Year' & 'Run For Cover' & 2 album tracks on album 'One Touch' – Writer/Producer
Sophie Ellis Bextor – album track 'I Believe' on album 'Read My Lips' – Writer
Rhianna – single 'Oh Baby' – Writer/Producer

RICHARD 'BIFF' STANNARD
(Songwriter – topline/producer)
Gabrielle Forthcoming mid-2004 Album, 7 tracks. Production/Co-Writer
Kylie Minogue 'Loving Days' from L.P. 'Body Language' Writer/Production
Atomic Kitten 'If You Come To Me' single Writer/Production
Holly Valance 'Connect' from 'Footprints' LP Writer/Production
Abs 'What You Got' single Writer/Production
Sarah Whatmore singles 'When I Lost You' and 'Automatic' Production/Writer
Blazing Squad tracks from LP 'In The Beginning' Writer/Production
Will Young tracks from 'You and I' LP Writer/Production
Kylie Minogue tracks from 'Fever' LP inc 'In Your Eyes' and 'Love At First Sight' singles. Light Years' LP tracks inc 'Please Stay' Writer/Production
U2 'All That You Can't Leave Behind' LP track 'In A Little While' Additional Production
Bono/Gavin Friday 'Children of the Revolution' from 'Moulin Rouge' LP Producer
David Gray 'Sail Away' & 'This Year's Love' singles Additional Produstion
Gabrielle 'Rise' LP tracks inc 'When a Woman', 'Falling', 'Tell Me What You Dream' and forthcoming tracks Writer/Production
Emma Bunton 'What Took You So Long' No.1 single & 'A Girl Like Me' LP tracks Writer/Production
Five 'Kingsize' LP inc No. 1 single 'Let's Dance', 'Invincible' LP inc Five/Queen No. 1 single 'We Will Rock You', '5ive' LP inc 'Got The Feelin' Writer/Production
Westlife 'World Of Our Own' LP tracks Writer/Production
Melanie C 'Northern Star' LP tracks inc 'Going Down' single Writer
The Corrs 'Little Wing' Additional Production
Spice Girls 'Spiceworld' and 'Spice' LP tracks (Ivor Novello Award Winner 1999) Writer/Production
Jimmy Somerville 'Dare To Love' LP 'By Your Side', 'Heartbeat' Writer/Production
East 17 'Steam' LP & 'Steam', 'It's Alright' Writer/Production
East 17 'All Around The World', 'Hold My Body Tight' Writer

WARNER/CHAPPELL MUSIC LIMITED

GREGG ALEXANDER
New Radicals, Enrique, Ronan Keating, Sophie Ellis Bextor, Texas, Gerri Halliwell

CHRIS BRAIDE
Will Young's "Anything Is Possible" (1.78m singles sold), American Idol runner up Clay Aiken's 'Measure Of A Man' album (the 1st single which CB co-wrote sold an excess of 60,000 on week of release. The album did about 2.5m in the US alone

DAN CAREY & EMILIANA TORRINI
(who are an up-and-coming writing duo AKA Sunny Roads)
Credits: Kylie "Slow" (first collaboration was their Kylie single)

JOHNNY DOUGLAS
George Michael, Kylie Minogue, All Saints, Damage, Gemma Fox, Tina Turner

BRIAN HIGGINS
Cher's "Believe" (1.72m singles sold), Sugababes, Girls Aloud, Abs, Moonbaby, St Etienne, Mel B

ROB HOWES AKA OVERSEER
Music score to 'Every Given Sunday', Matrix 'Reloaded', Smirnoff Ice Ad, Snatch

EMI MUSIC PUBLISHING

ANDERS BAGGE
JLo 'Play', Jessica Simpson 'Irresistible', Celine Dion 'A New Day Has Come'
Stargate – Mis-teeq 'Scandalous' & 'One Night Stand', Blue 'All Rise'

CATHY DENNIS
Kylie Minogue 'Can't get you out of my head', Britney Spears 'Toxic', Rachel Stevens 'My L.A Ex'

MICHELLE ESCOFFERY
Liberty X 'Just A Little', Jamieson 'Take Control', cuts also on forthcoming Beverly Knight album

FELIX HOWARD
Sugababes 'Stronger' and 'Overload', Amy Winehouse 'Amy, Amy, Amy' & 'You Sent Me Flying', also has cuts on both Beverly Knight & Alex Parkes albums

TV COMMERCIAL WRITERS

SAM BABENTA
c/o Air – Edel associates,
18 Rodmarton St, London W1U 8BJ
T: 020 7486 6466 F: 020 7224 0344
Email: air-edel@air-edel.co.uk

JOHN BELL
132 Brondesbury Villas, London NW6 6AE
T: 020 7372 3860
Email: jbell.music@virgin.net

RAY DAVIES
10 Princess Mews, Hampstead, London NW3 5AP
T: 020 7431 8422
Email: rayd@buttondownfsnet.co.uk

BRIAN GASCOIGNE
c/o Air – Edel associates,
18 Rodmarton St, London W1U 8BJ
T: 020 7486 6466 F: 020 7224 0344
Email: air-edel@air-edel.co.uk

TONY HILLER
8 Garden Flat, 15 Westbourne Terrace, London W2 3UN
T: 020 7723 6104
Email: tony@tonyhiller.com

TOBY JARVIS
c/o Mcasso music
Productions Ltd, 9 Carnaby St,
London W1F 9PE
T: 020 7734 3664 F: 020 7439 2375
Email: music@mcasso.com

TONEY KINSEY
5 The Pennards, Sunbury-on-Thames, Middx, TW16 5JZ
T: 01932 78345

JULIAN MOORE
c/o Ronnie Bond Music, Churchwood Studio, 1 Woodchurch Rd,
London NW6 3PL
T: 020 7372 3339
Email: rbm@easynet.co.uk

RICHARD NILES
c/o Air – Edel associates,
18 Rodmarton St, London W1U 8BJ
T: 020 7486 6466 F: 020 7224 0344
Email: air-edel@air-edel.co.uk

MIKE OLDFIELD
c/o Air – Edel Associates,
18 Rodmarton St, London W1U 8BJ
T: 020 7486 6466 F: 020 7224 0344
Email: air-edel@air-edel.co.uk

ALAN PARKER
c/o Hudson Music Co Ltd,
2nd floor, 11–20 Capper St,
London WC1E 6JA
T: 020 7631 3700
Email: info@hudsonmusic.co.uk

TIM STONE
13 Clapton Common, Hackney, London E5 9AA
T: 0208 806 6037
M: 07855 370471
Email: www.stonemusic.co.uk

DORAN SYERS
c/o Ronnie Bond Music, Churchwood
Studio, 1 Woodchurch Rd,
London NW6 3PL
T: 020 7372 3339

MARTIN VISNICK
12 Watling St,
St Albans, Herts AL1 2PX
T: 01869 866507
Email: mvish@waitrose.com

1

2

3

4

5

6

7

8

9

10

11

12

13

14

15

MUSIC PUBLISHING

WHAT IS THE ROLE OF THE PUBLISHER?

Without publishing, songwriters would be unable to create value and income from their work. Like labels, publishing is dominated by a few large players, most connected to major labels, such as EMI, or Sony Publishing, but like labels, there is a flourishing independent business.

Although seemingly a traditional business, publishing is undergoing considerable change as it extends into development. Increasingly it isn't just providing studio time for clients to record demos, but is putting out records in limited editions to attract record company interest. Realising that good product needs to be nurtured, contributions to press and promotion are now possible, subject to recoupment against royalties of course.

IT'S GOOD FOR NEW TALENT

Publishers are now taking on record companies and prepared to invest in raw talent. The accepted wisdom of leaving a publishing deal until after a record deal is becoming questionable. Sometimes this development funding might be a 'top up' to an existing record deal, and labels are increasingly happy to share the risk.

Often this is being done for defensive reasons. Traditionally, publishers brought artists and writers together, but increasingly artists who also write have set up their own publishing companies with the help of their management, keeping control and a greater share of their income.

PUBLISHERS CAN AFFORD TO DO MORE

There has probably never been a better time for exploiting publishing rights. Synchronisation rights (all rights outside recording and live) are benefiting from the explosion of new types of musical application from ring-tones to computer games, the growth in cinema audiences and DVDs. These rights are showing double digit growth for many publishers opposed to negative growth from mechanical rights (recording rights) that fund the record companies, altering the balance of power between labels and publishing.

Publishers are also benefiting from the increase in performance rights, because live and broadcast are both growing, with over thirty music TV stations and a resurgence in the live circuit. That's even before back catalogue is considered. All media industries have a growing hunger for content. The advertising industry really pushed this with Hamlet cigars in the 1970s and the Levi campaign in the '80s; more recently brands such as Peugeot have built strong awareness through use of music. Compilations continue to sell well from *Chill Out Ibiza*, to Sony Music's School Disco.com and all boost the value of back catalogue.

THE FUTURE OF PUBLISHING

Publishing generates income for artists who own their own rights in a way that traditional labels never can. Even on the Internet labels cannot compete with how MCPS has improved its ability to secure income from paid-for-downloading sites. Publishing's strength is that it doesn't rely on an old-fashioned form of physical distribution like the major record companies are tied into. Whether it's ring-tones or broadcast, it can collect income for its clients without having to duplicate CDs, load vans, deliver to stores, or merchandise anything on the shelf.

TIPS FOR NEWCOMERS

- ***Protecting your copyright:*** Protecting copyright isn't easy. Although the 1988 Copyright Designs and Patents Act automatically grants copyright to the originator, i.e. the writer, proving that you were the originator is another thing entirely. There's no UK legislation to protect songwriters in this respect. That's why we recommend joining the Guild of International Songwriters and Composers who run a copyright service that is free for their members. It issues a copyright certificate and registers members' work.
- ***Other services provided by the Guild:*** The Guild run a collaboration service enabling songwriters to collaborate with composers and artists with songwriters. Publishers will sometimes put songwriting teams together, but this service can help individuals make their own contacts and partnerships. The Guild also provides practical advice on issues of songwriting; a 'Song Assessment Service' helps members by looking at the strengths and weaknesses of songs and compositions and considering whether they have commercial value. They offer advice, consultancy, information and contact service to help members get published.
- ***Why do you need a publisher?*** A publishing deal is important if you want to exploit the value of your song or composition. Increasingly publishers are putting songwriters and artists together to help them get a record deal. They market and collect revenue from a catalogue of publishing rights, collecting and distributing royalties earned by their clients from the Performing Right Society (PRS) and Mechanical Copyright Protection Society (MCPS). Legally you don't need to work through a publishing company, but someone has to be identified as the publisher/copyright owner of the song, especially if it's successful, as credits have to be identified on commercial record releases. If your song has been taken up by an artist or record label and you do not need a

publishing company to do a deal or market it, it might be worth forming a publishing facility to retain 100% of royalties. Remember, you could always do a deal later to exploit back catalogue rights.

- ***How do royalties work?*** The biggest royalty for most songwriters comes from issuing a licence to record a performance of their song. This means that even if you are the performer as well as songwriter, the record label will have to get permission to record the track and must pay a licence fee to the owner of what is known as mechanical rights, from the days when recording was done mechanically on mechanical piano-rolls. The MCPS control the collection of these royalties, operating a scheme approved by the Copyright Tribunal set up by the 1988 Copyright, Designs and Patents Act. The licence fee is 8.5% of the dealer price of a record, usually meaning 60–80p an album – although obviously depending on dealer price. There's no membership fee to join MCPS; instead they deduct a commission of 4.75–12.5% depending on members' income. As Internet downloading has increased, MCPS has had to introduce a licence for this new distribution medium. Since 2002 they've issued blanket licences averaging 10% of revenue for the relevant track. Many sites still dispute this and operate one-off licences, but this should eventually be clarified.

  Synchronisation rights are another important source of income for songwriters. These license use of your songs and compositions for films, adverts, computer games, ring-tones and any other application other than live performance and records. They are called synchronisation rights because they grant the licence to synchronise your music with visual images. Royalties can be considerable; advertising agencies will pay £70,000–£100,000 for an important track. Although technically payable for promos, the publisher will usually give the record company free synchronisation rights, as it's in their interest if this is successful. In the UK these rights are negotiated on a case-by-case basis. How much you get depends on how good your publisher and lawyer is at negotiation.

Performance rights are the third source of income for songwriters. These are the rights to perform a song in a public place, including playing music in shops, restaurants, clubs, airplanes and anywhere else you can hear music in public as well as live concerts. PRS (the Performing Right Society) administers these rights and is solely responsible for the collection of income generated. If you become a member of PRS you assign performing rights in your songs over to them. PRS knows what is played on TV and radio by checking cue sheets, completed by station producers after each show. They rely on a random sampling policy for live shows. Most broadcaster and major venues have a blanket agreement with PRS; these cover all songs controlled by PRS and are negotiated as a single annual fee, divided among members from cue sheets and random sampling. Membership of PRS is £50 for songwriters and £250 for publishers. Additionally they take a commission on revenue collected.

The last source of income comprises direct fees paid for composing or writing special music for film tracks or adverts.

- ***How do you interest a publisher?*** Publishers' prime interest is the same as record labels – to sign clients who'll make them money. Nobody's interested in songwriters who write or compose in a vacuum. Songwriters who are successful get their songs performed by persuading artists to sing them, or co-writing with them. Increasingly they're not just songwriters but writer/producers or writer/performers. If not they have to be connected to the business; in many ways they have to be as determined to create a career as a new artist.
- ***How does a publishing deal work?*** In most publishing contracts the songwriter signs a contract transferring ownership of the musical composition to the publisher concerned. These contracts can take the form of single-song agreements or term songwriter agreements.

Unknown songwriters tend to sign single-song agreements while major songwriters tend to be offered the latter unless it's for a film, which takes the form of a different agreement.

However, administration deals are becoming popular with songwriters with a relatively small but valuable catalogue, or those that are very successful. Here the administrator usually doesn't ask for the copyright to be transferred, but is given a licence for an agreed period. But like artists, songwriters are looking for the 'publishing' deal that means they have arrived and someone rates them enough to invest in their success. This is known as an 'exclusive publishing agreement'.

- ***What should you expect in an exclusive publishing deal?*** The most important thing you should expect from a publisher, if you sign over your copyright for a significant period, is that it should be pro-active on your behalf. Not all are, and you need to check them out first.

The period you sign up for is often less than for record deals. Quite often it's for an initial period of a year, with options for the publisher to extend this for a further two or three years. In exchange for this the publisher usually pays an advance. This is not repayable as long as you fulfil the agreed minimum commitment to write a minimum number of songs. There may be additional requirements you have less control over. You could have to commit to one or more songs being commercially exploited in a certain way; perhaps to be released as an A-side of a single or an album track. Unlike record deals, recoupment is much simpler and usually faster because there's little to recoup apart from the advance, other than some demo costs and personal expenses.

The size of the advance depends on many factors. Your commercial potential will be the most effective. That's why the best way to get a deal is to get out there and be part of the scene. If you've already co-written material with an interesting artist and persuaded others to use your material, you will have some bargaining power.

Publishers' shares of your royalties are open to negotiation. Usually they are 20–25% although some publishers charge more like 25–35% for synchronisation fees because they believe they have to do more to find these projects, which is arguable. In terms of Performance Rights, the PRS send 50% of fees direct to the songwriter, which can be an invaluable source of income to songwriters whose advance is spent, but who have not recouped. The remainder will be sent to the publisher who will try to keep it unless you negotiate otherwise. On top of this share of royalties, your publisher will also charge you at least a further 10% fee for 'administration'. So in effect your publisher will take 40–50% of your royalties. More than 50% is not a good deal.

- ***How not to get screwed by your publisher:*** The biggest area where you can get screwed by your publisher is for them not to do anything with your songs. If you've been granted an exclusive contract, you're not free to go anywhere else until the end of the contract term. It's always harder to rectify problems after you've entered a contract even though it's possible to serve a notice of dissatisfaction and give a time period during which the publisher must show signs of positive action.

You must do your homework about the publisher. Understanding how commercial they see your work, what plans they have for you to collaborate and ideas for exploiting your synchronisation rights should all be part of your negotiation and are as important as negotiating the advance and the royalties split.

If you're an artist with a record deal and your label also owns a publishing company or has a long-term relationship with one, beware! It's not unknown for labels' publishing operations to issue a 'sweetheart licence', allowing them to have mechanical rights at below market rates, and to keep more of the dealer price. This could also apply to their film company or any other exploitation. If you look at the varied interests of the majors you'll see how this could happen. There have been several court cases where bands have been in dispute with labels about packaging issues (i.e. when their record deals are tied to publishing deals) that are unfavourable.

It's not just majors that are the problem. If you perform your own songs, sometimes independents just want to get your publishing rights because they see it as another income source, but they are not real publishers, and haven't the resources to exploit your rights properly. In these cases, often they just contract a major publisher to administer your songs, when you could have done a better deal direct, or at their worst they are just incompetent and don't collect your royalties properly. It's best not to give your publishing away in an independent deal, if you don't have to. Try to limit the deal to mechanical rights.

Publishers can screw you on overseas royalties. Make sure wherever you can you get royalties calculated 'at source' and not on 'receipts'. This means that there are no deductions other than VAT, collection societies and translation costs from your income, which means overseas sub-publishers are paid out of the publisher's split and not yours. If it's not possible to have this deal on some overseas territories, at least limit the deduction that a sub-publisher can take off the top.

What if your publisher pushes your songs inappropriately? A song can be murdered by the wrong association or a bad performance. If you waive your moral rights or performer rights, you could lose creative control. Be aware of this when you negotiate your contract. Some songwriters have total control of which ads or films can use their songs; others have an agreement that they are not to be used for certain categories such as erotic films or tobacco advertising.

If you're writing most of an album that is already part of a record deal and is commercial, then anything from £40,000 to £80,000 is possible; highly rated and established songwriters could expect much more.

THE VIEW FROM WITHIN

GUY MOOT – EXECUTIVE VICE PRESIDENT, HEAD OF A&R UK AND EUROPE, EMI MUSIC PUBLISHING

Guy Moot has a long, successful track record in publishing. He's one of the few senior music industry executives who combine sincere passion for music with business efficiency and professionalism.

How do publishers assess the potential of a song?
There are tracks you hear that make the hairs stand up on the back of your neck. Often discovering a hit song is about being around the vibe or scene as it is developing. These days I don't go clubbing much because I've a department to run, but when I can – I do. If I'm in Jamaica, I must go to a dance hall party. To hear a tune go off in those places and see everybody react is what it's all about. Some A&R people try to be scientific about signing artists. They research and study it like a university degree. For me it's down to gut instincts that come from listening to the right music. If an artist walks in the door with hit songs – that's just the start. We look for other factors such as their image and whether they have a strong desire to be famous. These things add up.

How important are lyrics?
Very! American songwriters have always reflected and coined what's going on in the street and embodied it in their songs. It's really important to touch people with songs related to their everyday lives. Look at the way Eminem can use his lyrics to relate his own personal experiences in a way that people all over the world can understand.

How active are you in artist development, especially as the labels seem to be turning away from spending any money in this area?
It's a huge part of what we do. Jamiroquai, Ms Dynamite and So Solid Crew were all signed to EMI Publishing before they had any record deal. Nurturing talent and helping them get placed with the right record deal is a big part of what we do. The industry is full of people who will always say: **'Ah I could**

have signed that, but they didn't let me.' I don't have any sympathy for people like that. It's easy to blame people above you for not signing stuff. I want people to come to me and say, 'I fucking love this', rather than 'This could be big' or 'What do you think?' This business is about one person's enthusiasm taking a vision and pushing it forward with conviction.

Once you have made up your mind that the writer or artist has what it takes, you have to look at the business side of the deal. Before we get to that point, we will look at which record company is involved, or interested, and what their track record is at delivering that sort of act, and other factors such as how strong they are internationally. Obviously it's easier to make a decision if the act already has a good record deal, or the chairman of the label wants to give them a big push.

Isn't there a temptation just to follow the latest bandwagon being chased by the major labels?

What we try to do here is to set our own A&R agenda. We were the first into the garage scene, and have signed up the best writers and artists. We didn't do this because we said, 'Oh look, garage is getting big now.' Instead we signed up people based on our instincts and their reputation within the underground, not whether the press said they were hot. We look for artist–writers who are culturally, socially and lyrically important to British youth. Too often American acts relate better to our youth than our own artists. So I want some artists from the UK who can say the right thing. That's why I think there will be a big Asian scene this year and I think a UK rapper will burst through soon. I really prefer to do deals before any record deal has been signed, not just because you can do a better deal, but it gives you a chance to play a part in suggesting which teams the artists can work with to create the hit.

We're getting in there early not because it's cheaper, but because it feels right. It gives us a chance to pass on our knowledge to help their career, which in return means that we all have a chance in creating success.

So you're almost acting like a management company?

I think managers, production and publishing companies are more likely to develop acts than major labels. It's not easy being a major, it's very expensive for them. That's why they want no-brainers, that they can just plug into the machine.

How developed does an artist have to be to interest you?
I want the production to be good, and it needs to be a great song with contemporary lyrics. We know who's looking for the right song, so if they play us something that is hot, we can introduce them to the right people, and help it become a hit. It's not just about the song – that's a big myth. It has to be well produced, because you need to show what it's going to sound like when it is properly produced. If a writer–producer comes looking for a deal, their material must be brilliant. I don't think it's going to work these days, going to a record label with a fairly unproduced track.

For a band to get our attention, there's got to be a buzz about them. You have to create your own community and jibe. You have to do it yourself. So Solid Crew created their own pirate radio station and released records, to do just that. The White Stripes released independently in Detroit. It's all about doing something to get noticed. My department gets about 100 demos a day, so you have to do something special.

So how many hit songs do there have to be on a demo before you would sign?
It varies, sometimes one, preferably three to four. It's not just about having a hit single, it's about having three to four to sell an album. These tracks should open out really slowly and show the artist's capabilities and diversity.

You must get a real buzz when one of your writer–artists does well in the charts?
Absolutely! I love it. I'm a junkie for it. It's not just from a chart perspective, but also from a financial level. It's not all about us making money, but also for the artist, especially when we sign underground stuff that crosses over. Money is a by-product of sucess and spreading your music to more people.

So how do you create opportunities for your writers?
Mainly by building profile and awareness for them. Sometimes by sending out

a whole song to an established artist to cover, or by introducing writers to record company A&R people. We like to think at EMI Music Publishing that we can really make a difference in terms of our writers' careers. We go the extra distance to make them successful. We provide some of the less obvious services a publisher can provide, such as radio mixes, and white labels, in fact anything that an array of our contacts can provide to help their careers.

You've obviously been very successful but have you ever messed up?
Yeah, but I think 80% of what I've signed has been a success not just as a hit, but also for the careers of the artists. I'm ashamed of the other 20%, as it's often our fault, although sometimes the artists don't do the best to realise their full potential.

How does a publishing deal work at EMI?
They'll get an advance, in return for a product commitment. This means that you have to get five whole songs released on a major label. They might not be five whole songs but ten half ones that add up to five. Then we go to the next option period, when we decide if we want to go on; if we do we have to pay more money.

What keeps you in the business?
I'm driven to find new artists and to bring an exciting team together, to create those hits. My friends think I'm crazy because I'm obsessed by what I do. When I did a deal with Eminem for the *8 Mile* soundtrack, it was such a thrill. They have built their own thing from the underground. The best thing about this job is that you can do a project like that one day, and another meet a new act that's going to be the next best thing.

PUBLISHERS

AIR MUSIC AND MEDIA GROUP LIMITED
Chiltern House, 184 High Street, Berkhamsted, Hertfordshire HP4 3AP
T: 01442 877018 F: 01442 877015
Email: info@airmusicandmedia.com
Website: airmusicandmedia.com
Michael Infante

AIR TRAFFIC CONTROL MUSIC PUBLISHING
29 Harley St, London W1G 9QR
T: 0870 20 200 20
Email: mark@airtrafficcontrolhq.com
Director: Mark Barker

ALARCON MUSIC LTD
The Old Truman Brewery, 91 Brick Lane, London E1 6QL
T: 020 7377 9373 F: 020 7377 6523
Email: AlarconMusic@aol.com
Director: Byron Orme

ALAW
4 Tyfila Road, Pontypridd, RCT CF37 2DA
T: 01443 402178 F: 01443 402178
Email: sales@alawmusic.ndo.co.uk
Website: alawmusic.ndo.co.uk
Director: Brian Raby

ALFRED PUBLISHING CO (UK) LTD
Burnt Mill, Elizabeth Way, Harlow, Essex CM20 2HX
T: 01279 828960 F: 01279 828961
Email: music@alfredpublishing.demon.co.uk
Website: alfreduk.com
Mktng Mgr: Andrew Higgins

ALL ACTION FIGURE MUSIC
Unit 9 Darvells Works, Common Rd, Chorleywood, Herts WD3 5LP
T: 01923 286010 F: 01923 286070
Email: songs@allactionfigure.co.uk
MD: Steve Lowes

ALPADON MUSIC
Shenandoah, Manor Park, Chislehurst, Kent BR7 5QD
T: 020 8295 0310 F: 020 8295 0311
Email: don@dpap.demon.co.uk
MD: Don Percival

AMAZING FEET PUBLISHING
Interzone House, 74-77 Magdalen Road, Oxford OX4 1RE
T: 01865 205600 F: 01865 205700
Email: amazing@rotator.co.uk
Website: rotator.co.uk/amazingfeet
MD: Richard Cotton

ANGLO PLUGGING MUSIC
Fulham Palace, Bishops Avenue, London SW6 6EA
T: 020 7384 7373 F: 020 7736 4237
Email: sue@asongs.co.uk
Director: Sue Crawshaw

ANGUS PUBLICATIONS
14 Graham Terrace, Belgravia, London SW1W 8JH
T: 07850 845280 F: 020 7730 3368
Email: bill.puppetmartin@virgin.net
Chairman: Bill Martin

ARCADIA PRODUCTION MUSIC (UK)
Greenlands, Payhembury, Devon
EX14 3HY
T: 01404 841601 F: 01404 841687
Email: admin@arcadiamusic.tv
Website: arcadiamusic.tv
Prop: John Brett

ARIEL MUSIC
Malvern House, Sibford Ferris, Banbury, Oxon 0X15 5RG
T: 01295 780679 F: 01295 788630
Email: jane@arielmusic.co.uk
Website: arielmusic.co.uk
Managing Partner: Jane Woolfenden

ARISTOCRAT MUSIC LTD
Elstree Business Centre, Elstree Way, Borehamwood, Hertfordshire WD6 1RX
T: 020 8624 6166 F: 020 8624 6167
Email: AristocratMusic@KingdomRecords.co.uk
MD: Terry King

ARPEGGIO MUSIC
Bell Farm House, Eton Wick, Windsor, Berkshire SL4 6LH
T: 01753 864910 F: 01753 884810
MD: Beverley Campion

ARTEMIS MUSIC LTD
Pinewood Studios, Iver Heath, Bucks
SL0 0NH
T: 01753 650766 F: 01753 654774
Email: info@artemismusic.com
Website: artemismusic.com
MD: Mike Sheppard

ARTFIELD
5 Grosvenor Square, London W1K 4AF
T: 020 7499 9941 F: 020 7499 9010
Email: info@artfieldmusic.com; bbcooper@artfieldmusic.com
Website: artfieldmusic.com
MD: BB Cooper

ARTS MUSIC PUBLISHING
335 Upton Lane, London E7 9PT
T: 020 8586 0314
Email: renkrecords@msn.com
MD: Junior Hart

ASHLEY MARK PUBLISHING COMPANY
1-2 Vance Court, Trans Britannia Enterprise Pk, Blaydon on Tyne, Tyne & Wear NE21 5NH
T: 0191 414 9000 F: 0191 414 9001
Email: mail@ashleymark.co.uk
Website: ashleymark.co.uk
MD: Simon Turnbull

ASSOC. BOARD OF THE ROYAL SCHOOLS OF MUSIC (PUB'G)
24 Portland Place, London W1B 1LU
T: 020 7636 5400 F: 020 7637 0234
Email: publishing@abrsm.ac.uk
Website: abrsmpublishing.co.uk
Director of Publishing: Leslie East

ASTWOOD MUSIC LTD
Latimer Studios, West Kington, Wilts
SN14 7JQ
T: 01249 783 599 F: 0870 169 8433
Email: DolanMAP@aol.com
CEO: Mike Dolan

ASYLUM SONGS
PO Box 121, Hove, East Sussex
BN3 7WP
T: 01273 774468 F: 08709 223099
Email: info@AsylumGroup.com
Website: AsylumGroup.com

AUTOMATIC SONGS LTD
41-49 Canalot Studios, 222 Kensal Road, London W10 5BN
T: 020 8964 8890 F: 020 8960 5741
Email: mail@automaticrecords.co.uk
Website: automaticrecords.co.uk
MD: Russell Coultart

BANKS MUSIC PUBLICATIONS
The Old Forge, Sand Hutton, York, North Yorkshire YO41 1LB
T: 01904 468472 F: 01904 468679
Email: banksramsay@cwcom.net
Website: banksmusicpublications.cwc.net
Proprietor: Margaret Silver

BARDIC EDITION
6 Fairfax Crescent, Aylesbury, Buckinghamshire HP20 2ES
T: 01296 428609 F: 01296 581185
Email: info@bardic-music.com
Website: bardic-music.com
Proprietor: Barry Peter Ould

BARE TUNES
5 Warren Mews, London W1T 6AU
T: 020 7388 5300 F: 020 7388 5399
Email: bare.tunes@virgin.net
MD: Saul Galpen

BARN PUBLISHING (SLADE) LTD
1 Pratt Mews, London NW1 0AD
T: 020 7267 6899 F: 020 7267 6746
Email: partners@newman-and.co.uk
Pub: Colin Newman

BBC MUSIC PUBLISHING
A2033 Woodlands, 80 Wood Lane, London W12 OTT
T: 020 8433 1723 F: 020 8433 1741
Email: victoria.watkins@bbc.co.uk
Catalogue Manager: Victoria Watkins

BEARSONGS
PO Box 944, Birmingham, West Midlands B16 8UT
T: 0121 454 7020 F: 0121 454 9996
Email: bigbearmusic@compuserve.com
Website: bigbearmusic.com
MD: Jim Simpson

BEECHWOOD MUSIC PUBLISHING LTD
Littleton House, Littleton Rd, Ashford, Middx TW15 1UU
T: 01784 423214 F: 01784 251245
Email: melissa@beechwoodmusic.co.uk
Website: beechwoodmusic.co.uk
MD: Tim Millington

BEIJING PUBLISHING
105 Emlyn Road, London W12 9TG
T: 020 8749 3730
Email: brianleafe@aol.com
Owner: Brian Leafe

BIG FISH SONGS LTD
5, Astrop Mews, London W6 7HR
T: 020 8746 4040 F: 020 8746 4060
Email: bigfish@music-village.com
Website: music-village.com
MD: John Carnell

BIG LIFE MUSIC
67-69 Chalton Street, London NW1 1HY
T: 020 7554 2100 F: 020 7554 2154
Email: biglife@biglife.co.uk
Website: biglife.co.uk
MD: Tim Parry

BIG NOTE MUSIC LIMITED
Comforts Place, Tandridge Lane,
Lingfield, Surrey RH7 6LW
T: 01342 893046 F: 01342 893562
Email: ahillesq@aol.com
Deborah Beaton

BIGTIME MUSIC PUBLISHING
86 Marlborough Road, Oxford OX1 4LS
T: 01865 249 194 F: 01865 792 765
Email: info@bejo.co.uk
Website: bejo.co.uk
Administrator: Tim Healey

BISWAS MUSIC
24 Pepper St, London SE1 0EB
T: 020 7928 9777 F: 020 7928 9222
Email: guy@guyrippon.org
MD: Guy Rippon

BLACK HEAT MUSIC
13a Filey Avenue, London N16 6JL
T: 020 8806 4193
Email: tmorgan@ntlworld.com
Director: Tony Morgan

BLASTER! MUSIC
77 Nightingale Shott, Egham, Surrey
TW20 9SU F: 01784 741 592
Email: martinw@netcomuk.co.uk
MD: Martin Whitehead

BLUE MOUNTAIN MUSIC LTD
8 Kensington Park Road, London
W11 3BU
T: 020 7229 3000 F: 020 7221 8899
Email: bluemountain@islandlife.co.uk
Website: bluemountainmusic.tv
MD: Alistair Norbury

BMG MUSIC PUBLISHING LTD
Bedford House, 69-79 Fulham High
Street, London SW6 3JW
T: 020 7384 7600 F: 020 7384 8164
Email: firstname.lastname@bmg.com
Website: bmgmusicsearch.com

BMG MUSIC PUBLISHING INTERNATIONAL
Bedford House, 69-79 Fulham High
Street, London SW6 3JW
T: 020 7384 7600 F: 020 7384 8162
Email: (firstname).(lastname)@bmg.co.uk

BMG ZOMBA PRODUCTION MUSIC
10-11 St Martin's Court, London
WC2N 4AJ
T: 020 7497 4800 F: 020 7497 4801
Email: musicresearch@bmgzomba.com
Website: bmgzomba.com
Senior Music Researcher: Andrew Stannard

BOOSEY & HAWKES MUSIC PUBLISHERS LTD
295 Regent Street, London W1B 2JH
T: 020 7291 7222 F: 020 7291 7109
Email: booseymedia@boosey.com
Website: booseymedia.com
Mktg Mgr: Caroline Buss

BOURNE MUSIC LTD
2nd Floor, 207/209 Regent Street,
London W1B 4ND
T: 020 7734 3454 F: 020 7734 3385
Email: bournemusic@supanet.com
Office Manager: John Woodward

BRASS WIND PUBLICATIONS
4 St Mary's Road, Manton, Oakham,
Rutland LE15 8SU

T: 01572 737409 F: 01572 737409
Email: info@brasswindpublications.co.uk
Website: brasswindpublications.co.uk :

BRIGHT MUSIC LTD
21c Heathmans Road, Parsons Green, London SW6 4TJ
T: 020 7751 9935 F: 020 7731 9314
Email: brightmusic@aol.com
Website: brightmusic.co.uk
MD: Martin Wyatt

BRIGHTLY MUSIC
231 Lower Clapton Road, London E5 8EG
T: 020 8533 7994 F: 020 8986 4035
Email: abrightly@yahoo.com
Website: brightly.freeserve.co.uk
MD: Anthony Brightly

BROADLEY MUSIC (INT) LTD
Broadley House, 48 Broadley Terrace, London NW1 6LG
T: 020 7258 0324 F: 020 7724 2361
Email: admin@broadleystudios.com
Website: broadleystudios.com
MD: Ellis Elias

BUCKS MUSIC GROUP
Onward House, 11 Uxbridge Street, London W8 7TQ
T: 020 7221 4275 F: 020 7229 6893
Email: info@bucksmusicgroup.co.uk
Website: bucksmusicgroup.com
MD: Simon Platz

BUDDING MUSIC `LEIGH'
Brompton Ralph, Taunton, Somerset TA4 2SF
T: 01984 623968 F: 01984 623711
MD: John Marshall

BUFFALO SONGS
120 Ashurst Rd, North Finchley, London N12 9AB
T: 07887 983 452 F: 020 8342 8213
Email: jonathan@buffalosongs.com
Website: buffalosongs.com
Creative Director: Jonathan Morley

BUGLE PUBLISHING
1 Water Lane, London NW1 8NZ
T: 020 7267 1101 F: 020 7267 8879
Email: legalark21@aol.com
Website: milescopeland.com
Head of Publishing: Andy Graham

BULK MUSIC LTD
9 Watt Road, Hillington Park, Glasgow, Strathclyde G52 4RY
T: 0141 882 9986 F: 0141 883 3686
Email: krl@krl.co.uk
Website: krl.co.uk
MD: Gus McDonald

CANDLE MUSIC LTD
44 Southern Row, London W10 5AN
T: 020 8960 0111 F: 020 8968 7008

CARIBBEAN MUSIC LIBRARY
Sovereign House, 12 Trewartha Road, Penzance, Cornwall TR20 9ST
T: 01736 762826 F: 01736 763328
Email: panamus@aol.com
Website: panamamusic.co.uk
Director: Roderick Jones

CARITAS MUSIC PUBLISHING
28 Dalrymple Crescent, Edinburgh EH9 2NX
T: 0131 667 3633 F: 0131 667 3633
Email: caritas@caritas-music.co.uk

Website: caritas-music.co.uk
Proprietor: Katharine H Douglas

CARLIN MUSIC CORPORATION
Iron Bridge House, 3 Bridge Approach, London NW1 8BD
T: 020 7734 3251 F: 020 7439 2391
Email: enquiries@carlinmusic.com
MD: David Japp

CATHEDRAL MUSIC
King Charles Cottage, Racton, Chichester, West Sussex PO18 9DT
T: 01243 379968

CHAIN MUSIC
24 Cornwall Road, Cheam, Surrey SM2 6DT
T: 020 8643 3353 F: 020 8643 3353
Email: gchurchill@c-h-a-ltd.demon.co.uk
Chairman: Carole Howells

CHANDOS MUSIC LTD
Chandos House, Commerce Way, Colchester, Essex CO2 8HQ
T: 01206 225200 F: 01206 225201
Email: shogger@chandos.net
Website: chandos.net Music/Copyright Admin: Stephen Hogger

CHANTELLE MUSIC
3A Ashfield Parade, London N14 5EH
T: 020 8886 6236
MD: Riss Chantelle

CHEEKY MUSIC
181 High Street, Harlesden, London NW10 4TE
T: 020 8961 5202 F: 020 8965 3948
Email: eddie@championrecords.co.uk
Website: championrecords.co.uk
Business Affairs: Eddie Seago

CHELSEA MUSIC PUBLISHING CO LTD
124 Great Portland St, London W1N 5PG
T: 020 7580 0044 F: 020 7580 0045
Email: eddie@chelseamusicpublishing.com
Website: chelseamusicpublishing.com
MD: Eddie Levy

CHESTER MUSIC
8-9 Frith Street, London W1D 3JB
T: 020 7434 0066 F: 020 7287 6329
Email: promotion@musicsales.co.uk
Website: chesternovello.com
MD: James Rushton

CHESTNUT MUSIC
Smoke Tree House, Tilford Road, Farnham, Surrey GU10 2EN
T: 01252 794253 F: 01252 792642
Email: keynote@dial.pipex.com
MD: Tim Wheatley

CHRISTABEL MUSIC
32 High Ash Drive, Alwoodley, Leeds, West Yorkshire LS17 8RA
T: 0113 268 5528 F: 0113 266 5954
MD: Jeff Christie

CHRYSALIS MUSIC LTD
The Chrysalis Building, 13 Bramley Rd, London W10 6SP
T: 020 7221 2213 F: 020 7465 6178
Email: firstname.lastname@chrysalis.com
Website: chrysalis.com
MD: Alison Donald

CHUCKLE MUSIC
6 Northend Gardens, Kingswood, Bristol BS15 1UA
T: 0117 783 7586

Email: ply501@netscapeonline.co.uk
MD: Peter Michaels

COLUMBIA PUBLISHING WALES LTD
Glen More, 6 Cwrt y Camden, Brecon, Powys LD3 7RR
T: 01874 625270 F: 01874 625270
Email: dafydd@columbiapublishing.co.uk
Website: columbiapublishing.co.uk
MD: Dafydd Gittins

CONGO MUSIC LTD
17A Craven Park Road, Harlesden, London NW10 8SE
T: 020 8961 5461 F: 020 8961 5461
Email: congomusic@hotmail.com
Website: congomusic.com
A&R Director: Root Jackson

CONSTANT IN OPAL MUSIC PUBLISHING
Sovereign House, 12 Trewartha Road, Penzance, Cornawall TR20 9ST
T: 01736 762826 F: 01736 763328
Email: panamus@aol.com
Website: songwriters-guild.co.uk
MD: Roderick Jones

THE CONTEMPORARY MUSIC CENTRE
19 Fishamble Street, Temple Bar, Dublin 8, Ireland
T: +353 1 673 1922
F: +353 1 648 9100
Email: info@cmc.ie
Website: cmc.ie
Director: Eve O'Kelly

COOKING VINYL LTD
10 Allied Way, London W3 0RQ
T: 020 8600 9200 F: 020 8743 7448
Email: Francisco@cookingvinyl.com
Website: cookingvinyl.com
A&R Assistant: Francisco Garcia

CORNERWAYS MUSIC
Ty'r Craig, Longleat Avenue, Craigside, Llandudno LL30 3AE
T: 01492 549759 F: 01492 541482
Email: gordonlorenz@compuserve.com
Gordon Lorenz

COURTYARD MUSIC
22 The Nursery, Sutton Courtenay, Oxfordshire OX14 4UA
T: 01235 845800 F: 01235 847692
Email: andy@cyard.com
Website: courtyardmusic.net
A&R Mgr: Andy Ross

CREATIVE WORLD ENTERTAINMENT LTD
PO Box 2206, Lichfield, Staffordshire WS14 0GZ
T: 01543 253576 F: 01543 253576
Email: mail@creative-world-entertainment.co.uk
Website: creative-world-entertainment.co.uk
MD: Mervyn Spence

CREOLE MUSIC LTD
The Chilterns, France Hill Drive, Camberley, Surrey GU15 3QA
T: 01276 686077 F: 01276 686055
Email: creole@clara.net
MD: Bruce White

CSA WORD
6a Archway Mews, 241a Putney Bridge Rd, London SW15 2PE
T: 020 8871 0220 F: 020 8877 0712

Email: clive@csaword.co.uk
Website: csatelltapes.demon.co.uk
Audio Manager: Victoria Williams

CUTTING EDGE MUSIC LTD
3rd Floor, 36 King St, London
WC2E 8JS
T: 020 7759 8550 F: 020 7759 8560
Email: philipm@cutting-edge.uk.com
Website: cutting-edge.uk.com
MD: Philip Moross

CWMNI CYHOEDDI GWYNN
Cyf Y Gerlan, Heol-y-Dwr, Penygroes,
Caernarfon, Gwynedd LL54 6LR
T: 01286 881797 F: 01286 882634
Website: gwynn.co.uk
Administrator: Wendy Jones

DALMATION SONGS LTD
The Chapel, 57 St Dionis Road, London
SW6 4UB
T: 020 7731 2100 F: 020 7371 7722
Email: gooner@netcomuk.co.uk
Directors: Bill Stonebridge, Marc Fox

DARAH MUSIC LTD
21C Heathmans Rd, Parsons Green,
London SW6 4TJ
T: 020 7731 9313 F: 020 7731 9314
Email: admin@darah.co.uk
MD: David Howells

DE HASKE MUSIC (UK) LTD
Fleming Road, Earlstrees, Corby,
Northamptonshire NN17 4SN
T: 01536 260981 F: 01536 401075
Email: music@dehaske.co.uk Sales &
Marketing Mgr: Mark Coull

DEADWOOD PUBLISHING LTD
1 Trafalgar Mews, Eastway, London
E9 5JG
T: 020 8985 8427 F: 020 8985 8472
Email: info@almafame.co.uk
Website: almafame.co.uk
GM: Nick B. Collie

DECEPTIVE MUSIC
PO Box 288, St Albans, Hertfordshire
AL4 9YU
T: 01727 834130
MD: Tony Smith

DELICIOUS PUBLISHING
Fourth Floor, Voysey House, Barley Mow
Passage, London W4 4GB
T: 020 8987 6181 F: 020 8987 6182
Email: ollie@deliciousdigital.com
Website: deliciousdigital.com
MD: Ollie Raphael

DEMI MONDE PUBLISHING
Llanfair Caereinion, Powys, Wales
SY21 0DS
T: 01938 810758 F: 01938 810758
Email: demi.monde@dial.pipex.com
Website: demimonde.co.uk
MD: Dave Anderson

DESILU PUBLISHING LTD
6 Rookwood Park, Horsham, West
Sussex RH12 IUB
T: 01403 240272 F: 01403 263008
Email: gbowes@desilurecords.com
MD: Graham Bowes

DHARMA MUSIC
36 Sackville Street, London W1S 3EQ
T: 020 7851 0900 F: 020 7851 0901
Email: zen@instantkarma.co.uk
Chairman: Rob Dickins

DICK LEAHY MUSIC LTD
1 Star Street, London W2 1QD
T: 020 7258 0093 F: 020 7402 9238
Email: info@playwrite.uk.com Office Manager: Nicky McDermott

DIGGER MUSIC
34 Great James St, London WC1N 3HB
T: 020 7404 1422 F: 020 7242 2555
Email: tills@globalnet.co.uk
CEO: Tilly Rutherford

DINOSAUR MUSIC PUBLISHING
5 Heyburn Crescent, Westport Gardens, Stoke On Trent, Staffordshire ST6 4DL
T: 08707 418651 F: 08707 418652
Email: alan@dinosaurmusic.co.uk
Website: dinosaurmusic.co.uk
MD: Alan Dutton

DIVERSE MUSIC LTD
Creeting House, All Saints Road, Creeting St Mary, Ipswich, Suffolk IP6 8PR
T: 01449 720 988 F: 01449 726 067
Email: steve@eastcentral.one.co.uk
MD: Diana Graham

EATON MUSIC LTD
Eaton House, 39 Lower Richmond Road, Putney, London SW15 1ET
T: 020 8788 4557 F: 020 8780 9711
Email: info@eatonmusic.com
Website: eatonmusic.com
MD: Terry Oates

EDEL PUBLISHING
12 Oval Road, London NW1 7DH
T: 020 7482 9700 F: 020 7482 4846
Email: phil_hope@edel.com
Website: edel.com
MD: Phil Hope

EG MUSIC LTD
PO Box 4397, London W1A 7RZ
T: 020 8540 9935
MD: Sam Alder

ELA MUSIC
Argentum, 2 Queen Caroline Street, London W6 9DX
T: 020 8323 8013 F: 020 8323 8080
Email: ela@ela.co.uk
Website: ela.co.uk
MD: John Giacobbi

EMI MUSIC PUBLISHING
127 Charing Cross Road, London WC2H 0QY
T: 020 7434 2131 F: 020 7434 3531
Email: firstinitial+lastname@emimusicpub.com
Website: emimusicpub.co.uk :

EMI MUSIC PUBLISHING CONTINENTAL EUROPE
Publishing House, 127 Charing Cross Road, London WC2H 0QY
T: 020 7434 2131 F: 020 7287 5254
Email: firstinitial+lastname@emimusicpub.com
Website: emimusicpub.co.uk

ENDOMORPH MUSIC PUBLISHING
29 St Michael's Rd, Leeds, West Yorkshire LS6 3BG
T: 0113 274 2106 F: 0113 278 6291
Email: dave@bluescat.com
Website: bluescat.com
MD: Dave Foster

ENGLISH WEST COAST MUSIC
The Old Bakehouse, 150 High Street, Honiton, Devon EX14 8JX

T: 01404 42234 F: 07767 869029
Email: Studio@ewcm.co.uk
Website: ewcm.co.uk
Studio Manager: Sean Brown

ESOTERICA MUSIC LTD
20 Station Road, Eckington Road, Sheffield, South Yorkshire S21 4FX
T: 01246 432507 F: 01246 432507
Email: richardcory@lineone.net
MD: Richard Cory

ESQUIRE MUSIC COMPANY
185A Newmarket Road, Norwich, Norfolk NR4 6AP
T: 01603 451139
MD: Peter Newbrook

EVOLVE MUSIC LTD
The Courtyard, 42 Colwith Road, London W6 9EY
T: 020 8741 1419 F: 020 8741 3289
Email: firstname@evolverecords.co.uk
Co-MD: Oliver Smallman

EXPRESS MUSIC (UK) LTD
Matlock, Brady Road, Lyminge, Kent CT18 8HA
T: 01303 863185 F: 01303 863185
Email: siggyjackson@onetel.net.uk
MD: Siggy Jackson

FAMOUS MUSIC PUBLISHING
Bedford House, 69-79 Fulham High Street, London SW6 3JW
T: 020 7736 7543 F: 020 7471 4812
Email: luke.famousmusic@bigfoot.com
Website: syncsite.com
A&R Director: Luke McGrellis

FASHION MUSIC
17 Davids Road, London SE23 3EP
T: 020 8291 6253 F: 020 8291 1097
Producer: Chris Lane

FAST WESTERN LTD
Bank Top Cottage, Meadow Lane, Millers Dale, Derbyshire SK17 8SN
T: 01298 872462 F: 01298 872461
Email: fast.west@virgin.net
MD: Ric Lee

FASTFORWARD MUSIC PUBLISHING LTD
1 Sorrel Horse Mews, Ipswich, Suffolk IP4 1LN
T: 01473 210555 F: 01473 210500
Email: sales@fastforwardmusic.co.uk
Sales Director: Neil Read

FAT FOX MUSIC
24a Radley Mews, off Stratford Rd, London W8 6JP
T: 020 7376 9555 F: 020 7376 9555
Email: nick@fatfox.co.uk
Website: fatfox.co.uk
Director: Nick Wilde

FRIENDLY OVERTURES
Walkers Cottage, Aston Lane, Henley-on-Thames, Oxfordshire RG9 3EJ
T: 01491 574457 F: 01491 574457
Creative Director: Michael Batory

FUNDAMENTAL MUSIC LTD
The Old Lampworks, Rodney Place, London SW19 2LQ
T: 020 8542 4222 F: 020 8542 9934
Email: info@fundamental.co.uk
MD: Tim Prior

FUNTASTIK MUSIC
43 Seaforth Gardens, Stoneleigh, Surrey KT19 0LR
T: 020 8393 1970 F: 020 8393 2428
Email: info@funtastikmusic.com
Website: funtastikmusic.com
John Burns

FUTURE EARTH MUSIC PUBLISHING
59 Fitzwilliam Street, Wath Upon Dearne, Rotherham, South Yorks S63 7HG
T: 01709 872875
Email: david@future-earth.co.uk
Website: future-earth.co.uk
MD: David Moffitt

FYNE MUSIC
2 Chester Avenue, Southport, Merseyside PR9 7ET
T: 01704 224666 F: 01704 224666
Lou Fyne

GEORGE MARTIN MUSIC LTD
Air Studios, Lyndhurst Rd, London NW3 5NG
T: 020 7794 0660 F: 020 7916 2784
Email: info@georgemartinmusic.com
Website: georgemartinmusic.com
A&R: Adam Sharp

GOOD GROOVE SONGS LTD
Unit 217 Buspace Studios, Conlan Street, London W10 5AP
T: 020 7565 0050 F: 020 7565 0049
Email: gary@goodgroove.co.uk
Gary Davies

GOOD MOVE MUSIC
27 Spedan Close, London NW3 7XF
T: 020 7435 5302 F: 020 7435 7152
Email: philsimmonds@excite.co.uk
MD: Philip Simmonds

GRAPEDIME MUSIC
28 Hurst Crescent, Barrowby, Grantham, Lincolnshire NG32 1TE
T: 01476 560241 F: 01476 560241
Email: grapedime@pjbray.globalnet.co.uk
A&R Manager: Phil Bray

GRAPEVINE MUSIC LTD
1 York Street, London W1U 6PA
T: 020 7486 2248 F: 020 7486 8515
Email: enquiries@eastcentralone.com
Website: eastcentralone.com
MD: Steve Fernie

GRASS ROOTS MUSIC PUBLISHING
29 Love Lane, Rayleigh, Essex SS6 7DL
T: 01268 747 077
MD: Gerald Mahlowe

GREENSLEEVES PUBLISHING LTD
Unit 14, Metro Centre, St John's Road, Isleworth, Middlesex TW7 6NJ
T: 020 8758 0564 F: 020 8758 0811
Email: clare@greensleeves.net
Website: greensleeves.net
MD: Chris Sedgwick

GREGSONGS
T: 020 8767 9076 F: 020 8672 6195
Email: mail@gregsongs.com
Administrator: John Martin

GUT MUSIC
Byron House, 112A Shirland Road,
London W9 2EQ
T: 020 7266 0777 F: 020 7266 7734
Email: info@gut-intermedia.com
Website: gutrecords.com
Chairman: Guy Holmes

HALCYON MUSIC
233 Regents Park Road, Finchley,
London N3 3LF
T: 07000 783633 F: 07000 783634
MD: Alan Williams

TONY HALL GROUP OF COMPANIES
16-17 Grafton House, 2-3 Golden Sq,
London W1F 9HR
T: 020 7437 1958 F: 020 7437 3852
Email: tony@tonyhallgroup.com
MD: Tony Hall

HARLEQUIN MUSIC
69 Eversden Road, Harlton, Cambridge
CB3 7ET
T: 01223 263795 F: 01223 263795
Director: Val Bell

HATTON & ROSE PUBLISHERS
46 Northcourt Avenue, Reading,
Berkshire RG2 7HQ
T: 0118 987 4938 F: 0118 987 4938
Graham Hatton

HEAVENLY SONGS
47 Frith Street, London W1D 4SE
T: 020 7494 2998 F: 020 7437 3317
Email: info@heavenlyrecordings.com
Website: heavenly100.com
MD: Jeff Barrett

HIT & RUN MUSIC (PUBLISHING) LTD
11 Denmark Street, London WC2 8TD
T: 020 7240 2408 F: 020 7240 1818
Email: firstname@hit-and-run.com
Jon Crawley

HORNALL BROTHERS MUSIC LTD
1 Northfields Prospect, Putney Bridge
Road, London SW18 1PE
T: 020 8877 3366 F: 020 8874 3131
Email: stuart@hobro.co.uk
Website: hobro.co.uk
MD: Stuart Hornall

HQ
4 The Hamlet, The Bank, Marlcliff,
Bidford on Avon, Warwickshire B50 4NT
T: 01789 778 482 F: 01789 778 482
Email: thehamlet@freeserve.co.uk
John Tully

HYDE PARK MUSIC
110 Westbourne Terrace Mews, London
W2 6QG
T: 020 7402 8419 F: 020 7723 6104
Chairman: Tony Hiller

IQ MUSIC LTD
Commercial House, 52 Perrymount
Road, Haywards Heath, West Sussex
RH16 3DT
T: 01444 452807 F: 01444 451739
Email: kathie@iqmusic.co.uk
Director: Kathie Iqbal

IRMA UK
8 Putney High Street, London SW15 1SL
T: 020 8780 0906 F: 020 8780 0545
Email: irmauk@btinternet.com
Website: irmagroup.com
Managing Director: Corrado Dierna

JAMDOWN MUSIC LTD
Stanley House Studios, 39 Stanley Gardens, London W3 7SY
T: 020 8735 0280 F: 07970 574924
Email: othman@jamdown-music.com
Website: jamdown-music.com
MD: Othman Mukhlis

JAVELIN MUSIC LTD
Satril House, 3 Blackburn Road, London NW6 1RZ
T: 020 7328 8283 F: 020 7328 9037
Email: licensing@hho.co.uk
Website: hho.co.uk
MD: Henry Hadaway

KICKSTART MUSIC
12 Port House, Square Rigger Row, Plantation Wharf, London SW11 3TY
T: 020 7223 3300 F: 020 7223 8777
Email: info@kickstart.uk.net
Director: Frank Clark

KILA MUSIC PUBLISHING
Charlemont House, 33 Charlemont Street, Dublin 2
T: +353 1 476 0627
F: +353 1 476 0627
Email: info@kilarecords.com
Website: kila.ie
Director: Colm O'Snodaigh

KINGSWAY MUSIC
Lottbridge Drove, Eastbourne, East Sussex BN23 6NT
T: 01323 437700 F: 01323 411970
Email: music@kingsway.co.uk
Website: worshiptogether.com
Label Mgr: Stephen Doherty

KRISTANNAR MUSIC
33 Park Chase, Wembley, Middlesex HA9 8EQ
T: 020 8902 5523 F: 020 8902 5523
Email: kristannar@freenetname.co.uk
MD: Eddie Stevens

LEAF MUSIC PUBLISHING LTD
Reverb House, Bennett Street, London W4 2AH
T: 020 8747 0660 F: 020 8747 0880
Email: liam@leafsongs.com
Website: leafsongs.com
MD: Liam Teeling

MARKET SQUARE MUSIC
Market House, Market Square, Winslow, Bucks MK18 3AF
T: 01296 715228 F: 01296 715486
Email: msmpub@pmpr.co.uk
Adminstrator: Patrick Rob

MAXWOOD MUSIC LTD
Regent House, 1 Pratt Mews, London NW1 0AD
T: 020 7267 6899 F: 020 7267 6746
Email: partners@newman-and.co.uk
MD: Colin Newman

MCGUINNESS WHELAN
30-32 Sir John Rogersons Quay, Dublin 2, Ireland
T: +353 1 677 7330
F: +353 1 677 7276
Email: jenn@numb.ie
MD: Paul McGuinness

MCI MUSIC PUBLISHING LTD
4th Floor, Holden House, 57 Rathbone Place, London W1T 1JU
T: 020 7396 8899 F: 020 7470 6659
Email: info@mcimusic.co.uk
Creative Manager: James Bedbrook

MCS MUSIC LTD
(A Division of Music Copyright, Solutions plc), 32 Lexington Street, London W1F 0LQ
T: 020 7255 8777 F: 020 7255 8778
Email: info@mcsmusic.com
Website: mcsmusic.com

MEMNON MUSIC
Habib House, 3rd Floor, 9 Stevenson Square, Piccadilly, Manchester M1 1DB
T: 0161 237 3360 F: 0161 236 6717
Email: rudi@grayand.co.uk
Website: memnonentertainment.com
Director: Rudi Kidd

MEMORY LANE MUSIC LTD
Independent House, 54 Larkshall Rd, London E4 6PD
T: 020 8523 9000 F: 020 8523 8888
Email: erich@independentmusicgroup.com
Website: independentmusicgroup.com
CEO: Ellis Rich

MERINGUE PRODUCTIONS LTD
37 Church St, Twickenham, Middlesex TW1 3NR
T: 020 8744 2277 F: 020 8744 9333
Email: meringue@meringue.co.uk
Website: meringue.co.uk
Director: Lynn Earnshaw

METROPHONIC
Tithebarns, Tithebarns Lane, Send, Surrey GU23 7LE
T: 01483 225 226 F: 01483 479 606
Email: info@metrophonic.com
Website: metrophonic.com
MD: Brian Rawling

MIKE MUSIC LTD
Freshwater House, Outdowns, Effingham, Surrey KT24 5QR
T: 01483 281500 F: 01483 281502
Email: yellowbal@aol.com
MD: Mike Smith

MIKOSA MUSIC
9-10 Regent Square, London WC1H 8HZ
T: 020 7837 9648 F: 020 7837 9648
Email: mikosapanin@hotmail.com
MD: Mike Osapanin

MINDER MUSIC LTD
18 Pindock Mews, London W9 2PY
T: 020 7289 7281 F: 020 7289 2648
Email: songs@mindermusic.com
Website: mindermusic.com

MINISTRY OF SOUND MUSIC PUBLISHING LTD
103 Gaunt Street, London SE1 6DP
T: 020 7378 6528 F: 020 7403 5348
Email: publishing@ministryofsound.com
Website: ministryofsound.com
Publishing Manager: Tony Moss

MIX MUSIC LTD
PO Box 89, Slough, Berkshire SL1 6DQ
T: 01628 667124 F: 01628 605246
Email: info@dmcworld.com
Website: dmcworld.com
Business Affairs Mgr: Bud Nidjar

MOGGIE MUSIC LTD
101 Hazelwood Lane, London N13 5HQ
T: 020 8886 2801 F: 020 8882 7380
Email: artistes@halcarterorg.com
Website: halcarterorg.com
Owner: Hal Carter

MONUMENT MUSIC LTD
Creeting House, All Saints Road, Creeting St Mary, Ipswich, Suffolk IP6 8PR
T: 01449 723 244 F: 01449 726 067

Email: info@monumentmusic.co.uk
A&R Manager: Steve Lindsey

MOONROCK MUSIC PRODUCTIONS LTD
PO Box 883, Liverpool L69 4RH
T: 0151 922 5657 F: 0151 922 5657
Email: bstratt@mersinet.co.uk
Website: mersinet.co.uk
Publishing Manager: Billy Stratton

MOONSUNG MUSIC
PO Box 369, Glastonbury, Somerset BA6 8YN
T: 01749 831 674 F: 01749 831 674
Sheila Chandra

MORRISON BUDD MUSIC
1 Star Street, London W2 1QD
T: 020 7706 7304 F: 020 7706 8197
Email: morrison@powernet.co.uk
MD: Carol Smith

MOTHER MUSIC
30-32 Sir John Rogersons Quay, Dublin 2, Ireland
T: 00 353 1 677 7330
F: 00 353 1 677 7276
Email: jenn@numb.ie
MD: Paul McGuinness

MOVING SHADOW MUSIC
PO Box 2551, London SE1 2FH
T: 020 7252 2661 F: 0870 051 2594
Email: info@movingshadow.com
Website: movingshadow.com
MD: Rob Playford

MRM LTD
Cedar House, Vine Lane, Hillingdon, Middx UB10 0BX
T: 01895 251515 F: 01895 251616
Email: mail@mrmltd.co.uk
MD: Mark Rowles

MUIRHEAD MUSIC / IPA
Michelin House, 81 Fulham Road, London SW3 6RD
T: 020 7351 5167 F: 0870 136 3878
Email: info@muirheadmanagement.co.uk
Website: muirheadmanagement.co.uk
CEO: Dennis Muirhead

MUSIC HOUSE (INTERNATIONAL)
2nd Floor, 143 Charing Cross Road, London WC2H 0EH
T: 020 7434 9678 F: 020 7434 1470
Website: playmusichouse.com
Gen Mgr: Simon James

MUSIC LIKE DIRT
9 Bloomsbury Place, East Hill, Wandsworth, London SW18 2JB
T: 020 8877 1335 F: 020 8877 1335
Email: mld@bigworldpublishing.com
Website: bigworldpublishing.com
MD: Patrick Meads

MUSISCA PUBLISHING
34 Strand, Topsham, Exeter, Devon EX3 0AY
T: 01392 877737 F: 01453 751911
Email: musisca@printed-music.com
Website: printed-music.com/musisca
Prop: Philippe Oboussier

MUSIWORKS SERVICES LTD
The Old Boiler House, Brewery Courtyard, High St, Marlow, Bucks SL7 2FF
T: 01628 488808 F: 01628 890777
Email: mark@musiworks.com
Website: musiworks.com
Director: Mark Mumford

MUTE SONG
429 Harrow Road, London W10 4RE
T: 020 8964 2001 F: 020 8968 4977
Email: info@mutehq.co.uk
Website: mute.com
MD: Daniel Miller

MUZIKMEDIA PUBLISHING LTD
Haslemere, 40 Broomfield Road,
Henfield, W. Sussex BN5 9UA
T: 01273 491416 F: 01273 491417
Email: info@muzikmedia.co.uk
Website: muzikmedia.co.uk
Director: Robin Scott

NCOMPASS PUBLISHING
113 Chewton Rd, Walthamstow, London
E17 7DN
T: 07941 331181
Email: rich@ncompass.freeserve.co.uk
MD: Richard Rogers

NEW MUSIC ENTERPRISES
Meredale, Reach Lane, Heath And
Reach, Leighton Buzzard, Bedfordshire
LU7 0AL
T: 01525 237700 F: 01525 237700
Email: Pauldavis@newmusic28.freeserve.co.uk
Prop: Paul Davis

NILES PRODUCTIONS
34 Beaumont Rd, London W4 5AP
T: 020 8248 2157
Email: smiles@richardniles.demon.co.uk
Website: richardniles.com
Director: Richard Niles

19 MUSIC
Unit 33, Ransomes Dock, 35-37
Parkgate Road, London SW11 4NP
T: 020 7801 1919 F: 020 7801 1920
MD: Simon Fuller

NO KNOWN CURE PUBLISHING
45 Kings Road, Dover Court, Harwich,
Essex CO12 4DS
T: 07760 427306
MD: Mr TF McCarthy

NOISE OF SHADE
46 Spenser Rd, London SE24 0NR
T: 020 7274 6618 F: 020 7326 5464
Email: noise@charmenko.net
Website: charmenko.net
Mgr: Nick Hobbs

NOTTING HILL MUSIC (UK) LTD
Bedford House, 8B Berkeley Gardens,
London W8 4AP
T: 020 7243 2921 F: 020 7243 2894
Email: info@nottinghillmusic.com
MD: David Loader

NOVELLO & CO LTD
8-9 Frith Street, London W1D 3JB
T: 020 7434 0066 F: 020 7287 6329
Email: promotion@musicsales.co.uk
MD: James Rushton

NOWHERE PUBLISHING
30 Tweedholm Ave East, Walkerburn,
Peeblesshire EH43 6AR
T: 01896 870284
Email: michaelwild@btopenworld.com
MD: Michael Wild

OBELISK MUSIC
32 Ellerdale Road, London NW3 6BB
T: 020 7435 5255 F: 020 7431 0621
MD: Mr H Herschmann

OFF THE PEG SONGS
42 Winsford Gardens, Westcliff-on-Sea,
Essex SS0 0DP

T: 01702 390353 F: 01702 390355
Prop: Will Birch

ONLINE MUSIC
Unit 18, Croydon House, 1 Peall Road, Croydon, Surrey CR0 3EX
T: 020 8287 8585 F: 020 8287 0220
Email: publishing@onlinestudios.co.uk
Website: onlinestudios.co.uk
MD: Rob Pearson

OPAL MUSIC
Studio 1, 223A Portobello Rd, London W11 1LU
T: 020 7221 7239 F: 020 7792 1886
Email: opal-chant@dial.pipex.com
MD: Anthea Norman-Taylor

ORANGE SONGS LTD
1st Floor, 28 Denmark Street, London WC2H 8NJ
T: 020 7240 7696 F: 020 7379 3398
Email: cliff.cooper@omec.com
MD: Cliff Cooper

PALAN MUSIC PUBLISHING LTD
Greenland Place, 115-123 Bayham Street, London NW1 0AG
T: 020 7446 7439 F: 020 7446 7421
Email: chrisg@palan.com
Website: palan.com
A&R/Aquisitions Mgr: Chris Gray

PANAMA MUSIC LIBRARY
Sovereign House, 12 Trewartha Rd, Praa Sands, Penzance, Cornwall TR20 9ST
T: 01736 762826 F: 01736 763328
Email: panamus@aol.com
Website: panamamusic.co.uk
MD: Roderick Jones

PARTISAN SONGS
c/o Mute Song, 429 Harrow Road, London W10 4RE
T: 020 7357 8416 F: 020 8968 8437
Email: emusic.com
MD: Caroline Butler

PAUL RODRIGUEZ MUSIC LTD
61 Queen's Drive, London N4 2BG
T: 020 8802 5984 F: 020 8809 7436
Email: paul@paulrodriguezmus.demon.co.uk
MD: Paul Rodriguez

PEERMUSIC (IRELAND) LTD
The Peer House, 12 Lower Pembroke St, Dublin 2 Ireland
T: +353 1 662 9337
F: +353 1 662 9339
Email: Dublin@peermusic.com
Website: peermusic.com
MD: Darragh M Kettle

PEERMUSIC (UK)
Peer House, 8-14 Verulam Street, London WC1X 8LZ
T: 020 7404 7200 F: 020 7404 7004
Email: peermusic@peermusic.com
Website: peermusic.com
MD/European VP: Nigel Elderton

PERPETUITY MUSIC
21A Maury Rd, London N16 7BP
T: 020 7394 4493
Email: mowhock@aol.com
Website: fucdk.com
MD: Michael Gordon

PETERS EDITION
Hinrichsen House, 10-12 Baches Street, London N1 6DN
T: 020 7553 4000 F: 020 7490 4921

Email: sales@uk.edition-peters.com
Website: edition-peters.com
Marketing Manager: Linda Hawken

PLAN C MUSIC LTD
Covetous Corner, Hudnall Common, Little Gaddesden, Herts HP4 1QW
T: 01442 842851 F: 01442 842082
Email: christian@plancmusic.com
Website: plancmusic.com
MD: Christian Ulf-Hansen

PLANGENT VISIONS MUSIC LTD
27 Noel Street, London W1F 8GZ
T: 020 7734 6892 F: 020 7439 4613
Email: info@noelstreet.com
MD: Peter Barnes

PLUS MUSIC PUBLISHING
36 Follingham Court, Drysdale Place, London N1 6LZ
T: 020 7684 8594 F: 020 7684 8740
Proprietor: Desmond Chisholm

POP MUSIC
22 Newbank Towers, Salford, Manchester M3 7JZ
T: 0161 839 4366
Email: info@poprecordings.co.uk
Website: poprecordings.co.uk
Director: Martin Isherwood

PURE GROOVE MUSIC
679 Holloway Road, London N19 5SE
T: 020 7263 4660 F: 020 7263 9669
Email: puregroove@puregroove.co.uk
Website: puregroove.co.uk
Head of A&R: Mick Shiner

RAK PUBLISHING LTD
42-48 Charlbert St, London NW8 7BU
T: 020 7586 2012 F: 020 7722 5823
Email: rakpublishing@yahoo.com
General Manager: Nathalie Hayes

RANDM MUSIC
72 Marylebone Lane, London W1U 2PL
T: 020 7486 7458 F: 020 8467 6997
Email: roy@randm.co.uk
MDs: Roy Eldridge, Mike Andrews

REAL WORLD MUSIC LTD
Box Mill, Mill Lane, Box, Corsham, Wiltshire SN13 8PL
T: 01225 743188 F: 01225 744369
Email: publishing@realworld.co.uk
Website: realworld.co.uk/publishing
Publishing Manager: Rob Bozas

THE REALLY USEFUL GROUP
22 Tower St, London WC2H 9TW
T: 020 7240 0880 F: 020 7240 8977
Email: robinsond@reallyuseful.co.uk
Website: reallyuseful.com
Music Publishing Manager: David Robinson

REALLY WICKED PUBLISHING
8 Martin Dene, Bexleyheath, Kent DA6 8NA
T: 020 8301 2828 F: 020 8301 2424
Email: mholmes822@aol.com
Website: htdrecords.com
A&R Director: Barry Riddington

REDEMPTION PUBLISHING
516 Queslett Road, Great Barr, Birmingham B43 7EJ
T: 0121 605 4791 F: 0121 605 4791
Email: bhaskar@redemption.co.uk

Website: redemption.co.uk
MD: Bhaskar Dandona

RELIABLE SOURCE MUSIC
6 Kenrick Place, London WIU 6HD
T: 020 7486 9878 F: 020 7486 9934
Email: library@reliable-source.co.uk
Website: reliable-source.co.uk
MD: Dr Wayne Bickerton

REVOLVER MUSIC PUBLISHING
152 Goldthorn Hill, Penn, Wolverhampton, West Midlands WV2 3JA
T: 01902 345345 F: 01902 345155
Email: Paul.Birch@revolver-e.com
Website: revolvermusic.com
MD: Paul Birch

RG MUSIC PUBLISHING
2nd Floor, 98 White Lion St, London N1 9PF
T: 020 7278 5698 F: 020 7278 6009
Email: paula@rgrmusic.com
Website: rgrmusic.com
Professional Mgr: Paula Greenwood

RIGHT MUSIC
177 High Street, Harlesden, London NW10 4TE
T: 020 8961 3889 F: 020 8961 4620
Email: johnkaufman@totalise.co.uk
Directors: David Landau, John Kaufman

RITA (PUBLISHING) LTD
12 Pound Court, The Marld, Ashtead, Surrey KT21 1RN
T: 01372 276293 F: 01372 276328
Email: thebestmusicis@ritapublishing.com
Website: ritapublishing.com
MD: Ralph Norton

RIVERBOAT (UK) MUSIC
6 Abbeville Mews, 88 Clapham Park Road, London SW4 7BX
T: 020 7498 5252 F: 020 7498 5353
Email: phil@worldmusic.net
Website: worldmusic.net
MD: Phil Stanton

ROBERTON PUBLICATIONS
The Windmill, Wendover, Aylesbury, Buckinghamshire HP22 6JJ
T: 01296 623107 F: 01296 696536
Website: impulse-music.co.uk/roberton.htm
Proprietor: Kenneth Roberton

ROEDEAN MUSIC LTD
16-17 Grafton House, 2-3 Golden Sq, London W1F 9HR
T: 020 7437 1958 F: 020 7437 3852
Email: tony@tonyhallgroup.com
MD: Tony Hall

RONDOR MUSIC (LONDON) LTD
The Yacht Club, Chelsea Harbour, London SW10 0XA
T: 020 7349 4750 F: 020 7376 3670
Email: firstname.surname@umusic.com
MD: Richard Thomas

ROUGH TRADE PUBLISHING
81 Wallingford Rd, Goring, Reading, Berks RG8 0HL
T: 01491 873612 F: 01491 872744
Email: info@rough-trade.com
Website: rough-trade.com
MD: Matt Wilkinson

RYKOMUSIC LTD
329 Latimer Road, London W10 6RA
T: 020 8960 3311 F: 020 8960 4334
Email: info@rykodisc.co.uk

Website: rykomusic.com
GM: Paul Lambden

SANCTUARY MUSIC PUBLISHING LTD
Sanctuary House, 45-53 Sinclair Rd, London W14 0NS
T: 020 7602 6351 F: 020 7300 6650
Email: firstname.lastname@sanctuarygroup.com
Website: sanctuarygroup.com
Director of A&R: Jamie Arlon

SCO MUSIC
29 Oakroyd Avenue, Potters Bar, Hertfordshire EN6 2EL
T: 01707 651439 F: 01707 651439
Email: constantine@steveconstantine.freeserve.co.uk
MD: Steve Constantine

SEA DREAM MUSIC
Sandcastle Productions, PO Box 13533, London E7 0SG
T: 020 8534 8500
Email: sea.dream@virgin.net
Snr Partner: Simon Law

SERIOUS MUSIC
Bajonor House, 2 Bridge Street, Peel, Isle of Man IM5 1NB
T: 01624 844134 F: 01624 844135
Email: rwcc@tesco.net
Website: rwcc.com
Director: Candy Atcheson

SERIOUSLY GROOVY MUSIC LTD
3rd Floor, 28 D'Arblay Street, Soho, London W1F 8EW
T: 020 7439 1947 F: 020 7734 7540
Email: admin@seriouslygroovy.com
Website: seriouslygroovy.com
Director: Dave Holmes

SGO MUSIC PUBLISHING LTD
PO Box 34994, London SW6 6WF
T: 020 7385 9377 F: 020 7385 0372
Email: sgomusic@sgomusic.com
Website: sgomusic.com
MD: Stuart Ongley

SHADE FACTOR PRODUCTIONS LIMITED
4 Cleveland Square, London W2 6DH
T: 020 7402 6477 F: 020 7402 7144
Email: mail@shadefactor.com
Website: shadefactor.com
MD: Ann Symonds

SHALIT MUSIC
Cambridge Theatre, Seven Dials, London WC2H 9HU
T: 020 7379 3282 F: 020 7379 3238

Email: info@shalitglobal.com
MD: Jonathan Shalit

SHARP END MUSIC LTD
Grafton House, 2-3 Golden Square, London W1F 9HR
T: 020 7439 8442 F: 020 7434 3615
Email: sharpend2@aol.com
Director: Robert Lemon

SIGNIA MUSIC
20 Stamford Brook Avenue, London W6 0YD
T: 020 8846 9469 F: 020 8741 5152
Email: info@signia.com
Website: signiamusic.com
MD: Dee Harrington

SILVA SCREEN MUSIC PUBLISHERS
3 Prowse Place, London NW1 9PH
T: 020 7428 5500 F: 020 7482 2385

Email: info@silvascreen.co.uk
Website: silvascreen.co.uk
MD: Reynold D'Silva

SINGLE MINDED MUSIC PUBLISHING
11 Cambridge Court, 210 Shepherds Bush Rd, London W6 7NJ
T: 0870 011 3748 F: 0870 011 3749
Email: tony@singleminded.com
Website: singleminded.com
MD: Tony Byrne

SKRATCH MUSIC PUBLISHING
Skratch Music House, 81 Crabtree Lane, London SW6 6LW
T: 020 7381 8315 F: 020 7385 6785
Email: les@skratchmusic.co.uk
Website: passionmusic.co.uk
Head of Publishing: Les McCutcheon

SONGLINES LTD
PO Box 20206, London NW1 7FF
T: 020 7284 3970 F: 020 7485 0511
Email: doug@songlines.demon.co.uk
MD: Doug D'Arcy

SONGMATIC MUSIC PUBLISHING
PO Box 562, London N10 3BR
T: 020 7482 5036
Email: poppy@poptel.org
Website: poppyrecords.com
GM: Jason Clark

SONIC ARTS NETWORK
Jerwood Space, 171 Union Street, London SE1 0LN
T: 020 7928 7337
Email: darryl@sonicartsnetwork.org
Website: sonicartsnetwork.org
Exec Director: Phil Hallett

SONY/ATV MUSIC PUBLISHING
13 Great Marlborough Street, London W1F 7LP
T: 020 7911 8200 F: 020 7911 8600
Email: firstname_lastname@uk.sonymusic.com
MD: Charlie Pinder

SOUNDS LIKE A HIT LTD
Studio 222, Canalot Production Studios, 222 Kensal Rd, London W10 5BN
T: 020 8962 0000 F: 020 8962 0011
Email: steve@soundslikeahit.com
Website: soundslikeahit.com
Director: Steve Crosby

SPECTRUM MUSIC
7 Brunswick Close, Thames Ditton, Surrey KT7 0EU
T: 020 8398 1450 F: 020 8398 1450
Email: smd.music@virgin.net
Director: Al Dickinson

SPLIT MUSIC
13 Sandys Road, Worcester WR1 3HE
T: 01905 29809 F: 01905 613023
Email: split.music@virgin.net
Website: splitmusic.com
MD: Chris Warren

SPRINT MUSIC LTD
High Jarmany Farm, Jarmany Hill, Barton St David, Somerton,Somerset TA11 6DA
T: 01458 851010 F: 01458 851029
Email: info@sprintmusic.co.uk
Website: sprintmusic.co.uk
Consultant: John Ratcliff

STANZA MUSIC
11 Victor Road, Harrow, Middlesex HA2 6PT

T: 020 8863 2717 F: 020 8863 8685
Email: bill.ashton@virgin.net
Website: nyjo.org.uk
Director: Bill Ashton

STAR STREET MUSIC LTD
PO Box 375, Chorleywood, Herts
WD3 5ZZ
T: 01923 440608
Email: StarstreetUK@aol.com
Website: Starstreetmusic.com
MD: Nick Battle

STATE MUSIC
6 Kenrick Place, London WIU 6HD
T: 020 7486 9878 F: 020 7486 9934
Email: songs@statemusic.co.uk
MD: Wayne Bickerton

STEELWORKS SONGS
218 Canalot Studios, 222 Kensal Road,
London W10 5BN
T: 020 8960 4443 F: 020 8960 9889
Email: steelworks@frdm.demon.co.uk
MD: Martyn Barter

STICKYSONGS
Great Oaks Granary, Kennel Lane,
Windlesham, Surrey GU20 6AA
T: 01276 479255 F: 01276 479255
Email: stickysong@aol.com
MD: Peter Gosling

STILL WORKING MUSIC
Covetous Corner, Hudnall Common,
Little Gaddesden, Herts HP4 1QW
T: 01442 842039 F: 01442 842082
Email: mhaynes@orbison.com
Website: orbison.com
European Consultant: Mandy Haynes

STOP DROP & ROLL MUSIC LTD
Colbury Manor, Jacobs Gutter Lane,
Eling, Southampton SO40 9FY
T: 0845 658 5006 F: 0845 658 5009
Email: frontdesk@stopdroproll.com
Website: stopdroproll.com
Publishing Executive: Howard Lucas

STUDIO MUSIC COMPANY
PO Box 19292, London NW10 9WP
T: 020 8830 0110 F: 020 8451 6470
Email: sales@studio-music.co.uk
Ptnr: Stan Kitchen

SUB ROSA
13 Cotswold Mews, 30 Battersea
Square, London SW11 3RA
T: 020 7978 7888 F: 020 7978 7808
Email: auto@automan.co.uk
MD: Jerry Smith

SUBLIME MUSIC PUBLISHING
77 Preston Drove, Brighton, East
Sussex BN1 6LD
T: 01273 560605 F: 01273 560606
Email: info@sublimemusic.co.uk
Website: sublimemusic.co.uk
MD: Patrick Spinks

SUGARSTAR MUSIC LTD
Park View House, 64 Murray St, York
YO24 4JA
T: 08456 448424 F: 0709 222 8681
Email: info@sugarstar.com
Website: sugarstar.com
MD: Mark J. Fordyce

SUN-PACIFIC MUSIC (LONDON) LTD
PO Box 5, Hastings, E. Sussex
TN34 IHR
T: 01424 721196 F: 01424 717704

Email: aquarius.lib@clara.net
MD: Gilbert Gibson

SYLVANTONE MUSIC
17 Allerton Grange Way, Leeds, West Yorkshire LS17 6LP
T: 0113 268 7788 F: 0709 235 9333
Email: sylvantone@hotmail.com
Website: countrymusic.org.uk./tony-goodacre/index.html
Prop: Tony Goodacre

TABITHA MUSIC LTD
39 Cordery Road, Exeter, Devon EX2 9DJ
T: 01392 499889 F: 01392 498068
Email: graham@tabithamusic.fsnet.co.uk
Website: eyespyonline.net
MD: Graham Sclater

TELEVISION MUSIC LTD
Yorkshire Television, TV Centre, Leeds, West Yorkshire LS3 1JS
T: 0113 243 8283 F: 0113 222 7166
Email: sue.clark@granadamedia.com
Sue Clark

TEMA INTERNATIONAL
151 Nork Way, Banstead, Surrey SM7 1HR
T: 01737 219607 F: 01737 219609
Email: music@tema-intl.demon.co.uk
Website: temadance.com Production Manager: Amanda Harris

TEMPLE RECORDS & PUBLISHING
Shillinghill, Temple, Midlothian EH23 4SH
T: 01875 830328 F: 01875 830392
Email: robin@templerecords.co.uk
Website: templerecords.co.uk
Prop: Robin Morton

THAMES MUSIC
445 Russell Court, Woburn Place, London WC1H 0NJ
T: 020 7837 6240 F: 020 7833 4043
MD: C W Adams

THREE 4 MUSIC PUBLISHING
c/o DWL (Dave Woolf Ltd), 19a Goodge Street, London W1T 2PH
T: 020 7436 5529 F: 020 7637 8776
Email: dwoolf@dircon.co.uk
MD: Dave Woolf

3MV MUSIC PUBLISHING
81-83 Weston Street, London SE1 3RS
T: 020 7378 8866 F: 020 7378 8855
Email: guyv@theknowledge.com
Website: 3mvmusic.com
MD: Guy Van Steene

TIDY TRAX
Hawthorne House, Fitzwilliam St, Parkgate, Rotherham, South Yorks S62 6EP
T: 01709 710022 F: 01709 523141
Email: firstname.lastname@tidy.com
Website: tidy.com
MD: Andy Pickles

TIMBUKTU MUSIC
(see V2 Music Publishing Ltd.)
MD: Mark Bond

TKO MUSIC GROUP LTD
PO Box 130, Hove, E. Sussex BN3 6QU
T: 01273 550088 F: 01273 540969
Email: management@tkogroup.com
Website: tkogroup.com
Creative Manager: Warren Heal

TMR PUBLISHING
PO Box 3775, London SE18 3QR
T: 020 8316 4690 F: 020 8316 4690
Email: marc@wufog.freeserve.co.uk
Website: wufog.freeserve.co.uk
MD: Marc Bell

TOWNHILL MUSIC
Ty Cefn, Rectory Road, Canton, Cardiff
CF5 1QL
T: 029 2022 7993 F: 029 2034 1622
Email: huwwilliams@townhillmusic.com
Director: Huw Williams

TOYBOX INTERNATIONAL LTD
2nd Floor, 12 Mercer St, London
W2H 9QD
T: 020 7240 8848 F: 020 7240 8864
Email: toyboxint@aol.com
MD: Lenny Zakatek

TRACK MUSIC
PO Box 107, South Godstone, Redhill,
Surrey RH9 8YS
T: 01342 892178 F: 01342 893411
Email: ig@btconnect.com
Website: trackrecords.tv
MD: Ian Grant

TRAX ON WAX MUSIC PUBLISHERS
Glenmundar House, Ballyman Road,
Bray, Co. Wicklow, Ireland
T: +353 86 257 6244
F: +353 1 216 4395
Email: picket@iol.ie
Director: Deke O'Brien

TRIAD PUBLISHING
PO Box 150, Chesterfield S40 0YT
T: 0870 746 8478
Email: traid@themanagementcompany.biz
Website: themanagementcompany.biz
MD: Tony Hedley

TRIPLE A PUBLISHING LTD
GMC Studio, Hollingbourne, Kent
ME17 1UQ
T: 01622 880599 F: 01622 880020
Email: publishing@triple-a.uk.com
Website: triple-a.uk.com
CEO: Terry Armstrong

TRUELOVE MUSIC
19F Tower Workshops, Riley Rd,
London SE1 3DG
T: 020 7252 2900 F: 020 7252 2890
Email: music@truelove.co.uk
Website: truelove.co.uk A&R: Bob

TSUNAMI SOUNDS LTD
The Gables, Avenue Road, Cranleigh,
Surrey GU6 7LE
T: 01483 506114 F: 01483 506113
Email: info@tsunami-sounds.com
Website: tsunami-sounds.com
Director: Ken Easter

TUMI MUSIC (EDITORIAL) LTD
8-9 New Bond St. Place, Bath,
Somerset BA1 1BH
T: 01225 464736 F: 01225 444870
Email: info@tumimusic.com
Website: tumimusic.com
MD: Mo Fini

UNITED MUSIC PUBLISHERS LTD
42 Rivington Street, London EC2A 3BN
T: 020 7729 4700 F: 020 7739 6549
Email: info@ump.co.uk
Website: ump.co.uk
MD: Shirley Ranger

UNIVERSAL EDITION (LONDON)
38 Eldon Way, Paddock Wood,
Kent TN12 6BE
T: 01892 833422 F: 01892 836038
Website: uemusic.co.uk
Sales/Mktng Mgr: Andrew Knowles

UNIVERSAL MUSIC PUBLISHING LTD ELSINORE HOUSE, 77 FULHAM PALACE ROAD, LONDON W6 8JA
T: 020 8752 2600 F: 020 8752 2601
Email: firstname.lastname@umusic.com
MD & Exec VP Europe: Paul Connolly

URBAN G
PO Box: 45821, London E11 3YZ
T: 07904 255244
Email: urbangospel@hotmail.com
Website: urbangospel.com
Head of A&R: P Mac

URBANSTAR MUSIC
Global House, 92 De Beauvoir Rd,
London N1 4EN
T: 020 7288 2239 F: 020 7288

V2 MUSIC PUBLISHING LTD
131 Holland Park Avenue, London
W11 4UT
T: 020 7471 3000 F: 020 7471 3110
Email: betul.al-bassam@v2music.com
MD: Mike Sefton

VANESSA MUSIC CO
35 Tower Way, Dunkeswell, Devon
EX14 4XH
T: 01404 891598
MD: Don Todd MBE

VAUGHAN WILLIAMS MEMORIAL LIBRARY (SOUND ARCHIVE)
Cecil Sharp House, 2 Regent's Park Rd,
Camden, London NW1 7AY
T: 020 7485 2206 F: 020 7284 0534
Email: info@efdss.org
Website: efdss.org
Publications Manager: Felicity Greenland

VERY POSITIVE MUSIC
St Peter's Chambers, St Peter's Street,
Huddersfield, West Yorks HD1 1RA
T: 01484 452013 F: 01484 435861
Email: info@beaumontstreet.co.uk
Website: beaumontstreet.co.uk
Professional Manager: Katherine
Canoville

VITAL SPARK MUSIC
1 Waterloo, Breakish, Isle Of Skye
IV42 8QE
T: 01471 822484 F: 01471 822952
Email: chris@vitalspark.demon.co.uk
CEO: Chris Harley

WALK ON THE WILD SIDE
8 Deronda Road, London SE24 9BG
T: 020 8674 7990 F: 020 8671 5548
MD: Dave Massey

WALL OF SOUND MUSIC
Office 2, 9 Thorpe Close, London
W10 5XL
T: 020 8969 1144 F: 020 8969 1155
Email: general@wallofsound.uk.com
Website: wallofsound.net
MD: Mark Jones

WARNER/CHAPPELL MUSIC LTD
The Warner Building, 28 Kensington
Church St, London W8 4EP
T: 020 7938 0000 F: 020 7368 2777
Email: firstname.surname@warnerchappell.com
Website: warnerchappell.com

1 2 3 4 5 6 7 8 9 10 11 12 13 14 15

WATER MUSIC PRODUCTIONS
6 Erskine Road, London NW3 3AJ
T: 020 7722 3478 F: 020 7722 6605
Email: splash@watermusic.co.uk
Producer: Tessa Lawlor

JEFF WAYNE MUSIC GROUP
Oliver House, 8-9 Ivor Place, London
NW1 6BY
T: 020 7724 2471 F: 020 7724 6245
Email: info@jeffwaynemusic.com Group
Director: Jane Jones

WEBSONGS
The Troupe Studio, 106 Thetford Road,
New Malden, Surrey KT3 5DZ
T: 020 8949 0928 F: 020 8949 0928
Email: kip@websongs.co.uk
Website: websongs.co.uk
MD: Kip Trevor

WELSH MEDIA MUSIC
Gorwelion, Llanfynydd, Carmarthen,
Dyfed SA32 7TG
T: 01558 668525 F: 01558 668750
Email: dpierce@welshmediamusic.f9.co.uk
MD: Dave Pierce

WESTBURY MUSIC LTD
Suite B, 2 Tunstall Road, London
SW9 8DA
T: 020 7733 5400 F: 020 7733 4449
Email: enquiries@westburymusic.net
Website: westburymusic.net
MD: Caroline Robertson

WINCHESTER MUSIC LTD
3 Sovereign Court, Graham Street,
Birmingham B1 3JR
T: 0121 233 9192 F: 0121 233 0135
Email: david.alldridge@winchesterent.co.uk
Website: winchesterfilms.com
Music Supervisor: David Alldridge

WINDSWEPT MUSIC (LONDON) LTD
Hope House, 40 St Peter's Road,
London W6 9BD
T: 020 8237 8400 F: 020 8741 0825
Email: firstname@windswept.co.uk
Website: windsweptpacific.com

WIPE OUT MUSIC LTD
PO Box 1NW, Newcastle-Upon-Tyne
NE99 1NW
T: 0191 266 3802 F: 0191 266 6073
Email: johnesplen@btconnect.com
Manager: John Esplen

WORD MUSIC
9 Holdom Avenue, Bletchley, Milton
Keynes, Buckinghamshire MK1 1QR
T: 01908 364210 F: 01908 645141
Email: grahamword@aol.com
Website: premieronline.co.uk
MD: Graham Williams

YOSHIKO PUBLISHING
Estate Office, Great Westwood, Old
House Lane, King's Langley,
Hertfordshire WD4 9AD
T: 01923 261545 F: 01923 261546
Email: yoouchi@globalnet.co.uk
MD: Yoshiko Ouchi

ZOMBA MUSIC PUBLISHERS
Zomba House, 165-167 High Rd,
Willesden, London NW10 2SG
T: 020 8459 8899 F: 020 8830 2801
Email: firstname.lastname@zomba.co.uk
Website: zomba.co.uk
MD: Steven Howard

HIGHLY RECOMMENDED INDEPENDENT PUBLISHERS

Carlin Music Cooperation

MCS

Peer Music

Windswept

1

2

3

4

5

6

7

8

9

10

11

12

13

14

15

MARKETING & PROMOTION

WHAT IS THE ROLE OF THE PROMOTER?

Marketing in the music business is probably more competitive than anywhere else. If you're the marketing manager for a baked beans company, you don't have to launch new products every week, nor worry about hundreds of new competitors each year. Like opening movies, **if you don't get it right in the first week, you are finished and like movies, everyone knows the figures during that week, and so there's nowhere to hide.**

Although quick impact and mass exposure is essential to make a single a hit, it's only ever a minimum requirement. Marketing in the true sense is a failure if it doesn't manage to position the artist's desired image and capture the right audience's imagination.

THE BUSINESS LIVES ON HYPE

Music is the home of hype. It's fuelled by continually launching new bands and new albums. To the public this hype seems completely random, but those behind it know differently. Every major album launch is planned and agonised over by a large team of specialists and their expertise backed by increasing levels of investment by the major labels. However, even in this part of the business the majors dominate many of the available marketing channels and try to use their muscle to control the hype.

BUILDING A BRAND

Too many corporate marketing executives chase exposure without understanding that their artist is a brand and needs to be created with as much ingenuity as the music they make. You can't build a brand unless you understand it intimately. **Beware of marketing executives, pluggers and press officers in major labels that treat artists like products on a production line. They'll want to fit you into a neat box** like R&B or pop and then press the right button and activate one of their tried and trusted marketing and promotional plans.

Good marketing is a team process. The artist or band has to be central to everything. Too many newly signed artists neglect this area. They're too busy finishing off their first album in the studio to attend the early strategy meetings when the key decisions that determine the campaign are being set. You must remember you are a brand and brands need to be managed carefully or they die. If you had a baby, would you be happy to leave it in the care of many record executives? Exactly, don't do it to your brand.

Branding requires attention to detail. Just as we encourage you to find a distinct voice and work with a good producer to create your own sound, it's important to define your own style. If you're an artist, this needs to come from inside, that expresses the real you, because the public can always spot a fake. Of course if you're a manufactured pop entertainer, packaged to pieces, forget your own style – follow your manager, he probably created you.

If you can't communicate and define your brand, don't complain if your marketing programme isn't to your liking. Nobody can be expected to know telepathically what your brand is. That's why marketing companies and advertising agencies in the food and drink industries spend so long defining their brands, with lots of pretentious terminology like brand essence and brand frame. You don't need to swallow a business book, but you do need to let people know simply and clearly what you are and what you are not.

Write it down. Decide where the boundaries are. What are you comfortable and uncomfortable doing? Why are you different, and why do your fans like to come to your gigs and buy your records?

MARKETING AN ARTIST AS A BRAND

Every representation of the brand needs to reflect the brand. From the artist logo, to the CD cover, to the live set to the video promo. It's no coincidence that the artists with the longest careers are the most 'hands on' when it comes to marketing their image. Think Madonna, Bowie, the Stones, even Kylie. Their images change over time, but their attitude doesn't, nor does their fixation with every piece of their projected brand image.

Behind this marketing there are exceptional graphic artists, stylists and promo directors. From Brian Eatwell who art-directed the most famous Beatles films in the Sixties like *Help!*, to Roger Deane who defined record covers in the Seventies to Jamie Reid who created the graphics of punk to modern promo directors, music marketing has attracted some of the world's greatest artists. So it should.

The Ministry of Sound is not an artist, but it's virtually everything else from venue to label, and most of all it is a brand. Jamie Palumbo understood early on that it was possible to brand a whole music genre, and did. Then he proved that if you have a strong brand you can extend it into virtually anything as long as you understand your target market.

Huge multinational brands understand the power of music brands. That's why Pepsi signs up megastars and Mastercard sponsors awards ceremonies. Ministry of Sound is interesting because, unlike other labels, it is more famous than its artists. With the exception of Motown and perhaps Island, it's one of the few label brands that have built a consumer brand.

So what if you're not Madonna, Bowie or the Stones?

So what. If anything you have to be even more obsessive about marketing. Your fans are your fans because you offer them something different, something they can identify with. But like all relationships they do not want their artists to be weak and sycophantic. Artists need to have a strong image and attitude.

Record labels are increasingly looking for artists who haven't just produced a highly finished demo, but also have created a clearly defined image. **In the twenty-first century all artists have to be marketers to attract attention and do the right record deal.**

WHY ISN'T MARKETING BETTER IN THE MUSIC BUSINESS?

Although there are exceptions, the general standard of marketing in the business is declining. Short-term pressures have built distrust and a lack of interest in strategic marketing. A good example of distrust is the relationship between in house marketing and promotion and 'plugging' companies. There is a common distrust of pluggers because they seem to collect £2,000 a month from ten clients and although they get bonuses for getting on playlists they appear only to push the easiest tracks or the ones from their latest clients. They don't make it to the main playlist 70% of the time, but there's a continual suspicion from the labels that the pluggers haven't tried hard enough.

When you talk to young smart pluggers you begin to realise that labels often have unrealistic expectations and don't give pluggers enough ammunition to do their jobs. Good marketers find an angle to get exposure, they don't expect to get it by pushing someone and paying them a bonus.

However many labels will argue their case, too many tracks and albums are marketed before they're ready or when they're just not good enough. No amount of spend can paper over a bad decision or a bland album. Too many bands have pressure put on them to finish quickly in the studio, resulting in too little time to properly think through the marketing properly. Most people we talk to point to a lack of communication between the artist and the label, and in turn between the label and outside agencies such as pluggers, for bad marketing and promotion. Once you lose your faith in what you're marketing, you might as well be selling baked beans.

THE FIVE Ps: WHO'S WHO IN MARKETING AND PROMOTION

1. PUBLICISTS

A good publicist can be invaluable to an artist. You have to be successful enough to afford one of your own, or lucky enough to be with a label that has a good in house one. The best have experience in both journalism and the business. They have to be discreet and totally trustworthy, because they will be your mouthpiece to the media. They have to be brilliant at spotting an angle to make a story or a great picture. The best can take the driest bio or box of contact sheets and find a 'hook' for a media story.

Publicists often do more than just find ways of communicating a story. Increasingly they're involved in creating an artist's image. They often have a say in the visual image of the artist that needs to be projected in a photo shoot, promo, or live performance. In this way the publicist can win much more of the artist's trust than a record executive.

2. PRESS OFFICERS

These are usually employed in house. While publicists have a broader role in terms of the whole image and public projection, press officers are more focused in terms of taking a brief and getting maximum exposure with the bands in the media. But there is a huge overlap. The real difference is that publicists are more concerned with individual clients and their longer term image, while press officers are more about the label's interests, work across all artists and often don't look past the specific activity they are concerned with, e.g. an album launch. Cynics may say the only difference is publicists get out more and hang out with artists, so are usually more charming and better looking, but we couldn't possibly comment.

3. PLUGGERS

Without pluggers radio and TV stations would just feature the same old bands and music. Really their job is the same as press officers, except that they're trying to get publicity for their clients on broadcast media rather than press.

Because broadcast media is so much more powerful than press in building the impact and awareness that makes a hit, they are better paid and have to deliver against higher expectations.

Pluggers can be employed in or out of house, although the best are independent. They have a tough job. It's impossible for most of the singles plugged to get played on the key stations, Radio I or MTV, because there just aren't enough slots for the number of potential hit records being made. Generally this is more of a face-to-face job than in the press, as it's much more than just sending out a press release.

4. PROMO DIRECTORS

Since the birth of MTV, promo directors have never looked back. Videos can cost anything from £20,000 to £100,000, although some videos have cost even more. Michael Jackson's 'Thriller' video in the '80s had a feature-film-type budget, but then he did sell quite a few albums.

The right promo is critical to secure the right airplay on the TV stations like MTV. For a breaking band it's even more crucial because it's going to establish the band's style and image in the minds of the public. For pop acts they are probably as important as the song itself. Kylie's the best example: she does video like nobody else.

Promo directors often have to pitch a treatment or storyboard to the label. They work with a producer and the shoot itself takes one or two days. The shoot will involve a stylist, who will be key to making the artist's look work.

Promos are probably the most dangerous medium for a new band. Never trust it to turn out right. Once it's in the can it's too late. Never do anything you're uncomfortable with. It's easy to look stupid and difficult to be cool. Like your producer, directors have to understand you, your vision and your music if they're going to make it all come to life on film. If you feel they don't, make sure you sit them down long enough to make them understand. Remember it's easier to make changes at treatment stage, than in the editing studio.

5. PRODUCT MANAGERS

For our final P we've cheated slightly: we mean marketing managers and directors too. They are important as they are the third part of the triangle that forms the artist's inner circle, along with the manager and A&R.

Good marketing people understand both the artist's unique attributes and the profile and attitudes of their target market. It's important to understand whom the artist wants to target and work out what's going to appeal to them. It sounds like common sense, but many times they get it wrong. Lazy marketing just tries to get exposure and doesn't create a distinctive image, or brand.

Marketing people have to understand the media. They need to know which publications, posters or TV to use to reach the audience. Increasingly new media is important, like viral marketing online, or creative stunts and ambient ideas. We believe that compared with political campaign marketing, music marketing plays it much too safe. Political PR is continually using stunts and clever photo opportunities to get their message across, so why can't music marketing do it better?

As in all types of marketing, there needs to be better coordination between all different types of promotion from plugging, PR, promo video, to paid-for advertising and online. Somehow the huge machine of the major label keeps these too compartmentalised and the good marketing executive manages to pull all this together in a coherent strategy.

SELF-PROMOTION

Just because you can't get on to Kiss FM or *CD:UK* and can't afford a heavyweight marketing campaign doesn't mean you can't put together an effective marketing campaign for your unsigned band. You have two things going for you that most smug marketing executives don't – ingenuity and intelligence. They're worth more than a fat budget.

GUERRILLA MARKETING

Ironically huge multinational companies have just discovered guerrilla marketing, and it's the buzzword among their brightest young marketing executives. All it means is that you break with convention and find ways of marketing and promotion at street level, not with national marketing. It relies on non-traditional advertising. It might use graffiti or stickers on lamp posts, or perhaps a projection onto a building at night. Whatever it takes to cut through the fug of boring advertising.

This is exactly what you need to promote your band. Start with the basics. Design a logo and a strong look, so whether it's spray painted on a wall or on a club flyer, it stands out and is memorable. Think about the graphic images that stick in everyone's minds: the graphic image of Che Guevara, the cover of *Tubular Bells*, the Nike swoosh, they all have a power and simplicity that get under your skin. Don't make it too fussy, or like it's been seen before. If you get it right you've saved yourself £1 million already. That's why a blue chip company will pay a design company to develop a corporate logo.

The next thing you need is a press release – something to send out to promoters, venues and local press, radio and more – a 'hook' to make people want to book you or write about you. It might be somewhere you've played, someone you've supported or something unique about a member of the band, maybe a background of overcoming the odds – you work it out.

Make the release upbeat. Add some good lyrics if you've got any and make sure you put in all the right information, like website, contact details, where you're playing next. Remember, words are not enough. You need pictures. The sort that give an impression of your music and your act. You need to think of how they're going to be used. A newspaper or magazine is more likely to do an article if they have an interesting picture.

If you can make a record in your bedroom you can make a video too. If you can get hold of a DV camera, you can shoot to broadcast quality. There are enough new digital TV stations or websites that stream video to make it worthwhile, plus it's a great calling card for a promoter (soon you'll be able to send it via your mobile phone) and even a small indie label. If you can't do it find a friend who can, there's always someone in a post-production studio, who fancies himself or herself as a director – grab them.

HOW DOES A GUERRILLA CAMPAIGN WORK?

It's about making your presence felt where your fans and potential fans hang out. It could be the street or the Internet. By associating your message with places that your fans think of as their own, you show you're part of their world and understand them.

Owning the street can be about stickering or flysheeting or it could be about the coolest people wearing your T-shirt, or the coolest bar having your poster on their door. Some big brands have shown how it should be done. Sony Play Station spray-painted pavements with stencilled messages, and to publicise Sony's film *Godzilla*, Saatchi & Saatchi bought smashed-up cars from scrapyards and parked them in the street with yellow tape round them saying 'Godzilla', as if the monster itself had stepped on them. It didn't cost much except lots of creativity.

It's worth thinking about a cheap teaser campaign. Sometimes it's best to build up an anticipation that something's happening. Maybe stickering your graphic everywhere in your neighbourhood will give you a familiarity before your flyers hit the street.

Genius marketers from the past are worth considering. Malcolm McLaren, probably the most controversial and successful, understood the publicity potential of having your own distinctive fans. The Sex Pistols were always accompanied by the Bromley Contingent, the most bizarre-looking collection of fans. Sue Cat Woman was the original punk cat, and Siouxsie, later of the Banshees, was a goth before it had been invented. It probably helped that Vivienne Westwood made their clothes, but the Bromley Contingent was a great form of guerrilla marketing. McLaren realised that when you manage to get exposure you have to exploit it for all it's worth, whether it's swearing on TV or getting arrested on a river boat. If it suits, go for it – ruffle a few middle-aged, middle-class feathers. **Music is too nice these days.**

Behaving as if you're bigger and more successful is a classic market tactic and works just as well for an unsigned band. Build a website, make the band look established. Get your friends to review your last gig. Load it with great photos, and sell some merchandise.

Don't wait to do a deal to design merchandise. T-shirt printing shops will print a few shirts. Get postcards printed with a stunning picture and your website details. Get the best-looking girls (and boys) to wear your T-shirt to other people's gigs and the best bars.

The Sex Pistols wouldn't have been the Sex Pistols without Westwood. Get to know someone at art or fashion college, or someone who wants to be, to design you some great clothes and a look for the stage. Get your fans wearing them. See if you can develop one iconic T-shirt or other fashion item that will make your fans instantly recognisable, like the Oasis haircut. Don't be scared to think up a motto or a phrase to go on everything. Not enough bands do it, but it works, like Girl Power. Building this crowd and making them yours will do more than anything else to create buzz. It starts a momentum that convinces promoters and venue owners that you're going to be the next big thing. It will set you apart.

Get sponsorship. It might be your local bar. They can pay for your petrol and your merchandising, in return for a certain number of free gigs. There's no instruction manual so you have to invent it.

Get into the national music press. Send them your brilliant press pack and promo and tell them your tour dates; you'll probably get a mention. Target one music journalist, send him or her your stuff, invite them to gigs – they won't come but you're slowly seeping into their consciousness. Then try the flattery approach. Write them a letter and say you think what they write is brilliant, quote examples and say you would like some advice about the business. Either try to establish a letter relationship first or ask if you can come to see the paper and have a coffee. Remember, everybody's vain and love a chance to show off, even hard-bitten journalists or radio DJs.

This is a 'leapfrogging' strategy. It means that whatever stage you're at, you exceed expectations. So if you're an unsigned band starting out, people don't expect you to have great merchandise, the best-looking, weirdest fan base, an interesting promo, and your logo sprayed on every available space. A&R won't expect it, but might like it, and if your music isn't too bad they'll think they've found the latest street thing … good for them.

TIPS FOR NEWCOMERS

- Never work a record/artist you don't like.
- Always under-promise and over-deliver.
- Treat all your contacts equally.
- Eat, breathe, sleep music.
- Don't confine yourself to London – get out and around the UK.
- Be honest with your feedback to clients; negative reactions are as important as positive reactions.

THE VIEW FROM WITHIN

JODIE DALMEDA – INDEPENDENT PR CONSULTANT

Jodie was previously Head of Press at Arista, overseeing publicity across the whole label, working with artists from Pink and Whitney Houston to P Diddy.

How do you put together a press strategy for a client?
It depends on the artist, the type of music and audience you're targeting. Different magazines and papers will impact sales depending on genre. However, it's usually very important to get the support of the relevant underground publications before moving into the mainstream to establish a strong fan base. In terms of establishing an artist's credibility the style magazines have a powerful role to play, especially *The Face*, *iD*, *Dazed and Confused*, *Straight No Chaser* and of course *Q Magazine*.

Give us an example of one of your most successful campaigns.
For me the success of a campaign is not how many covers or column inches you secure, it's about breaking ground and getting covers and features in magazines you wouldn't expect. It's about being creative and changing perceptions and prejudices. Sean 'P Diddy' Combs was one of my most successful campaigns. The challenge of working with such a high-profile artist is securing time for interviews and photo shoots. This campaign saw P Diddy grace the cover of *Vogue* alongside Naomi Campbell shot by Mario Testino as the first black man to appear on a cover of *Vogue* magazine. I secured covers in the urban and music press, as well as the *Telegraph* magazine, and features running in *FHM*, *Glamour*, *NME* and teen press.

What is your experience of working in the music industry?
There's always pressure to have successful campaigns and a press person is always working with many artists at one time. When working with an artist there's always a certain amount of unpredictability even though you may plan for certain factors. With the recent mergers and staff cutbacks many people are doing the work of two people.

The sad thing about the record industry is the lack of resources at the major labels to develop new talent. The independents are trying to address this, and are in tune with the talents they are nurturing. The fact that the majors are in trouble is only change, and change is necessary for progress and growth.

Tell us about Future Youth and the Music Bus project.
This aims to inspire and empower young people through music. It is aimed at young people from inner cities and uses music to engage and enthuse them to do more with their life. I feel passionately that music can have a positive impact on people's lives. It's the soundtrack of our lives. Personally I have been inspired by many artists and their music and lyrics, as much today as when I was young.

BRAD LAZARUS – LM2

Brad Lazarus is in his late twenties. He is one of a new breed of music entrepreneurs. He runs a management and promotions company (LM2). Before setting it up, he was at Nonstop Promotions where he helped break many high-profile bands.
We looked after Badly Drawn Boy after he had put together his first single. He was always a strange one to look after. Very wisely his management restricted his TV exposure in the early days. They were able to do this and still have hits, because he could always get national radio exposure. My strategy for placing him on TV was only to place him on shows that would showcase his talent, especially as a live performer. So this meant that I arranged for him to play an acoustic version of his single on the Pepsi Chart Show. There was just him and a grand piano. It worked brilliantly. The impact of a performance like that can be brilliant. It was fantastic and set him apart from all the other acts on the show who were performing run-of-the-mill stuff. Later we put him on *Later with Jools Holland*, which he did lots of times.

Saying no to a TV show must be completely the opposite of the normal way you work as a plugger?

In terms of how we sold him to the media, it was more a case of having to tell producers that he wasn't going to be able to do their show. The trick was to be able to manage the process while maintaining relationships with the producers for the future when I would want to place an act. In this situation it's easy for a TV plugger to make more enemies than friends if they are not careful.

What are the biggest pressures of the job?

It can be a horrible job sometimes. TV is the largest and most effective medium when it comes to breaking an act. Of course the record label pays a lot of attention to TV and therefore much rides on getting the exposure. The pressure can be extreme for an act they consider high priority. Labels can have very unreasonable expectations about what a plugger can achieve. There are approximately 60–70 videos landing on a desk of one booker. The most slots they will have in one week will be three to six, so the chances of your act getting one of those slots without an exceptional marketing plan is very slim. It can be demoralising, but occasionally that extra phone call can make all the difference.

With so much riding on TV exposure, the labels must need good TV pluggers, so there must be plenty of work for people like you.

Sometimes work is hard to come by, sometimes not. As you build a relationship with a label they tend to trust your judgement more. They know if you work hard and tend to give the people they rate more work. But the competition among indie promo companies is fierce.

Take CD:UK *or MTV. What would you send them in terms of a pitch?*

First of all I'd send them the full PR and marketing package, including the CD, video, press release, biog, and a general plot/progress marketing report. This would cover what radio play the band is getting nationally and regionally, and substantial press features in demographically relevant magazines and newspapers. You need to do this if you're going to convince the booker or producer that the record or band is going to be a hit, or at least successful enough to justify the kind of exposure you're looking to get.

When you pitch an artist to MTV, what are the key points you're trying to get across?
First and foremost I want to tell them how good the artist is; then I want to convince them that they'll fit well within their playlist. Then I will want them to realise that there's a fit between their audience and that of the programme. They also need to be reassured about the long-term commitment of the record label to the artist. This is needed to give the producer or channel the confidence to 'stick their neck out', or take a chance on a new act. This must be backed up with a summary of the positive history of the band. This helps the producer feel he is not taking too much of a risk and gives him the confidence to go with the artist.

Can they sometimes change minds if you pitch and pitch again?
They can definitely do this. That's when a plugger's skills really come into play. Eight weeks before a single is released, the booker may like the band, have gone to see them live a couple of times, even played their record on his stereo at home, but there's no certainty that he'll book the act for his show. The bookers need to be convinced that they have sufficient familiarity among the show's audience and that they will be into the single. The plugger's job is to convince them that their audience will know who they are. The reason why the second pitch could have a better chance of success is that the marketing plot may have picked up pace. The record may have made the playlist on national radio, and picked up substantial press. At this stage there's a real opportunity to change the booker's mind.

MARK RICHARDSON – INDEPENDIENTE

Mark is in charge of marketing at Independiente, an independent label with high-profile artists including Travis and So Solid Crew. Mark is one of the best marketing guys in the business and previously worked with Muff and Lincoln at Sony. He's passionate about innovation and bands that have some edge. He has high standards and hates mediocrity. We want to know about the maddest marketing campaign he has pulled off.

Probably the biggest and the best laugh was the 'Travelling Without Moving' campaign I did for Jamiroquai. The idea was born out of the fact that Jay Kay refused to do any interviews on the previous album. To begin with I just took the Ferrari logo and drew one rainman on it on a WordPerfect drawing package. I used the Ferrari logo because Jay Kay was into his cars at that point and I thought it would be a good way of getting him interested in the campaign. Then we got sued by Ferrari and managed somehow to arrange for them to do an international launch of the album in the Ferrari tent at Monza. Ferrari won at Monza, so everybody wanted to be in the tent when the album was launched. It was huge. But the overall campaign was even better.

We were able to develop the branding so strongly that we actually launched the first single without the name of the single, or the name of the artist. All we did was put the logo on the front cover and on the poster. It worked. I proved you could brand a band as if it was Nike or Coca Cola. It had been my goal to do just that with a visual. The first single was a hit, and then the album was huge. I had achieved everything I wanted. It was a high point creatively.

Do you prefer working for an independent?

At Sony there is a pressure to release albums in a timeline for other reasons apart from quality. At the time it was a system I had to go with, but ultimately that is why I left. When we worked on 'Travelling Without Moving' it sold eight million copies worldwide. As soon as that happened everyone was peeking over the fence.

How important is it to be innovative in marketing?

Sometimes it's essential. Recently we worked with a great artist, but she would not tour live. This was seriously hindering her profile, so I gave some video directors five grand each to make a film for each track. Then I toured it around the cinemas, and released it as a DVD and an album so you were getting more. It was not a big deal, but it was about innovation. The great thing about being an independent label is that you have the focus and time to innovate your tactics and your marketing strategy, whereas with a major label you cannot.

NEIL FERRIS – LEGENDARY PLUGGER

He's managed to get more bands more airplay than anyone else. In the 1980s and '90s his Brilliant Group represented virtually every major act from UB40, the Stones, Bowie, Van Morrison, Moby, Prince to Madness. In 1997 Neil became MD of EMI Records and then tried to retire in 2000. However, unable to keep away from a business that is in his blood, he's promoting a number of new artists. His judgement is trusted and sought by labels and stations alike. If you have him plugging your act, your chances of making it good have just gone through the roof.

What do you think of the current state of the music business?

The problem with the industry is that it doesn't listen like it used to. There's no sense of working with the artist to develop their talent, which is bad. It's not that there's a shortage of talent, it's definitely out there, it's all about finding it. The problem is that it's become a *Pop Idol* culture which is all about ratings and not music.

What's the secret of being a great plugger?

The secret of plugging is to create a myth, by not revealing too much. You need to keep everyone guessing about the artist, and wonder what they are going to do next. David Bowie has been great at this. He's always been an enigma, so he's kept the media hungry. If you can keep the mystery and have the nerve to stand back, you'll do well. Remember familiarity breeds contempt.

What excites you about the business?

I love working inside the music business because the most exciting thing in the world is finding an artist who is amazing. Whenever I have been let down by people in the business it usually comes down to them not having the passion for the creative side of the business and for the integrity of the artist.

You talk about the importance of understanding and believing in the artist you are plugging. Why?

Because having faith and believing in the band or the artist is everything. If you have this then other people will follow this energy and you'll achieve the visibility you need. It's all about belief. That's why when I started I didn't want to work on one huge artist but on a handful of interesting acts. To work with people I thought had potential and help them achieve it.

How did you do this?

I had to get radio and television to understand that I represented the best bands. We didn't do this by hanging around pubs. It was about building relationships and providing a level of service that nobody else could offer. It helped that I had a background with the BBC which gave me a unique insight in how to service radio.

What should pluggers today learn from your experience?

That there are no shortcuts. You must really understand and get under the skin of the artist and the radio and TV station. You need the confidence and trust of both to be successful. The only way to do this is to spend time and deliver to earn the respect and trust that is essential to do a good job.

WOOLFIE – PLUGGER

Please explain what you do and how you started in the business.

I am a record plugger for national radio. I promote bands to radio stations that are London-based and broadcast across the country and London. I started as a roadie for a mate's band and ended up working for their management company. I was there for about a year before I realised it wasn't going anywhere and decided to learn a bit more about the business as a whole. I found an advert in the back of a music magazine for a global music business course and spent a couple of hundred pounds on a three-day course. Various people from all different sides of the industry talk for a couple of hours about what they do and there's a questions section at the end of their presentation. This gives you an overview of the industry and how it works from A&R to retail to management to promotion. After the course ends you're given a pack like a mini trade directory with contacts to the industry and you're encouraged to get in touch with them for possible positions. My CV ended up in the hands of one of the leading independent promotions companies and they offered me some work experience, which I took. After a few weeks they extended my work experience and soon after that offered me a position as promotions assistant. I then worked my way to junior plugger and now eight years later have my own radio promotions company.

Why do record labels use you when they have in-house promotions?
Independent companies get to choose the bands they like and think will work. This is key if your relationships with DJs and producers are built on trust and you're trying to promote the artist by saying how good it is and why they should be playing them. If you're not into a band, how can you tell people how good they are and get excited by it? Small independent labels need outside promotion, as they don't have the luxury of in-house promotion. Independent promotion can be more specialised towards a certain genre. They might have contacts that they deal with regularly and better relationships. You aren't up against a massive roster and you're more likely to be a priority. You have to work hard to justify your position as an independent; consequently your clients get better value.

What bands are you working with?
I work with various clients. In no particular order, Fabric's monthly artists mix releases, ranging from Ali B to John Peel, and James Lavelle to Grooverider and everywhere in between. I work The Lostprophets for Visible Noise, several bands on Poptones including The Boxer Rebellion and The Others, Martina Topley Bird for Independiente, Coheed & Cambria for B-Unique, The Mint Chicks, Minus for Smekkleysa/Bad Taste SM, Adam Masterson for

BMG's Gravity label, At Large recordings artist Gisli and the Fallout Trust and various other new and developing artists.

How upfront do you like to work with the band before introducing them to radio?
I normally work with the artist for at least a month before introducing them to radio, but I like to grow with the artist. Always developing and introducing new areas of radio promotion. Most records are with tastemaker DJs about six weeks before release.

Why do pluggers go down to Radio 1?
Pluggers have set appointments with the producers and music team to discuss upcoming releases and playing them tracks they hope to get played or playlisted. They will also have appointments with heads of music and playlist personnel at other stations including XFM, Virgin, Radio 2, Capital, Kiss, 6 Music, etc.

What are the key stations for breaking an act?
There are different stations for breaking different acts. Radio is one part of a bigger picture of promotion. There are stations like Radio 1 who are key in taking music to a wide audience and use their specialist shows to great effect in crossing over potential artist to the mainstream. There are also stations like XFM who have a great alternative daytime playlist essential in getting new artists heard and building a buzz on an act as well as maintain support for core artist. Then you have stations like Radio 2 geared to artists and album-based projects rather than the singles market. I would say a combination of stations and everything else that goes with promotion is important.

What do you need from the label (marketing support, etc.) to help you plug the band?
A plot including live dates or PAs, press, TV, radio, club, regional, online and artist availability for promotion. Also ads later down the line.

What are the common reasons why a band doesn't make it onto the playlist?
How long is a piece of string? There can be so many factors: timing, wrong choice of single, no specialist support, no plot, bad record, too early, too late, too many of the same sound of record, fierce competition … the list is endless.

How do you charge and what's the bonus structure?
Each deal is structured differently depending on the amount of time it will take up. All the hard work is done early on in a band's career and, you guessed it, that's when people haven't got any funds! You generally take an act on in good faith, if this is the case, that when there are funds available you will get a good rate and a retainer. Something you should have first. Performance bonuses are normally charged for these early deals, on the basis that if the band does well, you do well. Equally later on in a band's career you may get sales or chart bonuses.

What's it like when the station informs you the band didn't make the playlist?
Gutting – this is normally months into a campaign you have been putting your heart and soul into. It's one of the lows of the job; the highs are obviously getting playlisted and early plays on a new artist. Swings and roundabouts are how you have to take it, otherwise it can seriously affect you. Saying that though, you have to brush it off and get back out there. Bands are here to have careers, hopefully, so you need to maintain support in other areas and come back with another single. You take the positives out of that situation and move forward.

What's it like telling the label they didn't make the playlist?
Obviously not nice, but most labels take a view of what's been happening and take into consideration other areas. If it's not happening elsewhere they have to be more understanding about the situation. If it is happening elsewhere you have to have a look at what you're doing.

1
2
3
4
5
6
7
8
9
10
11
12
13
14
15

PUBLICITY COMPANIES – PRESS & PROMOTIONS

APB STUDIO
18, Westbourne Studios, 242 Acklam Road, London W10 5JJ
T: 020 8968 9000 F:020 8968 8500
Email: apb.press@which.net
MD: Gordon Duncan

ASSASSINATION MUSIC PROMOTIONS
Tudor House, Pinstone Way, Gerrards Cross, Bucks SL9 7BJ
T: 01494 862770 F:01494 862770
Email: amp@assassination.co.uk
Website: assassination.co.uk
MD: Rupert Withers

BAD MOON PUBLICITY
19B All Saints Road, London W11 1HE
T: 020 7221 0499 F:020 7792 0405
Email: press@badmoon.co.uk
MD: Anton Brookes

BEATWAX COMMUNICATIONS
91 Berwick Street, London W1F 0NE
T: 020 7734 1965 F:020 7292 8333
Email: general@beatwax.com
Website: beatwax.com
Head of Music: Simon Bell

BEST PR
3rd Floor, 29-31 Cowper St, London EC2A 4AT
T: 020 7608 4590 F:020 7608 4599
Email: beast@bestest.co.uk; simon@bestest.co.uk
MD: John Best

BIG GROUP LTD
91 Princedale Road, Holland Park, London W11 4NS
T: 020 7229 8827 F:020 7243 1462
Email: info@biggroup.co.uk
Website: biggroup.co.uk
Account Director: Simon Broyd

BR-ASIAN MEDIA CONSULTING
45 Circus Rd, St Johns Wood, London NW8 9JH
T: 020 8550 9898 F:020 7289 9892
Email: moizvas@brasian.com
Website: brasian.com
MD: Moiz Vas

BRASSNECK PUBLICITY
31A Almorah Road, London N1 3ER
T: 020 7226 3399 F:020 7226 7557
Email: brassneckpr@aol.com
MD: Mick Houghton

CAKE GROUP LTD
The Mission Hall, 9-11 North End Rd, London W14 8ST
T: 020 7471 6666 F:020 7471 6677
Email: mail@cakemedia.com
Website: cakemedia.com
Director: Clare Craven

CELEBRATION PR LTD
Unit C7, 55/57 Boscombe Road, London W12 9HT
T: 020 8743 4238 F:020 7598 9092
Email: celebration@dial.pipex.com
Publicist: James Doheny

IAN CHEEK PRESS
Suite 5, 51D New Briggate, Leeds, West Yorkshire LS2 8JD

T: 0113 246 9940 F:0113 246 9960
Email: iancheek@talk21.com
Head of Press: Ian Cheek

MAX CLIFFORD ASSOCIATES
49-50 New Bond Street, London
W1Y 9HA
T: 020 7408 2350 F:020 7409 2294
MD: Max Clifford

COALITION GROUP
Devonshire House, 12 Barley Mow
Passage, London W4 4PH
T: 020 8987 0123 F:020 8987 0345
Email: pr@coalitiongroup.co.uk
MD, Music Division: Tony Linkin

CREATIVE PR
Unit 53, Simla House, Weston St,
London SE1 3RN
T: 020 7378 1642 F:020 7378 1642
Email: general@creativepruk.com
CEO: Dave Norton

JOHN CROSBY & MICK BOVEE PRESS & PROMOTIONS
21 Claremont, Hastings, East Sussex
TN34 1HA
T: 01424 434347 F:01424 434349
Email: johncrosby@pressproms.demon.co.uk
Website: pressproms.demon.co.uk
MD: John Crosby

CYPHER PRESS & PROMOTIONS
Unit 2A Queens Studios, 121 Salusbury
Road, London NW6 6RG
T: 020 7372 4464 F:020 7372 4484
Email: info@cypherpress.uk.com
Website: cypherpress.uk.com Directors:
Simon Ward/Marion Sparks

DARLING DEPT
4th floor, 19 Denmark Street, London
WC2H 8NA
T: 020 7379 8787 F:020 7379 5737
Email: info@darlinguk.com
Website: darlingdepartment.com

DIFFUSION PR
PO Box 2610, Mitcham, Surrey
CR4 2YH
T: 020 8286 9654 F:0871 277 3055
Email: jodie@diffusionpr.co.uk
Website: diffusionpr.co.uk
MD: Jodie Stewart

DUROC MEDIA
Riverside House, 10-12 Victoria Rd,
Uxbridge, Middx UB8 2TW
T: 01895 810831 F:01895 231499
Email: info@durocmedia.com
Website: durocmedia.com
MD: Simon Porter

DWL (DAVE WOOLF LTD)
53 Goodge St, London W1T 1TG
T: 020 7436 5529 F:020 7637 8776
Email: dwoolf@dircon.co.uk;
kizzidwl@dircon.co.uk
Account Manager: Kizzi Alleyne-Stewart

SARAH J. EDWARDS PR
PO Box 2423, London WC2E 9PG
T: 0870 138 9430 F:0870 138 9430
Email: blag@blagmagazine.com
Website: blagmagazine.com/sarahjedwardspr.html
Dir: Sarah J. Edwards

EMMS PUBLICITY
100 Aberdeen House, 22-24 Highbury
Grove, London N5 2EA
T: 020 7226 0990 F:020 7354 8600

Email: info@emmspublicity.com
Website: emmspublicity.com
MD: Stephen Emms

EXCESS PRESS
72-80 Leather Lane, London EC1N 7TR
T: 020 7405 6226 F:020 7405 6116
Email: excess@excesspress.com
Press: Jon Wilkinson

FIFTH ELEMENT PUBLIC RELATIONS
258 Belsize Road, London NW6 4BT
T: 020 7372 2128 F:020 7624 3629
Email: info@fifthelement.biz
Website: fifthelement.biz
Directors: Chris Hewlett/Cat Hockley

FLEMING CONNOLLY LANDER PR
Music House Group, Host Europe House, Kendal Avenue, London W3 0TT
T: 020 8896 8200 F:020 8896 8201
Website: music-house.co.uk
Directors: Nick Fleming, Judd Lander

FRONTIER PROMOTIONS
The Grange, Cockley Cley Rd, Hilborough, Thetford, Norfolk IP26 5BT
T: 01760 756394 F:01760 756398
Email: frontier@frontierUK.fsnet.co.uk
MD: Sue Williams

JACKIE GILL PROMOTIONS
2-3 Fitzroy Mews, London W1P 5DQ
T: 020 7383 5550 F:020 7383 3020
Email: jackie.gill@bigfoot.com
MD: Jackie Gill

GLASS CEILING PR
50 Stroud Green Rd, London N4 3ES
T: 020 7263 1240 F:020 7281 5671
Email: promo@glassceilingpr.com
MD: Harriet Simms

GONE COUNTRY PROMOTIONS
9 Preston Road, Leytonstone, London E11 1NL
T: 020 8989 5005 F:020 8989 5006
Email: jeffrey@gonecountry.net
Website: gonecountry.net
MD: Jeffrey Stothers

HALL OR NOTHING
11 Poplar Mews, Uxbridge Rd, London W12 7JS
T: 020 8740 6288 F:020 8749 5982
Email: press@hallornothing.com
Website: hallornothing.com
MD: Terri Hall

HALL WALLACE PRESS & PROMOTION
The Corner House, Cidermill Lane, Chipping Campden, Gloucestershire GL55 6HL
T: 01386 841453 F:01386 841453
Email: successpr@hotmail.com
Jane Wallace

JENNIE HALSALL CONSULTANTS
PO Box 22467, London W6 0SG
T: 020 8741 0003 F:020 8846 9652
Email: jhc@dircon.co.uk
MD: Jennie Halsall

HARDZONE PR
The Business Village, 3 Broomhill Rd, London SW18 4JQ
T: 020 8870 8744 F:020 8874 1578
Email: info@hardzone.co.uk
Website: hardzone.co.uk
Marketing Dir: Reggie Styles

KATHERINE HOWARD PR
Hope House, Pettaugh Lane, Gosbeck,

Suffolk IP6 9SD
T: 01473 892007 F:08700 511772
Email: info@katherinehoward.co.uk
Website: katherinehoward.co.uk
MD: Katherine Howard

DAVID HULL PROMOTIONS
46 University St, Belfast BT7 1HB
T: 028 9024 0360 F:028 9024 7919
Email: info@dhpromotions.com
Website: davidhullpromotions.com
MD: David Hull

HUSH-HUSH SUITE
34, Old Truman Brewery, 91 Brick Lane, London E1 6QL
T: 020 7770 6175 F:020 7770 6176
Email: danielle@hush-hush.org.uk
Press Officer: Danielle Richards

ID PUBLICITY
25 Britannia Row, London N1 8QH
T: 020 7359 4455 F:020 7704 1616
Email: info@idpublicity.com
MD: Lisa Moskaluk

IMPRESSIVE
9 Jeffrey's Place, Camden, London NW1 9PP
T: 020 7284 3444 F:020 7284 1840
Email: mel@impressivepr.com
MD: Mel Brown

IN HOUSE PRESS
4th Floor, 20 Dale Street, Manchester M1 1EZ
T: 0161 228 2070 F:0161 228 3070
Email: info@inhousepress.com
Website: inhousepress.com
MD: David Cooper

LD COMMUNICATIONS
58-59 Gt. Marlborough St, London W1F 7JY
T: 020 7439 7222 F:020 7734 2933
Email: info@ldpublicity.com
Website: ldpublicity.com
CEO: Bernard Doherty

LEYLINE PROMOTIONS
Studio 24, Westbourne Studios, 224 Acklam Road, London W10 5JJ
T: 020 7575 3285 F:020 7575 3286
Email: info@leylinepromotions.com
Website: leylinepromotions.com
Dir: Adrian Leigh

M P PROMOTIONS
22 Hill St, Stockport, Cheshire SK6 3AH
T: 0161 494 7934 F:0161 406 8500
Email: maria@mppromotions.co.uk
MD: Maria Philippou

MAGNUM PR
41 Halcyon Wharf, 5 Wapping High St, London E1W 1LH
T: 020 7709 0914
Email: Tammy@magnumpr.co.uk
MD: Tammy Arthur

MEDIA RESEARCH (UK)
Kiln House, 210 New Kings Road, London SW6 4NZ
T: 020 7731 2020 F:020 7731 1100
Email: jon@mediagroup.com
Website: mediagroup.com
MD: Jon Mais

MERCENARY PR
Suite 4, Canalot Studios, 222 Kensal Road, London W10 5BN
T: 020 8354 4111 F:020 8354 4112

Email: kas@mercenarypr.com
Website: mercenarypr.com
Dir: Kas Mercer

MI LIVE
55 St Albans Road, S.C.R., Dublin 8, Ireland
T: +353 1 416 9418
F:+353 1 416 9418
Email: info@milive.net
MD: Bernie McGrath

MONKEY BUSINESS PR
Suite 410, Cumberland House, 80 Scrubs Lane, London NW10 6RF
T: 020 8960 9500 F:020 8964 3600
Email: monkey.pr@clara.net
MD: Pippa Hall

MONOPOLY PR
34B Halliford Street, London N1 3EL
T: 020 7354 1057 F:020 7288 1571
Email: monopolyPR@aol.com
Kate Comoshevski

NELSON BUSTOCK
Compass House, 22 Redan Place, London W2 4SA
T: 020 7229 4400 F:020 7727 2025
Email: pr@nelsonbostock.com
Website: nelsonbostock.com
Snr Acc Exec: Kelly Finlay

NOBLE PR
1 Mercers Mews, London N19 4PL
T: 020 7272 7772 F:020 7272 2227
Email: suzanne@noblepr.co.uk
Website: noblepr.co.uk
Dirs: Suzanne & Peter Noble

THE OUTSIDE ORGANISATION LTD
Butler House, 177-178 Tottenham Court Rd, London W1T 7NY
T: 020 7436 3633 F:020 7436 3632
Email: info@outside-org.co.uk
Website: outside-org.co.uk
Chairman: Alan Edwards

THE PARTNERSHIP
57-63 Old Church Street, London SW3 5BS
T: 020 7761 6005 F:020 7761 6035
Email: billy@partnership2.com
Partner: Billy Macleod

PLANET EARTH PUBLICITY
49 Rylstone Way, Saffron Walden, Essex CB11 3BL
T: 01799 501347 F:01799 501347
Email: info@planetearthpublicity.com
Website: planetearthpublicity.com
MD: Dave Clarke

PLATINUM PR
42 Cheriton Close, Queens Walk, Ealing, London W5 1TR
T: 020 8997 8851 F:020 8997 8851
Email: carolyn@platinum.fsnet.co.uk
MD: Carolyn Norman

POPLICITY
100 Aberdeen House, 22-24 Highbury Grove, London N5 2EA
T: 020 7226 0990 F:020 7354 8600
Email: info@poplicity.com
Website: poplicity.com
MD: Stephen Emms

POWER PROMOTION
Unit 11, Impress House, Mansell Road, London W3 7QH

T: 020 8932 3030 F:020 8932 3031
Email: info@power.co.uk
Website: power.co.uk
MD: Terry Marks

PRECIOUS PR
3 Eliot Place, Blackheath, London
SE3 OQL
T: 020 8318 0368
Email: jack@preciouspr.plus.com
MD: Jack McKillion

PRESS COUNSEL PR
5-7 Vernon Yard, Off Portobello Rd, London W11 2DX
T: 020 7792 9400 F:020 7243 2262
Email: info@presscounsel.com
Website: presscounsel.com
Partner: Charlie Caplowe

QUITE GREAT PUBLICITY
1C Langford Arch, London Rd Trading Estate, Cambridge CB2 4EG
T: 01223 830111
Email: news@quitegreat.co.uk
Website: quitegreat.co.uk
MD: Pete Bassett

RADICAL PR
Suite 421, Southbank House, Black Prince Rd, London SE1 7SJ
T: 020 7463 0677 F:020 7463 0670
Email: info@radicalpr.com
Website: radicalpr.com
Dirs: Paul Ruiz & Mark Nicholls

RAZZLE PR
66 Red Lion Street, Holborn, London
WC1R 4NA
T: 020 7430 0444 F:020 7405 4391
Email: karen@razzlepr.com
Head of Press: Karen Childs

THE RED CONSULTANCY
77 Wimpole Street, London W1G 9RU
T: 020 7465 7700 F:020 7486 5260
Email: red@redconsultancy.com
Website: redconsultancy.com
MD: David Fuller

RED HOT PR
62 Bell Street, London NW1 6SP
T: 020 7723 9191 F:020 7723 6423
Email: info@redhotpr.co.uk
MD: Liz Bolton

RED SQUARE
147 Drummond St, London NW1 2PB
T: 020 7388 1880 F:020 7388 1889
Email: davidfisher@bigfoot.com
MD: David Fisher

SALLY REEVES PR
27 Burgess Rd, Waterbeach, Cambridge
CB5 9ND
T: 01223 864710 F:01223 864727
Email: sally.reeves@easynet.co.uk
MD: Sally Reeves

RMP
9 Ivebury Court, 325 Latimer Rd, London W10 6RA
T: 020 8969 2600 F:020 8969 1588
Email: rmp@easynet.co.uk
MD: Regine Moylett

ROCKETSCIENCE MEDIA
First Floor, 24 Porden Road, London
SW2 5RT
T: 020 7737 1777 F:020 7346 8417
Email: office@rocketsciencemedia.com
Website: rocketsciencemedia.com
Directors: Paul Coleman & Alex Black

MATTHEW RYAN
Criel House, St. Leonards Road, London
W13 8RG
T: 020 8566 3426 F:020 8567 3699
Email: mail@matthewryan.co.uk
Website: matthewryan.co.uk
MD: Matthew Ryan

SAINTED PR
Office 3, 9 Thorpe Close, London
W10 5XL
T: 020 8962 5700 F:020 8962 5701
Email: heatherfinlay@saintedpr.com
MD: Heather Finlay

SAVAGE & SAVIDGE LTD
9 Little Portland Street, London
W1W 7JF
T: 020 7636 6996 F:020 7636 6998
Email: phill@savageandsavidge.com
Website: savageandsavidge.com
Director of Press: Phill Savidge

SERIOUS PRESS AND PR
30 West Street, Stoke-sub-Hamdon,
Somerset TA14 6PZ
T: 01935 823719 F:01935 823719
Email: janehamdon@yahoo.co.uk
MD: Jane Osborne

SHARP END MUSIC GROUP
Grafton House, 2-3 Golden Square,
London W1F 9HR
T: 020 7439 8442 F:020 7434 3615
Email: sharpend2@aol.com
Dir: Robert Lemon

SILVER PR
33 Belmont Court, 93 Highbury New
Park, London N5 2HA
T: 020 7503 3920 F:020 7503 3920
Email: rachel.silver@silverpr.co.uk
Website: silverpr.co.uk
Dir: Rachel Silver

SLICE
The Clockhouse, 220 Latimer Road,
London W10 6QY
T: 020 8964 0064 F:020 8964 0101
Email: slice@slice.co.uk
Website: slice.co.uk
Simone Young/Damian Mould

SLIDINGDOORS PR
PO Box 21469, Highgate, London
N6 4ZG
T: 020 8340 3412 F:020 8340 3413
Email: annie@slidingdoorspr.com
Website: slidingdoorspr.com
MD: Annie Donnelly

SMASH PRESS
56 Ackroyd Road, London SE23 1DL
T: 020 8291 6466
Email: nick@smashpress.com
Website: smashpress.com
MD: Nick White

SOHO PR LTD
2D Millman St, London WC1N 3EB
T: 020 7405 6515 F:020 7813 7180
Email: anita@sohopr.com
Website: sohopr.com
Partner: Anita Strymowicz

SOUL 2 STREETS
36-38 Rochester Place, London
NW1 9JX
T: 020 7485 7694 F:020 7284 0166
Email: jamie@soul2soul.co.uk
Jamie Binns

ST PIERRE PUBLICITY
24 Beauval Road, Dulwich, London
SE22 8UQ
T: 020 8693 6463 F:020 8299 0719
Email: stpierre.roger@ukf.net
MD: Roger St Pierre

STARFISH COMMUNICATIONS
76 Oxford Street, London W1D 1BS
T: 020 7323 2121 F:020 7323 0234
Email: fearfield@star-fish.net
Website: star-fish.net
Managing Partner: Sally Fearfield

STREET LIFE
PO Box 23351, London SE16 4YQ
T: 020 7231 1393 F:020 7232 1373
Email: info@interactivem.co.uk
Website: interactivem.co.uk
MD: Jo Cerrone

TALK LOUD PR
6-10 Lexington Street, London W1F 0LB
T: 020 7734 1133 F:020 7734 7787
Email: talkloud@talkloud.co.uk
Website: talkloud.co.uk
MD: Addie Churchill

VELOCITY COMMUNICATIONS
Ground Floor, 4 Bourlet Close, London
W1W 7BJ
T: 020 7323 1744 F:020 7436 4199
Email: info@velocitypr.co.uk
Website: velocitypr.co.uk
MD: Andy Saunders

MARKETING COMPANIES

ANGLO PLUGGING
Fulham Palace, Bishops Avenue,
London SW6 6EA
T: 020 7384 7373 F:020 7371 9490
Email: firstname@angloplugging.co.uk
Website: angloplugging.co.uk
Promotions Co-ordinator: Alice Schofield

AUTOMATIC PROMOTIONS
First Floor, 151 City Road, London
EC1V 1JH
T: 020 7490 0666 F:020 7490 0660
Email: roger@automaticpromotions.co.uk
Website: automaticpromotions.co.uk
Dir: Roger Evans

BEATWAX COMMUNICATIONS
91 Berwick Street, London W1F 0NE
T: 020 7734 1965 F:020 7292 8333
Email: general@beatwax.com
Website: beatwax.com
Head of Music: Simon Bell

BRICKWERK YOUTH MARKETED EVENTS
19, Wynell Road, London SE23 2LN
T: 020 7381 3524 F:020 8291 5053
Email: events@brickwerk.co.uk
Website: brickwerk.co.uk
Directors: Maria Walker/ Jo Brooks-Nevin

CYPHER PRESS & PROMOTIONS LTD
Unit 2A Queens Studios, 121 Salusbury Road, London NW6 6RG
T: 020 7372 4464 F:020 7328 3808
Email: info@cypherpress.uk.com
Website: cypherpress.uk.com
Simon Ward/Marion Sparks

DEVOLUTION
25 Pinehurst Court, Colville Gardens,
London W11 2BH
T: 020 7229 5021 F:020 7229 5021
Email: geremy@devolution.freeserve.co.uk
MD: Geremy O'Mahony

TERRIE DOHERTY PROMOTIONS
40 Princess St, Manchester M1 6DE
T: 0161 234 0044 F:01625 418 746
Email: terriedoherty@zoo.co.uk
Director: Terrie Doherty

ESSENTIAL ENTERTAINMENTS LTD
9 Church Street, Brighton, E. Sussex
BN1 1US
T: 01273 888787 F:01273 888780
Email: info@essentialents.com
Website: essentialfestival.com
Events Organiser: Ish Ali

EUROSOLUTION MUSIC HOUSE GROUP
Host Europe House, Kendal Avenue,
London W3 0TT
T: 020 8896 8200 F:020 8896 8201
Email: craig.eurosolution@music-house.co.uk
Website: music-house.co.uk
Craig Jones

FLEMING CONNOLLY AND LANDER (FCL) MUSIC HOUSE GROUP
Host Europe House, Kendal Avenue,
London W3 0TT

T: 020 8896 8200 F:020 8896 8201
Email: nick@fclpr.com; judd@fclpr.com
Website: music-house.co.uk
Nick Fleming/Judd Lander

FLYING SPARKS PROMOTION
Garden House, Hayters Way, Alderholt, Hampshire SP6 3AX
T: 01425 658 000 F:01425 658 222
Email: flyingsparks@promotion100.fsnet.co.uk
MD: Ian Brown

FUTURE STUDIOS INTERNATIONAL
PO Box 10, London N1 3RJ
T: 020 7241 2183 F:020 7241 6233
Email: ladybelle888@blueyonder.co.uk
Website: gigsonline.co.uk
Director: Michelle L Goldberg

HALL WALLACE ENTERTAINMENT
The Corner House, Cidermill Lane, Chipping Campden, Gloucestershire GL55 6HL
T: 01386 841453 F:01386 841453
Email: successpr@hotmail.com
Dir Press/Promo: Jane Wallace

HARDZONE FULL SERVICE MARKETING
The Business Village, Gardiner House, 3-9 Broomhill Road, London SW18 4JQ
T: 020 8870 8744 F:020 8874 1578
Email: info@hardzone.co.uk
Website: hardzone.co.uk
Head of Marketing: Reggie Styles

HART MEDIA LTD
Primrose Hill Business Centre, 110 Gloucester Avenue, London NW1 8JA
T: 020 7209 3760 F:020 7209 3761
Email: info@hartmedia.co.uk
Website: hartmedia.co.uk
MD: Jo Hart

HYPER ACTIVE MUSIC HOUSE GROUP
Host Europe House, Kendal Avenue, London W3 0TT
T: 020 8896 8200 F:020 8896 8201
Email: matt.hyperactive@music-house.co.uk
Website: music-house.co.uk
Matt Waterhouse

IMPACT VENTURES
24 Porden Rd, London SW2 5RT
T: 020 7274 8509
Email: info@impactventures.co.uk
MD: Rachel Bee

INSTINCTIVE PROMOTIONS
Byron House, 112A Shirland Rd, London W9 2EQ
T: 020 7266 7720 F:020 7266 7734
Email: chrisslade@instinctivepr.com
Website: instinctivepr.com
MD: Chris Slade

INTERMEDIA REGIONAL
Byron House, 112A Shirland Road, London W9 2EQ
T: 020 7266 0777 F:020 7266 7726
Email: info@intermediaregional.com
MD: Steve Tandy

ISH-MEDIA
1 Devonport Mews, Devonport Road, London W12 8NG
T: 020 8742 9191 F:020 8742 9102
Email: eden@ish-media.com
Website: ish-media.com
Director: Eden Blackman

PHIL LONG PR
2/14 Park Terrace, The Park,
Nottingham NG1 5DN
T: 0115 947 5440 F:0115 947 5440
Email: phil.long@pipemedia.co.uk

MEGA BULLET ARCHWAY
74, Ranelagh Gardens, London
SW6 3UR
T: 020 7384 3222 F:020 7384 3223
Email: info@megabullet.com
Website: platin-m.com
MD: Marilyn Rosen

LES MOLLOY
22 Grafton St, Mayfair, London
W1S 4EX
T: 020 7355 1884 F:020 7355 1884
Email: lmolloy@dircon.co.uk
Les Molloy

MP PROMOTIONS
Bexley Cottage, Haselor, Warwickshire
B49 6LU
T: 01789 488988 F:01789 488998
Email: mppromotions@btinternet.com
MD: Mike Perry

MVPD
Queens House, 1 Leicester Place,
Leicester Square, London WC2H 7BP
T: 020 7534 3340 F:020 7534 3341
Email: chris@mvpd.net
Website: mvpd.net Dir: Chris Page

NONSTOP PROMOTIONS STUDIO
39, Aaron Business Centre, 6 Bardolph
Road, Richmond, Surrey TW9 2LS
T: 020 8334 9994 F:020 8334 9995
Email: info@nonstop1.co.uk
Niki Sanderson, Rachel Dicks

STEVE OSBORNE PROMOTIONS
PO Box 69, Daventry, Northamptonshire
NN11 4SY
T: 07000 243 243
Email: steve@daventrynet.co.uk
Website: holierthanthourecords.com
Proprietor: Steve Osborne

OUTSIDE MEDIA PROMOTIONS LTD
Butlers House, 177-178 Tottenham
Court Rd, London W1T 7NY
T: 020 7462 2900 F:020 7462 2901
Email: omp@outside-org.co.uk
Website: outside-org.co.uk :

PACIFIC EDGE PROMOTIONS & PUBLIC RELATIONS
Charlestone House, 34 Poppleton Road,
London E11 1LR
T: 020 8530 7748 F:020 8530 2571
Email: pacific.edge@btinternet.com
MD: Jill Cramer

THE PARTNERSHIP
57-63 Old Church Street, London
SW3 5BS
T: 020 7761 6005 F:020 7761 6035
Email: matthew@partnership2.com
Partner: Matthew Austin

PHUTURE TRAX
11 Savant House, 63-65 Camden High
Street, London NW1 7JL
T: 020 7387 2545 F:020 7387 2392
Email: nicky@phuturetrax.co.uk
Website: phuturetrax.co.uk
MD: Nicky Trax

PLANETLOVEMUSIC
2 Gregg St, Lisburn, Co Antrim
BT27 5AN

T: 02892 667 000 F:02892 668 000
Email: eddie@planetlovemusic.com
Website: planetlovemusic.com
Dir: Eddie Wray

POWER PROMOTIONS
Unit 11, Impress House, Mansell Road, London W3 7QH
T: 020 8932 3030 F:020 8932 3031
Email: info@power.co.uk
Website: power.co.uk MD: Terry Marks

RADIO PROMOTIONS
T: 0129 581 4995
Email: music@radiopromotions.co.uk
Website: radiopromotions.co.uk
Steve Betts

ROCKET
The Brix at St Matthews Church, Brixton Hill, London SW2 1JF
T: 020 7326 1234
Email: Radio@Rocketpr.co.uk
Website: rocketpr.co.uk
MD: Prudence Trapani

RPPR AND PROMOTIONS
The Collective, 2nd Floor, Chiswick High Rd, London W4 1SY
T: 020 8995 5544 F:020 8995 1133
Email: rppr1@ukonline.co.uk
Head of Radio/TV: Richard Perry

RUSH RELEASE LTD
The Music Village, 11B Osiers Road, London SW18 1NL
T: 020 8870 0011 F:020 8870 2101
Email: info@rush-release.co.uk
Website: rushrelease.com
Jo Underwood (MD)

SERIOUS PROMOTIONS
PO Box 13143, London N6 5BG
T: 020 8731 7300 F:020 8458 0045
Email: firstname@seriousdjs.co.uk
Website: seriousdjs.co.uk :

SHARP END MUSIC GROUP
Grafton House, 2-3 Golden Square, London W1F 9HR
T: 020 7439 8442 F:020 7434 3615
Email: sharpend2@aol.com
Dir: Robert Lemon

SIZE NINE MUSIC HOUSE GROUP
Host Europe House, Kendal Avenue, London W3 0TT
T: 020 8896 8200 F:020 8896 8201
Email: paul.sizenine@music-house.co.uk
Website: music-house.co.uk
Paul Kennedy (Radio)....top list

SOUL2STREETS
Unit 219, Canalot Production Studios, Kensal Rd, London W10 5BN
T: 020 8960 8950 F:020 8964 5968
Email: doug@soul2soul.co.uk
Website: ukmusicworldwide.com
Promotions Mgr: Doug Cooper

TOMKINS PR
The Old Lampworks, Rodney Place, London SW19 2LQ
T: 020 8540 8166 F:020 8540 6056
Email: info@tomkinspr.com
MD: Susie Tomkins

WAXWORKS MUSIC HOUSE GROUP
Host Europe House, Kendal Avenue, London W3 0TT
T: 020 8896 8200 F:020 8896 8201
Email: aidan.waxworks@music-house.co.uk

Website: music-house.co.uk
Aidan Byrne

WAY TO BLUE
1st Floor, Suna House, 128-132 Curtain Road, London EC2A 3AR
T: 020 7749 8444 F:020 7749 8420
Email: lee@waytoblue.com
Website: waytoblue.com
Director: Lee Henshaw

WHITENOISE PROMOTIONS
8 Southam Street, London W10 5PH
T: 020 8964 0020 F:020 8964 0021
Email: info@whitenoisepromo.com
Website: whitenoisepromo.com
Promotions Mgr: Colin Hobbs

MERCHANDISING COMPANIES

ADRENALIN MERCHANDISING
Unit 5, Church House, Church Street,
London E15 3JA
T: 020 8503 0634 F:020 8221 2528
Email: scott@adrenalin-merch.demon.co.uk
Website: adrenalin-merch.demon.co.uk :
Scott Cooper

ALISTER REID TIES
9 Applegate House, Applegate,
Brentwood, Essex CM14 5PL
T: 01277 375329 F:01277 375331
Email: colin@arties.fsbusiness.co.uk
Sales Manager: Colin Stoddart

THE BIZZ
14 Finlay Street, London SW6 6HD
T: 020 7384 1528 F:020 7371 5651
Email: mail@the-bizz.demon.co.uk
Dir: Anne Loates

BLOWFISH U.V.
29 Granville St, Loughborough, Leics.
LE11 3BL
T: 07900 262 052 F:01509 560 221
Email: anna@blowfishuv.co.uk
Website: blowfishuv.co.uk
MD: Anna Sandiford

CATERPRINT LTD
Unit 3, Chaseside Works,, Chelmsford
Rd, Southgate, London N14 4JN
T: 020 8886 1600 F:020 8886 1636
Email: info@caterprint.co.uk
Website: caterprint.co.uk
Leonard

CHESTER HOPKINS INTERNATIONAL
24 Fulham Palace Road, London
W6 9PH
T: 020 8741 9910 F:020 8741 9914
Email: office@chesterhopkins.co.uk
Website: chesterhopkins.co.uk
MD: Adrian Hopkins

DE-LUX MERCHANDISE COMPANY LTD
2nd Floor Zetland House, 5-25 Scrutton
Street, London EC2A 4HJ
T: 020 7613 3555 F: 020 7613 3550
Email: jeremy@delux.net
Website: de-lux.net
Contact: Jeremy Joseph

EMC ADVERTISING GIFTS
Derwent House, 1064 High Road,
Whetstone, London N20 0YY
T: 020 8492 2200 F:020 8445 9347
Email: sales@emcadgifts.co.uk
Website: emcadgifts.co.uk
Sales Dir: John Kay

FIFTH COLUMN T SHIRT DESIGN & PRINT
276 Kentish Town Road, London
NW5 2AA
T: 020 7485 8599 F:020 7267 3718
Email: fifthc@globalnet.co.uk
Website: fifthcolumn.co.uk
MD: Rodney Adams

FINALLY FAN-FAIR LTD
PO Box 153, Stanmore, Middx HA7 2HF
T: 01923 896 975 F:01923 896985
Email: hrano@fan-fair.freeserve.co.uk
MD: Mike Hrano

GMERCH
2 Glenthorne Mews, London W6 0LJ
T: 020 8741 7100 F:020 8741 1170
Email: Paula.Campbell@gmerch.com
Website: gmerch.com
MD: Mark Stredwick

GREEN ISLAND PROMOTIONS LTD
Unit 31, 56 Gloucester Rd, Kensington, London SW7 4UB
T: 0870 789 3377 F:0870 789 3414
Email: greenisland@btinternet.com
Dir: Steve Lucas

INDEPENDENT POSTERS
PO Box 7259, Brentwood, Essex CM14 5ZA
T: 01277 372000 F:01277 375333
Email: info@independentposters.co.uk
Publishing Manager: Kim Miller

LOGO PROMOTIONAL MERCHANDISE LTD
10 Crescent Terrace, Ilkley, West Yorkshire LS29 8DL
T: 01943 817 238 F:01943 605 259
Email: alan@logomerchandising.co.uk
Director: Alan Strachan

PPA (PAIVA PENNICK ASSOCIATES)
62 Oliver Road, Hemel Hempstead, Hertfordshire HP3 9PZ
T: 01408 641777 F:01408 641775 :

PROMOTIONAL CONDOM CO
PO Box 111, Croydon, Surrey CR9 6WS
T: 0033 29751 2950
F:0033 29739 3306
Email: promotionalcondoms@btopenworld.com
Dir: Andrew Kennedy

RTG BRANDED APPAREL
The Old Dispensary, 36 The Millfields, Plymouth, Devon PL1 3JB
T: 01752 253888 F:01752 255663
Email: sales@rtg.co.uk
Website: rtg.co.uk Sales
Dir: Andy Moulding

STOP PRESS SCREEN PRINTING
38 Torquay Gardens, Redbridge, Ilford, Essex IG4 5PT
T: 020 8551 9005 F:020 8551 9005
Email: g4gql@aol.com.uk
Alan Shipman

HIGHLY RECOMMENDED PR COMPANIES

Dave Wolf Ltd

Purple PR

Outside Organization

Amanda Williams PR

Sainted PR

Mercenary PR

1

2

3

4

5

6

7

8

9

10

11

12

13

14

15

PRODUCTION

WHAT IS THE ROLE OF THE PRODUCER?

Producers have a central place in the music business. In many ways they combine the functions of a director and producer in the film business. The best are incredibly creative and visionary, as they have to translate the artist's ideas into reality. It's not an easy role because often they have to bear in mind both the artists' creativity and the record label's commercial motives.

The term producer is often misused. To our mind a producer is a strong figure who has a major influence on the artist's creativity and also administers all aspects of production; however, increasingly the term is being attached to 'mixers'. These are technical wizards who take tracks and remix them to create a better sound, but for real producers this is just one of their functions.

In this book we're quite hard on producers, because we believe too many of them play it safe. We're particularly critical of the production of British urban music. Here we believe the sound produced is too derivative of America and not enough of its producers have managed to create a signature sound. To understand how this could change, we've interviewed two of the producer greats, Sly and Robbie who've managed to produce a signature sound for Jamaican reggae and dance hall that has made it world famous.

In some ways the major labels are to blame for the relative blandness of UK producers. A&R often impose producers on bands to keep them 'on the straight and narrow'. Record labels are expecting producers to nursemaid bands, to produce instant hits and think there's a simple formula to make this happen.

A good producer requires a real understanding of an artist's vision for their music. They need to create a sound uniquely right for that band and a mix that allows them to be the very best they can. Howie B talks about listening to the music, but in practical terms he is ensuring the band works properly together. He tries to simplify the sound and find space for 'dynamics' or the emotion and energy to be brought out of the track. When an artist and producer have collaborated well, you can hear it in the music.

So has technology made it easier for producers?

When Phil Spector invented his 'Wall of Sound' it took days to lay down track after track. Nowadays you can buy equipment that he never dreamed of and put it in your bedroom for just over a thousand pounds and make a record. Logically you would expect modern tracks to be better produced and have a much better sound, but this is often not the case.

It's not the fault of modern technology, but how it's used. We're strongly behind technology that enables anyone to produce music in their own bedroom, but also we are passionate about ensuring that British music is the best in the world.

In a way, computer technology requires more musical skill than the old analogue days. Making changes or laying on sounds, makes it harder to keep it sounding real. A strong vision is needed, to keep true to your instinct when it is so easy to over-produce a track.

It's not just old-school producers who prefer analogue to digital technology. An increasing number of American R&B producers are using analogue because they realise it has a warmer and more organic sound.

If the new generation of British producers want to create the sort of international success enjoyed by Sly and Robbie they won't do it because of technology, but because they've had the courage and the musicality to produce their own unique sound.

DON'T SHOOT ME, I'M ONLY THE PRODUCER

Being a producer isn't as easy as it seems. They have to work hard for their money. Although they need to be very creative they have to be good at logistics, working to details and getting the best out of people. The responsibility for delivering the finished creative product, on time and on budget.

You have to be prepared to work with ego-driven artists and unreasonably demanding A&R guys. The producer will virtually live in the studio while the album is in production. Hardest of all are the unrealistic expectations placed on producers to keep getting elusive hits. As shareholders push the majors harder, a producer cannot afford to have an unsuccessful run, even though a lack of success might be outside their control. It's not their fault the marketing programme didn't work or the plugger didn't manage to secure enough radio play. These expectations lead to producers coming in and out of fashion and a naive belief that they're only as good as the last album they produced.

This explains why too many producers are scared to experiment or be different, and produce the sort of unique sounds we were talking about earlier. However, the demand for fully developed material by the majors and the growing importance of small labels are slowly changing the way producers work.

Increasingly they work on a speculative basis with artists before they've signed a major deal. Often a manager or publishing company will fund the costs. The producer here has extremely high levels of creative input as the artist's style and sound are usually much less formed. Obviously it's important for them to negotiate a good deal if the artist is successful, but at least they haven't got a blinkered A&R executive on their back.

WHO HIRES THE PRODUCER?

Traditionally producers are hired by the A&R department of the labels, but this is changing. In the US, record companies are increasingly insisting they contract directly to the artist, to sidestep any legal costs and contractual difficulties. In the UK the trend towards artists having to develop at least three tracks with hit potential before securing a deal means that they often need to collaborate with a producer at this stage.

In terms of contracts, the MMF Producer Managers Group and the RPA (the Record Producers' Association) have produced a preferred form of producer contract that is increasingly being used, and conforms to the basics of most producer deals.

Generally producers are entitled to a royalty to reward them directly for the success of their efforts. The fee for their work will be treated as an advance against royalties. Advances for successful producers are usually about £40,000 to £50,000 per album. Producer royalties range from 2% to 5% of the dealer price, though 3–4% is more normal. Importantly both the advance and royalty are actually paid by the artist and not the record company as under the terms of the artist contract it comes out of their recoupment.

This can lead to conflict. Arguably producers are valued more highly by record companies. This is often because the producer earns more than the band. If a producer's on a 4% royalty and works with four band members on a 16% royalty, they will in effect earn more than each band member. This is even worse when you consider that often a band only produces an album every two years, while producers often work on at least three or four a year.

It's important that artists are careful not to allow a record company to select a producer they don't want, or at too high a percentage, as this can be one of the most expensive mistakes they make. On the other hand the right producer could ensure their first single and album is a hit and their career assured. Whichever, the producer could be one of the most important factors in an artist's career.

So how rich can you get being a producer? If you complete four projects a year as a successful producer you could be looking to earn £200,000 before any accumulated royalties. Out of this you have to pay a manager, legal and professional fees, but this is for experienced and successful producers. A less experienced but recognised producer may only command about £1,000 per track and perhaps £2,000 if they're lucky.

TIPS FOR NEWCOMERS

- ***Be interested in sound and dynamics:*** You must have a sense of how to make a good tune great. The best producers care about music, to the extent that a badly produced track will send them into despair.
- ***Experiment:*** The range of skills required by a good producer is immense, but it has to begin and end with the music. Experiment with putting music together with different sounds. Even though we've been disparaging about computers, they can be great to experiment with, as long as you don't expect them to take over. Daniel Bedingfield proved that you can get a long way with a basic computer and the right software.
- **Create a sound of your own:** It's worth looking for old secondhand analogue equipment to increase your range. Try getting hold of an old Korg or Moog keyboard from the 1970s or '80s to play with a different sound. Go back through your record collection and reproduce some of the different sounds.
- ***Understand the business:*** You'll need to know how a studio runs, how artists operate and the machinations of an A&R department. Get to know your local studio, see if you can help. Understand what an engineer does, and a mixer. How all the equipment works, what it can and can't do. Then offer to produce some tracks on spec and see how it goes. Hooking up with a new band or artist can help. It gives you a chance to collaborate and learn how to develop their sound.

NEGOTIATING A PRODUCER'S CONTRACT

- ***A-side protection:*** If the producer doesn't produce the B-side, s/he should suffer no pro rata reduction of her/his royalty rate. Record companies can be reluctant to grant this, but successful producers usually get it.
- **Secondary exploitation:** The producer should insist s/he receives

money from secondary exploitation, i.e. any income outside record sales e.g. ring-tones. It should be possible to negotiate a pro rata share of what is payable to the artist. So if his or her royalty represents 15% of the artist's royalty s/he should get this share of their exploitation income.

- ***European deals:*** These are often different. The royalty is often unrelated to the artist's deal and therefore the royalty paid to the producer is not subject to the recoupment of recording costs. However Germany is beginning to follow the UK model.
- ***Performance income:*** Currently producers are excluded from the PPL collection agreement that distributes performance income, such as radio play, 50% to the record company and 50% to the artist. Neither are likely to give any to the producer.
- ***UK v US recoupment:*** Most UK agreements only expect producers to recoup their advance to trigger royalty payment. In the USA producers have to wait until all recording costs have been recouped, and sometimes the producer's royalty will actually be used towards the recoupment of these costs.

THE VIEW FROM WITHIN

HOWIE B – PUSSY FOOT RECORDS, PRODUCER, ENGINEER, SONGWRITER, DJ

Howie started his career by making tea and then had a break and became an assistant engineer. His first project was to be engineer on a Siouxsie and the Banshees track, 'Peeka Blue'. Since then he's become a successful songwriter and DJ, and has run a record label. Most importantly Howie is a brilliant producer, having produced for U2 and Soul II Soul's first and second album, as well as writing songs on the second. With his partner Dick Young, he owns Pussy Foot Records and has released 22 albums and 48 twelve inches to date.

How do you create the right vibe in the studio to produce a great track?
It's about chemistry. If that flows then hit 'record'. It doesn't matter what type of studio you use; if the vibe's right, you'll capture the energy on the track. For instance, when I worked with U2 it was about making them feel comfortable and encouraging them about being the best they can be. I would rehearse them and rehearse them through tracks until I felt they were talking to each other through their instruments to the point they were bouncing off each other without thinking and creating dynamics in the room. With a singer it's about getting them to sing deeper and from within.

Going on tour with U2 allowed me to get deeper into the songs as they performed them. I would give them instructions to play tighter as a band or scale down the sound to the bare basic with no reverb. It would just be the drum, guitar, bass and keyboard with Bono on mike.

The less and the quieter they played as a band, the more air they would have to move in. It's the space between and around the notes that allows the real essence of the music to breathe. This can only be achieved when a band plays organically and really listens to each other so that they can hear the song.

Do bands today manage to achieve this?

Many bands today cannot write songs with dynamics that breathe. I don't mean drama, but dynamics that allow the artist to express the song with emotion and energy. It's about playing as a unit and being able to play with very little effects. Less is better because it forms a chemistry and a bond around the track.

So how do you put together a great track, how do you put the elements together?

I look at it like a pyramid. At the bottom you have the groove, bass, chords, strings, guitar licks and vocals and then you must decide what goes on top. It depends on what signature sound you are going for. It could be the guitar or strings, but as a simple rule of thumb, your groove has got to be slamming if you want to have any sort of dynamic. It's about being emotional and getting into the mood of the track and surrendering yourself to its energies. If I'm producing for someone it's not a Howie B tune, it's a U2 or Björk tune. I just listen to the song and what the song tells me to do. A lyric will help with the direction and tell you where the mood is going. It is about turning a band on to themselves and getting them to express their feelings.

Someone with your strong sense of the right sound must have had some run-ins with record labels.

I was dropped by Polydor from a third album I had done for them. They gave me no notice, no phone calls, no meetings and no signals. Polydor said there were no singles, but I thought there were at least six. I thought it was a great album, probably the finest I had done at the time. They had even given a big party for me a week before they gave me the boot. You get massive kicks in this business and that was one of the worse.

There must be huge pressure on producers to be constantly churning out hits.

Of course, every record I make I want to be a hit, I don't want to make a record that is average, because I want everyone in the world to hear it. But thinking a hit record can be written to a formula is wrong. I have learnt that creating a unique signature sound is what sets you apart in the business and gives you the money to eat. Many times labels are wrong and records they don't rate end up being a real hit with the public.

Has there ever been a job you've taken on just for the money rather than because you really wanted to do it?
Yes, I did a track for BT with a mate of mine called Major, he's a real grafter and a brilliant producer. I don't think either of us were really into the track, but the money was very good. In the end it was a waste of time because our hearts weren't in it. Not that I don't like doing adverts. I enjoyed doing the Lloyds ones with my mate Jeremy. The agency were good to work with, they were on the same level. In many ways the advertising industry has kept independent music alive in Britain over the past five or six years.

What does someone need to produce their own track?
You need a microphone, keyboard, drum machine, and a four-track cassette recorder. You can work off either a Mac or a sequencer that comes in a good keyboard or drum machine. However, I do think computers can rob the soul and spirit of production, so you have to use them in a balanced way.

Is it true you can make a decent record from your bedroom?
Yes you can. Miles Davis created some of his greatest tracks from his basement. You can travel around with just an acoustic guitar and record tracks wherever. Bob Dylan did just that and produced great songs. Yes, you can produce a great track in your bedroom, because it's not about the technology it's about the soul. Everything can make a difference to the sound, whether you're using digital or analogue. It can even depend on which digital tape you use, what protocols and who's actually doing the recording. **The important thing is that you understand the tools you have and know how to use them to get the sound you want and not let them dictate to you.**

Some people feel that digital is not as warm as analogue in sound. Do you agree?

In many ways, but not because of analogue itself, but the fact that it makes you really focus on the arrangement. Often this is what makes the tune tighter and gives you different dynamics. In America they still use a lot more analogue especially with hip hop. Analogue enables them to produce a much more organic and sincere sound. The trouble is that with digital there is more room to manipulate and manufacture what you want and this can sound artificial if you are not careful. Both approaches to recording work, but it depends how you use the equipment.

What advice would you give to someone starting out?
You have to be prepared to do jobs on spec. They'll pay for it if it's good. If not then cool, at least you've learnt more about the process of producing a track. You have to be proactive, bands and labels like it if you offer to produce tracks on spec. I still call people or get my manager to call and say, let me do a track for you. No matter how many tracks you do it's important to keep pushing yourself to do the tracks more creatively. Don't just turn out the same style of tracks. You have to challenge yourself and do things with your music that might at first seem weird. It's not until you're really experimenting that you're going to discover new directions or vibes.

There's no short cut. You have to work hard and be persistent. When I started I worked seven days a week in the studio for around 18 hours a day where I learnt all I could assisting engineers for at least three years. To be successful you have to see being a producer as learning a craft. You have to learn from those around you and then have a sense of conviction to adopt your own style or signature. Of course, it's good to read about this business and to go on a course, but at the end of the day you have to go and do it.

SLY AND ROBBIE – PRODUCERS

Sly and Robbie are legends. They produced Bob Marley and most of the other reggae greats. They are the only Jamaican producers that have crossed over to mainstream contemporary music, having produced the Rolling Stones, Simply Red, No Doubt and Grace Jones. Our interview is conducted by transatlantic phone call. When we thank them for talking to us, Sly replies, 'No problem guys, the UK's got so much unsigned talent and I'm pleased to do anything that might help them.' Sly's right: so much urban talent in the UK is unsigned because it's not being properly produced or managed. He is passionate about the UK's need to get its act together.

I am always confused why so much UK talent are not in deals. Especially as in the UK the music structure is so much more advanced than in Jamaica in terms of marketing talent, but in Jamaica our talent is more recognised around the world. **The UK urban scene should be looking to create legends like Marvin Gaye, Michael Jackson or even Frank Sinatra.** When you look at British black music I can't think of one icon like The Beatles or the Rolling Stones. Look at America, you have Motown and Earth Wind & Fire and in Jamaica at least we created Bob Marley.

Jazzie B from Soul II Soul is the only person who comes close, but I thought he would have taken it further like Sean Puffy Coombs or Berry Gordy. The UK needs someone like Puffy who understands the culture, music and how to package it in a way that people round the globe will buy. Black British musicians need to think about developing their own sound and not focus so much on producing an American sound. It's important for them to believe in their own culture and sound. To be proud of it.

Jamaican music will keep growing because it has universal appeal. It comes down to great songs and hook lines. Just look at the great hooks Marley used like 'Stir It Up, Little Darling' or 'No Woman No Cry'. His songs were popular because they were catchy and everyone could understand what he was singing.

Of course Jamaicans migrating around the world have helped spread the culture and music. DJs have helped: in the last few years they're the ones who have pushed the music. It was always my dream for reggae to be played on popular radio around the world and now that is happening.

In Jamaica we're not afraid to express our Jamaican culture, just look at the Sean Paul video with dance hall. People who never understood or knew what dance hall is, watch those videos and then buy into the culture because it's packaged in a way that makes people want to have fun and forget about their worries. American music does this even better. One of the reasons it does so well around the world is because its music and videos express their surroundings.

Sly is definitely on to something. Jazzie B sold in America because of his British sensibility, not because he was trying to be American. But Sly feels Jamaican music could go further if it had better backing.

Jamaican music could be so much bigger if we had the money or support of a major label to really market it to its full potential. If a major backed a production team like us in the way Clive Davis backed P Diddy then nothing could stop us. The only person who ever really invested in Jamaican music was Chris Blackwell of Island Records.

The best thing about Jamaican music is that you can't help dancing to it. How important is this to you?

If you can't dance to a tune then what is the point? A tune must be able to work in the clubs, the home or on radio. I judge a track by its energy and the way it makes people want to move to it. I'm not making music for people to sit down and listen to. It's about creating a vibe that makes them have to dance whether they are at home or in a club. When that Jamaican vibe touches an artist you feel the influence. I worked with Gwen Guthrie when she created some of the first dub–R&B tunes. I was with Gwen chilling out. I asked her to sing behind a drum track. It was amazing. If you listen to the original track of 'Nothing Going On But The Rent', it was quite empty and sounded like a typical American R&B song, but we added that heavy bass line to fatten it up. I wasn't the official producer of the track, but since we were friends I didn't mind giving it that dub vibe.

How do you create a track with the warm and organic feel that you have made your own?

This generation of artists are from the technology generation, but **artists like Bob Marley were from the organic generation. They had to go out there and learn their craft, whereas the technology generation has everything**

presented to them on a platter. That's why so many of them don't have the depth and warmth that's organic and sounds warm and natural when you listen to it.

It's about where you get your inspiration from and what you're tuning in to. If you're listening to computer-generated music all the time, that's what you're learning from. Your production will be so structured and formatted that it does not encourage your mind or spirit to think organic. With live music it's about the raw energy. Soul and chemistry created around the song and the vocal. You can hear live instruments almost responding to every breath the singer takes. So if an artist or producer wants to create tracks with that warm and organic feel, they must soak their mind into music that gives off that energy.

What music inspires you?
I listen to a lot of Philadelphia records and Stax for their grooves. I think about how I can adapt that style into reggae. I have always found inspiration in other music styles. Even when I was sixteen years old and playing drums on a record called 'Double Barrel'. I listened to the bass-line on the Isley Brothers' 'It's Your Thing'. It inspired us to create the track. We played a funk bass line on top of drum groove.

Sly sings the bass line to make his point.
The Isleys were the inspiration, but we did the track in our own way, without losing our own Jamaican sound or culture. Producers and artists should listen to other styles of music, not to recreate it, but to see how to use a bit of this influence in their music but always keeping to their own sound.

So what are you listening to at the moment?
I listen to lots of music – hip hop, R&B, but also Brazilian and world music and English-sounding records. I try to take everything and use it for reggae and dance hall. I've been doing this since being a kid. It has to fit my vibe. I think Robbie's and my success is because we create our own sound. In most of our tracks you'll hear our signature sound. People that listen to our music will say 'that's Sly and Robbie.'

You must have been asked this so many times but how did you get to work with Bob Marley?
I was coming from Channel One studio and I stopped by Joe Giggs studio for a chat. When I walked in he said Rudy Thomas was looking for me because every good drummer was trying to play on a track for Bob, but none of them could get the groove. I said, let me hear the track. There was no count. I told him to press record and when Bob's vocals came on I started to fill in and lock into how he was singing. I said to myself, boy me not going to move from this groove. You know I got that track laid down in five minutes.

Then we spoke to Robbie. What makes you so successful?
Our love for music and making sure we do not overplay on tracks, because less is more. It's about making sure the songs breathe and matching your playing to the song and the singer. Feeling what they are doing, instead of playing something that just sounds great, but on its own doesn't fit the energy of the song.

What inspires you, Robbie?
I am music (we laugh). My channel flows directly from God and my channel isn't broken. If you have a nice mind with a free and open spirit, then you can allow the energy and music to flow out to the people. Playing is a spiritual experience and God is always with me wherever I go.

Is there any advice you can give to someone wanting to be a producer?
The best advice I can give is that when I work with an artist, I try to be a part of that artist and listen to what they are about creatively and spiritually. It's important an artist knows who he is. Once you is you, you can't change you and once you open your mouth and sing, you is what comes out.

STEPHEN BUDD – RECORD PRODUCER AND SONGWRITER MANAGEMENT

Stephen Budd was one of the first people to offer a management service for producers. Today his company is the largest producer management company in Europe. Running this business has given him a unique insight into what makes a good producer. In his office itself there are fifty CDs evenly spaced on the wall, each representing a major hit, for Steve's clients.

How did you come to manage producers?
After setting up a record company in my bedroom, I managed bands. In the mid-eighties I began working with Tony Visconti, David Bowie's producer. He owned his own studios and was a real gear freak. He had an expensive SSL console and had bought one of the first samplers for £25,000. We needed to keep the studio busy thirty days a month, just to pay for it all. I thought the only way to keep the studio full was to manage producers and encourage them to work there.

Did it work?
Not the way I expected. I discovered good producers wanted the flexibility to work with different studios. However, I did find out that there was a real need for someone to manage producers, help them to sell themselves and with all the paperwork and planning. When Tony left the UK I decided to concentrate on this, and it went from strength to strength.

So what makes a good producer?
There are so many different skills and talents that can make a difference, because there are so many types of music and artists. Good producers can have very different approaches. I have worked with some who are totally hands on, some who are more artists than the artists themselves, and others who rarely set foot in the studio. What makes them good is having hit records. It's as simple as that.

How do they get hits?
Hits come from a whole variety of qualities. It can be because they're ruthless or nice, but for me the most important skill is to be able to spot a hit song, especially when others can't, and be able to communicate with the artist so he feels included, not dominated. **A good producer has to be able to create an environment where artists feel supported to achieve what they want to achieve.**

How do producers choose their projects?
The best ones know that it's important to have the right management involved and the support of the record label. Clever producers know how to position themselves to pick up projects that have the greatest chance of success. It might be that they decide that because the project is run by the right A&R person. If they're going to commit three to four months to a project they want to know if they can really make a difference and if this will give it a realistic chance of being a hit. Of course there are others who just let it happen and those who are primarily interested in money.

How do you educate your producers about how to succeed in the music business?
They must be objective. They have got to ask themselves who they are competing against, who their peers are. We're a comparison business. If I ask you if you like a piece of music, you'll say it's like this or that. This is happening in multi layers. When an A&R guy listens to a track he makes comparisons to the sound of The Neptunes or Flood or whoever. As a producer you have to think about what makes it unique. The skilled producer is making his own comparisons and finding out what he can add to the music.

You must have picked up a deep knowledge of producing?
One of the great joys of this business is spending time in studios with producers who are generally interested in what I say and where I think I can make a contribution. There was one team of producers from Italy with whom I made many hit records in the nineties with Take That, who worked so closely with me that I was even credited and received royalties for some of the tracks. It was like my early days working with Toni Visconti. That had been an amazing opportunity to work with one of the world's best producers, who'd worked with Bowie and T Rex.

I've always found that the best producers are open and collaborative. At the moment I work with many of the biggest songwriters around, and they're often asking what do you think of this and interested in feedback. 'I'm right' people seem to come and go, whereas the people who want to find out more and do better tend to survive fifteen years or longer.

So what's the most important trait you see in a successful producer?
Behaviour patterns are the most important indicator. I've never met a successful producer who has not been extremely intelligent, way more than me. The ability to deal with artists is paramount. Also they have to be able to sell themselves. My job is to set up the job, but they have to be able to clinch it. They have to make the artist trust them. Of course it's very different for producers who deal with made-up artists; then the producer is much more in charge.

What happens when the artist doesn't get what they want from a producer?
The producer is always striking a delicate balance between achieving the artist's vision and adding to it. It's more difficult when the artist doesn't have a clear vision. It helps that these days the artist, songwriter and management have usually worked together on the demo before they even get into the studio. It's the job of the A&R guy to liaise with the artist and the producer and to know where the thing is going. The relationships in the studio can be delicate and I often have to be diplomatic and sort them out carefully if there's a problem. I can usually tell when an A&R man is not in control and doesn't understand the process. There are times when you have to face up to problems before they get too big and destroy the project. You have to find out what the cause of the problem is, even if it's as fundamental as the artist can't sing.

So what advice do you have for aspiring producers, who are still at the stage of creating music in their bedrooms?
The music business is one of the two or three most competitive businesses in the world. The people who succeed are the ones who can generate activity for themselves and not have to rely on others to do it for them. Nowadays they need a range of skills, and they have to be very good musically. If they're producing in the bedroom it has to be great.

Don't you think there needs to be more mentoring and education?
No amount of education is going to change the fact that you're either talented or you are not. Nowadays there are many producer courses,

resources on the Internet and endless TV programmes, but the most important thing is to learn what's good and what's not. It's about creating your own confidence and knowingness. Of course you have to learn skills. I had to learn all about contracts and the detail of how the business worked. Ironically I had already picked up lots of music knowledge, like what makes a good chorus. Why does it stick in your head? Does it have a good lyric?

What are the key elements of your job?
There are four parts to it – first I have to find projects for my producers that they like, pay properly, happen at the right time and are going somewhere. Then secondly we have to negotiate the terms and conditions of the contract. This is when we have to agree the budget. Thirdly the right studios, facilities and equipment need to be planned and booked. Lastly everything needs to be communicated to everybody and every potential pitfall thought about and sorted out. Then if you have the artist and the label happy you have contributed to the right conditions to create a hit record.

Don't most people take all this for granted?
They might, but unless all this is done properly an artist's career can be completely buggered up. Gone are the days when you can remake an album. You only get one shot these days. Setting everything right is essential. It's a bit like setting up a mini movie. The producer is like the movie director and the A&R like the movie producer, except we don't have as much money as the movies of course!

What is the most difficult part of producing a record?
In many projects you reach a point where you're not sure it's all going to come together and you're not sure if you are going to achieve the original vision. This can be very frightening, especially for a first-time artist. Often they're not sure who to trust. This is when the producer needs to give them confidence. The problem for the artist is they fear the unknown, is they don't know what they don't know, whereas the producer has been there many times before.

How many No. 1s have your producers been responsible for?
Over twenty, but then we are the biggest. I have eight staff, and have continually reinvested in the business. I demand excellence from them as I do from my clients.

You are passionate about the music business. What is the most important thing you want to say about it to people considering it as a career?
I always ask, 'What are you doing in the music business if you don't love music?' **The business needs to get back to core values. I do what I do because I'm insanely in love with music.** Even when I was a kid I loved playing people a record and saying this is great, listen to this. That's what got me into the business. The biggest kick for me is when someone walks into the room with a song and you know it's a masterpiece. It's probably happened to me about ten or fifteen times out of all the hundreds and hundreds of songs I've been involved in.

MASTERING

ALCHEMY MASTERING LTD
29-30 Windmill Street, London W1T 2JL
T: 020 7692 0214 Fax:020 7436 3735
Email: info@alchemymastering.com
Website: alchemymastering.com
Mastering Engineer: Martin Giles

AUDIO EDIT PRODUCTIONS (AEP)
Littleton House, Littleton Road, Ashford, Middlesex TW15 1UU
T: 01784 421996 F: 01784 247542
Email: clive@audioedit.co.uk
Website: audioedit.co.uk
MD: Phil Kerby

BOOMTOWN (PROTOOLS) STUDIO
Valetta Road, London W3 7TG
T: 020 8723 9548 F: 020 8723 9548
Email: boomtown@dircon.co.uk
Website: boomtownstudio.co.uk
Simon Wilkinson

CUT AND GROOVE
Prospect Farm,
Main Rd, Bosham, Chichester, W. Sussex PO18 8PN
T: 01243 572381 F: 01243 575861
Email: info@cutandgroove.com
Website: cutandgroove.com
Dirs: Duncan Davis, Adam Twine

DIAMOND BLACK PRESSINGS
91 Brick Lane, London E1 6QL
T: 020 7053 2179 F: 010 7053 2179
Email: diamondblackpressings@hotmail.com
Sales Manager: Katrina Smith

EDIT VIDEOS
2A Conway Street, London W1T 6BA
T: 020 7637 2288 F: 020 7637 2299
Email: mail@editvideo.co.uk
Website: editvideo.co.uk
MD/Editor: Henry Stein

FIREBIRD SUITE
11 Osram Road, East Lane Business Park, Wembley, Middx. HA9 7NG
T: 020 8904 4422 F: 020 8904 3777
Email: info@thefirebirdsuite.com
Website: thefirebirdsuite.com

FLARE DVD
Ingestre Court, Ingestre Place, London W1F 0JL
T: 020 7343 6565 F: 020 7343 6555
Email: katy@flare-dvd.com
Website: flare-dvd.com
Manager: Katy Deegan

HILTONGROVE MULTIMEDIA
Hiltongrove Business Centre, Hatherley Mews, London E17 4QP
T: 020 8521 2424 F: 020 8521 4343
Email: info@hiltongrove.com
Website: hiltongrove.com
MD: Guy Davis

INTIMATE RECORDING STUDIOS
The Smokehouse, 120 Pennington St, London E1 9BB
T: 020 7702 0789 F: 020 7813 2766
Email: p.madden1@ntlworld.com
Website: intimatestudios.com
Paul Madden, Gerry Bron

JTS
73 Digby Road, London E9 6HX
T: 020 8985 3000 F: 020 8986 7688
Email: sales@jts-uk.com
Website: jts-uk.com
Studio Mgr: Keith Jeffrey

KEYNOTE AUDIO SERVICES LTD
Smoke Tree House, Tilford Rd, Farnham, Surrey GU10 2EN
T: 01252 794253 F: 01252 792642
Email: admin@keynoteaudio.co.uk
Website: keynoteaudio.co.uk
MD: Tim Wheatley

LANSDOWNE STUDIOS
Lansdowne House, Lansdown Road, London W11 3LP
T: 020 7727 0041 F: 020 7792 8904
Email: mastering@cts-lansdowne.co.uk
Website: cts-lansdowne.co.uk/mastering
Mastering Engineer: Mike Brown

LIQUID MASTERING
Unit 6Q, Atlas Business Centre, Oxgate Lane, London NW2 7HU
T: 020 8452 2255 F: 020 8422 4242
Email: sales@liquidmastering.co.uk
Website: liquidmastering.co.uk
Director: Bob Kane

THE MACHINE ROOM
54-58 Wardour Street, London W1D 4JQ
T: 020 7734 3433 F: 020 7287 3773
Email: paul.willey@themachineroom.co.uk
Website: themachineroom.co.uk
Paul Willey

METROPOLIS DVD
The Power House, 70 Chiswick High Road, London W4 1SY
T: 020 8742 1111 F: 020 8742 2626
Email: reception@metropolis-group.co.uk
Website: metropolis-group.co.uk
Producer: Alex Sanders

METROPOLIS MASTERING
The Power House, 70 Chiswick High Road, London W4 1SY
T: 020 8742 1111 F: 020 8742 2626
Email: reception@metropolis-group.co.uk
Website: metropolis-group.co.uk
Mastering Bookings: Beta Ratel/Michelle Conroy

MOLINARE
34 Fouberts Place, London W1F 7PX
T: 020 7478 7000 F: 020 7478 7299
Website: molinare.co.uk

NICK MORGAN AUDIO PRODUCTION SERVICES
7 Overhill Road, London SE22 0PQ
T: 07939 052 689
Email: morgancom@aol.com
Nick Morgan

PORKY'S MASTERING
55-59 Shaftesbury Avenue, London W1D 6LD
T: 020 7494 3131 F: 020 7494 1669
Email: george@porkysprimecuts.com
Website: porkysprimecuts.com
Studio Mgr: George Peckham

REDWOOD STUDIOS
20 Great Chapel St, London W1F 8FW
T: 020 7287 3799 F: 020 7287 3751
Email: andrestudios@yahoo.co.uk
Website: redwoodstudios.co.uk
MD/Prod: Andre Jacquemin

REFLEX MEDIA SERVICES LTD
Unit 5, Cirrus, Glebe Road, Huntingdon
PE29 7DL
T: 01480 412222 F: 01480 411441
Email: roger@reflex-media.co.uk
Dir: Roger Masterson

REPEAT PERFORMANCE RPM
6 Grand Union Centre, West Row,
London W10 5AS
T: 020 8960 7222 F: 020 8968 1378
Email: info@rpmuk.com
Website: rpmuk.com
MD: Robin Springall

REVOLUTION DIGITAL
33 St James's Square, London
SW1Y 4JS
T: 020 7661 9303 F: 020 7661 9413
Email: laura@rdigital.co.uk
Website: rdigital.co.uk
MD: Laura Gate-Eastley

REYNOLDS MASTERING
55 Albert Street, Colchester, Essex
CO1 1RX
T: 01206 562655 F: 01206 761936
MD: Peter Reynolds

SANCTUARY
Town House Mastering Sanctuary Town
House, 140 Goldhawk Road, London
W12 8HH
T: 020 8932 3200 F: 020 8932 3209
Email: mastering@sanctuarystudios.co.uk
Website: sanctuarystudios.co.uk
Booking Co-ordinators: Sophie Nathan/
Lavinia Burrell

SOUND DISCS CD MASTERING & MANUFACTURING LTD
5 Barley Shotts Business Park, 246
Acklam Road, London W10 5YG
T: 020 8968 7080 F: 020 8968 7475
Email: info@sound-discs.co.uk
Website: sound-discs.co.uk Production
Director: Peter Bullick

SOUND GENERATION
Unit 3, Clarence Road, Greenwich,
London SE8 3EY
T: 020 8691 2121 F: 020 8691 3144
Email: at@soundperformance.co.uk
Website: soundperformance.co.uk
Studio Mgr: Andrew Thompson

SOUND PERFORMANCE
Unit 3, Clarence Road, Greenwich,
London SE8 3EY
T: 020 8691 2121 F: 020 8691 3144
Email: sales@soundperformance.co.uk
Website: soundperformance.co.uk
Sales

SOUNDS GOOD LTD
12 Chiltern Enterprise Centre, Station
Rd, Theale, Reading, Berks RG7 4AA
T: 0118 930 1700 F: 0118 930 1709
Email: sales-info@sounds-good.co.uk
Website: sounds-good.co.uk
Dir: Martin Maynard

STREAM DIGITAL MEDIA LTD
61 Charlotte St, London W1P 1LA
T: 020 7208 1567 F: 020 7208 1555
Email: info@streamdm.co.uk
Website: streamdm.co.uk
Head of Stream: Paul Kind

TRANSFERMATION LTD
63 Lant Street, London SE1 1QN
T: 020 7417 7021 F: 020 7378 0516
Email: trace@transfermation.com
Website: transfermation.com
Co-ordinator: Tracey Roper

VDC GROUP
VDC House, South Way, Wembley,
Middx HA9 0HB
T: 020 8903 3345 F: 020 8900 1427
Email: enquiries@vdcgroup.com
Website: vdcgroup.com
Sales Executive: Aaron Williamson

VIDEOSONICS
13 Hawley Crescent, London NW1 8NP
T: 020 7209 0209 F: 020 7419 4460
Email: info@videosonics.com
Website: videosonics.com
Studio Mgr: Peter Hoskins

WATERFALL STUDIOS
2 Silver Road, London W12 7SG
T: 020 8746 2000 F: 020 8746 0180
Email: sam@waterfall-studios.com
Website: waterfall-studios.com
Director: Samantha Leese

HIGHLY RECOMMENDED MASTERING

Alchemy

Metropolis

Abbey Road

The Exchange

Sound Masters

Transfermation

Townhouse

1 2 3 4 5 6 7 8 9 10 11 12 13 14 15

MUSIC PRODUCTION COMPANIES

ADMAX MUSIC
25 Heathmans RD, London SW6 4TJ
T: 020 7371 5756 F: 020 7371 7731
Email: stirling@stakis.com
Website: pureuk.com
Ian Ferguson Brown

AIR-EDEL ASSOCIATES
18 Rodmarton Street, London W1U 8BJ
T: 020 7486 6466 F: 020 7224 0344
Email: mrodford@air-edel.co.uk
Website: air-edel.co.uk
MD: Maggie Rodford

ARCLITE PRODUCTIONS
Unit 303, Safe Store 5-10 Eastman Rd, London W3 7YG
T: O20 8743 4000
Email: info@arcliteproductions.com
Website: arcliteproductions.com
Prod: Alan Bleay

DAVID ARNOLD MUSIC LTD
Unit 9, Dry Drayton Industries, Dry Drayton, Cambridge CB3 8AT
T: 01954 212020 F: 01954 212222
Email: alex@davidarnoldmusic.com
Website: davidarnoldmusic.com

ARTEMIS MUSIC LTD
Pinewood Studios, Pinewood Rd, Iver Heath, Bucks SL0 0NH
T: 01753 650766 F: 01753 654774
Email: info@artemismusic.com
Website: artemismusic.com
MD: Mike Sheppard

BAZZA PRODUCTIONS
116 Ember Lane, Esher, Surrey KT10 8EL
T: 020 8398 1274 F: 020 8398 1353
Email: bsguard@aol.com
Website: barrieguard.com
MD: Barrie Guard

BEETROOT MUSIC
3/4 Portland Mews, D'Arblay St, London W1F 8JF
T: 020 7437 7889 F: 020 7734 9230
Email: info@beetrootmusic.com
Website: beetrootmusic.com Co
MD: Tish Lord

BMG PRODUCTION MUSIC
Bedford House, 69-79 Fulham High Street, London SW6 3JW
T: 020 7384 8188 F: 020 7384 2744
Email: Production.Music@bmg.com
Website: bmgmusicsearch.com
Head of Mktg: Juliette Richards

BOOM! MUSIC LTD
16 Blackwood Close, West Byfleet, Surrey KT14 6PP
T: 01932 336212
Email: Phil@music4media.tv
Website: music4media.tv
Composer: Phil Binding

BRILLIANT MUSIC PRODUCTION
Unit 2, The Quarry, Kewstoke Road, Worle, Weston-Super-Mare BS22 9LS
T: 01761 470023
Email: davidrees@brilliantmusicproductions.co.uk
Partner: David Rees

CALECHE STUDIOS
175 Roundhay Road, Leeds LS8 5AN
T: 0113 219 4941 F: 0113 249 4941
Email: caleche.studios@virgin.net
MD: Leslie Coleman

CANDLE
44 Southern Row, London W10 5AN
T: 020 8960 0111 F: 020 8968 7008
Email: email@candle.org.uk
Website: candle.org.uk
MD: Tony Satchell

CARITAS MEDIA MUSIC (INC CARITAS MUSIC LIBRARY)
28 Dalrymple Crescent, Edinburgh EH9 2NX
T: 0131 667 3633 F: 0131 667 3633
Email: media@caritas-music.co.uk
Website: caritas-miusic.co.uk
MD: James Douglas

CHICKEN SOUNDS
19 Lyncroft Gardens, London NW6 1LB
T: 020 7209 2586 F: 020 7209 2586
Email: suewhitehouse@ukonline.co.uk
Website: chickensounds.co.uk
Director: Sue Whitehouse

DELICIOUS DIGITAL
Fourth Floor, Voysey House, Barley Mow Passage, London W4 4GB
T: 020 8987 6181 F: 020 8987 6182
Email: ed@deliciousdigital.com
Website: deliciousdigital.com
Creative Director: Ed Moris

DIGITAL VISION
India House, 45 Curlew St, London SE1 2ND
T: 020 7378 5555 F: 020 7378 5735
Email: sales@digitalvisiononline.co.uk
Website: digitalvisiononline.co.uk
UK Sales: Joanne Rees

DAVID DUNDAS MUSIC LTD
142 Battersea Park Road, London SW11 4NB
T: 020 7627 8017 F: 020 7627 5412
Email: tai.dundas@virgin.net
Producer: Tai Dundas

EAGLE EYE PRODUCTIONS
Unit 8, Lots Road, Chelsea, London SW10 0QS
T: 020 7351 6429 F: 020 7351 1018
Email: mail@eagle-rock
Website: eagle-rock.com
Dir Of Intl Acquisitions: John Gaydon

G3 MUSIC
13 Hales Prior, Calshot Street, London N1 9JW
T: 020 8361 2170 F: 020 8361 2170
Email: g3music@g3music.com
Website: g3music.com Creative Dir: Greg Heath

HIGHER GROUND MUSIC PRODUCTIONS
The Stables, Albury Lodge, Albury, Ware, Herts SG11 2LH
T: 01279 776 019
Email: info@highergrounduk.com
Website: highergrounduk.com
Creative & Commercial Dir: Greg Newman

HOWARTH & JOHNSTON
61 Timber Bush, Leith, Edinburgh, Lothian EH6 6QH

T: 0131 555 2288 F: 0131 555 0088
Email: doit@redfacilities.com
Website: redfacilities.com
Partner: Max Howarth

HYDRAPHONIC
127, Tottenham Road, London N1 4EA
T: 020 7923 7638
Email: info@hydraphonic.net
Manager: Brian Betts

IN A CITY
Unit 49, Carlisle Business Centre, 60 Carlisle Rd, Bradford BD8 8BD
T: 01904 438753 F: 01274 223204
Email: cc@inacity.co.uk
Website: inacity.co.uk
MD: Carl Stipetic

INSTANT MUSIC
14 Moorend Crescent, Cheltenham, Gloucestershire GL53 0EL
T: 01242 523304 F: 01242 523304
Email: info@instantmusic.co.uk
Website: instantmusic.co.uk
MD: Martin Mitchell

JOE & CO (MUSIC)
59 Dean Street, London W1D 6AN
T: 020 7439 1272 F: 020 7437 5504
Email: justine@joeandco.com
Website: joeandco.com
Office Mgr: Justine Campbell

LBS MANCHESTER
11-13 Bamford Street, Stockport, Cheshire SK1 3NZ
T: 0161 477 2710 F: 0161 480 9497
Email: info@lbs.co.uk
Website: lbs.co.uk
Prod: Adders

LIVING PRODUCTIONS
39 Tadorne Road, Tadworth, Surrey KT20 5TF
T: 01737 812922 F: 01737 812922
Email: Livingprods@ukgateway.net
Dir/Co Sec: Norma Camby

MAD HAT STUDIOS IN TOWN
off Lichfield Street, Walsall, West Midlands WS1 1SQ
T: 01922 616244 F: 01922 616244
Email: music@madhat.co.uk
Website: madhat.co.uk
Dir: Clair Swan

MCASSO MUSIC PRODUCTION
9 Carnaby Street, London W1V 9PE
T: 020 7734 3664 F: 020 7439 2375
Email: music@mcasso.com
Website: mcasso.com
Producer: Dan Hancock

MISOUND LTD STUDIO
7, Fort Box, 25-31 Penrose Street, London SE17 3DW
T: 020 7701 0293 F: 020 7701 0293
Website: eliotj.co.uk
Music Prod: Jim Eliot

MOMENTS MUSIC LIBRARY
7 Brunswick Close, Thames Ditton, Surrey KT7 0EU
T: 020 8398 1450 F: 020 8398 1450
Email: smd.music@virgin.net
Dir: Al Dickinson

MURFIN MUSIC INTERNATIONAL
1 Post Office Lane, Kempsey, Worcestershire WR5 3NS
T: 01905 820659 F: 01905 820015
Email: muff.murfin@virgin.net

Website: muffmurfin.com
MD: Muff Murfin

NORTH STAR MUSIC PUBLISHING LTD
PO Box 868, Cambridge CB1 6SJ
T: 01787 278256 F: 01787 279069
Email: info@northstarmusic.co.uk
Website: northstarmusic.co.uk
MD: Grahame Maclean

PANAMA PRODUCTIONS
Sovereign House, 12 Trewartha Road, Praa Sands, Penzance, Cornwall TR20 9ST
T: 01736 762826 F: 01736 763328
Email: panamus@aol.com
Website: panamamusic.co.uk
MD: Roderick Jones

PRIMROSE MUSIC PUBLISHING
1 Leitrim House, 36 Worple Rd, London SW19 4EQ
T: 020 8946 7808 F: 020 8946 3392
Email: jestersong@msn.com
Website: primrosemusic.com
Director: R B Rogers

PROPHET MUSIC
147 Drummond Street, London NW1 2PB
T: 020 7383 5003 F: 020 7383 5004
Email: info@prophetmusic.co.uk
Website: prophetmusic.co.uk
MD: Jonathan Brigden

RBM COMPOSERS
Churchwood Studios, 1 Woodchurch Road, London NW6 3PL
T: 020 7372 2229 F: 020 7372 3339
Email: rbm@easynet.co.uk
MD: Ronnie Bond

SAVIN PRODUCTIONS
164 Streetsbrook Road, Solihull, Birmingham, West Midlands B90 3PH
T: 0121 240 1100 F: 0121 240 4042
Email: info@savinproductions.com
Website: savinproductions.com
Prop: Brian Savin

SOMETHIN' ELSE SOUND DIRECTION
Unit 1-4, 1A Old Nichol Street, London E2 7HR
T: 020 7613 3211 F: 020 7739 9799
Email: info@somethin-else.com
Website: somethin-else.com
Dir: Steve Ackerman

SOUND ILLUSTRATION
St Nicholas Cottage, Hedsor Priory, Bourne End, Buckinghamshire SL8 5JW
T: 01628 526562
Website: music4media.co.uk
MD: Jamie Perkins

SOUNDBYTES PROMOTIONS
PO Box 1209, Stafford ST16 1XW
T: 01785 222382 F: 0871 277 3060
Email: soundbytes@btinternet.com
Creative Dir: Robert L Hicks

SOUNDSCAPE MUSIC & SOUNDDESIGN
7 Goodge Place, London W1P 1FL
T: 020 7436 2211 F: +31 35 622 9826
Email: info@soundscape.nl
Website: soundscape.nl
Producer: Alex Nijmolen

SOUNDTREE MUSIC LTD
Unit 124, Canalot Studios, 222 Kensal Road, London W10 5BN

T: 020 8968 1449 F: 020 8968 1500
Email: post@soundtree.co.uk
Business Mgr: Jo Feakes

TOWNEND MUSIC
44 Eastwick Crescent, Rickmansworth, Hertfordshire WD3 8YJ
T: 01923 720083 F: 01923 710587
Email: townendmus@aol.com
MD: Mike Townend

TRIMMER MUSIC
13 Outram Road, London N22 7AB
T: 020 8881 7510
Email: trimmer@thejazzangels.fsnet.co.uk
MD: Akane Abe

TRIPLE M PRODUCTIONS
31 Elmar Rd, Aigburth, Liverpool L17 0DA
T: 0151 727 7405 F: 0151 727 7405
Email: mikemoran@breathemail.net
Website: triplemproductions.mersinet.co.uk
Producer/Composer: Mike Moarn

ULTIMATE UNIT
6 Belfont Trading Estate, Mucklow Hill, Halesowen, West Midlands B62 8DR
T: 0121 585 8001 F: 0121 585 8003
Email: info@ultimate1.co.uk
Website: ultimate1.co.uk
Manager: Andy Tain

VISUAL MUSIC
West House, Forthaven, Shoreham by Sea, W Sussex BN43 5HY
T: 01273 453422 F: 01273 452914
Email: visualmusic@richard-durrant.com
Website: richard-durrant.com
Composer: Richard Durrant

WAVSUB MUSIC
Penvose Cottage, Summers Street, Lostwithiel, Cornwall PL22 0DH
T: 08700 702 265
Email: info@wavsub.com
Website: wavsub.com
Projects Manager: Lisa Baker

RECORDING STUDIOS

ABBEY ROAD STUDIOS
3 Abbey Road, London NW8 9AY
T: 020 7266 7000 F: 020 7266 7250
Email: bookings@abbeyroad.com
Website: abbeyroad.com
Studio Mgr: Colette Barber

AIR STUDIOS (LYNDHURST)
Lyndhurst Hall, Lyndhurst Road, London
NW3 5NG
T: 020 7794 0660 F: 020 7794 8518
Email: info@airstudios.com
Website: airstudios.com
Bookings Mgr: Alison Burton

AIR TANK STUDIOS
138A Chiswick High Road, London
W4 1PU
T: 020 8994 4443 F: 020 8995 1051
Email: info@airtank.co.uk
Website: airtank.co.uk
Studio Mgr: Bootus McManus

AIRTIGHT PRODUCTIONS UNIT
16, Albany Rd Trading Estate, Albany
Rd, Chorlton M21 OAZ
T: 0161 881 5157
Email: info@airtightproductions.co.uk
Website: airtightproductions.co.uk
Director: Anthony Davey

ANGEL STUDIOS
The Brainyard, 156-158 Gray's Inn
Road, London WC1X 8ED
T: 020 7209 0536
Email: info@arriba-records.com
Dir: S-J Henry

ANGELSWORD PRODUCTIONS LTD
Little Barn, Plaistow Road, Loxwood,
West Sussex RH14 0SX
T: 01403 751 862 F: 01403 753 564
Email: jonn@jonnsavannah.co.uk
Website: jonnsavannah.co.uk
Dir: Jonn Savannah

ARRIBA STUDIOS
256-258 Gray's Inn Road, London
WC1X 8ED
T: 020 7713 0998
Email: info@arriba-records.com
Website: arriba-records.com
SJ/Baby Doc

AUDIOLAB WEST STREET
3 West St, Buckingham, Bucks
MK18 1HL
T: 01280 822814 F: 01280 822814
Email: office@alab.co.uk
Website: alab.co.uk
Studio Manager: Jamie Masters

AXIS RECORDING STUDIOS
3 Brown Street, Sheffield, South
Yorkshire S1 2BS
T: 0114 275 0283 F: 0114 275 4915
Email: axis@syol.com
Website: axisrecordingstudios.co.uk
Studio Mgr: Paul R Bower

BARK STUDIO
1A Blenheim Road, London E17 6HS
T: 020 8523 0110 F: 020 8523 0110
Email: Brian@barkstudio.co.uk
Website: barkstudio.co.uk
Studio Manager: Brian O'Shaughnessy

BBC RESOURCES (LONDON)
Maida Vale Music Studios, Delaware Road, London W9 2LH
T: 020 7765 3374 F: 020 7765 3203
Email: adam.askew@bbc.co.uk
Ops Mgr: Adam Askew

BEIGE PHUNK PRODUCTIONS
54 Great Marlborough St, London W1F 7JU
T: 020 7434 9199 F: 020 7434 3994
Email: info@beigephunk.com
Website: beigephunk.com
Director: Khaled Bin Ali

BIFFCO
20 Ringsend Road, Dublin 4, Ireland
T: 00 353 1 668 5567
F: 00 353 1 667 0114
Email: biffco1@indigo.ie
Website: biffco.net
Studio Mgr: Dave Morgan

BIG BOSS PRODUCTIONS
9 Parade Mews, Norwood Road, London SE27 9AX
T: 020 8671 6134 F: 020 8671 6134
Email: studio@bigbossproductions.co.uk
Website: bigbossproductions.co.uk
MD: Yiannis Constantinou

BLAH STREET STUDIOS
The Hop Kiln, Hillside, Odiham, Hants RG29 1HX
T: 01256 701112 F: 01256 701106
Email: studio@blahstreet.co.uk
Website: blahstreet.co.uk
Producer: Nick Hannan

BLAKAMIX INTERNATIONAL
Garvey House, 42 Margetts Road, Bedford MK42 8DS
T: 01234 302115 F: 01234 854344
Email: blakamix@aol.com
Website: blakamix.co.uk
MD: Dennis Bedeau

BLUEPRINT STUDIOS
Elizabeth House, 39 Queen Street, Salford, Manchester M3 4DQ
T: 08700 11 27 60 F: 08700 11 27 80
Email: info@blueprint-studios.com
Website: blueprint-studios.com
Studio Manager: Tim Thomas

BLUESTONE RECORDING STUDIO
11 Uxbridge Street, London W8 7TQ
T: 020 7243 4101 F: 020 7243 4131
Email: bluestudio@cs.com
Website: bluestonestudio.co.uk
Manager: Chris Wyles

THE BRIDGE FACILITIES LTD
55-57 Great Marlborough St, London W1F 7JX
T: 020 7434 9861 F: 020 7494 4658
Email: bookings@thebridge.co.uk
Website: thebridge.co.uk
Facilities Mgr: Tom McConville

THE BRILL BUILDING
Kings Court, 7 Osborne Street, Glasgow G1 5QN
T: 0141 552 6677 F: 0141 552 1354
Email: info@brillbuilding.pair.com
Website: brillbuilding.pair.com
Studio Mgr: Angela Ross

BRYN DERWEN STUDIO
Coed-y-Parc, Bethesda, Gwynedd LL57 4YW
T: 01248 600234 F: 01248 601933
Email: Laurie@brynderwen.co.uk

Website: brynderwen.co.uk
Manager: Laurie Gane

CASTLESOUND STUDIOS
The Old School, Park View, Pencaitland, East Lothian EH34 5DW
T: 0131 666 1024 F: 0131 666 1024
Email: info@castlesound.co.uk
Website: castlesound.co.uk
Studio & Bookings Mgr: Freeland Barbour

THE CAVE STUDIO
155 Acton Lane, Park Royal, London NW10 7NJ
T: 020 8961 5818 F: 020 8965 7008
Email: cavestudio@jet-star.co.uk
Danny Ray

CENT MUSIC
Melbourne House, Chamberlain St, Wells BA5 2PJ
T: 01749 689074 F: 01749 670315
Email: kevin@centrecords.com
Website: centrecords.com
MD: Kevin Newton

CHAPEL STUDIOS
Bryants Corner, South Thorseby, Lincolnshire LN13 0AS
T: 01507 480305 F: 01507 480752
Studio Mgr: Andy Dransfield

CHEM19 RECORDING STUDIOS
Unit 5C, Peacock Cross Trading Estate, Burnbank Road, Hamilton ML3 9AQ
T: 01698 286882
Email: mail@chem19studios.co.uk
Website: chem19studios.co.uk
Manager: Peter Black

THE CHURCH STUDIOS
145H Crouch Hill, London N8 9QH
T: 020 8340 9779 F: 020 8348 3346
Email: juliec@eligiblemusic.com
Studio Mgr: Julie O'Shea

THE DAIRY
43-45 Tunstall Road, London SW9 8BZ
T: 020 7738 7777 F: 020 7738 7007
Email: thedairy@dircon.co.uk
Website: thedairy.co.uk
Mark Evans

DEBRETT STUDIOS
42 Wood Vale, Muswell Hill, London N10 3DP
T: 020 8372 6179
Email: jwest@debrett41.freeserve.co.uk
Proprietorr: Jon West

DEEP RECORDING STUDIOS
187 Freston Road, London W10 6TH
T: 020 8964 8256 F: 020 8969 1363
Email: deep.studios@virgin.net
Website: deeprecordingstudios.com
Studio Manager: Mark Rose

DELTA RECORDING STUDIOS
Deanery Farm, Bolts Hill, Chatham, Kent CT4 7LD
T: 01227 732140 F: 01227 732140
Email: delta.studios@virgin.net
Website: deltastudios.co.uk
Julian Whitfield

DEP INTERNATIONAL STUDIOS
1 Andover Street, Birmingham, West Midlands B5 5RG
T: 0121 633 4742 F: 0121 643 4904
Email: enquiries@ub40.co.uk
Website: ub40.co.uk
Bkngs/Studio Mgr: Dan Sprigg

EARTH PRODUCTIONS
163 Gerrard Street, Birmingham, West Midlands B19 2AP
T: 0121 554 7424 F: 0121 554 9250
Email: earth.p@virgin.net
Studio Mgr: Natasha Godfrey

EBONY & IVORY PRODUCTIONS
11 Varley Parade, Edgware Road, Colindale, London NW9 6RR
T: 020 8200 7090
Email: SVLProds@aol.com
Studio Manager: Alan Bradshaw

EDEN STUDIOS LTD
20-24 Beaumont Road, Chiswick, London W4 5AP
T: 020 8995 5432 F: 020 8747 1931
Email: eden@edenstudios.com
Website: edenstudios.com
Studio Mgr: Natalie Horton

EMS AUDIO LTD
12 Balloo Avenue, Bangor, Co Down BT19 7QT
T: 028 9127 4411 F: 028 9127 4412
Email: ems@musicshop.to
Website: musicshop.to
Director: William Thompson

FOURFIVES MUSIC
21d Heathman's Rd, London SW6 4TJ
T: 020 7731 6555 F: 020 7371 5005
Email: mp@fourfives-music.com
Website: fourfives-music.com
Bookings Mgr: Mia Pillay

GATEWAY STUDIO
Kingston Hill Centre, Kingston, Surrey KT2 7LB
T: 020 8549 0014 F: 020 8547 7337
Email: studio@gsr.org.uk
Website: gsr.org.uk Studio
Administrator: Katy Burton

GOLDEN ACRID
78 Albion Road, Edinburgh, Lothian EH7 5QZ
T: 0131 659 6673
Email: info@goldenacrid.com
Website: goldenacrid.com
Studio Mgr: James Locke

GREAT LINFORD MANOR
Great Linford Manor, Great Linford, Milton Keynes, Buckinghamshire MK14 5AX
T: 01908 667432 F: 01908 668164
Email: bookings@greatlinfordmanor.com
Website: greatlinfordmanor.com
Studio Manager: Sue Dawson

THE HANGER RECORDING STUDIO
Unit H, 4 Doman Rd, Yorktown Ind Est., Camberley, Surrey GU15 3DF
T: 01276 685808 F: 01276 683060
Email: info@thehanger.co.uk
Website: thehanger.co.uk
Owner: Tom Gibbs, Barry Scott

HEADROOM STUDIOS LTD
23 Gatton Rd, Bristol BS2 9TF
T: 0117 983 8050 F: 0117 983 8063
Email: info@headroomstudios.co.uk
Website: headroomstudios.co.uk
Studio/Bookings Mgr: Ralph Ruppert

HEARTBEAT RECORDING STUDIO
Guildie House Farm, North Middleton, Gorbridge, Mid Lothian EH23 4QP
T: 01875 821102 F: 01875 821102
Email: eddie@logane.freeserve.co.uk
Engineer/Prod: David L Valentine

HIGH BARN STUDIO
The Bardfield Centre, Great Bardfield,
Braintree, Essex CM7 4SL
T: 01371 811291 F: 01371 811404
Email: info@bmn-music.com
Website: bmn-music.com
Studio Manager: Iain Court

IMPULSIVE STUDIO
71 High Street East, Wallend,
Tyne and Wear 7RJ
T 0191 262 4999 F 0191 263 7082
MD: David Wood.
Soundtracks 32-16-24

INSTANT MUSIC
14 Moorend Crescent, Cheltenham,
Gloucestershire GL53 0EL
T: 07957 355630 F: 01242 523304
Email: info@instantmusic.co.uk
Website: instantmusic.co.uk
MD: Martin Mitchell

JACOB'S STUDIOS LTD
Ridgway House, Dippenhall, Farnham,
Surrey GU10 5EE
T: 01252 715546 F: 01252 712846
Email: andy@jacobs-studios.co.uk
Website: jacobs-studios.co.uk
Studio Mgr: Andy Fernbach

JINGLE JANGLES
The Strand, 156 Holywood Rd, Belfast,
Co Antrim BT4 1NY
T: 028 9065 6769 F: 028 9067 3771
Email: steve@jinglejangles.tv
Website: jinglejangles.tv
MD: Steve Martin

KINGSIZE RECORDS
28 Lyon Road, Hersham, Surrey
KT12 3PU
Tel:01932 700400 F: 01932 702144
Email: info@ kingsize.co.uk
Website: Kingsize.co.uk
Lbl Mgr: Richard Crowmains.
Studio Mgr: Julian Shay.
Bookings Mgr Richard Crow-Mains.
Soundtracks Solitaire

KONK STUDIOS
84-86 Tottenham Lane, London N8 7EE
T: 020 8340 4757 or 020 8340 7873
F: 020 8348 3952
Email: Linda@konkstudio.com
Studio Mgr: Sarah Lockwood.
Bookings Mgr: Linda McBride.
STUDIO 1: Neve with GML Automation.
Studio 2 SSL G series.

LANSDOWNE RECORDING STUDIOS
Lansdowne House, Lansdowne Road,
London W11 3LP
T: 020 7727 0041 F: 020 7792 8904
Email: info@cts-lansdowne.co.uk
Website: cts-lansdowne.co.uk
Studio Mgr: Chris Dibble

THE LEISURE FACTORY LTD
The Leisure Factory, Oldfields, Cradley
Heath, West Midlands B64 6BS
T: 01384 637776 F: 01384 637227
Email: music@therobin.co.uk
Director: Mike Hamblett

THE LIBRARY
2 Sybil Mews, London N4 1EP
T: 07956 412 209
Email: jules@librarystudio.com

Website: librarystudio.com
Owner: Julian Standen

LINDEN STUDIO
Laurel Bank, Motherby, Penrith, Cumbria
CA11 0RL
T: 01768 483181 F: 01768 483181
Email: guy@lindenstudio.co.uk
Website: lindenstudio.co.uk
Producer/Engineer: Guy Forrester

MAD HAT STUDIOS IN TOWN
off Lichfield Street, Walsall, West
Midlands WS1 1SQ
T: 01922 616244 F: 01922 616244
Email: studio@madhat.co.uk
Website: madhat.co.uk
Prop: Claire Swan

MAP MUSIC LTD
46 Grafton Road, London NW5 3DU
T: 020 7916 0544 F: 020 7284 4232
Email: info@mapmusic.net
Website: mapmusic.net
MD: Chris Townsend

MAYFAIR RECORDING STUDIOS
11A Sharpleshall Street, London
NW1 8YN
T: 020 7586 7746 F: 020 7586 9721
Email: bookings@mayfair-studios.co.uk
Website: mayfair-studios.co.uk
Bkings/Studio Mgr: Daniel Mills

MCS STUDIO
7 Northington Street, London
WC1N 2JF
T: 020 7404 2647 F: 020 7404 2647
Email: kevin.delascasas@lineone.net
Prod/Engineer: Kevin de Las Casas

METROPOLIS STUDIOS
The Power House, 70 Chiswick High
Road, London W4 1SY
T: 020 8742 1111 F: 020 8742 2626
Email: reception@metropolis-group.co.uk
Website: metropolis-group.co.uk Studio
Bookings: Sophie Downs

MIGHTY ATOM STUDIOS
Dylan Thomas House, 32 Alexandra Rd,
Swansea SA1 5DT
T: 01792 476567 F: 01792 476564
Email: info@mightyatom.co.uk
Website: mightyatom.co.uk
Producer/Engineer: Joe Gibb

MILL HILL RECORDING COMPANY LTD
Unit 7, Bunns Lane Works, Bunns Lane,
Mill Hill, London NW7 2AJ
T: 020 8906 5038 F: 020 8906 9991
Email: enquiries@millhillmusic.co.uk
Website: millhillmusic.co.uk
MD: Roger Tichborne

MILOCO
36 Leroy Street, London SE1 4SP
T: 020 7232 0008 F: 020 7237 6109
Email: info@milomusic.co.uk
Website: miloco.co.uk
Bookings Mgr: Jess Gerry

MONNOW VALLEY STUDIOS
Old Mill House, Rockfield Road,
Monmouth NP25 5QE
T: 01600 712761 F: 01600 712761
Email: studio@monnowvalley.freeserve.co.uk
Website: monnowvalleystudios.com
Studio Mgr: Paul Durrant

MONROE PRODUCTION CO
103-105 Holloway Road, London
N7 8LT
T: 020 7700 1411
Email: monroehq@netscapeonline.co.uk
Studio Mgr: Halina Ciechanowska

MOTHER DIGITAL STUDIO
30 Redchurch St, Shoreditch, London
E2 7DP
T: 020 7739 8887
Email: studio@motherdigitalstudio.com
Website: motherdigitalstudio.com
Owner: Justin Morey

MUCHMOREMUSIC STUDIOS
Unit 29, Cygnus Business Centre,
Dalmeyer Road, London NW10 2XA
T: 020 8830 0330 F: 020 8830 0220
Email: info@muchmoremusic.net
Website: robert-miles.com
MD: Sandra Ceschia

MUSOWIRE
PO Box 100, Gainsborough DN21 3XH
T: 01427 628826
Email: info@musoswire.com
Website: musoswire.com
Proprietorr: Dan Nash

MWA STUDIOS
20 Middle Row, Ladbroke Grove,
London W10 5AT
T: 020 8964 4555 F: 020 8964 4666
Email: studios@musicwithattitude.com
Website: musicwithattitude.com
Studio Engineer: Matt Foster

NIMBUS PERFORMING ARTS CENTRE
Wyastone Leys, Monmouth,
Monmouthshire NP25 3SR
T: 01600 891090 F: 01600 891052
Email: adrian@wyastone.co.uk
Website: wyastone.co.uk
Director: Adrian Farmer

NO U TURN STUDIOS
Safestore, London W3 7YG
T: 020 8746 0998 F: 020 8743 3003
Email: nick@nouturnrecords.fsnet.co.uk
Website: nouturnrecords.com
Studio Mgr: Nick

NUCOOL STUDIOS
34 Beaumont Rd, London W4 5AP
T: 020 8248 2157
Email: smiles@richardniles.demon.co.uk
Website: richardniles.com
Director: Richard Niles

ODESSA WHARF STUDIOS
38 Upper Clapton Road, London
E5 8BQ
T: 020 8806 5508 F: 020 8806 5508
Email: odessa@mathias.idps.co.uk
Website: surf.to/odessa
MD: Gwyn Mathias

OLYMPIC STUDIOS
117 Church Road, Barnes, London
SW13 9HL
T: 020 8286 8600 F: 020 8286 8625
Email: siobhan@olympicstudios.co.uk
Website: olympicstudios.co.uk
Studio Mgr: Siobhan Paine

ONLINE STUDIOS UNIT
18-19 Croydon House, 1 Peall Road,
Croydon, Surrey CR0 3EX
T: 020 8287 8585 F: 020 8287 0220
Email: info@onlinestudios.co.uk
Website: onlinestudios.co.uk
MD: Rob Pearson

OPEN EAR PRODUCTIONS LTD
Main Street, Oughterard, Co Galway, Ireland
T: +353 91 552816 F: +353 91 557967
Email: info@openear.ie
Website: openear.ie
MD: Bruno Staehelin

OVNI AUDIO
33-37 Hatherley Mews, London E17 4QP
T: 020 8521 9595
Email: flavio.uk@ukonline.co.uk
Website: curiousyellow.co.uk
Owner: Flavio Curras

OXRECS DIGITAL MAGDALEN
Farm Cottage, Standlake, Witney, Oxfordshire OX29 7RN
T: 01865 300347 F: 01865 300347
Email: info@oxrecs.com
Website: oxrecs.com
Dir: Bernard Martin

PANTHER RECORDING STUDIOS
5 Doods Road, Reigate, Surrey RH2 0NT
T: 01737 210848 F: 01737 210848
Email: panther@dial.pipex.com
Website: dialspace.dial.pipex.com/sema/panther.htm

PARK LANE
974 Pollokshaws Road, Glasgow, Strathclyde G41 2HA
T: 0141 636 1218 F: 0141 649 0042
Email: graccounts@btconnect.com
Website: pls.uk.com
Studio Mgr: Alan Connell

PARR STREET STUDIOS
33-45 Parr Street, Liverpool L1 4JN
T: 0151 707 1050 F: 0151 707 1813
Email: info@parrstreet.co.uk
Website: parrstreet.co.uk
Bookings Manager: Paul Lewis

THE PIERCE ROOMS
Pierce House, London Apollo Complex, Queen Caroline Street, London W6 9QH
T: 020 8563 1234 F: 020 8563 1337
Email: meredith@pierce-entertainment.com
Website: pierce-entertainment.com
Studio Mgr: Meredith Leung

PLANET AUDIO STUDIOS
Travel House, Spring Villa Road, Edgware, London HA8 7EB
T: 020 8952 4355 F: 020 8952 4548
Email: helen@planetaudiostudios.com
Website: planetaudiostudios.com
GM: Helen Gammons

PLUTO STUDIOS
Hulgrave Hall, Tiverton, Tarporley, Cheshire CW6 9UQ
T: 01829 732427 F: 01829 733802
Email: info@plutomusic.com
Website: plutomusic.com
Studio Mgr: Keith Hopwood

POLLEN STUDIOS
97 Main Street, Bishop Wilton, York, North Yorkshire YO42 1SQ
T: 01759 368223
Email: sales@pollenstudio.co.uk
Website: pollenstudio.co.uk
Prop: Dick Sefton

THE PREMISES STUDIOS LTD
201-205 Hackney Road, Shoreditch, London E2 8JL

T: 020 7729 7593 F: 020 7739 5600
Email: info@premises.demon.co.uk
Website: premises.demon.co.uk
CEO: Viv Broughton

PRESSHOUSE
PO Box 6, Colyton, Devon EX24 6YS
T: 01297 553508 F: 01297 553709
Email: presshouse@zetnet.co.uk
Studio Mgr: Mark Tucker

PRIDEROCK RECORDING STUDIOS
Deppers Bridge Farm, Southam,
Warwicks CV47 2SZ
T: 01926 614640 F: 01926 614640
Email: studio@dreamville.demon.co.uk
Website: pride-rock.co.uk
MD: Dutch Van Spall

THE PRO TOOLS ROOM
Sanctuary House, 45-53 Sinclair Road,
London W14 0NS
T: 020 8932 3200 F: 020 8932 3207
Email: protools@sanctuarystudios.co.uk
Website: sanctuarystudios.co.uk
Studio Manager: Nikki Affleck

PULSE RECORDING STUDIOS
67 Pleasants Place, Dublin 8, Ireland
T: 00 353 1 478 4045
F: 00 353 1 475 8730
Email: pulse@clubi.ie
Website: pulserecording.com
Studio Mgr: Tony Perrey

PWL IN THE NORTH
380 Deansgate, Castlefield, Manchester
M3 4LY
T: 0161 833 3630 F: 0161 832 3203
Email: info@pwl-studios.com
Website: pwl-empire.com

QUO VADIS RECORDING STUDIO
Unit 1 Morrison Yard, 551A High Road,
London N17 6SB
T: 020 8365 1999
Email: quovadis_2002@yahoo.co.uk
Website: musicrecordingstudios.com
Studio Mgr: Dan MacKenzie

RAEZOR STUDIO
25 Frogmore, London SW18 1JA
T: 020 8870 4036 F: 020 8874 4133
Studio Mgr: Ian Wilkinson

RAK RECORDING STUDIOS
42-48 Charlbert Street, London
NW8 7BU
T: 020 7586 2012 F: 020 7722 5823
Email: trisha@rakstudios.co.uk
Website: rakstudios.co.uk Bookings
Mgr: Trisha Wegg

RAY HAYDEN PRODUCTIONS & STUDIOS
293 Mare Street, London E8 1EJ
T: 020 8986 8066 F: 020 8533 7978
Email: rayopaz@aol.com
Website: rayhayden.com
Prod: Ray Hayden

REACT STUDIOS
3 Fleece Yard, Market Hill, Buckingham
MK18 1JX
T: 01280 821840 F: 01280 821840
Email: info@reactstudios.co.uk
Website: reactstudios.co.uk
Studio Mgr: Tom Thackwray

THE REAL STEREO RECORDING COMPANY
14 Moorend Crescent, Cheltenham,
Gloucestershire GL53 0EL

T: 01242 523304 F: 01242 523304
Email: martin@instantmusic.co.uk
Website: instantmusic.co.uk
Prod Mgr: Martin Mitchell

REAL WORLD STUDIOS
Box Mill, Mill Lane, Box, Corsham, Wiltshire SN13 8PL
T: 01225 743188 F: 01225 743787
Email: studios@realworld.on.net
Website: realworld.on.net/studios
Studio Mgr: Owen Leech

RED FORT
The Sight And Sound Centre, Priory Way, Southall, Middlesex UB2 5EB
T: 020 8843 1546 F: 020 8574 4243
Email: kuljit@compuserve.com
Website: keda.co.uk
MD: Kuljit Bhamra

REVOLUTION STUDIOS
11 Church Road, Cheadle Hulme, Cheadle, Cheshire SK8 6LS
T: 0161 485 8942 F: 0161 485 8942
Email: revolution@wahtup.com
Prop: Andrew MacPherson

RIDGE FARM STUDIO
Rusper Road, Capel, Dorking, Surrey RH5 5HG
T: 01306 711202 F: 01306 711626
Email: info@ridgefarmstudio.com
Website: ridgefarmstudio.com
Bookings & Admin. Mgr: Ann Needham

RIVER RECORDINGS
3 Grange Yard, London SE1 3AG
T: 020 7231 4805 F: 020 7237 0633
Email: sales@riverproaudio.co.uk
Website: riverstudios.co.uk
MD: Joel Monger

RNT STUDIOS
Pinetree Farm, Cranborne, Dorset BH21 5RR
T: 01725 517204 F: 01725 517801
Email: info@rntstudios.com
Website: rntstudios.com
Studio Manager: Rick Parkhouse

ROGUE STUDIOS RA
4 Bermondsey Trading Estate, Rotherhithe New Road, London SE16 3LL
T: 020 7231 3257 F: 020 7231 7358
Email: info@RogueStudios.co.uk
Website: roguestudios.co.uk
Jon Paul Harper/Jim Down

ROLLOVER STUDIOS
29 Beethoven Street, London W10 4LJ
T: 020 8969 0299 F: 020 8968 1047
Email: bookings@rollover.co.uk
Studio Mgr: Phillip Jacobs

ROOSTER
117 Sinclair Road, London W14 0NP
T: 020 7602 2881 F: 020 7603 1273
Email: roosteraud@aol.com
Website: roosterstudios.com
Proprietorr: Nick Sykes

ROUNDHOUSE RECORDING STUDIOS
91 Saffron Hill, Clerkenwell, London EC1N 8PT
T: 020 7404 3333 F: 020 7404 2947
Email: roundhouse@stardiamond.com
Website: stardiamond.com/roundhouse
Studio Managers: Lisa Gunther & Maddy Clarke

SANCTUARY
Town House 150 Goldhawk Road,
London W12 8HH
T: 020 8932 3200 F: 020 8932 3207
Email: townhouse@sanctuarystudios.co.uk
Website: sanctuarystudios.co.uk
Studio Mgr: Nikki Affleck

SANCTUARY WESTSIDE STUDIOS
Olaf Centre, 10 Olaf Street, London
W11 4BE
T: 020 7221 9494 F: 020 7727 0008
Email: westside@sanctuarystudios.co.uk
Website: sanctuarystudios.co.uk
Booking Co-ordinator: Jo Buckley

SANCTUARY WESTWAY STUDIOS
8 Olaf Street, London W11 4BE
T: 020 7221 9041 F: 020 7221 9399
Email: westway@sanctuarystudios.co.uk
Website: sanctuarystudios.co.uk Asst
Studio Manager: Kathy Hunter

SAWMILLS STUDIO
Golant, Fowey, Cornwall PL23 1LW
T: 01726 833338 F: 01726 832015
Email: ruth@sawmills.co.uk
Website: sawmills.co.uk
Studio Mgr: Ruth Taylor

SILK STUDIOS
23 New Mount St, Manchester M4 4DE
T: 0161 953 4045 F: 0161 953 4001
Email: leesilkstudios@hotmail.com
Dir: Lee Stanley

SOLEIL STUDIOS
Unit 10, Buspace Studios, Conlan
Street, London W10 5AP
T: 020 7460 2117 F: 020 7460 3164
Email: soleil@trwuk.com
Proprietorr: Jose Gross

SOLITAIRE RECORDING STUDIO
45 Swiftbrook Drive, Tallaght, Dublin 24,
Ireland
T: +353 1 462 5544
F: +353 1 462 5545
Email: info@solitairestudio.com
Website: solitairestudio.com
MD: Alan Whelan

SONGWRITING & MUSICAL PRODUCTIONS
Sovereign House, 12 Trewartha Road,
Praa Sands, Penzance, Cornwall
TR20 9ST
T: 01736 762826 F: 01736 763328
Email: panamus@aol.com
Website: songwriters-guild.co.uk
MD: Colin Eade

SOUL II SOUL STUDIOS
36-38 Rochester Place, London
NW1 9JX
T: 020 7284 0393 F: 020 7284 2290
Email: sales@soul2soul.co.uk
Website: soul2soul.co.uk
Louise Howells/Ed Colman

THE SOUND JOINT
10 Parade Mews, London SE27 9AX
T: 020 8678 1404 F: 020 8671 0380
Email: info@soundjoint.fsnet.co.uk
Website: soundjoint.fsnet.co.uk
Director: Barnaby Smith

THE SOUND SUITE
92 Camden Mews, London NW1 9AG
T: 020 7485 4881 F: 020 7482 2210
Email: peterrackham@soundsuite.freeserve.co.uk
Studio Mgr: Peter Rackham

SOUNDTREE MUSIC
Unit 124, Canalot Studios, 222 Kensal Road, London W10 5BN
T: 020 8968 1449 F: 020 8968 1500
Email: post@soundtree.co.uk
Business Mgr: Jo Feakes

TALL ORDER STUDIOS
The Basement, 346 North End Road, London SW6 1NB
T: 020 7385 1816 F: 020 7385 1816
Email: paul@tallorder.org.uk
Website: tallorder.org.uk
Studio Mgr: Paul Southby

TAUREAN RECORDINGS LTD
Old Barn Studios, West Street Business Park, Stanford, Lincolnshire PE9 2PS
T: 01780 481353
Email: taurean@talk21.com Prod/MD: Brian Harris

TEMPLE MUSIC STUDIOS
48 The Ridgway, Sutton, Surrey SM2 5JU
T: 020 8642 3210 F: 020 8642 8692
Email: jh@temple-music.com
Website: temple-music.com
Chief Bottlewasher: Jon Hiseman

TRIBAL SOUND + VISION
66C Chalk Farm Road, London NW1 8AN
T: 020 7482 6945 F: 020 7485 9244
Email: tribal.sound@virgin.net
Website: tribaltreemusic.co.uk
Studio Manager: Kate Greenslade

TWIN PEAKS STUDIO
Ty Neuadd, Torpantau, Brecon Beacons, Mid Glamorgan CF48 2UT
T: 01685 359932 F: 01685 376500
Email: TwinPeaksStudio@aol.com
Website: TwinPeaksStudio.com
Director: Adele Nozedar

VERTICAL ROOMS
Road Farm, Ermine Way, Arrington, Herts SG8 3YY
T: 01223 207007 F: 01223 207007
Email: info@verticalrooms.com
Website: verticalrooms.com
Studio Manager: Phil Culbertson

VITAL SPARK STUDIOS
1 Waterloo, Isle Of Skye IV42 8QE
T: 01471 822484 F: 01471 822952
Email: chris@vitalspark.demon.co.uk
Manager: Chris Harley

WAREHOUSE
60 Sandford Lane, Kennington, Oxford OX1 5RW
T: 01865 736411
Email: info@warehousestudios.com
Website: warehousestudios.com
Studio Mgr: Steve Watkins

WATERRAT MUSIC STUDIOS
Unit 2 Monument Way East, Woking, Surrey GU21 5LY
T: 01483 764444
Email: jayne@waterrat.co.uk
Website: waterrat.co.uk
Proprietorr: Jayne Wallis

WELSH MEDIA MUSIC
Gorwelion, LLanfynydd, Carmarthen, Dyfed SA32 7TG
T: 01558 668525 F: 01558 668750
Email: dpierce@welshmediamusic.f9.co.uk
Studio & Bkings Mgr: Dave Pierce

WESTPOINT STUDIOS
39-40 Westpoint, Warple Way, London
W3 0RG
T: 020 8740 1616 F: 020 8740 4488
Email: respect@dircon.co.uk
Website: disc-studios.com
Studio Mgr: Cathy Gilliat

THE WINDINGS RESIDENTIAL RECORDING STUDIOS
Ffrwd Valley, Ffrwd, Wrexham, Clwyd
LL12 9TH
T: 01978 720420 F: 01978 757372
Email: windings@enterprise.net
Website: windings.co.uk
Studio Mgr: Max Rooks

WINDMILL LANE STUDIOS
20 Ringsend Road, Dublin 4, Ireland
T: +353 1 668 5567
F: +353 1 668 5352
Email: catherine@windmill.ie
Website: windmill.ie
Studio Mgr: Catherine Rutter

WISE BUDDAH CREATIVE
74 Great Titchfield St, London
W1W 7QP
T: 020 7307 1600 F: 020 7307 1601
Email: paul.plant@wisebuddah.com
Website: wisebuddah.com
Manager: Paul Plant

REHEARSAL ROOMS

ARIWA REHEARSAL STUDIOS
34 White Horse Lane, London
SE25 6RE
T: 020 8653 7744 F: 020 8771 1911
Email: info@ariwa.com
Website: ariwa.com
Studio Manager: Neil Fraser

BACKSTREET REHEARSAL STUDIOS
313 Holloway Road, London N7 9SU
T: 020 7609 1313 F: 020 7609 5229
Email: backstreet.studios@virgin.net
Website: backstreet.co.uk
Prop: John Dalligan

BLUEPRINT STUDIOS
Elizabeth House, 39 Queen Street,
Salford, Manchester M3 4DQ
T: 08700 11 27 60 F: 08700 11 27 80
Email: info@blueprint-studios.com
Website: blueprint-studios.com
Studio Manager: Tim Thomas

THE BRILL BUILDING
Kings Court, 7 Osborne Street, Glasgow
G1 5QN
T: 0141 552 6677 F: 0141 552 1354
Email: info@brillbuilding.pair.com
Website: brillbuilding.pair.com
Studio Mgr: Angela Ross

CHEM19 REHEARSAL STUDIOS
Unit 5C, Peacock Cross Trading Estate,
Burnbank Road, Hamilton ML3 9AQ
T: 01698 286882
Email: mail@chem19studios.co.uk
Website: chem19studios.co.uk
Manager: Peter Black

COLORSOUND AUDIO
68 Fountainbridge, Edinburgh,
Midlothian EH3 9PY
T: 0131 229 3588 F: 0131 221 1454
Email: r.heatlie@virgin.net
Website: colorsound.mu
MD: Bob Heatlie

DIAMOND DANCE STUDIO
6/8 Vestry Street, London N1 7RE
T: 020 7251 8858 F: 020 7251 8379
Email: gem@diamonddance.com
Website: diamondstudio.co.uk
Studio Mgr: Dawn Farrow

FALLING ANVIL STUDIOS
Unit 114 Stratford Workshops, Burford
Road, London E15 2SP
T: 020 8503 0415
Email: necker@falling-
anvil.freeserve.co.uk
Website: fallinganvil.co.uk
Studio Mgr: Necker

GOLDEN ACRID
78 Albion Road, Edinburgh, Lothian
EH7 5QZ
T: 0131 659 6673
Email: info@goldenacrid.com
Website: goldenacrid.com
Studio Mgr: James Locke

THE HANGER REHEARSAL ROOMS
Unit H, 4 Doman Rd, Yorktown Ind Est.,
Camberley, Surrey GU15 3DF
T: 01276 685808 F: 01276 683060
Email: info@thehanger.co.uk
Website: thehanger.co.uk
Studio Manager: Tom Gibbs

HOUSE OF MOOK STUDIOS
Unit 1, Authorpe Works, Authorpe Road,
Leeds LS6 4JB
T: 0113 230 4008
Email: mail@mookhouse.ndo.co.uk
Website: mookhouse.ndo.co.uk
Studio Mgr: Phil Mayne

ISLINGTON ARTS FACTORY
2 Parkhurst Road, Holloway, London
N7 0SF
T: 020 7607 0561 F: 020 7700 7229
Email: islington@artsfactory.fsnet.co.uk
Website: islingtonartsfactory.org.uk
Office Manager: Licy Clayden

JOHN HENRY'S LTD
16-24 Brewery Road, London N7 9NH
T: 020 7609 9181 F: 020 7700 7040
Email: johnh@johnhenrys.com
Website: johnhenrys.com
MD: John Henry

JUMBO MUSIC COMPLEX
387-389 Chapter Road, London
NW2 5NG
T: 020 8459 7256 F: 020 8459 7256
The Facilities Mgr

LAB 24
346 Kingsland Road, Ground Floor,
London E8 4DA
T: 07970 309470
Studio Mgr: Hamish Dzewu

MUSIC CITY LTD
122 New Cross Road, London
SE14 5BA
T: 020 7277 9657 F: 0870 7572004
Email: info@musiccity.co.uk
Website: musiccity.co.uk
Rehearsal Mgr: Chris Raw

OPUS23 SOUND STUDIO
23 New Mount Street, Manchester
M4 4DE
T: 0161 953 4077 F: 0161 953 4001
Email: info@opus23.co.uk
Website: opus23.co.uk
Owner: Sean Flynn

THE PREMISES STUDIOS LTD
201-205 Hackney Road, Shoreditch,
London E2 8JL
T: 020 7729 7593 F: 020 7739 5600
Email: info@premises.demon.co.uk
Website: premises.demon.co.uk
CEO: Viv Broughton

REACT STUDIOS
3 Fleece Yard, Market Hill, Buckingham
MK18 1JX
T: 01280 821840 F: 01280 821840
Email: info@reactstudios.co.uk
Website: reactstudios.co.uk
Studio Mgr: Tom Thackwray

RICH BITCH
505 Bristol Road, Selly Oak,
Birmingham, West Midlands B29 6AU
T: 0121 471 1339 F: 0121 471 2070
Email: richbitchstudios@aol.com
Website: rich-bitch.co.uk
Owner: Rob Bruce

RIVER STUDIOS
3 Grange Yard, London SE1 3AG
T: 020 7231 4805 F: 020 7237 0633
Email: sales@riverproaudio.co.uk
Website: riverstudios.co.uk
Joel Monger

ROGUE STUDIOS RA
4, Bermondsey Trading Estate,
Rotherhithe New Road, London
SE16 3LL
T: 020 7231 3257 F: 020 7231 7358
Email: info@roguestudios.co.uk
Website: roguestudios.co.uk
Jon-Paul Harper/Jim Down

THE SANCTUARY
Denbigh North Leisure, V7 Saxon
Street, Milton Keynes, Bukinghamshire
MK1 1SA
T: 01908 368984 F: 01908 277028
Email: sanctuary@xsleisure.co.uk
Mgr: Claire Vanneck

SOUNDBITE STUDIOS
Unit 32, 17 Cumberland Business Park,
Cumberland Avenue, London
NW10 7RG
T: 020 8961 8509 F: 020 8961 8994
Owner: Ranj Kumar

THE STUDIO
Tower Street, Hartlepool TS24 7HQ
T: 01429 424440 F: 01429 424441
Email: thestudiohartlepool@ntlworld.com
Website: studiohartlepool.com
Studio Manager: Liz Carter

SURVIVAL STUDIOS
Unit B18, Acton Business Centre,
School Road, London NW10 6TD
T: 020 8961 1977
Mgr: Simon Elson

SYNC CITY MEDIA LTD
16-18 Millmead Business Centre,
Millmead Road, Tottenham Hale,
London N17 9QU
T: 020 8808 0472
Email: sales@synccity.co.uk
Website: synccity.co.uk
Studio Manager: Ron Niblett

TERMINAL STUDIOS
4-10 Lamb Walk, London SE1 3TT
T: 020 7403 3050 F: 020 7407 6123
Email: info@terminal.co.uk
Website: terminal.co.uk
Prop: Charlie Barrett

WAREHOUSE
60 Sandford Lane, Kennington, Oxford
OX1 5RW
T: 01865 736411
Email: info@warehousestudios.com
Website: warehousestudios.com
Studio Mgr: Steve Watkins

WESTBOURNE REHEARSAL STUDIOS
The Rear Basement, 92-98 Bourne
Terrace, Little Venice, London W2 5TH
T: 020 7289 8142 F: 020 7289 8142
Studio Mgr: Chris Thomas

1
2
3
4
5
6
7
8
9
10
11
12
13
14
15

1

2

3

4

5

6

7

8

9

10

11

12

13

14

15

LIVE

WHAT IS THE ROLE OF THE LIVE VENUE?

LIVE IS ALIVE AND KICKING!

It is one area of the music business where the public's happy to pay more than ever before. They might only be prepared to pay £9.99 for a CD, but they'll pay more than £150 to go to a festival.

It's not surprising when you think about it. Live is a total experience and the experiential is a growth area in many aspects of life today. From restaurants to theme parks and cinemas, people are prepared to pay for an experience, especially one shared with many other people.

Like all experiential businesses, the live music scene is undergoing change and is dominated by big corporate players, but it still contains huge opportunities for breaking bands and for established bands to connect with their audiences and fans. There's nothing quite like the energy and atmosphere of a live performance.

THE IMPORTANCE OF LIVE TO THE REST OF THE BUSINESS

Record labels have always recognised the importance of live to their artists and have been prepared to provide hard cash in the form of tour support to get out there and make it happen. They know a tour is the best way to promote an album, and a band who regularly and successfully tour are much lower risk to a label, because they'll have a strong fan base that can be relied on to buy a minimum number of records.

They are just beginning to see that live is more than just a successful marketing tool: it's a major potential source of income in its own right. As CD revenues decline they are beginning to look at how they can get in on the act. It's no coincidence that Robbie Williams's huge record deal included a share of his live earnings, rather than just the traditional recoupment of tour support.

For a band starting out, live performance provides a unique opportunity. It enables you to develop material, your act and persona. Importantly it gives you instant feedback from your audience. Just as DJs talk about reading the crowd, the best live acts know how to connect with their audience. More importantly it is the best way of creating a buzz which, if it's strong enough and the band is good enough, will get them a record and publishing deal.

We're keen on live because it's the ultimate opportunity to do it for yourself, to be yourself and take risks. It's impossible not to get a kick when you go into a pub and are surprised by the raw talent of a band you have never heard of. It's enough to make you want to rush out and work in A&R. If anything, we want to encourage everyone to have a go and not be too planned or strategic about it. That's how you're more likely to develop your own style.

Live stretches from the biggest stadium to the smallest pub. Live offers unique opportunities for breaking bands to super groups. Obviously dinosaur bands make huge money from over-forties on heavily sponsored world tours. Even so, there are many opportunities for breaking bands to build a fan base and a buzz in smaller venues.

The level of support you need as a breaking band is minimal. As bands become more successful they need a more sophisticated team and booking agents become important.

LIVE IS BIG BUSINESS

Of course there's another side of live. One where money is counted in millions and bands are far away on stadium stages. There have always been big promoters, but in the USA and more recently in the UK they've been getting even bigger. The market was shaken up when Harvey Goldsmith went into receivership at the end of the 1990s. He left a large gap in the marketplace that was partially filled by SJM. The other big player was the US company SFX entertainments, the largest concert promoter in the US. It embarked on an aggressive acquisition programme in the UK, taking over the Midland Concert promotions group and the Marquee Group in 1999. This was followed by Barry Clayman Concerts, later that year. The next year SFX was sold to Clear Channel.

Clear Channel is huge in the US where it owns 1,170 radio stations, or 10% of the total. This is even higher in terms of music air play, it controls 60% of rock stations. Apart from being America's biggest concert-touring business, it owns radio research companies, an airplay monitoring system, syndicated programming, radio trade magazines, hundreds of thousands of outdoor billboards and 19 television stations.

In the UK Clear Channel controls large venues including Cardiff International Arena, the Sheffield Arena and the Carling Apollo venues in Manchester and Hammersmith. Clear Channel is important not just because of its size, but the way it integrates different parts of the business. In many ways it is operating like a major record label in live. Some might say it is becoming more important than a label, with the power to make or break bands.

MERCHANDISING AND SPONSORSHIP

As Clear Channel have identified, music remains a potent marketing tool. Pepsi and Coca Cola both compete to be part of the music scene. The biggest touring super bands are major sponsorship opportunities.

The Rolling Stones might be a generation older than most live audiences, but they have been masters at branding each of their tours and maximising sponsorship and advertising. From T-shirts to posters tour merchandising is actively sought after by fans.

The income from merchandising often makes the difference between a tour being in profit or not. Many artists have struck merchandising deals that extend far beyond live venues. J Lo Fragrance was the fastest-selling fragrance ever, with more than $160 million worth of Lopez's perfume sold in

1 2 3 4 5 6 7 8 9 10 11 12 13 14 15

three months and hip hop mogul Russell Simmons music merchandise labels have sales of over $300 million a year.

It's amazing to think that no T-shirts were sold at gigs or concerts until 1973 and even the Rolling Stones didn't catch on to this huge source of revenue until 1975. Now merchandising sales data is devoured as eagerly as CD or ticket sales.

As a band starting out there is much to learn from the Stones, whatever you think about them musically. They have their finger on the pulse when it comes to maximising their tour revenue, or at least their highly paid management do.

Many bands without a major deal make good money touring. They keep their fans informed through their website, and increasingly use it to sell tickets and merchandising.

THE FUTURE OF LIVE

In a business sense, live will probably follow the same trends as other leisure industries. The big players will get even bigger and the small players will get better, more distinctive and real.

As bigger players and more marketing and sponsorship money flows into the business, festivals and stadium concerts will become more packaged. Cheap flights and promoters who understand they can sell an experience not just a ticket will see a huge increase in ordinary fans travelling abroad to see bands. Promoters will arrange their whole trip. Tours will be branded more in their own right and fans will be better targeted. Promoters who are clever and managers who are smart will have better databases of fans and start to use more sophisticated methods of direct and viral marketing.

The balance of power is likely to shift more towards live and away from the major labels because live has the stronger relationship with the end consumer – the fan. They don't have to worry about Tesco pushing them on price, or illegal Internet downloads. Instead the Internet is a powerful promotional tool and the public seem to be prepared to pay significantly more for a better experience.

LIVE

So what are the big live players going to do with this shift in power, and what are the major labels going to do about it? **At least Clear Channel in America has a clear strategy. By dominating as many different channels as it can from radio, TV, theatre and venues to marketing and promotion, it cross-promotes**, giving artists profile across media, selling more to its consumers and offering a comprehensive package to corporate marketing clients. The end game for this sort of company could be similar to a huge entertainment company like Disney.

Other big players might expand their activities. Ministry of Sound started as a promoter in one venue, became a label and then went on to brand an island, Ibiza, and build an online community. There is no reason why other promoters shouldn't expand their activities. As labels lose touch with new bands because they scale back their A&R, there is an opportunity for live promoters to give more bands a break. It's not impossible that they will see the production of CDs and a recording contract as just another piece of merchandise and decide to expand into this area.

Major labels are already eyeing up live and will push to have a slice of it, either through acquisition or more contracts like Robbie Williams's, where a share of live earnings will be included in the deal.

At the other end of the business, live will get more interesting and real. We believe there will be more venues like Barfly at the Monarch in Camden where unsigned bands are staged and actively encouraged. The decline of dance music will bring live bands back to DJ-dominated venues and going to small gigs will come back to being a normal way of life, instead of clubbing or going to a huge stadium.

Not every pub will want to turn into a gastropub. More will realise that live music is back. Our prediction for 2005 is that pubs and venues will be the places to see the best bands.

TIPS FOR NEWCOMERS

- ***Booking your own tour:*** You can't afford an agent, and your manager's green, but that shouldn't stop you organising your own tour. The tour route plan needs to be carefully put together. You need to research the venues carefully. Don't go to the other end of the country for the sake of it. It's best to extend outwards in a radius from your local stronghold. It's more likely your fans will travel, and you might get away with less expensive nights away from home. If you don't have a manager, it's worth finding someone else to drive, so nobody is driving when they are exhausted. Ensure everything's agreed with the promoters at every venue. Send them a press pack, details of your website and a good demo to get the gig. Reputable venues will send you a contract ahead. This will set out the payment details.
- ***Playing festivals:*** It's virtually impossible to play big festivals without a reputation and an agent, except possibly Glastonbury. Even then your music has to be right, i.e. acoustic, ethnic or folk. You might get in if you're early enough, but there's stiff competition.

  Smaller festivals are easier and definitely worth playing, because the crowd and atmosphere are good. There's quite a circuit and it's a good idea to ask other bands where the next one is. There are many small festivals abroad: the Internet is the best way to get details.
- ***Playing colleges*:** The college circuit has been responsible for giving many bands their first break.

  In many ways the circuit is not what it used to be. Student unions don't have the money they used to, and aren't prepared to take such risks. The circuit is crying out for better promotion. Avalon have shown how it can be done with standup comedy, where they have attracted good sponsors and organised a proper schedule across the country.
- ***Showcases for unsigned bands:*** Going on tour is important to get experience, meet other bands and build up a fan base. When you're

ready you'll want to consider raising your profile in the business. That's why you're going to consider a showcase.

Some venues have proper showcase evenings for unsigned artists. The PRS sometimes supports these events and is a good source of information about where to find them. It's worth trying to get in on the unsigned acts part of 'In the City', an annual conference for the music industry held in mid-September, set up and run by Tony Wilson, which probably has more talent scouts and A&R per metre than any other gig or event. Thirty or forty bands are selected for the event, so if you want to be considered make sure you get a good demo and press pack to Tony as early as possible. A similar event has started in Glasgow and there's talk of something in Wales.

- ***Getting an agent:*** As you build up a reputation, consider getting an agent. If you don't you won't get into the best venues. It's best to take an agent on recommendation. Ask around, especially other bands. It's important that the agent works in your type of music and with bands at your level, otherwise s/he is not going to know the right venues and promoters.

  Increasingly bands are getting agents before they get a record deal, because they are using live to build a buzz to eventually get the right deal. It's worth talking to several before you make up your mind which to choose. Invite them to gigs and see what they think. Different agents have different levels of clout, so you have to check out their reputation as well as use your gut instinct.

  If you have a record deal you'll probably find booking agents are approaching your label. Most record companies will be keen to find you a good booking agent to maximise your live exposure, to help publicise your album or single. Often they'll get a financial kickback from the label in the form of a retainer or a small percentage of record sales. This is usually no more than 1% and often less. It's important to make sure this is the label's expense and not deducted from your royalty.

- ***Booking agents' fees and contracts:*** Booking agents typically charge 10–15% of gross tour income. They have no interest in merchandising or sponsorship income. The manager takes his commission from the remainder. There's a clear distinction between roles and responsibilities of the manager and the agent on a tour. The manager looks after all aspects of the tour other than the actual booking which is the agent's job. Booking agents can be contracted for a single tour, but the best ones look for a fixed term. Most are looking for three- to five-year terms. They will expect this to be an exclusive contract, and therefore to handle all your live work. Obviously you'll have the right to turn down their recommendations, but once agreed you must fulfil your obligations.
- ***Promoters' fees and contracts:*** Promoters may own the venue, or they may be a third party who have a deal with a venue. They are responsible for security and selling tickets. Their profit comes from what's left from paying the venue on one side and the artist and their team on the other. In addition the promoter can control merchandise and food and drink sales, and make money from these as well. They need to promote actively to maximise ticket sales, minimise risk and make money.

  Promoters' contracts should specify any agreements about equipment and personnel. If it's an overseas venue they should provide all relevant work permits. It's their responsibility to provide insurance cover for any accidents among members of the public. For established artists there's an agreed guaranteed minimum fee negotiated with the promoter regardless of sales. Fees vary, usually being about 10% of net ticket sales.
- ***Funding a tour:*** There are ways to fund a tour other than just relying on ticket sales. Merchandising doesn't have to be the big bands' prerogative. T-shirts can be printed in small batches and sold on your website. CDs can be easily duplicated and a little expense can make their packaging look professional. You'll probably need everything you

can raise from these to fund your transport and equipment when you start. Artists who are smart and know how to control their costs can make a good living from touring.

It's possible but not easy for unsigned bands to get sponsorship. Beer companies are worth a try, and if nothing else you will probably end up with some free product. If you have a record deal, you can probably get support from your record company to get out on the road. Although it's not usually in the contract, it's in their interest for you to be out touring and promoting your latest album. Often they'll be prepared to underwrite any shortfall from the costs of touring; this is known as tour support and is usually 100% recoupable from royalties from record sales. In terms of new bands if they have real potential, their record label may be prepared to pay a buy-on fee to the headline band for the privilege of allowing them to be their support band. (A buy-on fee is when a supporting band pays a fee to perform live in concert before the main headline act goes on stage.) That's why you often see a support band from the same label as the headline band. It's another way the label can use its muscle.

- ***Other personnel:*** When you're successful you'll probably employ a tour manager who works alongside your manager to handle the tour details and be in charge of the tour on a daily basis, dealing with problems as they happen. Usually they receive a fixed fee.

  Your performance can be wrecked by the wrong sound levels and bad lighting. As soon as you can afford it, or make your record company pay for it, you should get your own sound engineer and not rely on pot luck at every venue. Then when you reach another level get your own lighting engineer.

  If you're a solo artist you'll need to engage backing musicians for the tour. They will be employed on fixed retainers and fees. There are different types of retainers. If they are really important you will pay them enough to have them on a first-call basis.

- ***Publicising the tour:*** You and your promoter are jointly responsible for this. If you have a label deal they will also want to get involved. If your record company is already planning a marketing campaign, you will want to make sure it's coordinated with your tour, for example, to increase the posters where you're playing. The label's press office should help you get appearances to promote the tour.

  Your website and record company are important in terms of promoting the tour and where possible selling tickets online. Getting your fan base out on tour with you is important to maximise the buzz. Established groups with large fan clubs do deals with promoters to give them special offers, such as transport and accommodation packages.

THE VIEW FROM WITHIN

BARRY DICKINS – ITB

Barry is founder of ITB, the biggest, most respected music agency in Europe. At 17 he was agent for The Who and later Jimi Hendrix and The Kinks.

How does today's music business differ from when you started out?

Punk was great because it had anarchy and energy. Most bands today feel as if they come off a conveyer belt. People in the business say artists of today are legends and icons, but what a load of bollocks. Artists like Dylan and Marley are legends, because they have something to say and are leaders. Youth around the world want someone who can challenge the establishment and social conditions. For me it's about saying something that matters.

I've probably lost lots of money from not working with typical pop bands, and probably gained certain acts because of it. I'm fortunate that my client roster has included people like Bob Dylan, Neil Young, Joni Mitchell and Alanis Morissette. Before I finish in this business I want to find one more artist who is important to music and the world. Then I'd be very happy.

What should a new artist look for in an agent?

Someone who knows their music, knowledge of the scene and has the hunger. The problem with this business is that there are people working in the music business who don't understand it or what they're talking about.

How do you work with promoters to make sure your artists play to full venues?

It depends on the act and the venue. If you have a new act, especially with a different type of audience, where you don't know the buying pattern, our advice to promoters is to promote your concert intensely from the start. Make sure that during the last two to three weeks leading up to the day of the concert, you increase the intensity of the campaign even more, especially the last few days. The general rule is not to stop promoting until you've sold out of tickets. Whatever you do, I tell them not to sell more tickets than the venue holds. It might sound crazy, but promoters do it all the time.

Do you think the music business is changing?
Any change must come from the artists. I think the business is swinging back to the indies. But with the majors, there's no room for development. Did you know Supertramp's first two albums with A&M flopped, but their third sold millions all around the world? If Supertramp started out today they'd have been dropped and never would have succeeded.

SIMON MORAN – SJM

Simon Moran is one of the biggest players in the live part of the music business. SJM promotes a staggering 1,400 concerts a year.

How did you get started?
When I started out sixteen years ago, the thought of promoting one gig seemed hard enough. I used to wonder how someone could do a whole tour. But like everything you've got to start off small and learn the ropes. The small gigs at the beginning taught me loads of lessons and prepared me for the bigger concerts. When I was at university, I wanted to see The Farm play, but no one was putting them on, so I managed to organise it. I made a bit of money from the gig, so I thought why not do it again?

From then on I went around organising tiny gigs with unknown bands. It was really hard work in the beginning. That first year I started, 1988, was hard. I was living with my mum and dad. I had to go everywhere by train. I had to carry bits of equipment in plastic bags. I felt like shit. Lots of the bands I looked after were so new that they couldn't fill a venue. I was getting £50 a week from the Enterprise Allowance Scheme. Money and everything was shit.

Then, when I was 19, I hassled the manager of New Order until he agreed that I could put them on at Sheffield University. Then I wanted Smiley Culture, who had that 'Police Office' hit. I tracked him down at a gig in Manchester, and waited for him after the show. I said, 'Look I'm putting on New Order. Will you do a concert in Sheffield University?' He gave me a number, I called it and was put through to a record shop in Clapham. I went down and we agreed a deal, but although the gig was meant to start at 9.30, he still hadn't turned up at 10.30. I thought, there's going to be a riot in here, but he turned up just before the headline act went on.

There must have been some tough times?
We did a concert and only 27 people turned up. We'd expected 500. I was so pissed off I stood outside for more than two hours kicking the Calor gas. When you're young you just don't have the contacts and relationships to secure artists who are guaranteed to sell out, so you just have to take a risk on unknown bands. Although even now we will work with new unsigned bands if we believe in them.

How did you get to build such a successful business?
It's all about hard work and providing a good service for the artist. You need to understand what they want and make sure you have an efficient team, so that everything runs smoothly. Unlike a record company, you have no long-term contracts with an artist. It means you have to find the right balance, because the last thing you want to do is to get into a fight with the band over crap, because if you do, you'll probably never work with them again. It's all about relationships and working with the right professional people.

What's been your favourite gig?
I suppose early on Stone Roses in Blackpool was an important point in their career. My first outdoor gig was James at Alton Towers – we sold out 35,000 tickets. It was nearly a disaster. The weather was terrible: the wind was so strong the top blew off the stage. We thought we would have to cancel it because of the rain and the electrics, but in the end we managed to get the top back on.

Later Oasis at Knebworth was a highlight and The Verve in Wigan outdoors was good and Radiohead outdoors for 45,000 people was great. Sometimes we persuade bands to tour, when they're not even considering it. Take M People – they never did a tour and I remember thinking they could. It was early on and at the time they didn't have a manager or an agent. I managed to track down Mike Pickering in Manchester, and then I kept ringing and hassling him, telling him that it would work really well if he was to do something live. We met Pete Hatfield at Deconstruction and then organised a small tour. In the end we took them on to do five Arena tours. We sold out 40,000 in Crystal Palace, 35,000 in Alton Towers, then did three nights in MEM Arena and sold out 50,000 tickets. It was 1998. I really liked doing that because it wouldn't have happened without me.

What about the artists? How does touring help their careers?
Touring helps artists establish a proper fan base. It means their fans are more likely to buy their albums regardless of chart position. Our service for artists often includes providing strategic advice about how to build their career through touring. We look at things like which small venues they should target to build a fan base, and later when to start their first stadium tour. It's important they don't go into stadiums too early. It's important to make sure they can achieve what they want.

What do you look for in an employee?
To get a job with me, I'm not interested in how good you can talk. You've got to prove you can do it for yourself. I need to see if you like putting on gigs and if you're any good at it. You have to be able to work night and day putting out flyers and do everything. It's no different than if you're an artist and want to be a big star. You don't just become it, you have to get out there, do some gigs, write songs and make it happen. That's the sort of person I'm looking for.

JEREMY JOSEPH – DE-LUX

Jeremy Joseph runs the worldwide merchandise company, De-lux. His clients include U2, Madonna, Bjork, Britney, Kylie, J-Lo, The Chemical Brothers, Bruce Springsteen, Underworld, Jay Kay, Kiss, Slipknot, Busted, Scissor Sisters, PJ Harvey, Annie Lennox, Lemonjelly, Slipknot, System of a Down and all Simon Fuller's clients at 19 Management.

How powerful is artist endorsement?
It's huge. If it wasn't for merchandise most concerts wouldn't make any money.

THE VIEW FROM WITHIN

How did you build your business?

Record labels used to own their own merchandising companies. When the artist came to them asking for more money, the label would acquire the artist's merchandise rights.

Then we came onto the scene as a young company with a fresh approach and very quickly we became a player in the field. If we saw a band we liked we would approach the management and introduce ourselves.

Now we exclusively acquire the worldwide rights to manufacture and distribute all items of merchandise, which include key items such as T-shirts, sweatshirts, books, perfume and other fan appreciation items. We then distribute these items in four distribution channels:

- The first is on the road – manufacturing and distributing merchandise at live performances.
- The second is to retail, where we manufacture and distribute approved licensed merchandise to high-street retailers. Giving music artists high-street brand recognition i.e. Def Jam – Phat Farm apparel, and The Beastie Boys – XLarge Collection.
- The third is appointing third-party licensees that manufacture and distribute to retail. By example a poster or Perfume Company, who specialise in their product field, and come to us to use the image or name of an artist such as Kylie or Madonna.
- The fourth, and fastest growing is online, whereby we manufacture and sell approved products via the official artist or band website. This is now extending to selling tickets for concerts.

How do you find a suitable band to do a merchandising deal?

First of all you have to look for a band that you know will sign a merchandising deal. Then you have to sign them early on in their career so you can build a relationship with them. Then we'd want to sign them up to a touring cycle that can be anything from a year to eighteen months. Our company is all about relationship.

How does the typical deal work?

We pay an advance against a royalty, based on a per head figure for the concerts. If a band plays to 100,000 people you estimate the average spend per head, so if this was £3, the estimated gross would be £300,000. The band would then get an advance based upon the expected royalty from this amount.

Who approves the merchandise – the manager or the artist?

With a band, there's usually one band member who'll lead the way in terms of how merchandise should look, even though everyone will have his or her say.

Planning starts up to three months in advance of the first show. We want to understand everything such as the album, the lyrics within the songs, what the set's going to look like and the audience demographics.

It's important to know whether it's predominant male or female. Are they under fourteen or over forty?

It's essential to have something for sale from 50p to £50, and sometimes we sell limited-edition items such as signed lithographs for up to £100.

Typically we'll have around 16 different items for sale, but by the end of the tour we might have more or less than this amount due to customer and artist demands.

Does the merchandise vary according to the music?

If it's a rock audience 80% of what you do will be T-shirts. That type of audience love to buy something that says they were there. Rock bands will sell millions of T-shirts in one touring year.

Pop acts are different. Fifty per cent of sales will be from a 36-page tour brochure containing pictures of the artist and a bio.

How do you produce the merchandise?

Everything's approved from the quality of paper printed on, to the pictures used and the artwork. Everything you see on the official stand is seen and directly approved by the artist in writing. What you don't want to do is start manufacturing too much of any one item. If you can't distribute it is worthless. For the first show you do a minimum run that will cover you for the first three shows. Then after show two or three you have to gauge what's going on and what items are the ones to focus on. Its not easy because what sells well in Manchester is not what sells well in Nottingham. On the U2 tour we sell different T-shirts in Norway than we do in the UK. Every single day we give financial statements on what's happened that day, reviewing sales of all the items. It's such a major income stream for artists that it's very important they know what's going on.

What's the breakdown of sales on a general night?
Sixty per cent of business is done as people go into the show and 40% on the way out. The amount of business done on the way out will depend on what time the show finishes, whether it's a weekday or weekend, and if the show was good or not.

Artists and management are interested in these figures because it's a good indicator of their performance.

CONCERT PROMOTERS

ARTSUN
18 Sparkle Street, Manchester M1 2NA
T: 0161 273 3435 F: 0161 273 3695
Email: mailbox@pd-uk.com
MD: Gary McClarnan

ASGARD PROMOTIONS
125 Parkway, London NW1 7PS
T: 020 7387 5090 F: 020 7387 8740
Email: info@asgard-uk.com
Jnt MDs: Paul Fenn, Paul Charles

BDA
32 Chiltern Road, Culcheth, Warrington, Cheshire WA3 4LL
T: 01925 766655 F: 01925 765577
Email: brian.durkin@btinternet.com
MD: Brian Durkin

THE BIG GIG/CENT EVENTS
500 Chiswick High Rd, London W4 5RG
T: 020 8956 2391 F: 020 8956 2394
Email: anne@centevents.com
Website: thebiggig.biz
Events Manager: Anne Jones

BKO PRODUCTIONS LTD
The Old Truman Brewery, 91 Brick Lane, London E1 6QL
T: 020 7377 9373 F: 020 7377 6523
Email: bkoprod@aol.com
Director: Byron Orme

DEREK BLOCK ARTISTES AGENCY LTD
70-76 Bell St, Marylebone, London NW1 6SP
T: 020 7724 2101 F: 020 7724 2102
Email: dbaa@derekblock.demon.co.uk
MD: Derek Block

BUGBEAR PROMOTIONS
21a Maury Rd, London N16 7BP
T: 020 8806 2668 F: 020 8806 6444
Email: info@bugbear18.freeserve.co.uk
Website: bugbearbookings.com
Jim Mattison/Tony Gleed

CLEAR CHANNEL ENTERTAINMENT MUSIC
1st Floor, Regent Arcade House, 252-260 Regents Street, London W1B 3BX
T: 020 7009 3333 F: 0870 749 3191
Email: info@clearchannel.co.uk
Website: cclive-europe.com
New Media Manager: Mark Yovich

CMC
PO Box 3, Newport NP20 3YB
T: 07973 715875 F: 01633 677672
Email: alan.jones@amserve.com
Principal: Alan Jones

CONCORDE INTERNATIONAL ARTISTES
Concorde House, 101 Shepherds Bush Road, London W6 7LP
T: 020 7602 8822 F: 020 7603 2352
Email: cia@cia.uk.com
MD: Paul Fitzgerald

DEAD OR ALIVE
PO Box 34204, London, N NW5 1FS
T: 020 7482 3908
Email: gigs@deadoralive.org.uk
MD: Nicholas Barnett

TONY DENTON PROMOTIONS LTD
19 South Molton Lane, Mayfair, London
W1K 5LE
T: 020 7629 4666 F: 020 7629 4777
Email: mail@tdpromo.com
Website: tdpromo.com
MD: Tony Denton

DIG PROMOTIONS
115 Otley Road, Leeds LS6 3PX
T: 0113 230 2113 F: 0113 278 9452
Email: eddie@digleeds.com
Website: digleeds.com
Partners: Eddie Roberts, Gip Dammone

DOMAIN MUSIC
Unit 9, TGEC, Town Hall Approach
Road, London N15 4RX
T: 020 8375 3608 F: 020 8375 3487
Email: info@domainmusic.co.uk
Website: domainmusic.co.uk
Dir: Michael Lowe

ESSENTIAL ENTERTAINMENTS LTD
9 Church Street, Brighton, E Sussex
BN1 1US
T: 01273 888787 F: 01273 888780
Email: info@essentialents.com
Website: essentialfestival.com
Promoter: Ish Ali

THE FLYING MUSIC COMPANY LTD
110 Clarendon Road, London W11 2HR
T: 020 7221 7799 F: 020 7221 5016
Email: info@flyingmusic.co.uk
Website: flyingmusic.com
Joint MD: Paul Walden

GERONIMO!
29 Gillian Avenue, Aldershot, Hampshire
GU12 4HS
T: 07960 187529 F: 01252 408041
Email: barneyjeavons@supanet.com
Website: geronimo-music.net
Promoter: Barney Jeavons

GLOBAL UNDERGROUND PROMOTIONS
Forth Banks Offices, Forth Banks,
Newcastle upon Tyne, Tyne and Wear
NE1 3PA
T: 0191 232 4064 F: 0191 232 5766
Email: info@globalunderground.co.uk
Website: globalunderground.co.uk
General Manager: Colin Tierney

HALLOGEN LTD
The Bridgewater Hall, Manchester
M2 3WS
T: 0161 950 0000 F: 0161 950 0001
Email: admin@bridgewater-hall.co.uk
Website: bridgewater-hall.co.uk
Programming Manager: Sara Unwin

HEAD MUSIC LTD
2 Munro Terrace, London SW10 0DL
T: 020 7376 4456 F: 020 7351 5569
Email: straight@freeuk.com
John Curd

THE HEADLINE AGENCY
30 Churchfields, Milltown, Dublin 14
T: +353 1 261 1879
F: +353 1 261 1879
Email: info@musicheadline.com
Website: musicheadline.com
MD: Madeleine Seiler

DAVID HULL PROMOTIONS
46 University St, Belfast BT7 1HB
T: 028 9024 0360 F: 028 9024 7919
Email: info@dhpromotions.com
Website: davidhullpromotions.com
MD: David Hull

HUTT RUSSELL ORGANISATION
PO Box 64, Cirencester, Gloucestershire
GL7 5YD
T: 01285 644622 F: 01285 642291
Email: shows@huttrussellorg.com
Website: huttrussellorg.com
Dir: Steve Hutt

INSANITY ARTISTS AGENCY
PO Box 292, Gillingham, Kent ME7 2WA
T: 08456 446625 F: 08456 446627
Email: info@insanitygroup.com
Website: insanitygroup.com
MD: Andy Varley

KENNEDY STREET ENTERPRISES LTD
Kennedy House, 31 Stamford Street,
Altrincham, Cheshire WA14 1ES
T: 0161 941 5151 F: 0161 928 9491
Email: kse@kennedystreet.com
Dir: Danny Betesh

LINE-UP PMC
9A Tankerville Place, Newcastle upon
Tyne, Tyne and Wear NE2 3AT
T: 0191 281 6449 F: 0191 212 0913
Email: c.a.murtagh@btinternet.com
Website: on-line-records.co.uk
Prop: Chris Murtagh

SCOTT MACKENZIE ASSOCIATES
6 Gardner Way, Kenilworth,
Warwickshire CV8 1QW
T: 01926 859102 F: 01926 858966
Email: scottmackenzie4u@hotmail.com
Website: scottmackenzie.co.uk
MD: Scott Mackenzie

MARSHALL ARTS
Leeder House, 6 Erskine Road, London
NW3 3AJ
T: 020 7586 3831 F: 020 7586 1422
Email: info@marshall-arts.co.uk
Website: marshall-arts.co.uk
MD: Barrie Marshall

PHIL MCINTYRE PROMOTIONS
2nd Floor, 35 Soho Square, London
W1D 3QX
T: 020 7439 2270 F: 020 7439 2280
Email: reception@pmcintyre.co.uk
Promoter: Paul Roberts

MEL BUSH ORGANIZATION LTD
Tanglewood, Arrowsmith Rd,
Wimbourne, Dorset BH21 3BG
T: 01202 691891 F: 01202 691896
Email: mbobmth@aol.com
MD: Mel Bush

MCLEOD HOLDEN PRESENTATIONS LTD
Priory House, 1133 Hessle High Road,
Kingston-upon-Hull, East Yorkshire
HU4 6SB
T: 01482 565444 F: 01482 353635
Email: peter.mcLeod@mcleod-holden.com
Website: mcleod-holden.com
Dir: Peter McLeod

MEAN FIDDLER CONCERTS
16 High Street, Harlesden, London
NW10 4LX
T: 020 8961 5490 F: 020 8961 9238
Website: meanfiddler.com

METROPOLIS MUSIC
69 Caversham Road, London NW5 2DR
T: 020 7424 6800 F: 020 7424 6849
Email: mail@metropolismusic.com
Website: gigsandtours.com
MD: Bob Angus

MUSICDASH
PO Box 1977, Manchester M26 2YB
T: 0161 724 4760
Email: jon@musicdash.co.uk
Website: manchestermusic.co.uk
Director: Jon Ashley

NEW VISION ARTS MANAGEMENT
Empire House, Penthouse Suite, 175 Piccadilly, London W1V 9DB
T: 0870 444 2506 F: 07000 785 845
Email: info@newvisionarts.com
Website: newvisionarts.com
Head of Promotions: Mark Foker

PARTNERS IN CRIME
18 Chenies St, London WC1E 7PA
T: 020 8521 7764
Email: saphron@msn.com
Promoter: Annette Bennett

PERFECT WORDS & MUSIC
6 Church St, Ventnor, Isle Of Wight PO38 1SW
T: 01983 855642
Email: philmurray.pac@talk21.com
Booker: Allison Longstaff

GORDON POOLE AGENCY LTD
The Limes, Brockley, Bristol, Somerset BS48 3BB
T: 01275 463222 F: 01275 462252
Email: agents@gordonpoole.com
Website: gordonpoole.com
Consultant: James Poole

REAL PROMOTIONS
140 Cross Lane, Crookes, Sheffield S10 1WP
T: 07989 347 645
Email: mark@realpromo.co.uk
Website: realpromo.co.uk
Promoter: Mark Roberts

REGULAR MUSIC
100B Constitution Street, Leith, Edinburgh EH6 6AW
T: 0131 554 7444 F: 0131 554 7222
Email: barry@regularmusic.co.uk
Website: regularmusic.co.uk
MD: Barry Wright

RIVERMAN CONCERTS
Top Floor, George House, Brecon Road, London W6 8PY
T: 020 7381 4000 F: 020 7381 9666
Email: info@riverman.co.uk
Website: riverman.co.uk
Dir: David McLean

RK PROMO
78 Church Rd, Northenden, Manchester M22 4WD
T: 0161 998 8903 F: 0161 998 8903
Email: JasonSingh78@aol.com
Website: RockKitchen.com
Promoter: Jason Singh

RLM PROMOTIONS
2A Old Mill Complex, Brown Street, Dundee DD1 5EG
T: 01382 224405 F: 01382 224406
Email: mail@rlm-promotions.com
Website: rlm-promotions.com
Owner: John Macdonald

SENSIBLE EVENTS
90-96 Brewery Road, London N7 9NT
T: 020 7700 9900 F: 020 7700 7845
Email: zweckaz@aol.com
Agent: Andrew Zweck

SHARK PROMOTIONS
23 Rolls Court Avenue, Herne Hill, London SE24 0EA
T: 020 7737 4580 F: 020 7737 4580
Email: mellor@organix.fsbusiness.co.uk
MD: MH Mellor

SJM CONCERTS
St Matthews, Liverpool Rd, Manchester M3 4NQ
T: 0161 907 3443 F: 0161 907 3446
Email: vicky@sjmconcerts.com
Website: gigsandtours.com
Office Manager: Vicky Potts

SOLO AGENCY & PROMOTIONS
1st Floor, Regent Arcade House, 252-260 Regent Street, London W1B 3BX
T: 020 7009 3361 F: 0870 749 3174
Email: solo@solo.uk.com
Website: solo.uk.com
MD: John Giddings

THE TALENT SCOUT
2nd Floor, Swiss Center, 10 Wardour Street, London W1D 6QF
T: 020 7864 1300 F: 020 7437 1029
Email: info@thetalentscout.co.uk
Website: thetalentscout.co.uk
Dir: Karen Smyth, Helen Douglas

TKO MUSIC GROUP LTD
PO Box 130, Hove, E. Sussex BN3 6QU
T: 01273 550088 F: 01273 540969
Email: management@tkogroup.com
Website: tkogroup.com
Warren Heal

TRUCK
15 Percy St, Oxford OX4 3AA
T: 01865 722333
Email: paul@truckrecords.com
Website: truckrecords.com
MD: Paul Bonham

WEEKENDER PROMOTIONS
PO Box 571, Taunton TA1 3ZW
T: 01823 321605 F: 01823 283389
Email: weekender@sotu.fsbusiness.co.uk
Website: weekenderlive.com
Director: Paul Dimond

THE WORLD MUSIC FOUNDATION (WMF)
Please, visit website for details
Email: events@musicaid.org
Website: musicaid.org

VENUES

THE ACADEMY
Cleveland Road, Uxbridge, Middlesex
UB8 3PH
T: 01895 462200 F: 01895 462301
Dan Harris

ACCRINGTON TOWN HALL
Blackburn Road, Accrington, Lancashire
BB5 1LA
T: 01254 380297 F: 01254 380291
Email: leisure@hyndburnbc.gov.uk
Website: leisureinhyndburn.co.uk
Mrktng & Events Officer: Nigel Green

THE ALBANY
Douglas Way, London SE8 4AG
T: 020 8692 0231 F: 020 8469 2253
Programmer: Geraldine Marsh

ALEXANDRA PALACE
Alexandra Palace Way, Wood Green,
London N22 7AY
T: 020 8365 4313 F: 020 8365 2662
Email: alexandrapalace@dial.pipex.com
Website: alexandrapalace.com
Head of Sales & Mkting: Chris Gothard

THE ALFRED MCALPINE STADIUM
Stadium Way, West Yorkshire HD1 6PG
T: 01484 450000 F: 01484 450144
Website: the_stadium.co.uk
Kevin Collinge

ALLOA TOWN HALL
Mars Hill, Alloa, Clackmannan FK10 1AB
T: 01259 213131 F: 01259 721313
Bookings Supervisor

ANGEL CENTRE
Angel Lane, Tonbridge, Kent TN9 1SF
T: 01732 359588 F: 01732 363677

APOLLO THEATRE
Shaftesbury Avenue, London W1V 7HD
T: 020 7494 5200 F: 020 7434 1217
Email: info@rutheatres.com
Website: rutheatres.com
Concerts & Hirings Mgr: Mike Townsend

APOLLO THEATRE
George Street, Oxford OX1 2AG
T: 01865 243041 F: 01865 791976
Gen Mgr: Louise

APOLLO VICTORIA
17 Wilton Road, London SW1V 1LG
T: 020 7834 6318 F: 020 7630 7716
Jamie Baskeyfield

ARTSLINK THEATRE
Knoll Road, Camberley, Surrey
GU15 3SY
T: 01276 707612 F: 01276 707644
Pat Pembridge

ASHCROFT THEATRE
Park Lane, Croydon, Surrey CR9 1DG
T: 020 8681 0821 F: 020 8760 0835
Email: dbarr@fairfield.co.uk
Nick Leigh

BAND ON THE WALL
25 Swan Street, Manchester M4 5JQ
T: 0161 832 6625 F: 0161 834 2559
Website: bandonthewall.com
The promotor

BAR ACADEMY
51 Dale End, Birmingham B4 7LS
T: 0121 262 3001
Email: baracademy@birmingham-academy.co.uk
Website: birmingham-academy.co.uk
Mgr: Stuart Strong

BARBICAN CENTRE
Silk Street, Barbican, London
EC2Y 8DS
T: 020 7638 4141 F: 020 7382 7037
Head of Music: Robert Van Leer

BARFLY CAMDEN
The Monarch, 49 Chalk Farm Road,
London NW1 8AN
T: 020 7691 4244 F: 020 7691 4245
Email: info@barflyclub.com
Website: barflyclub.com
MD: Be Rozzo

BARFLY CARDIFF
Ty Cefn, Rectory Road, Cardiff
CF5 1QL
T: 02920 667 658 F: 02920 341 622
Email: cardiff.info@barflyclub.com
Website: barflyclub.com
Booker: Jon Wing

BARFLY GLASGOW
Riverside House, 260 Clyde St,
Glasgow, Lanarkshire G1 4JH
T: 0141 221 0414 F: 0141 204 5711
Email: glasgow.info@barflyclub.com
Website: barflyclub.com
Manager: David Dempster

BATH PAVILION
North Parade Road, Bath BA2 4ET
T: 01225 462565 F: 01225 481306

BATH THEATRE
Royal St John's Place, Sawclose, Bath
BA1 1ET
T: 01225 448815 F: 01225 444080

BEACH BALLROOM
Beach Leisure Centre, Beach
Promenade, Aberdeen AB2 1NR
T: 01224 647647 F: 01224 648693

BECK THEATRE
Hayes Grange Road, Hayes, Middlesex
UB3 2UE
T: 020 8561 7506 F: 020 8569 1072
Website: tickest-direct.co.uk
Graham Bradbury

BELGRADE THEATRE
Belgrade Square, Coventry CV1 1GS
T: 024 7625 6431 F: 024 7655 0680
Email: admin@belgrade.co.uk
Website: belgrade.co.uk
GM: David Beidas

BIRBECK COLLEGE STUDENT UNION
Malet Street, London WC1E 7HX
T: 020 7631 6335 F: 020 7631 6270
Email: president@bcsu.bbk.ac.uk
Website: bbk.ac.uk/su
Lucy Reed

BIVOUAC @ THE DUKE OF WELLINGTON
37 Broadgate, Lincoln, Lincolnshire
LN2 5AE
T: 01522 539883 F: 01522 528964
Email: steve.hawkins@easynet.co.uk
Booker: Steve Hawkins

BLACKBURN ARENA
Blackburn Waterside, Lower Audley,
Blackburn, Lancashire BB1 1BB
T: 01254 263063 F: 01254 691516

BLACKHEATH HALLS
23 Lee Road, London SE3 9RQ
T: 020 8318 9758 F: 020 8852 5154
Email: mail@blackheathhalls.com
Website: blackheathhalls.com
Operation Mgr: Jenni Darwin

BLACKPOOL PLEASURE BEACH ARENA
Ocean Boulevard, Blackpool, Lancashire
FY4 1EZ
T: 01253 341033 F: 01253 401098
Email: michelle.barratt@bpbltd.com
Website: bpbltd.com
Michelle Barratt

BLOOMSBURY THEATRE
15 Gordon Street, London WC1H 0AH
T: 020 7679 2777 F: 020 7383 4080

THE BORDERLINE
Orange Yard, Off Manette Street,
Charing Cross Road, London W1V 5LB
T: 020 7395 0799 F: 020 7395 0766
Email: barry.borderline@virgin.net
Website: borderline.co.uk
Promoter: Barry Everitt

BRAEHEAD ARENA GLASGOW
Braehead, Kings Inch Rd, Glasgow
G51 4BN
T: 0141 561 0161 F: 0141 561 0009
Email: jfbraeheadarena@aol.com
General Manager: Jim Francis

BRAINTREE TOWERLANDS ARENA
Panfield Road, Braintree, Essex
CM7 5BJ
T: 01376 326802 F: 01376 552487
Mktg Mgr: Michael Smillie

BREWERY ARTS CENTRE
Highgate, Kendal, Cumbria LA9 4HE
T: 01539 725133 F: 01539 730257
Email: admin@breweryarts.co.uk
Website: breweryarts.co.uk
Music Officer: Gavin Sharpe

BRIDGE LANE THEATRE
Bridge Lane, London SW11 3AD
T: 020 7228 5185 F: 020 7262 0090
Artistic Dir: Terry Adams

THE BRIDGEWATER HALL
Lower Mosley Street, Manchester
M2 3WS
T: 0161 950 0000 F: 0161 950 0001
Email: admin@bridgewater-hall.co.uk
Website: bridgewater-hall.co.uk
Programming Manager: Sara Unwin

BRIDGWATER ARTS CENTRE
11-13 Castle Street, Bridgwater,
Somerset TA6 3DD
T: 01278 422700 F: 01278 447402
Charlie Dearden

BRIDLINGTON SPA THEATRE AND ROYAL HALL
South Marine Drive, Bridlington, East
Yorkshire YO15 3JH
T: 01262 678255 F: 01262 604625
Rob Clutterham

BRIGHTON DOME LTD
29 New Road Brighton, Brighton, East Sussex BN1 1UG
T: 01273 261530 F: 01273 261543
Email: robert.sanderson@brighton-dome.org.uk
Website: brighton-dome.org.uk
GM: Robert Sanderson

BRISTOL HIPPODROME
St Augustine's Parade, Bristol BS1 4UZ
T: 0117 926 5524 F: 0117 925 1661
Gen Mgr: John Wood

CAIRD HALL COMPLEX
City Square, Dundee, Tayside DD1 3BB
T: 01382 434451 F: 01382 434451
Susan Pasfield

CAMBRIDGE ARTS THEATRE
6 St Edward's Passage, Cambridge CB2 3PJ
T: 01223 578933 F: 01223 578997
Email: smarsh@cambridgeartstheatre.com
Website: cambridgeartstheatre.com
Ian Ross

CAMBRIDGE CORN EXCHANGE
3 Parsons Court, Wheeler Street, Cambridge CB2 3QE
T: 01223 457555 admin F: 01223 457559 admin
Email: admin.cornex@cambridge.gov.uk
Website: cornex.co.uk
Ents & Events Mgr: Mick Gray

CAMBRIDGE UNIVERSITY STUDENT UNION
11-12 Trumpington Street, Cambridge CB2 1QA
T: 01223 356454 F: 01223 323244

CAMDEN PALACE
1A Camden High Street, London NW1 7JE
T: 020 7387 0428 F: 020 7388 8850 : David Brindle

CANTERBURY CHRIST CHURCH UNIVERSITY COLLEGE STUDENT UNION
North Holmes Road, Canterbury, Kent CT1 1QU
T: 01227 782271 F: 01227 458287
Email: ents@cant.ac.uk
Website: su.cant.ac.uk
VP Ents & Communications: Matt Wynter

CARDIFF INTERNATIONAL ARENA
Mary Ann Street, Cardiff CF10 2EQ
T: 029 2023 4500 F: 029 2023 4501
Website: sfx-europe.com/cia
GM: Graham Walters

CARGO
Kingsland Viaduct, 83 Rivington St, Shoreditch, London EC2A 3AY
T: 020 7739 3440 F: 020 7739 3441
Email: info@cargo-london.com
Website: cargo-london.com
Events & Bookings Mgr: Ben Robertson

CARLING ACADEMY
Bristol Frogmore Street, Bristol BS1 5NA
T: 0117 9279 227 F: 0117 9279 295
Email: mail@bristol-academy.co.uk
Website: bristol-academy.co.uk
GM: Helen Spillane

CARLING ACADEMY
Brixton 211 Stockwell Road, Brixton, London SW9 9SL

T: 020 7771 3000 admin
F: 020 7738 4427
Email: mail@brixton-academy.co.uk
Website: brixton-academy.co.uk
Gen Mgr: Nigel Downs

CARLING ACADEMY
Glasgow 121 Eglinton St, Glasgow G5 9NT
T: 0141 418 3000 F: 0141 418 3001
Email: mail@glasgow-academy.co.uk
Website: glasgow-academy.co.uk
GM: David Laing

CARLING ACADEMY
Islington N1 Centre, 16 Parkfield St, London N1 0PS
T: 020 7288 4404
Email: mail@islington-academy.co.uk
Website: islington-academy.co.uk
GM: Graeme Nash

CARLING ACADEMY
Liverpool 11-13 Hotham Street, Liverpool L3 5UF
T: 0151 707 3200 F: 0151 707 3201
Email: post@liverpool-academy.co.uk
Website: liverpool-academy.co.uk
GM: Steve Hoyland

CARLING APOLLO
Manchester Stockport Road, Ardwick Green, Manchester M12 6AP
T: 0161 273 6921 F: 0870 749 0779
Email: manchester.apollo@clearchannel.co.uk
Website: ccLive.co.uk
GM: Rob O'Shea

CARLING BIRMINGHAM ACADEMY
52-54 Dale End, Birmingham, West Midlands B4 7LS
T: 0121 262 3000 F: 0121 236 2241
Email: mail@birmingham-academy.co.uk
Website: birmingham-academy.co.uk
GM: Richard Maides

CARLISLE SANDS CENTRE
The Sands, Carlisle, Cumbria CA1 1JQ
T: 01228 625208 F: 01228 625666
Email: sueb@carlisle-city.gov.uk
Website: 4leisure.org.uk
Ents Prog Mgr: Sue Baty

CARNEGIE HALL
East Port, Dunfermline, Fife KY12 7JA
T: 01383 314110 F: 01383 314131
Arts Co-ordinator: Evan Henderson

CARNEGIE THEATRE
Finkle Street, Workington, Cumbria CA14 2BD
T: 01900 602122 F: 01900 67143
Email: carnegie@allerdale.gov.uk
Gen Mgr: Paul Sherwin

THE CAVERN CLUB
8 Mathew Street, Liverpool, Merseyside L2 6RE
T: 0151 236 1964

CENTRAL LANCASHIRE UNIVERSITY STUDENT UNION
Fylde Road, Preston, Lancashire PR1 2TQ
T: 01772 513200 F: 01772 894975
Email: suents@uclan.ac.uk
Website: yourunion.co.uk
Ents Mgr: David Evans

CENTRAL PIER THEATRE
Promenade, Blackpool, Lancashire FY1 5BB
T: 01253 623422 F: 01253 752427

THE CENTRAL THEATRE
170 High Street, Chatham, Kent
ME4 4AS
T: 01634 848584 F: 01634 827711
Tony Hill

THE CHARLOTTE
8 Oxford Street, Leicester LE1 5XZ
T: 0116 255 3956
Email: charlotte@stayfree.co.uk
Website: thecharlotte.co.uk
Manager/Owner: Andy Wright

CHEESE & GRAIN
Market Yard, Frome, Somerset
BA11 1BE
T: 01373 455768 F: 01373 455765
Email: office@cheeseandgrain.co.uk
Website: cheeseandgrain.co.uk
Event Mgr: Nial Joyce

CHELTENHAM TOWN HALL
Imperial Square, Cheltenham,
Gloucestershire GL50 1QA
T: 01242 521621 F: 01242 573902
Email: TimHu@cheltenham.gov.uk
Website: cheltenham.gov.uk/events
Ents & Mktg Mgr: Tim Hulse

CHESTER COLLEGE - WARRINGTON CAMPUS STUDENT UNION
Padgate Campus, Fearnhead,
Warrington, Cheshire WA2 0DB
T: 01925 821336 F: 01925 838085
Email: studentsunion@warr.ac.uk
Entertainments Officer: Vasilis Stylianos

CHESTERFIELD ARTS CENTRE
Chesterfield College, Sheffield Road,
Chesterfield, Derbyshire S41 7LL
T: 01246 500578 F: 01246 500578
Co-ordinator: Bernie Hayter

CHINGFORD ASSEMBLY HALL
Station Road, Chingford, London
E4 8NU
T: 020 8529 0555
Halls Mgr

THE CITADEL ARTS CENTRE
Waterloo Street, St Helens, Merseyside
WA10 1PX
T: 01744 735436

CITY VARIETIES MUSIC HALL
Swan Street, Leeds LS1 6LW
T: 0113 242 5045 F: 0113 234 1800
Mr P Sandeman

CORBY FESTIVAL HALL AND THEATRE COMPLEX
George Street, Corby, Northamptonshire
NN17 1QB
T: 01536 402551 F: 01536 403748
Gen Mgr

THE CORN EXCHANGE
Market Place, Newbury, Berkshire
RG14 5BD
T: 01635 582666 F: 01635 582223
Email: admin@cornexchangenew.co.uk
Website: cornexchangenew.com
Dir: Michael Bewick

CORNWALL COLISEUM
Cornwall Leisure World, Carlyon Bay, St
Austell, Cornwall PL25 3RG
T: 01726 814004 F: 01726 817231
Gen Mgr: Sallie Polmounter

COVENTRY UNIVERSITY - THE PLANET NIGHTCLUB
Students Union, Priory Street, Coventry,
West Midlands CV1 5FJ

T: 01203 571231
Gen Mgr: William Blake

CRAWLEY LEISURE CENTRE
Haslett Avenue, Crawley, West Sussex RH10 1TS
T: 01293 552941 F: 01293 533362
Email: dave.watmore@crawley.gov.uk
Website: hawth.co.uk
Promotions & Ents Mgr: David Watmore

THE CRYPT
53 Robertson Street, Hastings, East Sussex TN34 1HY
T: 01424 444675 F: 01424 722847
Email: pete@the-crypt.co.uk
Website: the-crypt.co.uk

CUMBERNAULD THEATRE
Kildrum, Cumbernauld, Glasgow, Lanarkshire G67 2BN
T: 01236 737235 F: 01236 738408
Artistic Dir: Simon Sharkey

DARLINGTON ARTS CENTRE
Vane Terrace, Darlington, Co Durham DL3 7AX
T: 01325 483271 F: 01325 365794
Music Programmer: Lynda Winstanley

DARLINGTON CIVIC THEATRE
Parkgate, Darlington, Co Durham DL1 1RR
T: 01325 468006 F: 01325 368278
Email: marketing@darlington-arts.co.uk
Website: darlington-arts.co.uk
Head of Theatre & Arts: Peter Cutchie

DE LA WARR
Pavilion Marina, Bexhill-on-Sea, Sussex TN40 1DP
T: 01424 787900 F: 01424 787940
Email: dlwp@rother.gov.uk
Mike Jolly

DE MONTFORT HALL
Granville Road, Leicester LE1 7RU
T: 0116 233 3111 F: 0116 233 3182
Website: demontforthall.co.uk
Gen Mgr: Richard Haswell

DE MONTFORT STUDENT UNION DSU
Leicester City Campus, 4 Newarke Close, Leicester LE2 7BJ
T: 0116 255 5576 F: 0116 257 6309
Email: gnash@dsu.dmu.ac.uk
Website: dsu.dmu.ac.uk
Entertainment Manager: Graeme Nash

DE MONTFORT UNIVERSITY
Bedford Students Union, 21 Lansdowne Road, Bedford MK40 2BZ
T: 01234 211688 F: 01234 347357
Alan Barkbeck

EALING TOWN HALL
Halls & Events, Ground Floor, Perceval House, London W5 2HL
T: 020 8758 5624 F: 020 8566 5088
Email: HandM@Ealing.Gov.uk
Website: Ealing.Gov.uk/HE&M
Head of Halls & Events: M Hand

EARLS COURT/OLYMPIA GROUP LTD
Earls Court Exhibition Centre, Warwick Road, London SW5 9TA
T: 020 7370 8009 F: 020 7370 8223
Email: marketing@eco.co.uk
Website: eco.co.uk
Commercial Director: Nigel Nathan

EAST LONDON UNIVERSITY
Romford Road, London E15 4LZ
T: 020 8223 3000 F: 020 8223 3000

EDEN COURT THEATRE
Bishops Road, Inverness IV3 5SA
T: 01463 239841 F: 01463 713810
Email: ecmail@cali.co.uk
Website: edencourt.uk.com
Colin Marr

EDINBURGH INTERNATIONAL CONFERENCE CENTRE
The Exchange, Morrison Street,
Edinburgh EH3 8EE
T: 0131 300 3000 F: 0131 300 3030
Email: sales@eicc.co.uk
Website: eicc.co.uk
Snr Sales Team Leader: Lesley Stephen

EDINBURGH PLAYHOUSE
18-22 Greenside Place, Edinburgh
EH1 3AA
T: 0131 557 2692 F: 0131 557 6520
Website: edinburgh-playhouse.co.uk
Gen Mgr: Andrew Lyst

FAIRFIELD HALLS
Park Lane, Croydon, Surrey CR9 1DG
T: 020 8681 0821
Email: dbarr@fairfield.co.uk
Website: croydon.qou.uk/fairfield/
Head of Artistic Planning: Nick Leigh

FALMOUTH ARTS CENTRE
Church Street, Falmouth, Cornwall
TR11 3EG
T: 01326 212719
Email: jon@falmouthارts.org
Website: falmouthارts.org
GM: Shaun Kavanagh

FERNEHAM HALL
Fareham Osborn Road, Fareham,
Hampshire PO16 0TL
T: 01329 824864 F: 01329 281486
Email: rdavies@fareham.gov.uk
Website: fareham.gov.uk
Head of Arts & Ents: Russell Davies

FESTIVAL CITY THEATRES TRUST
13/29 Nicolson Street, Edinburgh
EH8 9FT
T: 0131 662 1112 F: 0131 667 0744
Email: empire@eft.co.uk
Website: eft.co.uk Acting
GM: David W S Todd

FORT REGENT LEISURE CENTRE
St Helier, Jersey, Channel Islands
JE2 4UX
T: 01534 500009 F: 01534 500225
Email: c.stanier@gov.je
Website: esc.gov.uk
Events Mgr: Colin Stanier

THE FORUM
9-17 Highgate Road, London NW5 1JY
T: 020 7284 1001 F: 020 7284 1102
Website: meanfiddler.com

THE FOUNDRY
Beak Street, Birmingham, West
Midlands B1 1LS
T: 0121 622 1894
Website: dr-p.demon.co.uk/foundry.html

THE FRIDGE
1 Town Hall Parade, Brixton Hill, London
SW2 1RJ
T: 020 7326 5100 F: 020 7274 2879
Email: info@fridge.co.uk
Website: fridge.co.uk
Gen Mgr: Gary Baker

FUTURIST THEATRE
Foreshore Road, Scarborough, North Yorkshire YO11 1NT
T: 01723 370742 F: 01723 365456

G-MEX CENTRE
Windmill Street, City Centre, Manchester M2 3GX
T: 0161 834 2700 F: 0161 833 3168
Email: email@g-mex.co.uk
Website: g-mex.co.uk
Paul Ashton

GARAGE
20-22 Highbury Corner, London N5 1RD
T: 020 8961 5490 F: 020 8961 9238
Email: joady@meanfiddler.co.uk
Bking Mgr: Joady Thornton

THE GARAGE
490 Sauchiehall Street, Glasgow G2 3LW
T: 0141 332 1120 F: 0141 332 1130
Website: cplweb.com
MD: Donald Macleod

GLASGOW CITY HALLS
32 Albion Street, Glasgow, Lanarkshire G1 1QU
T: 0141 287 5005 F: 0141 287 5533
Susan Deighan: Head of Programming

GLASGOW GARAGE
490 Sauchiehall Street, Glasgow, Lanarkshire G2 3LW
T: 0141 332 1120 F: 0141 332 1120
Donald Macleod

GLASGOW KING'S THEATRE
Glasgow City Council, Cultural and Leisure Services, 229 George Street, Glasgow G1 1QU
T: 0141 287 3922 F: 0141 287 5533
Pauline Murphy

GLASGOW PAVILION THEATRE
121 Renfield Street, Glasgow, Lanarkshire G2 3AX
T: 0141 332 7579 F: 0141 331 2745
Theatre Mgr: Iain Gordon

GLASGOW ROYAL CONCERT HALL
2 Sauchiehall Street, Glasgow, Lanarkshire G2 3NY
T: 0141 332 6633 F: 0141 333 9123
Email: grch@grch.scotnet.co.uk
Website: grch.com

GLASTONBURY FESTIVAL
Worthy Farm, Pilton, Shepton Mallet, Somerset BA4 4BY
Tel: 01749 890470 F: 01749 890285
Email: worthy@glastonbury-festivals.co.uk
Website: glastonburyfestivals.co.uk

THE GLOBE
Blackpool Pleasure Beach, Ocean Boulevard, Blackpool, Lancashire FY4 1EZ
T: 01253 341033 F: 01253 401098
Michelle Barratt

GOLDIGGERS
Timber Street, Chippenham, Wiltshire SN15 3BP
T: 01249 656444 F: 01249 443835
Email: goldinfo@aol.com

GRAND OPERA HOUSE
Great Victoria Street, Belfast, Co Antrim BT2 7HR

T: 028 9024 0411 F: 028 9023 6842
Website: goh.co.uk
Derek Nicholls

GRAND THEATRE
Church Street, Blackpool, Lancashire
FY1 1HT
T: 01253 290111 F: 01253 751767
Email: gm@blackpoolgrand.co.uk
Website: blackpoolgrand.co.uk
Stephanie Sir

GRAND THEATRE
Wolverhampton, West Midlands
T: 01902 429212

GREAT GRIMSBY TOWN HALL
Town Hall Square, Great Grimsby, North East Lincolnshire DN31 1HX
T: 01472 324109 F: 01472 324108
John Callison

GROUP THEATRE
Bedford Street, Belfast, Co Antrim
BT2 7FF
T: 028 9032 3900 F: 028 9024 7199
Pat Falls

GUILDFORD CIVIC
London Road, Guildford, Surrey
GU1 2AA
T: 01483 444720 F: 01483 301982
Email: info@guildford-civic.co.uk
Website: guildford-civic.co.uk
Dep Mgr, Sales & Dev't: Heather Richardson

HACKNEY EMPIRE LTD
291 Mare Street, London E8 1EJ
T: 020 8510 4500 F: 020 8510 4530
Email: info@hackneyempire.co.uk
Website: hackneyempire.co.uk
Programmer: Claire Muldoon

HALFMOON
Putney 93 Lower Richmond Road, London SW15 1EU
T: 020 8780 9383 F: 020 8789 7863
Email: office@halfmoon.co.uk
Website: halfmoon.co.uk
Bookings/Promotions Mgr: Carrie Davies

HARE AND HOUNDS
High Street, King's Heath, Birmingham
B14 7JZ
T: 0121 444 2081
The Manager

HARLOW BANDSTAND
Harlow Council Leisure Service, Latton Bush Centre, Southern Way, Harlow, Essex CM18 7BL
T: 01279 446404 F: 01279 446431
Recreation Services Officer

HAYMARKET THEATRE
1 Belgrave Gate, Garrick Walk, Leicester
LE1 3YQ
T: 0116 253 0021 F: 0116 251 3310

HEXAGON
Queen's Walk, Reading, Berkshire
RG1 7UA
T: 0118 939 0123 F: 0118 939 0028
Email: boxoffice@readingarts.com
Website: readingarts.com
Prog Co-ordinator: Charity Gordon

HIPPODROME
Leicester Square, London WC2 7JH
T: 020 7437 4311 F: 020 7434 4225
Website: londonhippodrome.com
Annette Morris

THE HIVE
Glasgow University Glasgow University,
32 University Avenue, Glasgow G12 8LX
T: 0141 339 8697 F: 0141 339 8931
Email: libraries@guu.co.uk
Website: guu.co.uk
The Porter's Box

THE HOPE & ANCHOR
207 Upper Street, London N1 1BZ
T: 020 8806 2668 F: 020 8806 6444
Email: info@bugbear18.freeserve.co.uk
Website: bugbearbookings.com
Promoters: Jim & Tony

HORSESHOE BAR
Blackpool Pleasure Beach, Ocean
Boulevard, Blackpool, Lancashire
FY4 1EZ
T: 01253 341033 F: 01253 401098
Email: michelle.barratt@bpbltd.com
Website: bpbltd.com
Michelle Barratt

HORSHAM ARTS CENTRE
North Street, Horsham, West Sussex
RH12 1RL
T: 01403 259708 F: 01403 211502
Gen Mgr: Michael Gattrell

HUDDERSFIELD UNIVERSITY STUDENT UNION
Queensgate, Huddersfield HD1 3DH
T: 01484 538156 F: 01484 432333
Email: j.curran@hud.ac.uk
Venue Mgr: Jerome Curran

HULL ARENA
Kingston Street, Hull, East Yorkshire
HU1 2DZ
T: 01482 325252 F: 01482 216066
Website: hullarena.co.uk
Linda Parker

HULL CITY HALL
Victoria Square, Hull, East Yorkshire
HU1 3NA
T: 01482 613880 F: 01482 613961
Programming Mgr: Mike Lister

HULL UNIVERSITY
University House, Cottingham Road,
Hull, East Yorkshire HU2 9BT
T: 01482 466253 F: 01482 466280
Email: j.a.brooks@hull.ac.uk
Website: hull.ac.uk
Ents Co-ordinator: James Brooks

ICA THEATRE
The Mall, London SW1Y 5AH
T: 020 7930 0493 F: 020 7306 0122
Email: jamiee@ica.org.uk
Website: ica.org.uk
Dir of Live Arts: Andrew Missingham

IMPERIAL COLLEGE UNION
Beit Quad, Prince Consort Road,
London SW7 2BB
T: 020 7594 8068 F: 020 7594 8065
Email: ents@ic.ac.uk
Website: union.ic.ac.uk
Ents Manager: Ham Al-Rubaie

IMPERIAL GARDENS
299 Camberwell New Road, London
SE5 0TF
T: 020 7252 6000 F: 020 7252 7180
Email: info@imperialgardens.co.uk
Website: imperialgardens.co.uk

INVERURIE TOWN HALL
Market Place, Inverurie, Aberdeenshire
T: 01467 621610

ION
161-165 Ladbroke Grove, London
W10 6HJ
T: 020 8960 1702
Website: meanfiddler.com

JAZZ CAFE
5 Parkway, Camden Town, London
NW1 7PG
T: 020 7916 6060 F: 020 7267 9219
Email: info@jazzcafe.co.uk
Website: jazzcafe.co.uk
Promoter: Adrian Gibson

JERSEY OPERA HOUSE
Gloucester Street, St Hellier, Jersey,
Channel Islands JE2 3QL
T: 01534 617521 F: 01534 610624
Ian Stephens

JOINER'S ARMS
141 St Mary Street, Southampton,
Hampshire SO14 1NS
T: 023 8022 5612 F: 01962 878812
Email: vic@liveattherailway.co.uk
Website: joinerslive.com
Promoter: Vic Toms

JUG OF ALE
43 Alcester Road, Moseley, Birmingham,
West Midlands B13 8AA
T: 0121 449 1082

THE JUNCTION
Clifton Road, Cambridge CB1 7GX
T: 01223 578000 F: 01223 565600
Email: spiral@junction.co.uk
Website: junction.co.uk
Commercial Prog Mgr: Rob Tinkler

KENDAL TOWN HALL
Highgate, Kendal, Cumbria LA9 4DL
T: 01539 725758 F: 01539 734457
Bookings: Debbie Mckee

KILMARNOCK PALACE THEATRE
9 Green Street, Kilmarnock KA1 3BN
T: 01563 537710 F: 01563 573047
Asst Theatre & Ents Mgr: Laura Brown

KING'S HALL EXHIBITION & CONFERENCE CENTRE
Balmoral, Belfast, Co Antrim BT9 6GW
T: 028 9066 5225 F: 028 9066 1264
Email: info@kingshall.co.uk
Website: kingshall.co.uk Comm
Dir: Philip M Rees

KING'S LYNN ARTS CENTRE
27-29 King Street, King's Lynn, Norfolk
PE30 1HA
T: 01553 765565 F: 01553 762141
Email: howard.barnes@dial.pipex.com
Website: west-norfolk.gov.uk
Gen Mgr: Mr Howard Barnes

KING'S THEATRE
Edinburgh 2 Leven Street, Edinburgh
EH3 9LQ
T: 0131 662 1112 F: 0131 667 0744
Email: empire@eft.co.uk
Website: eft.co.uk
Gen Mgr & Chief Exec: Stephen Barry

KING'S WC2
King's College London, Students Union,
Macadam Bldg, Surrey Street, London
WC2R 2NS

T: 020 7836 7132 F: 020 7379 9833
Email: Rob.Massy@kclsu.org
Website: kclsu.org/events
Events Mgr: Rob Massy

KINGSTON UNIVERSITY GUILD OF STUDENTS
Penrhyn Road, Kingston upon Thames, Surrey KT1 2EE
T: 020 8547 2000 F: 020 8255 0032
Website: kingston.ac.uk

KOMEDIA
44-47 Gardner Street, Brighton, East Sussex BN1 1KN
T: 01273 647100 F: 01273 647102
Email: komedia@dircon.co.uk
Website: komedia.dircon.co.uk
Co-Dir: Marina Kobler

LANCASTER UNIVERSITY (THE SUGAR HOUSE) STUDENT UNION
Slaidburn House, Lancaster LA1 4YT
T: 01524 593765 F: 01524 846732
Email: c.burston@lancaster.ac.uk
Website: lancs.ac.uk/lusu

LEEDS UNIVERSITY
PO Box 157, Leeds, West Yorkshire LS1 1UH
T: 0113 380 1334 F: 0113 380 1336
Email: ents@luu.leeds.ac.uk
Website: luuonline.com
Ents Mgr: Steve Keeble

LEICESTER UNIVERSITY STUDENT UNION
University Road, Leicester LE1 7RH
T: 0116 223 1169 F: 0116 223 1207
Email: jk69@le.ac.uk
Website: le.ac.uk/su
Bars & Ents Manager: Jo Kenning

THE LEMON TREE
5 West North Street, Aberdeen AB24 5AT
T: 01224 647999 F: 01224 630888
Email: info@lemontree.org
Website: lemontree.org
Music Programmer: Andy Shearer

LIGHTHOUSE POOLES' CENTRE FOR THE ARTS
Kingland Rd, Poole, Dorset BH15 1UG
T: 01202 665 334 F: 01202 670 016
Email: jamesm@lighthousepoole.co.uk
Website: lighthousepoole.co.uk
Programmer: James Makin

LIMELIGHT
17 Ormeau Aveue, Belfast, Co Antrim BT2 8HD
T: 028 9066 5771 F: 028 9066 8811
Eamonn McCann

LIMELIGHT THEATRE
Queens Park Centre, Queens Park, Aylesbury, Buckinghamshire HP21 7RT
T: 01296 431272 F: 01296 337363
Artistic Dir: Amanda Eels

LIVERPOOL HOPE UNIVERSITY COLLEGE STUDENTS UNION
Derwent House, Hope Park, Liverpool L16 9JD
T: 0151 291 3663 F: 0151 291 3535
Email: union@livhope.ac.uk
Chas Jenkins

LONDON APOLLO COMPLEX
Queen Caroline Street, London W6 9QH
T: 020 8748 8660 F: 020 8846 9320

LONDON ARENA
Limeharbour, London E14 9TH
T: 020 7538 8880 F: 020 7538 5572
Email: sales@londonarena.co.uk
Website: londonarena.co.uk
Dir of European Events: Eve Hewitt

LONDON ASTORIA
157 Charing Cross Road, London
WC2H 0EN
T: 020 7434 9592 F: 020 7437 1781
Email: chrisalexander@alexanderc.freeserve.co.uk
Bookings Mgr: Chris Alexander

LONDON GUILDHALL UNIVERSITY STUDENT UNION
2 Goulston Street, London E1 7TP
T: 020 7247 1441 F: 020 7247 0618
Email: studentunion@lgu.ac.uk
Website: lgu.ac.uk/studentunion

LONDON PALLADIUM
Argyll Street, London W1A 3AB
T: 020 7494 5020 F: 020 7437 4010
Gareth Parnell

THE LOWRY
Pier 8, Salford Quays, Manchester
M50 3AZ
T: 0161 876 2020 F: 0161 876 2021

LYRIC THEATRE
Hammersmith King Street, London
W6 0QL
T: 020 8741 0824 F: 020 8741 7694
Email: foh@lyric.co.uk
Website: lyric.co.uk
Theatre Mgr: Howard Meaden

MANCHESTER ACADEMY & UNIVERSITY STUDENT UNION
Oxford Road, Manchester M13 9PR
T: 0161 275 2930 F: 0161 275 2936
Email: maximum@umu.man.ac.uk
Website: umu.man.ac.uk
Events Manager: Sean Morgan

MANCHESTER BOARDWALK
Little Peter Street, Manchester M15 4PS
T: 0161 228 3555 F: 0161 237 1037
Email: colindsinclair@msn.com
Website: boardwalk.co.uk
Lee Donnelly

MANCHESTER EVENING NEWS ARENA
Victoria Station, Manchester M3 1AR
T: 0161 950 5333 F: 0161 950 6000
Email: john.knight@men-arena.com
Dir Sales/Mkting: John Knight

MANCHESTER MET STUDENTS' UNION
99 Oxford Road, Manchester M1 7EL
T: 0161 247 6468 F: 0161 247 6314
Email: s.u.ents@mmu.ac.uk
Website: mmsu.com
Ents Mgr: Ben Casasola

MANCHESTER OPERA HOUSE
Quay Street, Manchester M3 3HP
T: 0161 834 1787 F: 0161 834 5243
Website: manchestertheatres.co.uk

MANCHESTER PALACE THEATRE
Oxford Street, Manchester M1 6FT
T: 0161 228 6255 F: 0161 237 5746
Website: manchestertheatres.co.uk
Rachel Miller

MANSFIELD LEISURE CENTRE
Chesterfield Road South, Mansfield,
Nottinghamshire NG19 7BQ

T: 01623 463800 F: 01623 463912
Mgr: M Darnell

MARCO'S
An Aird, Fort William PH33 6AN
T: 01397 700707 F: 01397 700708

MARCUS GARVEY CENTRE
Lenton Boulevard, Nottingham NG7 2BY
T: 0115 942 0297 F: 0115 942 0297
Mr T Brown

MARGATE WINTER GARDENS
Fort Crescent, Margate, Kent CT9 1HX
T: 01843 296111 F: 01843 295180
Ops Mgr: Mr S Davis

MARINA THEATRE
The Marina, Lowestoft, Suffolk
NR32 1HH
T: 01502 533200 (Box) F: 01502
538179
Email: info@marinatheatre.co.uk
David Shepheard

THE MAYFLOWER
Commercial Road, Southampton,
Hampshire S015 1GE
T: 023 8071 1800 F: 023 8071 1801
Email: Dennis.hall@mayflower.org.uk
Website: the-mayflower.com
Chief Executive: Dennis Hall

MERCURY THEATRE
Balkerne Gate, Colchester, Essex
CO1 1PT
T: 01206 577006 F: 01206 769607
Email: info@mercurytheatre.co.uk
Marketing Director: Philip Bray

THE MET ARTS CENTRE
Market Street, Bury, Lancashire
BL9 0BW
T: 0161 761 7107 F: 0161 763 5056
Email: metarts.demon.co.uk
Dir: Alan Oatey

METRO CLUB
19-23 Oxford St, London
T: 020 7437 0964 F: 020 7494 4795
Email: bookings@blowupmetro.com
Website: blowupmetro.com
Dir: Paul Tunkin

THE METROPOLE GALLERIES
The Metropole Galleries, The Leas,
Folkestone, Kent CT20 2LS
T: 01303 255070 F: 01303 851353
Email: info@metropole.org.uk
Website: mertopole.org.uk
Dir: Nick Ewbank

MIDDLESBROUGH TOWN HALL
PO Box 69, Albert Road,
Middlesbrough, Cleveland TS1 1EL
T: 01642 263848 F: 01642 221866
Bookings Mgr: Jean Hewitt

MINISTRY OF SOUND
103 Gaunt Street, London SE1 6DP
T: 020 7378 6528 F: 020 7403 5348
Email: efitchett@ministryofsound.com
Website: ministryofsound.com
General Manager: Gary Smart

MITCHELL THEATRE
Exchange House, 229 George Street,
Glasgow, Lanarkshire G1 1QU
T: 0141 287 4855 F: 0141 221 0695

THE MUSICIAN
Clyde Street, Leicester LE1 2DE
T: 0116 251 0080 F: 0116 251 0474
Email: rideout@stayfree.co.uk

Website: themusicianpub.co.uk
Booker/Mgr: Darren Nockles

NAPIER STUDENT ASSOCIATION
12 Merchiston Place, Edinburgh
EH10 4NR
T: 0131 229 8791 F: 0131 228 3462
Email: e.reynolds@napier.ac.uk
Website: napierstudents.com
Ents Officer

THE NATIONAL BOWL AT MILTON KEYNES
c/o BS Group plc, Abbey Stadium, Lady Lane, Swindon, Wiltshire SW2 4DW
T: 0117 952 0600 F: 0117 952 5500
Gordon Cockhill

THE NATIONAL INDOOR ARENA
King Edward's Road, Birmingham, West Midlands B1 2AA
T: 0121 767 2754 F: 0121 644 7181
Email: tc-7002@mail.necgroup.co.uk
Website: necgroup.co.uk
Linda Barrow

NEC ARENA
Birmingham, West Midlands B40 1NT
T: 0121 780 4141
Email: nec-arena@necgroup.co.uk
Website: necgroup.co.uk
Sales: Linda Barrow

NEWMAN COLLEGE OF EDUCATION STUDENT UNION
Genners Lane, Bartley Green,
Birmingham B32 3NT
T: 0121 475 6714 F: 0121 475 6714
Email: ncsu@newman.ac.uk
Louise Beasley

NEWPORT CENTRE
Kingsway, Newport, Gwent NP20 1UH
T: 01633 662663 F: 01633 662675
Events Mgr: Roger Broome

NICE 'N' SLEAZY
421 Sauchiehall Street, Glasgow,
Lanarkshire G2 3LG
T: 0141 333 9637 F: 0141 333 0900
Email: sleazys@hotmail.com
Website: nicensleazy.com
Promoter: Mig

NORTH WALES THEATRE AND CONFERENCE CENTRE
The Promenade, Llandudno, Conwy
LL30 1BB
T: 01492 872000 F: 01492 879771
Email: info@nwtheatre.co.uk
Website: nwtheatre.co.uk
GM: Nick Reed

NORTH WORCESTERSHIRE COLLEGE STUDENT UNION
Burcot Lane, Bromsgrove,
Worcestershire B60 1PQ
T: 01527 570020 F: 01527 572900 :

NORTHGATE ARENA
Victoria Road, Chester CH2 2AU
T: 01244 377086 F: 01244 381693
Email: cadsart@compuserve.com
Website: northgatearena.com
Business Development Mgr: Jon Kelly

NORWICH ARTS CENTRE
Reeves Yard, St Benedicts, Norfolk
NR2 4PG
T: 01603 660387 F: 01603 660352
Centre Mgr: Pam Reekie

NOTTING HILL ARTS CLUB
21 Notting Hill Gate, London W11 3JQ
T: 020 7460 4459

NOTTINGHAM ALBERT HALL
North Circus Street, Off Derby Road, Nottinghamshire NG1 5AA
T: 0115 950 0411 F: 0115 947 6512
Events Mgr: Sarah Robinson

NOTTINGHAM TRENT UNIVERSITY STUDENT UNION
Byron House, Shakespeare Street, Nottingham NG1 4GH
T: 0115 848 6200 F: 0115 848 6201
Email: keri.stephenson@su.ntu.ac.uk
Ents Manager: Keri Stephenson

OASIS LEISURE CENTRE
North Star Avenue, Swindon, Wiltshire SN2 1EP
T: 01793 465148 F: 01793 445569
Bookings Mgr: G Byrne

ODYSSEY ARENA
2 Queen's Quay, Belfast BT3 9QQ
T: 028 9076 6000 F: 028 9076 6111
Email: info@smg-sheridan.com
Website: odysseyarena.com
Executive Director: Nicky Dunn

THE OLD VIC
The Cut, Waterloo, London SE1 8NB
T: 020 7231 1393 F: 020 7232 1373
Email: jo@interactivem.co.uk
Promoter: Jo Cerrone

100 CLUB
100 Oxford Street, London W1D 1LL
T: 020 7636 0933 F: 020 7436 1958
Email: info@the100club.co.uk
Website: the100club.co.uk
Prop: Jeff Horton

THE ORANGE
3 North End Crescent, North End Road, West Kensington, London W14 8TG
T: 020 7751 1044 F: 020 7348 3911
Email: livegigs@mail.com
Website: orangepromotions.com
Booker/Promoter: Phil Brydon

THE ORCHARD
Home Gardens, Dartford, Kent DA1 1ED
T: 01322 220099 F: 01322 227122
Theatre Mgr

ORMOND MULTI MEDIA CENTRE
14 Lower Ormond Quay, Dublin 1, Ireland
T: 00 353 1 872 3500
F: 00 353 1 872 3348

OXFORD UNIVERSITY STUDENT UNION
New Barnet House, Little Clarendon Street, Oxford 0X1 2HU
T: 01865 27077

PAISLEY ARTS CENTRE
New Street, Paisley, Renfrewshire PA1 1EZ
T: 0141 887 1010 F: 0141 887 6300
Email: artsinfo@renfrewshire.gov.uk
Principal Arts Officer: John Harding

PARADISE
19 Kilburn Lane, London W10 4AE
T: 020 8969 0098

PARADISE BAR
460 New Cross Road, London SE14 6TJ

T: 020 8692 1530 F: 020 8691 0445
Website: paradisebar.co.uk
David Roberts

PARR HALL
Palmyra Square South, Warrington, Cheshire WA1 1BL
T: 01925 442345 F: 01925 443228
Email: parrhall@warrington.gov.uk
Website: parrhall.co.uk
Arts & Project Mgr: John Perry

PATTI PAVILION/SWANSEA UNIVERSITY STUDENTS UNION
(see University of Wales - Swansea)

PAVILION
Argyle Street, Rothesay, Isle Of Bute
T: 01546 602127 F: 01700 504225

PAVILION THEATRE
Seafront, Felixstowe, Suffolk IP11 8AQ
T: 01394 282126 F: 01394 278978

PEACOCK ARTS AND ENTERTAINMENT CENTRE
Victoria Way, Woking, Surrey GU21 1GQ
T: 01483 747422 F: 01483 770477

PERTH CITY HALL
King Edward Street, Perth PH1 5UT
T: 01738 624055 F: 01738 630566
Gen Mgr: Drew Scott

PHILHARMONIC HALL
Hope Street, Liverpool, Merseyside L1 9BP
T: 0151 210 1945 F: 0151 210 2902
Email: publicity@rlps.co.uk
Website: liverpoolphil.com
Hall Dir: Pat Peter

THE PICKET
24 Hardman St, Liverpool L1 9AX
T: 0151 708 5318 F: 0151 708 8862
Email: picket@merseymail.com
Website: thepicket.co.uk
Venue Mgr: Neil Robinson

PLANET
Cox Street, Coventry, West Midlands CV1 5PH
T: 01203 571200 F: 01203 559146
Email: n.morgan@threelionsleisure.co.uk
Website: coventry.ac.uk/planet
Nick Morgan

THE PLATFORM
Old Station Buildings, Central Promenade, Morecambe, Lancashire LA4 4DB
T: 01524 582801 F: 01524 831704
Email: lancasterarts@tinyonline.co.uk
Website: artsandevents.co.uk
Head of Arts and Events: Jon Harris

PLYMOUTH PAVILIONS
Millbay Road, Plymouth, Devon PL1 3LF
T: 01752 222200 F: 01752 262226
Email: enquires@plymouthpavilions.com
Website: plymouthpavilions.com
Mktg Mgr: Shona Dipino

PLYMOUTH UNIVERSITY STUDENT UNION
Drake Circus, Plymouth, Devon PL4 8AA
T: 01752 663337 F: 01752 251669
Mark Witherall

PO NA NA HAMMERSMITH
242 Shepherd's Bush Road, London W6 7NL
T: 020 8600 2300 F: 020 86002332
Website: ponana.co.uk

THE POINT
The Plain, Oxford OX4 1EA
T: 01865 798794 F: 01865 798794
Email: mac@thepoint.oxfordmusic.net
Website: thepoint.oxfordmusic.net
Promoter: Mac

THE POINT ARENA AND THEATRE
East Link Bridge, Dublin 1, Ireland
T: 00 353 1 836 6777
F: 00 353 1 836 6422
Gen Mgr: Cormal Rennick

PORTOBELLO TOWN HALL
147 Portobello High Street, Edinburgh, Lothian EH15 1AF
T: 0131 669 5800 F: 0131 669 5800
Hall Keeper: Andrew Crazy

PORTSMOUTH GUILDHALL
Guildhall Square, Portsmouth, Hampshire PO1 2AB
T: 01705 834146 F: 01705 834177
Gen Mgr: Martin Dodd

PORTSMOUTH UNIVERSITY STUDENT UNION
Alexandra House, Museum Road, Portsmouth, Hampshire PO1 2QH
T: 02392 843679 F: 02392 843667
Email: janet.hillier@port.ac.uk
Website: upsu.net
Trad Op's Exec: Janet Hillier

PRINCE EDWARD THEATRE
Old Compton Street, London W1V 6HS
T: 020 7437 2024 F: 020 7734 1454

PRINCE OF WALES THEATRE
Coventry Street, London W1V 8AS
T: 020 7930 9901 F: 020 7976 1336
George Biggs

PRINCES HALL
Princes Way, Aldershot, Hampshire GU11 1NX
T: 01252 327671 F: 01252 320269
Website: rushmoor.gov.uk/princes/index.htm
Gen Mgr: Steven Pugh

PRINCESS PAVILION THEATRE & GYLLYNDUNE GARDENS
41 Melvill Road, Falmouth, Cornwall TR11 4AR
T: 01326 311277 F: 01326 315382
Mr RHD Phipps

PRINCESS THEATRE
Torbay Road, Torquay, Devon TQ2 5EZ
T: 01803 290288 F: 01803 290170
Gen Mgr: Wendy Bennett

PURCELL ROOM
Royal Festival Hall, Belvedere Road, London SE1 8XX
T: 020 7921 0952 F: 020 7928 2049
Email: calexander@rfh.org.uk
Website: rfh.org.uk
Prog Planning Mgr: Catherine Alexander

QUAY ARTS CENTRE
Sea Street, Newport, Isle Of Wight PO30 5BD
T: 01983 822490 F: 01938 526606
Email: info@quayarts.demon.co.uk
Website: quayarts.org
Centre Director: Virgil Philpott

QUEEN ELIZABETH HALL
Belvedere Road, London SE1 8XX
T: 020 7921 0815 F: 020 7928 2049
Email: pchowhan@rfh.org.uk
Website: rfh.org.uk
Prog Planning Mgr: Pam Chowhan

QUEEN ELIZABETH HALL
West Street, Oldham, Lancashire
OL1 1UT
T: 0161 911 4071 F: 0161 911 3094
Admin Mgr: Shelagh Malley

QUEEN MARGARET UNIVERSITY COLLEGE STUDENT'S UNION
36 Clerwood Terrace, Edinburgh
EH12 8TS
T: 0131 317 3403 F: 0131 317 3402
Email: stanpern@hotmail.com
Ents Mgr: Stan Pern

QUEEN'S HALL
Victoria Road, Widnes, Cheshire
WA8 7RF
T: 0151 424 2339 F: 0151 420 5762
Email: queenshall@halton-borough.gov.uk
Website: queenshall-widnes.com
Entertainments Manager: Brian Pridmore

QUEEN'S HALL ARTS CENTRE
Beaumont Street, Hexham,
Northumberland NE46 3LS
T: 01434 606787 F: 01434 606043
Arts Mgr: Geoff Keys

THE QUEENS HALL
Edinburgh Clerk Street, Edinburgh,
Lothian EH8 9JG
T: 0131 668 3456 F: 0131 668 2656
Hall Mgr: Iain McQueen

QUEEN'S THEATRE
Boutport Street, Barnstaple, Devon
EX31 1SY
T: 01271 327357 F: 01271 326412
Email: info@northdevontheatres.org.uk
Website: northdevontheatres.org.uk
Programming Dir: Karen Turner

QUEENS UNIVERSITY STUDENTS UNION
79-81 University Road, Belfast, Co
Antrim BT7 1PE
T: 028 9032 4803 F: 028 9023 6900
Email: info@qubsu-ents.com
Website: qubsu-ents.com

READING TOWN HALL
3 B's Bar and Cafe, Blagrave Street,
Reading, Berkshire RG1 1QH
T: 0118 939 9803 F: 0118 956 6719
Bookings Mgr: Stefano Buratta

READING UNIVERSITY
PO Box 230, Whiteknights, Reading,
Berkshire RG6 2AZ
T: 0118 986 0222 F: 0118 975 5283

THE RED BRICK THEATRE
Aqueduct Road, Blackburn, Lancashire
BB2 4HT
T: 01254 698859 F: 01254 265640
Miss C Kay

REDDITCH PALACE THEATRE
Alcester Street, Redditch,
Worcestershire B98 8AE
T: 01527 61544 F: 01527 60243
Bookings Mgr: Michael Dyer

THE REX
361 Stratford High Street, London
E15 4QZ
T: 020 8215 6003 F: 020 8215 6004
Website: meanfiddler.com

RICHMOND THEATRE
The Green, Richmond, Surrey TW9 IQJ
T: 020 8940 0220 F: 020 8948 3601
Theatre Dir: Karin Gartzke

THE RITZ BALLROOM
Whitworth Street West, Manchester
M1 5NQ
T: 0161 236 4355 F: 0161 236 7515
Email: eddieritz@hotmail.com
GM: Eddie Challiner

RIVERMEAD LEISURE COMPLEX
Richfield Avenue, Reading, Berkshire
RG1 8EQ
T: 0118 901 5014 F: 0118 901 5006

RIVERSIDE STUDIOS
Crisp Road, Hammersmith, London
W6 9RL
T: 020 8237 1000 F: 020 8237 1011
Email: jonfawcett@riversidestudios.co.uk
Website: riversidestudios.co.uk
Hires Mgr: Jon Fawcett

THE ROADHOUSE
8 Newton Street, Piccadilly, Manchester
M1 2AN
T: 0161 237 9789 F: 0161 236 9289
Email: live@theroadhouse.u-net.com
Website: theroadhouse.u-net.com
Owner: Katie Mountain

THE ROADMENDER
1 Ladys Lane, Northampton NN1 3AH
T: 01604 604 603 F: 01604 603 166
Website: roadmender.uk
Jon Dunn

THE ROBIN
1 The Robin Hood, Merry Hill, Brierley
Hill, West Midlands DY5 1TD
T: 01384 637747 F: 01384 637227
Email: music@therobin.co.uk
Website: therobin.co.uk
Prop: Mike Hamblett

ROCK CITY
8 Talbot St, Nottingham NG1 5GG
T: 0115 941 2544 F: 0115 941 8438
Email: jen@rock-city.co.uk
Website: rock-city.co.uk
Director: George Akins

ROCK GARDEN
6-7 The Piazza, Covent Garden, London
WC2E 8HA
T: 020 7257 8609 F: 020 7379 4793
Website: rockgarden.co.uk
Dir: Sean McDonnell

RONNIE SCOTT'S
47 Frith Street, London W1D 4HT
T: 020 7439 0747 F: 020 7437 5081
Email: ronniescotts@ronniescotts.co.uk
Website: ronniescotts.co.uk
Owner/Club Director: Pete King

ROTHERHAM CIVIC THEATRE
Catherine Street, Rotherham, South
Yorkshire S65 1EB
T: 01709 823640 F: 01709 823638

THE ROYAL
Pall Mall, Hanley, Stoke On Trent,
Staffordshire ST1 1EE
T: 01782 206000 F: 01782 204955
Website: webfactory.co.uk/theroyal/
Dir: Mike Lloyd

ROYAL ALBERT HALL
Kensington Gore, London SW7 2AP
T: 020 7589 3203 F: 020 7823 7725
Email: sales@royalalberthall.com
Website: royalalberthall.com
Head of Sales & Mkting: Tracy Cooper

ROYAL CENTRE
Theatre Square, Nottingham NG1 5ND
T: 0115 989 5500 F: 0115 947 4218
Email: enquiry@royalcentre-nottingham.co.uk
Website: royalcentre-nottingham.co.uk
Acting Director: James Ashworth

ROYAL COURT THEATRE
1 Roe Street, Liverpool, Merseyside L1 1HL
T: 0151 709 1808 F: 0151 709 7611
Email: Richard.Maides@iclway.co.uk
Website: royalcourttheatre.net
Theatre Manager: Richard Maides

ROYAL COURT THEATRE
Sloane Square, London SW1W 8AS
T: 020 7565 5050 F: 020 7565 5001
Email: info@royalcourttheatre.com
Website: royalcourttheatre.com
Exec Dir: Vikki Heywood

ROYAL EXCHANGE THEATRE
St Ann's Square, Manchester M2 7DH
T: 0161 833 9333 F: 0161 832 0881
Email: Philp.Lord@royalexchange.co.uk
Website: royalexchange.co.uk
Philip Lord

ROYAL FESTIVAL HALL
Belvedere Road, London SE1 8XX
T: 020 7921 0843 F: 020 7928 2049
Email: emcbain@rfh.org.uk
Website: rfh.org.uk
Head of Hall Prog Planner: Elspeth McBain

ROYAL HALL
Ripon Road, Harrogate, North Yorkshire HG1 2RD
T: 01423 500500 F: 01423 537210
Email: sales@harrogateinternationalcentre.co.uk
Website: harrogateinternationalcentre.co.uk
Dir: Paul Lewis

ROYAL LYCEUM THEATRE
Grindlay Street, Edinburgh EH3 9AX
T: 0131 248 4800 F: 0131 228 3955
Email: administration@lyceum.org.uk
Website: lyceum.org.uk
Admin Mgr: Ruth Butterworth

ROYAL VICTORIA HALL
London Road, Southborough, Tunbridge Wells, Kent TN4 0ND
T: 01892 529176 F: 01892 541402

ST ANDREWS MUSIC CENTRE
North Street, St Andrews, Fife KY16 9AJ
T: 01334 462226
Email: music@st-andrews.ac.uk
Website: st-andrews.ac.uk/services/music Office Manager: Alison Malcolm

ST DAVID'S HALL
The Hayes, Cardiff CF10 1SH
T: 029 2087 8500 F: 029 2087 8599
Head Arts & Cultural Serv: Judi Richards

ST GEORGE'S BRISTOL
Great George Street, (off Park Street), Bristol BS1 5RR
T: 0117 929 4929 F: 0117 927 6537
Email: administration@stgeorgesbristol.co.uk
Website: stgeorgesbristol.co.uk
Dir: Jonathan Stracey

ST GEORGE'S CONCERT HALL
Bridge Street, Bradford, West Yorkshire BD1 1JS

T: 01274 752186 F: 01274 720736
Email: christine.raby@bradford.gov.uk
Website: bradford-theatres.co.uk
Programme Booking Admin: Christine Raby

ST GEORGE'S HALL
Market Street, Exeter, Devon EX1 1BU
T: 01392 265866 F: 01392 422137
Email: markets.halls@exeter.gov.uk
Mgr: David Lewis

ST MARY'S COLLEGE STUDENT UNION
Waldergrave Road, Strawberry Hill, Twickenham, Middlesex TW1 4SX
T: 020 8240 4314 F: 020 8744 1700
Kieran Renihan

THE SANCTUARY LEISURE LTD
Denbigh North Leisure, V7 Saxon Street, Milton Keynes, Buckinghamshire MK1 1SA
T: 01908 368984 F: 01908 277028
Email: Sanctuary@xsleisure.co.uk
Mgr: Claire Vanneck

SCARBOROUGH UNIVERITY COLLEGE STUDENT UNION
Filey Road, Scarborough, North Yorkshire YO11 3AZ
T: 01723 362392 F: 01723 370815
Nick Evans

SCOTTISH EXHIBITION & CONFERENCE CENTRE
Glasgow, Lanarkshire G3 8YW
T: 0141 248 3000 F: 0141 226 3423
Acct Mgr, Concerts: Susan Verlaque

SHANKLIN THEATRE
Prospect Road, Shanklin, Isle of Wight PO37 6AJ
T: 01983 862739 F: 01983 867682
David Redston

SHEFFIELD ARENA
Broughton Lane, Sheffield, South Yorkshire S9 2DF
T: 0114 256 2002 F: 0114 256 5520
Email: info@clearchannel.co.uk
Website: sheffield-arena.co.uk
GM: David Vickers

SHEFFIELD CITY HALL
Barkers Pool, Sheffield, South Yorkshire S1 2JA
T: 0114 223 3740 F: 0114 276 9866
Email: info@sheffieldcityhall.co.uk
Website: sheffieldcityhall.com
GM: Jo Barnes

SHEFFIELD HALLAM UNIVERSITY STUDENT'S UNION
Nelson Mandela Building, Pond Street, Sheffield, South Yorksire S1 2BW
T: 0114 225 4122 F: 0114 225 4140
Email: a.sewell@shu.ac.uk
Website: shu.ac.uk/su
Ents Co-ordinator: Alice Sewell

SHEFFIELD UNIVERSITY STUDENTS UNION
Western Bank, Sheffield, South Yorkshire S10 2TG
T: 0114 222 8556 F: 0114 222 8574
Email: j.hann@sheffield.ac.uk
Ents Manager: James Hann

SHEPHERD'S BUSH EMPIRE
Shepherd's Bush Green, London W12 8TT

T: 020 8354 3300 F: 020 8743 3218
Email: mail@shepherds-bush-empire.co.uk
Website: shepherds-bush-empire.co.uk
GM: Bill Marshall

SHREWSBURY MUSIC HALL
The Square, Shrewsbury, Shropshire
SY1 1LH
T: 01743 281281 F: 01743 281283
Email: mail@musichall.co.uk
Website: musichall.co.uk
Marketing Officer: Adam Burgan

THE SPITZ
109 Commercial Street, Old Spitalfields
Market, London E1 6BG
T: 020 7392 9032 F: 020 7377 8915
Email: mail@spitz.co.uk
Website: spitz.co.uk
Music Promoter: Tris Dickin

THE SQUARE FOURTH AVENUE
Harlow, Essex CM20 1DW
T: 01279 305000 F: 01279 866151
Email: promotion@harlowsquare.com
Website: harlowsquare.com
Music Promoter: Tom Hawkins

STABLES THEATRE
Stockwell Lane, Wavendon, Milton
Keynes, Buckinghamshire MK17 8LU
T: 01908 280814 F: 01908 280827
Email: stables@stables.org
Website: stables.org
Penny Griffiths

STAFFORD GATEHOUSE
Eastgate Street, Stafford ST16 2LT
T: 01785 253595 F: 01785 225622
Mgr: Daniel Shaw

THE STANDARD MUSIC VENUE
1 Blackhorse Lane, London E17 6DS
T: 020 8523 0055 F: 020 8527 1944
Email: ngh354547@aol.com
Website: standardmusicvenue.co.uk
Nigel Henson

STANTONBURY LEISURE CENTRE
Purbeck, Stantonbury, Milton Keynes,
Buckinghamshire MK14 6BN
T: 01908 314466 F: 01908 318754
Mgr: Matthew Partridge

STOUR CENTRE
Tannery Lane, Ashford, Kent TN23 1PL
T: 01233 625801 F: 01233 645654

STOURBRIDGE TOWN HALL
Crown Centre, Stourbridge, West
Midlands DY8 1YE
T: 01384 812948 F: 01384 812963
Laurence Hanna

THE STUDIO
Tower Street, Hartlepool TS24 7HQ
T: 01429 424440 F: 01429 424441
Email: thestudiohartlepool@ntlworld.com
Website: studiohartlepool.com
Studio Manager: Liz Carter

SUBTERANIA
12 Acklam Road, London W10 5QZ
T: 020 8960 4590 F: 020 8961 9238
Promoter: Poorang Shahabi

SUNDERLAND UNIVERSITY STUDENT UNION
Manor Quay, Charles Street, Sunderland
SR6 0AN
T: 0191 515 3583 F: 0191 515 2499
Email: andy.fitzpatrick@sunderland.ac.uk

Website: mq@sunderland.co.uk
A Fitzpatrick

SUSSEX UNIVERSITY STUDENT UNION
Falmer House, Falmer, Brighton
BN1 9QF
T: 01273 678555 F: 01273 678875
Entertainments Dept

THE SWAN
215 Clapham Road, London SW9 91E
T: 020 7978 9778 F: 020 7738 6722
Website: swanstockwell.com
John McCormack

TAMESIDE HIPPODROME
Oldham Road, Ashton-under-Lyne,
Tameside OL6 7SE
T: 0161 330 2095 F: 0161 343 5839
Email: karen.whittick@clearchannel.co.uk
GM: Karen Whittick

TAMWORTH ARTS CENTRE
Church Street, Tamworth, Staffordshire
B79 7BX
T: 01827 53092 F: 01827 53092
The Arts Venue Mgr

TEESSIDE UNIVERSITY
University of Teesside Union, Southfield
Road, Middlesbrough, Cleveland
TS1 3BA
T: 01642 342234 F: 01642 342241
Email: L.Stretton@utsu.org.uk
Website: utsu.org.uk
Ent & Promotions Mgr: Luke Stretton

TELEWEST ARENA
Arena Way, Newcastle upon Tyne
NE4 7NA
T: 0191 260 6002 F: 0191 260 2200
Website: telewestarena.co.uk
Exec Dir: Colin Revel

TELFORD ICE RINK
Telford Town Centre, Telford, Shropshire
TF3 4JQ
T: 01952 291511 F: 01952 291543
Mgr: Robert Fountain

THAMES VALLEY UNIVERSITY STUDENTS UNION
St Mary's Road, London W5 5RF
T: 020 8231 2531 F: 020 8231 2589

THEATRE ROYAL
282 Hope Street, Glasgow G2 3QA
T: 0141 332 3321 admin
F: 0141 332 4477
Website: theatreroyalglasgow.com
Theatre Mgr: Martin Ritchie

THEATRE ROYAL
Corporation Street, St Helens,
Merseyside WA10 1LQ
T: 01744 756333 admin
F: 01744 756777
Gen Mgr: Basil Soper

THEATRE ROYAL
Royal Parade, Plymouth, Devon
PL1 2TR
T: 01752 668282 F: 01752 671179
Email: info@theatreroyal.com
Website: theatreroyal.com
Chief Exec: Adrian Vinken

THEATRE ROYAL
Grey Street, Newcastle upon Tyne, Tyne
and Wear NE1 6BR
T: 0191 232 0997 F: 0191 261 1906
Peter Sarah

TIVERTON NEW HALL
Barrington Street, Tiverton, Devon, Exeter EX16 6QP
T: 01884 253404 F: 01884 243677
Town Clerk: B Lough

TIVOLI
Brunswick Road, Buckley, Clwyd CH7 2EF
T: 01224 546201

TJ'S DISCO
16-18 Clarence Place, Newport, South Wales NP19 0AE
T: 01633 216608
Email: sam@tjs-newport.demon.co.uk
Website: tjs-newport.demon.co.uk
Manager: John Sicolo

THE TOP OF REILLY'S
10 Thurland Street, Nottingham NG1 3DR
T: 0115 941 7709 F: 0115 941 5604

TORBAY LEISURE CENTRE
Clennon Valley, Penwill Way, Paignton, Devon TQ4 5JR
T: 01803 522240
Website: torbay.gov.uk

TORQUAY TOWN HALL
Lymington Road, Torquay, Devon TQ1 3DR
T: 01803 201201 F: 01803 208856
Email: pete.carpenter@torbay.gov.uk
Mr P Carpenter

THE TOWER BALLROOM
Reservoir Road, Edgbaston, Birmingham, West Midlands B16 9EE
T: 0121 454 0107 F: 0121 455 9313
Email: tower@zanzibar.co.uk
Website: zanzibar.co.uk
MD: Susan Prince

TOWN HALL
High Street, Hawick TD9 9EF
T: 01450 364743
Alister Murdie

TRINITY & ALL SAINTS COLLEGE
The Base, Brownberrie Lane, Horsforth, Leeds, West Yorkshire LS18 5HD
T: 0113 258 5793 F: 0113 258 6831

TRURO HALL FOR CORNWALL
Back Quay, Truro, Cornwall TR1 2LL
T: 01872 262468 F: 01872 260246
Email: hallforcornwall@enterprise.net
Website: hallforcornwall.co.uk
Chief Exec

21 SOUTH STREET
21 South Street, Reading, Berkshire RG1 4QU
T: 0118 901 5234 F: 0118 901 5235
Website: readingarts.com
Venue Mgr: Matthew Linley

ULSTER HALL
Bedford Street, Belfast, Co Antrim BT2 7FF
T: 028 9032 3900 F: 028 9024 7199
Pat Falls

ULSTER UNIVERSITY STUDENTS' ASSOCIATION
York Street, Belfast, Co Antrim BT15 1ED
T: 028 9032 8515 F: 028 9026 7351
Club Sec: Joseph Mathews

ULU (UNIVERSITY OF LONDON UNION)
Malet Street, London WC1E 7HY
T: 020 7664 2022 F: 020 7436 4604
Email: entsinfo@ulu.lon.ac.uk
Website: ulu.lon.ac.uk
Ents Mgr: Graeme Nash

UMIST UNION
PO Box 88, Sackville Street, Manchester M60 1QD
T: 0161 200 3286 F: 0161 200 3268
Email: paul.parkes@su.umist.ac.uk
Paul Parkes

THE UNDERWORLD
174 Camden High Street, London NW1 0NE
T: 020 7267 3939 F: 020 7482 1955
Email: JonDowd@aol.com
Jon Vyner

UNIVERSITY OF EAST ANGLIA STUDENTS UNION
University Plain, Norwich, Norfolk NR4 7TJ
T: 01603 505401 F: 01603 593465
Email: ents@uea.ac.uk
Website: ueaticketbookings.co.uk
Ents Mgr: Nick Rayns

UNIVERSITY OF ESSEX STUDENTS' UNION
Students' Union, Uni of Essex, Colchester, Essex CO4 3SQ
T: 01206 863236 F: 01206 870915
Email: ents@essex.ac.uk
Website: su.essex.ac.uk
Ents & Venues Mgr: Clive Little

UNIVERSITY OF GLOUCESTERSHIRE STUDENTS' UNION
Student Union, PO Box 220, The Park, Cheltenham GL52 2EH
T: 01242 532848 F: 01242 361381
Email: union@uqsu.org; space@glos.ac.uk
Website: ugsu.org
VP Communications: Mathew Loach

UNIVERSITY OF GREENWICH STUDENT UNION
Bathway, Woolwich, London SE18 6QX
T: 020 8331 8268 F: 020 8331 8591

UNIVERSITY OF NOTTINGHAM STUDENT UNION
Portland Building, University Park, Nottingham NG7 2RD
T: 0115 935 1100
Social Sec: Tanya Nathan

UNIVERSITY OF PAISLEY - AYR CAMPUS STUDENT ASSOCIATION
Beech Grove, Ayr KA8 0SR
T: 01292 886330 office
F: 01292 886271
Email: dpa@upsa.org.uk
Deputy President: Kim Macintyre

UNIVERSITY OF STRATHCYLDE STUDENTS ASSOCIATION
90 John Street, Glasgow, Lanarkshire G1 1JH
T: 0141 567 5023 F: 0141 567 5033
Email: a.j.mawn@strath.ac.uk

UNIVERSITY OF SURREY UNION CLUB
Union House, University of Surrey, Guildford, Surrey GU2 7XH

T: 01483 689983
Email: ents@ussu.co.uk
Website: ussu.co.uk
Events Mgr: Alan Roy

UNIVERSITY OF ULSTER
Cromore Road, Coleraine, Co Antrim
BT52 1SA
T: 028 9036 5121 F: 028 9036 6817

UNIVERSITY OF WALES - CARDIFF CENTRAL UNION OFFICES
Cyncoed Site, Cyncoed Road, Cardiff
CF2 6XD
T: 029 2055 1111 F: 029 2050 6199 :

UNIVERSITY OF WALES - SWANSEA STUDENT UNION
Fulton House, Singleton Park, Swansea
SA2 8PP
T: 01792 295485 F: 01792 513006
Email: suents@swansea.ac.uk
Website: swansea-union.co.uk/ents
Ents Mgr: Lee Pugh

UNIVERSITY OF WALES - LAMPETER STUDENT UNION
Ty Ceredig, Lampeter, Ceredigion
SA48 7ED
T: 01570 422619 F: 01570 422480

UNIVERSITY OF WEST ENGLAND STUDENT UNION
Coldharbour Lane, Frenchay, Bristol
B16 1QY
T: 0117 965 6261 x 2580
F: 0117 976 3909
Email: union@uwe.ac.uk
Website: gate.uwe.ac.uk:8000/union/ents/index.html
Programming Asst

UNIVERSITY OF WESTMINSTER STUDENT UNION
32 Wells Street, London W1T 3UW
T: 020 7911 5000 x 2306
F: 020 7911 5848
Email: edfrith@hotmail.com
Events Mgr: Ed Frith

UPSTAIRS @ GARAGE
20/22 Highbury Corner, London N5 1RD
T: 020 7607 1818 F: 020 7609 0846
Email: joady@meanfiddler.co.uk
Bking Mgr: Joady Thornton

USHER HALL
Lothian Road, Edinburgh EH1 2EA
T: 0131 228 8616 F: 0131 228 8848
Mgr: Moira McKenzie

THE VENUE
Bath University, Students Union,
Claverton Down, Bath BA2 7AY
T: 01225 826613 F: 01225 444061
Email: ents@union.bath.ac.uk
Website: bath.ac.uk/~su4su/ent/
Ents Co-ordinator: Steve Backman

THE VENUE AT KENT UNIVERSITY
Kent Student Union, Mandela Building,
Canterbury, Kent CT2 7NW
T: 01227 824235 F: 01227 824207
Email: d.stepto@ukc.ac.uk
Entertainments Manager: Danny Stepto

VENUE 1 THEATRE STUDENT UNION
St Mary's Place, St Andrews KY16 9UZ
T: 01334 462700 F: 01334 462740
Email: nhll@st-and.ac.uk
Website: st-and.ac.uk/union
Bldg Supervisor: Bruce Turner

VERDIS
38A Maiden Street, Weymouth, Dorset
DT4 8AZ
T: 01305 779842 F: 01305 776869
Email: schultzy@verdis.co.uk
Website: verdis.co.uk
Prop: Michael Shalts

VIBE BAR
91-95 Brick Lane, London E1 6QL
T: 020 7247 3479 F: 020 7426 0641
Email: info@vibe-bar.co.uk
Website: vibe-bar.co.uk
Events Manager: Adelle Stripe

VICTORIA HALL
Akeman Street, Tring, Hertfordshire
HP23 6AA
T: 01442 228951

THE VICTORIA HALL
Bagnall Street, Hanley, Stoke-on-Trent, Staffordshire ST1 3AD
T: 0117 932 1952 F: 0117 932 1953
Email: Paul.Mazy@ukonline.co.uk

VICTORIA COMMUNITY CENTRE
Oakley Building, West Street, Crewe, Cheshire CW1 2PZ
T: 01270 211422 F: 01270 537960
Centre Mgr: Mrs E McFahn

VICTORIA THEATRE
Wards End, Halifax, West Yorkshire
HX1 1BU
T: 01422 351156 F: 01422 320552
Email: admin@victoria-theatre.yorks.co.uk
George Candler

WARWICK ARTS CENTRE
University Of Warwick, Coventry, West Midlands CV4 7AL
T: 024 7652 4524 F: 024 4652 4777
Email: box.office@warwick.ac.uk
Website: warwickartscentre.co.uk
Dir: Alan Rivett

WARWICK UNIVERSITY STUDENT UNION
Gibbet Hill Road, Coventry, West Midlands CV4 7AL
T: 024 7657 3179 F: 024 7669 0893
Email: dwalter@sunion.warwick.ac.uk
Ents Ops Mgr: Darren Walter

THE WATER RATS THEATRE
328 Grays Inn Road, London
WC1X 8BZ
T: 020 7837 7269

THE WATERFRONT
139 King St, Norwich, Norfolk NR1 1QH
T: 01603 632717 F: 01603 662144
Email: thewaterfront@uea.ac.uk
Website: ueaticketbookings.co.uk
Programmer: Paul Ingleby

WATERMANS ARTS CENTRE
40 High Street, Brentford, Middlesex
TW8 0DS
T: 020 8847 5651 F: 020 8569 8592
Lorna O'Leary

WATFORD COLOSSEUM
Rickmansworth Road, Watford, Hertfordshire WD1 7JN
T: 01923 445300 F: 01923 445225
John Wallace

THE WEDGEWOOD ROOMS
147B Albert Road, Southsea, Portsmouth, Hampshire P04 0JW
T: 023 9286 3911 F: 023 9285 1326

Email: tickets@wedgewood-rooms.co.uk
Website: wedgewood-rooms.co.uk
GM: Geoff Priestley

THE WELLY CLUB
105-107 Beverley Rd, Hull HU3 1TS
T: 01482 221113 F: 01482 221113
Email: thewelly@hull24.com
Website: yo-yo-indie.com
Promotions Mgr: Andrew Coe

WEMBLEY ARENA
Empire Way, Wembley, London
HA9 0DW
T: 020 8902 8833 F: 020 8585 3879
Email: venuebookings@wembley.co.uk
Website: wembley.co.uk/venues
Mgr: Caroline McNamara

WEMBLEY CONFERENCE AND EXHIBITION CENTRE
Wembley Conference, and Exhibition Centre, Wembley, Middlesex HA9 0DW
T: 020 8795 8073 F: 020 8585 3879
Email: venuebookings@wembley.co.uk
Website: wembley.co.uk/venues
Peter Tudor

WEST END CENTRE
Queens Road, Aldershot, Hampshire
GU11 3JD
T: 01252 408040 F: 01252 408041
Email: westendcentre@hants.gov.uk
Website: westendcentre.co.uk
Programme Co-ordinator: Barney Jeavons

WESTPOINT ARENA
Clyst St Mary, Exeter, Devon EX5 1DJ
T: 01392 446000 F: 01392 445843
Email: info@westpoint-devonshow.co.uk
Website: westpoint-devonshow.co.uk
Events Mgr: Sarah Symons

WEYMOUTH PAVILION
The Esplanade, Weymouth, Dorset
DT4 8ED
T: 01305 765218 F: 01305 789922
Arts & Entertainments Mgr: Stephen Young

THE WHEATSHEAF LIVE MUSIC VENUE
Church Street, Stoke On Trent, Staffordshire ST4 1BU
T: 01782 844438 F: 01782 410340
Anne Riddle

WHITE ROCK THEATRE
White Rock, Hastings, East Sussex
TN34 1JX
T: 01424 781010 F: 01424 781170
Andy Mould

WIGMORE HALL
36 Wigmore Street, London W1H 0BP
T: 020 7258 8200 F: 020 7258 8201
Email: info@wigmore-hall.org.uk
Website: wigmore-hall.org.uk
Management Office

WIMBLEDON THEATRE
93 The Broadway, London SW19 1QG
T: 020 8543 4549 F: 020 8543 6637
Email: live@wimbledontheatre.co.uk
Website: uktw.co.uk/info/wimbledon.htm
Gen Mgr: Ian Alexander

WINCHESTER GUILDHALL
The Broadway, Winchester, Hampshire
SO23 9LJ
T: 01962 840820
Email: cchurcher@winchester.gov.uk
Website: winchester.gov.uk/guildhall/index.htm
Sales & Events Mgr: Clare Churcher

WINDMILL BRIXTON
22 Blenheim Gardens, (off Brixton Hill), London SW2 5BZ
T: 020 8671 0700
Email: windmillbrixton@yahoo.co.uk
Website: windmillbrixton.co.uk
Booker: Tim Perry

WINDSOR ARTS CENTRE
St Leonard's Road, Windsor, Berkshire SL4 3BL
T: 01753 859421 F: 01753 621527 :
Debbie Stubbs

WOLVERHAMPTON CIVIC
North Street, Wolverhampton, West Midlands WV1 1RQ
T: 01902 552122 F: 01902 552123
Email: markb@wolvescivic.co.uk
Website: wolvescivic.co.uk
Gen Mgr: Mark Blackstock

WOLVERHAMPTON UNIVERSITY STUDENTS UNION
Wulfruna Street, Wolverhampton, West Midlands WV1 1LY
T: 01902 322021 F: 01902 322020
Website: wlv.ac.uk

WOODVILLE HALLS THEATRE
Woodville Place, Gravesend, Kent DA12 1DD
T: 01474 337456 F: 01474 337458
Email: woodville.halls@gravesham.gov.uk
Website: gravesham.gov.uk/woodvillehalls.htm
Rob Allen

WORTHING ASSEMBLY HALL
Stoke Abbott Road, Worthing, Sussex BN11 1HQ
T: 01903 239999 F: 01903 821124
Theatre Mgr: Peter Bailey

WORTHING PAVILION THEATRE
Marine Parade, Worthing, Sussex BN11 3PX
T: 01903 239999 F: 01903 821124
Theatre Mgr: Peter Bailey

WYVERN THEATRE
Theatre Square, Swindon, Wiltshire SN1 1QN
T: 01865 782900 F: 01865 782910
Nicky Monk

YEOVIL OCTAGON THEATRE
Hendford, Yeovil, Somerset BA20 1UX
T: 01935 422836 F: 01935 475281
Gen Mgr: John G White

YORK BARBICAN CENTRE
Barbican Road, York, North Yorkshire Y010 4NT
T: 01904 628991 F: 01904 628227
Email: craig.smart@york.gov.uk
Website: fibbers.co.uk/barbican
Craig Smart

YORK UNIVERSITY STUDENTS UNION
Goodricke College, Heslington, York, North Yorkshire YO1 5DD
T: 01904 433724 F: 01904 434664
Email: ents@york.ac.uk
Website: york.ac.uk/student/su/index.shtml
Andrew Windsor: Entertainments Officer

YOUNGER GRADUATION HALL
North Street, St Andrews KY16 9AJ
T: 01334 462226 F: 01334 462570
Email: music@st-and.ac.uk
Website: st-and.ac.uk/services/music
The Secretary

1

2

3

4

5

6

7

8

9

10

11

12

13

14

15

MEDIA

WHAT IS THE ROLE OF THE MEDIA?

The media and music go together like fish and chips. From the consumer's perspective both are changing all the time, but both are an essential part of their life. Of course there are always times when the relationship is strained, but that's just life.

WHY DOESN'T MUSIC MEDIA MOVE US LIKE IT USED TO DO?

There was a time in the UK when broadcast access to a band through TV and radio was an event we participated in nationally, watching *Top of the Pops* on Thursday and waiting for the Top 40 countdown on Sunday.

It wasn't until MTV arrived that we realised what we were missing. Suddenly music exploded as an audiovisual medium. It was the peak of Michael Jackson's dominance, when bored housewives danced along to the 'Thriller' video on thick pile carpets.

Meanwhile punk fanzines had spawned a new magazine sector. Nick Logan jumped straight from the photocopier to the studio, launching *The Face* and changing our perceptions of what a lifestyle magazine should be. *Q Magazine* understood this and transformed the mainstream music press.

But eventually the video tricks and slick production values of MTV began to pale as we discovered the street rawness of Kiss FM, born in the reality of a council flat. All those of us who'd been seeking out the latest music in illegal warehouse parties could suddenly find it on our radio. Kiss was a new type of pirate radio, harder edged than the generation before.

In theory there has never been a better time for media. Radio 1 has learnt from Kiss and uses specialist DJ presenters like Tim Westwood. Well-known DJs have brought it new credibility and audiences. Its website is one of the best in the business. Even good old *Top of the Pops* has revamped its format after having been shamed by the showmanship of *CD:UK*, and MTV has increased its offering with VH1 for the oldies, and MTV Base for the kids. Capital has bought Choice FM to get a credible urban music channel, and you can now listen to the radio on your mobile and get videos screened on it as well.

But somehow in general the music media has lost its ability to capture kids' imagination in the way it has in the past.

It may be our fault rather than the media itself, or a combination of both. We have become much more sophisticated consumers of all types of media. Research among kids indicates that unlike a previous generation they're looking for the editorial agenda behind the content. In other words they're cynical and just as they hate artists to be fake, they can't stand their media to be fake.

Although there are many more choices of stations and publications, the majority of the media is controlled by a relatively small number of large corporations that profile their audiences and market them to death. Understanding your audience statistically is not the same as knowing them or being connected to them.

It's amazing that with all the choices available to kids today there's still a very small core number of channels that dominate mainstream music. In the main they are most of the public's window on music and popular culture. MTV, *Top of the Pops*, Radio 1, *CD:UK* and *Q Magazine* are the media that make the hits and make the tills ring at the major labels. As such they have a huge responsibility. In this section we interview the main people responsible for these key channels. All of them are very smart, likeable individuals who are brilliant at what they do. However, their key objective is short-term, to get their ratings or their circulation up. They do this through clever formatting and featuring good acts. Their production values are higher than they have ever been, but they have lost some of the rawness and the connection with the audience that media had in the past.

In its way Channel U and hip hop underground magazines like *Tense* and *Rewind* are doing for their audience what Kiss did a decade ago and fanzines did a generation before that. What they have is a close identification with a particular culture and type of street style. Kids who consume this media don't think they are being sold to, or packaged. Channel U has increased this feeling by encouraging its viewers to participate, whether it's sending in videos of their band or just dancing, or on a simpler level texting the screen. Its what the dot com entrepreneurs were banging on about. They've facilitated their audience to produce their own content.

THE FUTURE

We see the future of media polarising. The mainstream channels will continue getting better at what they do. Their showmanship and packaging will carry on improving, as will their ability to present the next big thing to a mainstream market. But for a mainstream channel, it's important to get your timing right and find new bands just before they are crossing over to the mainstream and not before.

This leaves a huge gap for more street-based media. New technologies and new music forms will continue to spawn media that has a different agenda and a more targeted audience than the mainstream channels. Today it only costs £75,000 a year to rent a digital TV channel on the Sky platform, so the possibility of using broadcast medium to reach a street audience and to break unknown and unsigned bands is more feasible than ever before.

ONLINE MEDIA

With the coming of broadband, everyone's expecting the growth of Internet-based media. There has been an increase in 'virtual webcasting' with several artists like Madonna and Robbie Williams including part of their tours on virtual webcasts. A grander scheme, Now TV, set up by Richard Li who started Star TV in Asia, was closed last year. It had attempted to develop a number of broadband channels including one for music. In Italy Tiscali, the broadband provider, has been more successful. In many ways the artists' own websites probably have more influence, like Bowie's site, where he will regularly answer questions live, or radio and TV stations own sites, where they can offer more depth and interactivity than in the mainstream broadcast programming.

GENERAL MEDIA

Music plays an important role in non-specialist media. Too often people ignore the importance of exposure in image press, tabloids and general TV. Most style magazines review recent releases and are more trusted by their readers. Their special features play an important role in developing an artist's profile. This environment has huge advantages, because it is not cluttered with other artists and offers more opportunities to target a specific audience, especially for an artist like Norah Jones who appeals to a wider audience than regular consumers of music media.

TIPS FOR NEWCOMERS

- ***Newspaper journalist:*** Traditionally these are stars in their own right. There are some courses at colleges, e.g. London College of Printing. However, most successful journalists have been writing articles on bands for local papers or whoever will print them since they could first stand on tiptoe and blag their way into gigs.

  The trick is to become part of the scene, especially if it's a new scene that nobody else is covering. Caroline Coon got her big break in the macho 1970s world of music journalism because she spotted that punk was going to be big. She became a punk insider when everyone else thought it would never be more than a minor music scene.

  There are huge opportunities for would-be journalists to be part of the changing urban music scene. Start with the specialist underground mags like *Tense* and then offer articles to the national press, as their interest in the scene develops. Like songwriters, producers and anyone else who's part of the business, let go of the image of the writer sitting alone in a garret. If you want to be a successful music journalist you need to be part of what's going on.
- ***Radio or TV:*** The traditional way into radio has been hospital or college radio. That might still be the case, but increasingly the coolest stations are taking DJs from clubs and the street. The way into TV has usually been to start as a researcher and work your way up.

  Of course if you want to be a TV presenter none of this works. It's all about your look and presence. MTV presenters do not earnestly work their way up from being presenters. You have to treat yourself more as an artist. You'll need to produce a good demo reel. There's no point in producing a demo tape unless you can make it special. You'll need to persuade a high-profile band or artist to let you interview them. We don't mean just a sycophantic interview: you must show you have enough courage and charm to get them to be themselves with you and say something interesting and genuine or even provocative. Then you might have a chance of actually getting to meet someone.

- ***Music videos:*** There are lots of courses where you can learn to edit and direct. Pick a short one or a part-time one and spend the rest of the time actually doing it. Channels like Channel U give you an immediate audience for your material and there are enough unsigned bands who could do with a music video. Just do it!

THE VIEW FROM WITHIN

ALEX JONES DONELLY – RADIO 1, EDITOR OF MUSIC POLICY

When you walk into reception at Radio 1, the atmosphere hits you straight away. It has an intensity that can only be compared with the pressure you feel when you're waiting at the dentist to have your wisdom teeth removed. At least that's how the handful of pluggers feel who hang around the reception, waiting to hear the fate of their latest pitch. We're here to talk to Alex Donelly, Editor, Radio 1 Music Policy.

How did you get to where you are today?

I was brought up in South Manchester and from twelve was listening to John Peel, buying the *NME* and nicking my brother's new wave, mod and soul collection. At fifteen I was out gigging in Manchester every week and hanging out at the Hacienda. I went to university in Sheffield where I co-ran a dance club, DJ'd badly and worked for the entertainments committee. My career started by racking up various bits of experience in the music business first: working for Our Price records, being a discographer at MCPS, and then moving into radio by getting a job as a librarian at the newly legal Kiss Radio. From there I became Assistant Head of Music at Kiss, and left in 1997 to become Music Scheduler at Radio 1 and finally Head of Music in March 2000.

How do you feel now you're at the top? Do people try to sell you a line and soften you up to get on the playlist?

Of course they try. We have to keep our distance and keep our relationship with the labels in context. It's important for me to know every bit of information about a label and an artist that's in front of me. This gives me the opportunity to make the right call for the audience as well as studying whether this is going to be a breakthrough artist.

How difficult is it to decide what's going to make the grade?

All decisions are difficult. There are probably ten critical decisions you make in the year that make you think: 'Wow, man that was the right decision!' For example, we played Alicia Keys's 'Falling'. We loved the record, but we didn't know if it was going to work out for our audience, especially as it was brand new on the UK market. We went with it and that was a good decision. We have to make decisions about the playlist every day. We want to make sure we're selecting artists who mean something to our audience.

What do you consider to be a wrong decision?
There's a radio saying that you can't be damaged by records you don't play. If we miss out on a record our competitors play and it's a great success, we can just about get away with it. But if we get it wrong by missing out on a whole new style of music, that's bad. Spotting acts and a music style like Dizzy Rascal is important, but if we miss out on a Texas record then the impact is not so great.

What else helps you make a decision?
We need to know what the plot is, you need to have something happening as well as getting on our playlist. We want to know about a band's tour support. We want them to be gigging, and making things happen for themselves. It's important for us to know they're making a buzz on the street.

Does every song on the Radio 1 playlist have to be a chart hit?
Radio 1 is categorically not motivated by getting artists into the charts. Of course we need a percentage of chart artists on the playlist for our audience. This then allows us to take risks and bring through different forms of music that are new and challenging. Radio 1 does tend to be one of the leading stations in the world at breaking new artists who go on to become major stars.

Your job seems very pressured.
There is pressure on anyone who works for a music station that has a stated intention to play music that appeals to young people. Of course you could take the easy option and listen to the music the record labels and promotions tell you to listen to and whoever shouts the loudest. Or you can stay true to yourself, but it's not easy.

What do you mean by 'Whoever shouts the loudest'?
People who promote music get inside your mind. They seem very reasonable, and make sense. They might have had a hit in the past and seem to have plenty of money behind them now. It's tempting just to follow them, but that's not Radio 1's way. It might have been in the past. The way we do it is much harder. We analyse as much music as we can. Then we make sure we put the right records on at the right time. You might be playing the coolest band or you might not. You might be the hero and villain in one day or even in a minute.

Do labels try to wine and dine you or your team to persuade you of their case?
If any of my team go out to lunch or dinner with a label I expect them to represent Radio 1 by acting in a professional manner. They should not be susceptible to the charms of the label or a big expense account. These lunches are to talk about music, not to buy the label's views. It's important that we keep meeting all types of labels, large and small, to keep up with what's happening. Generally the labels want to know about the station's strategy and our music policy and if anything has changed since we last met. Understanding their strategy helps us understand why they bring certain types of music to us at certain times. This type of conversation would normally take place over lunch or dinner. If we were discussing a specific act, we would usually meet in my office.

Would a £1 million marketing plan influence your decision to playlist a record?
If the music was good it would. It's dangerous to play a record just because it's cool among a small number of people and get brownie points from the very judgemental British music press. If I playlisted them too much I'd be accused of over-exposing them.

How do your playlist meetings work?
Our playlist meetings are three hours long and involve fifteen to twenty people from producers to the music team. Also we get fed information from specialist producers such as Pete Tong and Tim Westwood. It's important that we get the right information fed into the playlist meeting, especially if a new form of music is about to break.

How do you know the right time to break new bands and new musical styles to your audience?

It's all about working out the best time to move on a tune. Sometimes it's better for a record to stay underground and then when it's ready move it into the mainstream. We have to sense when this time is right. We can't play a new form of music to our audience too early on or they'll just turn off, purely because they have no reference or context for the music. That's the beauty of the specialist shows: they allow us to play new music with full impact and authenticity. Then we sense when it's the right tipping point to introduce it into the mainstream playlist. Sometimes we get it wrong and do it too early. It's not an exact science, it's more intuitive, but I think we get it more right than not.

CHARLIE BEUTHIN – CHANNEL U

Charlie and his business partner Stuart started their digital TV channel in February 2003. It's an urban music station, and reached one million viewers in the first three months of launch. Channel U is independent, and financed privately. Before the interview took place, we had a meeting with Damon Dash and Channel U. His management had asked us to introduce him to Channel U. It was quite a crazy meeting: we couldn't work out if Damon wanted to buy the channel or start one of his own. At least it shows that Channel U is beginning to make waves.

How did you get the idea to start Channel U?

We knew there was a gap in the urban market. There wasn't anything that understood the kids, so we set up a channel so kids could see and listen to the music they couldn't usually find. Using the jukebox principle we could make sure they got exactly what they wanted, when they wanted it. Other people have used this idea, but the choice they have offered has always been too limited.

So how do you offer more choice?

We have two hundred videos on our playlist every day, as opposed to fifty to sixty, which is the most anyone else has had. That's not all. We don't limit ourselves to videos, we also show scratch tuition clips, from acts in the studio and behind the scenes, also dance. The channel shows that you don't have to limit urban music to music, because its much more, like fashion clips.

What have been the biggest problems so far?
The main difficulty has been to get the majors to take us seriously. For us to have the credibility for them to want us to show their videos. Pluggers aren't really in anything other than Radio 1 and MTV. We have to ring them up rather than them coming to us. Also we don't have the research data and facilities of the big channels. MTV and Viacom even know if a video makes someone turn over. It's harder for us to profile our audience with data. Still we probably know them much better as people.

Who's your audience?
Our core audience is a fifteen-year-old boy. He goes to a state school, in a city. He's too cool for school. He is mature musically, and socially intelligent rather than boringly academic. His school might not understand this. He is an informed viewer. He watches Channel U because he wants to, not because anyone or anything has told him he must. It's his own thing, he discovered it without any commercial hype.

How have you created the channel for them?
We try to make it as interactive as possible. There's a continual text conversation going on the screen. It's not basic like on other channels. We encourage our audience to text us, and as long as they're not too rude or libellous we put them all on. They're sometimes very comical, commenting on everything that's going on as it happens. They even slag off the bad adverts. We were the first channel to encourage everyone to email it about whatever they wanted, and we answer them all personally. They can send us videos about anything, it doesn't just have be just music, it can be dance, fashion , an ident or whatever, and if its good we'll put it on.

What other media are your audience into?

Typically they will watch T4 or MTV, there's not a huge choice out there. There are some specialist urban music magazines. *Rewind* and *Tense* are probably the best underground magazines. *Rewind* sells 28,000 according to the latest data, which is pretty good going, even if it is free.

How do you select your playlist?

We review the playlist every Monday. We don't listen to any hard sell from pluggers, we make up our own minds. We used to put 60% of what we received on air. Now we're trying to be more selective. The videos don't have to be expensively produced, but they do have to be imaginative and creative. We're keen to help our viewers produce better videos, because it's in our interest. We encourage them to send us their treatments, and we will give them advice about how to make them better. We will give them contacts of producers, directors and editors who are good, but don't charge much. This service doesn't make us any money, but it does increase the quality of our output, and helps us to move forward another step.

Do you think the British urban scene is trying too hard to copy America?

It's understandable that it looks to America, because its roots are American. But we have to work hard to catch up with their best music. It can be done, look at drum n base, Britain leads the world. The lack of media exposure has held it back. Kids need access to the whole scene to understand its real depth. Sure it's easy for a fifteen-year-old boy to buy a cap and feel part of a crew, but to push it further, he needs to understand that it's more than music, it's a whole culture. It needs radio play, and the visual identity of good music videos. Then people will begin to see that it's not just in America that you have great urban characters, who look and dance right like Bad Manner. The music is as strong as in America, but the culture is weaker it needs to be pushed further.

Who do you tip to be big in the urban scene in 2005?

A guy called Klashnekoff Kid from North London. He's part of the Terrafirma crew and he's about as hip hop as anyone can be, and he's taking it back to its roots. His first video, 'Murder', was in the Top 5 of our chart for the whole year and his second, 'Parrowdice', is currently No. 2. There is the biggest buzz about him on the street. In terms of sublo [garage] there's a guy called Whiley who's been a big part of the street scene and who's just signed to Excel. He's going a lot further. Then there is a female MC, just signed to Polydor, called Shyftie; she's worth watching out for.

What are your plans for 2005?
We're going to produce original programming to give us a character and a face. These programmes will be fronted and feature well-known artists and presenters like Tim Westwood. This programming is going to go behind the scenes and will include artists from America. On top of that we're putting together tours and compilations. We see Channel U as a brand, not just a channel. We want to raise the level of urban music in the UK. It's all about pushing forward a mix of UK and US artists, on tour together and collaborating . We intend to be what MTV is to the mainstream, to the underground. We'll stay cool, but that doesn't mean we can't be bigger. Look at BET in America, it got so big it was eventually sold to Viacom for $4 billion.

JAMIE CARING – MTV

Jamie is Head of Talent and Artist Relations at MTV Networks UK and Ireland. As such he's responsible for MTV's relationship with the UK music industry from the labels, management, promotional companies and artists. In many ways MTV has defined how music should look visually, and artists know that to be included in its playlists is important for their success.

How do you select bands for MTV?
We are primarily song based, so the song is virtually always the primary consideration. Marketing and image are very relevant when it comes to pop music. But when it comes to more cutting-edge styles of music other considerations are just as valuable if not more valuable. Indie and rock acts need to work the gig circuit and develop a grass roots live following. When they're

starting out, dance and to some extent urban acts need to develop a buzz in clubs with the right mixes and DJs. We need to know the artist is working from the street upwards. Overall the song quality is the most important consideration when it comes to video rotation. The ability for an artist to recreate their work live is crucial in credibility terms for new rock and urban acts, but as far as we're concerned it's only vital if we're planning them for a live performance or event.

What does an artist need to put together for a pitch?
It depends what we're booking them for. For a live p.a. of a single we might just need to hear the track and see them perform their single. It might even be good enough just on tape, as long as they are good. But if they wanted to play a live set at one of our events we'd normally want to hear their album. Plus we'd need to know a bit about them and go to a gig or two to make sure that they really delivered an impressive show.

How about an unsigned band, if they were good would you feature them?
Absolutely. By keeping an eye on the right clubs and gig circuits, we hear about many good unsigned acts out there trying to get noticed. Once in a while we pick one up. They usually get signed soon after. One of the bands we featured last year has done rather well since – The Darkness.

What is your advice to anyone presenting their artist to MTV?
I like to see passion for the artist, tempered a little by realism. A real understanding of what they're about and a plan for getting them off the ground. They must understand that we are not like other TV outlets. We have many ways to feature new artists other than solely being focused on performances.

How does the selection process work?
The Talent and Artist Relations and Music Programming departments have the task of deciding all artist bookings and the playlist, in conjuncton with various channel and production staff. It's difficult to say how many people get involved as it depends on the decision. We look at a whole range of factors,

from relevance and appeal to our target audience to the quality of the material and performance. It doesn't just stop there. We're interested in video quality and creativity, as well as their street level buzz, club reaction, press coverage and any other TV or radio exposure.

Do pluggers irritate you?

We prefer companies with vision. The ones that think laterally about how we can work together at all levels, not the ones that just want to tick the MTV box on their promo report. This means they must think about how we can incorporate their acts creatively and get involved in covering artists in greater depth. We want them to talk about tours, joint marketing activities and events. We definitely don't like companies that regard us as similar to other music video channels, which are solely based on viewer requests.

PHIL MOUNT – *CD:UK*

Phil is series producer of CD:UK. *His determination to improve continually and innovate in the production qualities of the programme have kept it a fresh and vital part of Saturday morning TV. The format is so successful that it's becoming a global brand. Phil invited us to see a show in action. Phil's at the control desk looking intently at the screens in front of him. He's in total control: 'Camera 4, try a shot behind the drums, lighting give me that funky graphic'. A girl rushes in and tells Phil she needs a decision now and it will cost £2,000. He does and she goes. Next, somehow the cameraman has made Alex Parks look as if she's floating across the stage. Eventually the show's over, and we catch Phil in wind-down mode.*

Who is the show aimed at?

Our target audience is 5–15 and 16–34. Our approach is to reflect what is going on in mainstream music, but just try to be a little bit ahead. We're keen to introduce new acts to our audience, but also to support established ones. At the end of the day we're governed by ITV's need to get high ratings. So it always has to be a balance between breaking new bands and having the most popular established acts. We were the first programme to feature many acts, from Busted to Craig David.

How important is the look of the show?
We pride ourselves on how it looks. At editorial meetings, we spend lots of time working out how we can make performances look fresh and exciting. We always want to make a big splash and try something new. We work with two great directors, Chris Howe and Phil Hayes. They're both young and know how to make things look good. Typically we sit down and discuss the act and they come up with a concept. We usually go back to the record company and discuss it with them.

They're always coming up with new ideas, like the concept we came up with for Blazing Squad a few weeks ago. We prerecorded their performance at half speed, then played it at double speed and dropped it into the performance subliminally. People were saying: 'How did they do that?' Both Phil and Chris are meticulous in the way they work; lots of what they come up with is carefully storyboarded.

Can you give us a sense of a normal week at CD:UK?
On Tuesday morning we have a debrief meeting about the show the previous Saturday. We all get together and talk about the show coming up. This is when we work out the nuts and bolts of the next show. By the end of Tuesday we agree the final line-up.

On Wednesday we have a script meeting and decide the editorial line and talk through the editorial plan. On Thursday we put all the VTs together and in the afternoon we discuss the Hot Shots Review, which is when a celebrity panel reviews the latest tracks. We have to find out who's available. By the end of Thursday we have nailed the guests and videos.

On Friday we're in the edit. Then we meet the lawyers to check compliance, to ensure none of our show is too raunchy, especially if we've someone like Kylie. Although we're getting pretty good at knowing the boundaries. In the afternoon we have a script review with Cat, our presenter. Even at this stage we might want some script changes.

Saturday starts early, we get called at 6.15 on Saturday morning. First we have a production meeting with sound and lighting, then at 6.45 we start to rehearse the bands and links. At 11.30 the show starts.

How do you work with the labels?
I like to have face-to-face meetings with the labels. I've known most of the people well. Once a month or every six weeks we go to all the major labels and see what's coming up. This helps us talk to them properly and do exclusive deals versus *Top of the Pops*. Sometimes in the early days labels tried to get us to take bands that they knew were weak, but if a record doesn't do well I'll never forget. It doesn't happen now. The relationship with the labels has to be based on trust. It's a two-way relationship. They know they can't pull a fast one, because the next time they may want to break a band and they'll want us to be open-minded about its pitch.

Do you only have relationships with the majors?
We can't just rely on the majors, especially as next year there'll probably be only four of them. Excel is a great label, from Prodigy to White Stripes. They'll be important for us. Road Runners records does well with Nickleback and Slipknot. But we have to remember our audience. We are the music window for the majority of people. We can't go too far away from the mainstream.

Do the majors contribute money towards staging their bands?
We only have a budget for so much. We explain what we can do for the money we have. If they want to pay for something extra special, that's fine. Anything they pay for is theirs to keep afterwards. We're happy if it adds to the performance. Also, we'll rent the studio out to more established artists, so they can record their latest tracks. They pay for the studio, so they own the footage. We're just the facility, though obviously we can use the footage on the programme. It's very cost effective for the record companies, because they get the footage and probably a Channel 4 special too. For major acts it's a good deal.

PAUL REES – Q MAGAZINE

Paul is Editor of Q Magazine, *the UK's most popular mainstream music magazine.*

Who are your target audience?

The philosophy of *Q* is simple: music matters. Our target audience is broad and simply defined as anyone who likes music and wants to be pointed towards it.

How do you decide who's featured in the magazine?

We pay no attention to marketing campaigns. It's based entirely on whether the editorial team thinks an artist's music has merit and if they have a story to tell. Obviously if your instinct is that something is going to be commercially successful, you're pretty sure a wide amount of people will want to read about it, but that doesn't preclude us from doing things that are more marginal. To select a band we need to see them or hear them, and like them. Simple as that.

How do you like a band to present themselves?

I just want them to say: 'Here's our music. What do you think?' We have to think a band is good and then that we trust a significant proportion of our readership will like them too. This decision is ultimately taken by the editorial team. We have daily and weekly meetings throughout the span of an issue; but we tend to work at least three to four issues up front.

Are you influenced by a telephone pitch from a PR?

It can perk up your interest if it is passionate enough. More normally I take it with a shovelful of salt. If you trust their judgement and they are not prone to 'record company bollocks speak' then you are far, far more likely to be receptive from the off. But ultimately, you can only ever trust and back your own judgement.

What is the worst part of how record companies behave?

They can be horribly obstructive when you are dealing with major artists. But they'd sell their grandmother to you if you are prepared to write about the rubbish band they've signed for pots of money that nobody likes.

1
2
3
4
5
6
7
8
9
10
11
12
13
14
15

MUSIC WEBSITES

BAND REGISTER
PO Box 594, Richmond, Surrey
TW10 6YT
T: 07973 297011
Email: peter@bandreg.com
Website: bandreg.com
MD: Peter Whitehead

BUYHEAR.COM
240 High Road, Harrow Weald,
Middlesex HA3 7BB
T: 020 8863 2520 F: 020 8863 2520
Email: steve@bluemelon.co.uk
steve@buyhear.com
Website: buyhear.com
Director: Steven Robert Glen

CHANNELFLY.COM
109X Regents Park Road, London
NW1 8UR
T: 020 7691 4555 F: 020 7691 4666
Email: info@channelfly.com
Website: channelfly.com
Editor: Will Kinsman

CLICKMUSIC LTD
58-60 Fitzroy Street, London W1T 5BU
T: 020 7554 9743 F: 0870 458 4183
Email: laurence@clickmusic.co.uk
Website: clickmusic.co.uk
Producer: Laurence Cooke

DROWNED IN SOUND
72 Palatine Rd, Stoke Newington,
London N16 8ST
Email: sean@drownedinsound.com
Website: drownedinsound.com
Managing Ed: Sean Adams

DRUM & BASS ARENA
Unit 27, Sheffield Science Pk, Arundel
St., Sheffield S1 2NS
T: 0114 281 4470 F: 0114 281 4471
Email: info@breakbeat.co.uk
ddias@breakbeat.co.uk
Website: breakbeat.co.uk
Commercial Director: Del Dias

EMAP DIGITAL
Mappin House, 4 Winsley Street,
London W1W 8HF
T: 020 7817 9690 F: 020 7312 8246
Email: tracy.thompson@emapdigital.com
Website: emap.com www.q4music.com
www.smashhits.net
Tracy Thompson

GET MEDIA
Wilsons House, Wilsons Park, Newton
Heath, Manchester M40 8WN
T: 0161 205 8885 F: 0161 205 8887
Email: enquiries@getmediaplc.com
Website: getmediaplc.com
CEO: John Doyle

THE LIVING TRADITION
PO Box 1026, Kilmarnock, Ayrshire,
Scotland KA2 0LG
T: 01563 571220 F: 01563 544855
Email: admin@livingtradition.co.uk
Website: folkmusic.net
Ed: Pete Heywood

LOSECONTROL LTD
177 Wager Street, London E3 4JR
T: 020 8980 1253 F: 020 7557 4771
Email: james@losecontrol.com

Website: losecontrol.com
Director: James Hay

MANCHESTERMUSIC.CO.UK
Musicdash, PO Box 1977, Manchester M26 2YB
T: 0161 724 4760
Email: mancmusic@hotmail.com
Website: manchestermusic.co.uk
Editor: Jon Ashley

MOBILETONES.COM
Unit 4, Handford Court, Garston Lane, Watford WD25 9EJ
T: 0870 444 7110 F: 01923 675 299
Email: info@mobiletones.com
Website: mobiletones.com
Music
Development Manager: Dominic Bignall

MP3.COM EUROPE
113 Farringdon Road, London EC1R 3BX
T: 020 7239 9310 F: 020 7239 9320
Email: leanne@mp3.com
Website: MP3.com
VP, Mktg & Commercial: Leanne Sharman

NME.COM
IPC Music Magazines, Kingsreach Tower, Stamford Street, London SE1 9LS
T: 020 7261 7875 F: 020 7261 6022
Email: news@nme.com
Website: nme.com
Editor: Anthony Thornton

ODYSSEY.FM
PO Box 18888, London SW7 4FQ
T: 020 7373 1614 F: 020 7373 1614
Email: info@outer-media.co.uk
Website: odyssey.fm
Dir: Gregory Mihalcheon

ONLINE CLASSICS
Gnd & 1st Floors, 31 Eastcastle Street, London W1W 8DL
T: 020 7636 1400 F: 020 7637 1355
Email: team@onlineclassics.com
Website: onlineclassics.com
CEO: Christopher Hunt

ONLINECONCERTS.COM
2 Valentine Cottages, Petworth Rd, Witley, Godalming, Surrey GU8 5LS
T: 01428 684537
Email: jdoukas@onlineconcerts.com
Website: onlineconcerts.com
Founder: John Doukas

POPEX.COM
109x Regents Park Road, London NW1 8UR
T: 020 7691 4555 F: 020 7691 4666
Email: pauly@popex.com
Website: popex.com
Administrator: Paul Clarke

POPWORLD LTD
21-23 Ransomes Dock, 35-37 Parkgate Road, London SW11 4NP
T: 020 7350 5500 F: 020 7350 5501
Email: promotions@popworld.com
Website: popworld.com
Gen Mgr: Emma Hill

PRIMAL SOUNDS.COM
PO Box 5, Alton, Hants GU34 2EN
T: 07967 155542
Email: mail@primalsounds.com
Website: primalsounds.com
Owner: Carl Saunders

RAFT, THE
Kensal House, 553-579 Harrow Road, London W10 4RH
T: 020 8964 6000 F: 020 8964 6003
Email: danny.van.emden@virginmusic.com
Website: the-raft.com
Multimedia Director: Danny Van Emden

REVOLUTION
211 Western Road, London SW19 2QD
T: 020 8646 7094 F: 020 8646 7094
Email: info@revolutionsuk.com
Website: revolutionsuk.com
Ed: John Lonergan

ROCK CITY
8 Talbot Street, Nottingham NG1 5GG
T: 0115 941 2544 F: 0115 941 8438
Email: claire@rock-city.co.uk
Website: rock-city.co.uk
Marketing Manager: Claire Dyer

SHAZAM ENTERTAINMENT LTD.
4th Floor, 136 Regent St, London W1B 5SX
T: 020 7851 9320

SPACED
Unit 2, New North House, 202-208 New North Road, London N1 7BJ
T: 020 7288 8150 F: 020 7288 8151
Email: info@spaced.co.uk
Website: spaced.co.uk
Sales & marketing Dir: Vanessa Vigar

THE SUN ONLINE
1 Virginia Street, London E98 1SN
T: 020 7782 4346 F: 020 7782 4597
Email: simon.rothstein@the-sun.co.uk
Website: thesun.co.uk
Staff Writer: Simon Rothstein

THEWHITELABEL.COM LIMITED
1-3 Croft Lane, Henfield, W. Sussex BN5 9TT
T: 01273 491761 F: 01273 491761
Email: contact@thewhitelabel.com
Website: thewhitelabel.com
CEO: Nic Vine

TOTP ONLINE
Room A400, Centre House, 56 Wood Lane, London W12 7SB
T: 020 8225 8917
Email: rob.cooper@bbc.co.uk
Website: bbc.co.uk/totp
Senior Producer: Rob Cooper

TRUSTTHEDJ.COM
Unit 13-14, Barley Shotts Bus.Park, 246 Acklam Road, London W10 5YG
T: 020 8962 5454 F: 020 8962 5455
Email: contact@trustthedj.com
Website: trustthedj.com
Editorial: Piers Linney

TURNROUND MULTI-MEDIA
16 Berkeley Mews, 29 High Street, Cheltenham, Gloucestershire GL50 1DY
T: 01242 224360 F: 01242 226566
Email: studio@turnround.co.uk
Website: turnround.co.uk
MD: Ross Lammas

UMUSIC.CO.UK
Universal UK, 22 St Peter's Square, London W6 9NW
T: 020 8910 3333 F: 020 8748 0948
Email: info@umusic.co.uk
Website: umusic.co.uk
Head of New Media: Rob Wells

VIRGIN.NET
The Communications Bld, 48 Leicester Square, London WC2H 7LT
T: 020 7664 6069 F: 020 7664 6006
Email: virgincontact@london.virgin.net
Website: virgin.net
Head of Content: Caroline Hugh

VITAMINIC
20 Orange St, London WC2H 7NN
T: 020 7766 4000 F: 020 7766 4001
Email: info@vitaminic.co.uk
Website: vitaminic.co.uk UK
MD: Chris Cass

WEB SHERIFF
Argentum, 2 Queen Caroline Street, London W6 9DX
T: 020 8323 8013 F: 020 8323 8080
Email: websheriff@websheriff.com
Website: websheriff.com
MD: John Giacobbi

YAHOO! UK & IRELAND
10 Ebury Bridge Rd, London SW1W 8PZ
T: 020 7808 4400 F: 020 7808 4203
Email: mccraw@uk.yahoo-inc.com
Website: yahoo.co.uk
Ent/Media Prod (UK): Beth McCraw

AMANDA WILLIAMS PR
Top Floor Office, 95 Waldegrave Road, Teddington, Middlesex TW11 8LA
T: 020 8943 2804 F:020 8943 8874
Email: amanda@amandawilliamspr.co.uk
Website: amandawilliamspr.co.uk
Dir: Amanda Williams

TV CONTACTS

ALL NEW TOP OF THE POPS
Room 267 – Design Building,
BBC Television Centre, Wood Lane,
London W12 7RJ
Jess Eldridge

CBBC
E178 (East Tower), BBC TV Centre,
Wood Lane, London W12 7RJ
T: 020 8743 8000
Jamie Sutcliffe

CD:UK
Blaze Television, 43-45 Dorset Street,
London W1U 7NA
T: 020 7224 2440
Phil Mount - Series Producer
T: 020 7664 1658
Tina O'Connor - Associate Producer

CHANNEL 4
124 Horseferry Road, London
SW1 P 2TX
T: 020 7396 444
Jo Wallace

CHANNEL U
VITV Plc, 18 Soho Square, London
W1D 3QA
T: 020 7253 2459
Stewart Lund

EMAP
3rd Floor, Mappin House, 4 Winsley
Street, London W1W 8HF
T: 020 7376 2000
Simon Sadler

GMTV
The London Studios
Upper Ground, London SE1 9LT
T: 020 7620 1620
Maurice Gallagher

INTIAL
Shepeheads Building Central, Charecroft
Way, London W14 OEE
T: 0870 333 1700
Malcolm Gerrie

LATER
Rm 385 (Design Bldg), BBC TV Centre,
Wood Lane, London W12 7RJ
T: 020 8743 8000
Mark Cooper
Alison Howe

MTV
17-19 Hawley Crescent, Camden Lock,
London NW1
T: 020 7284 7777
Jamie Caring

MTV / VH-1
17-19 Hawley Crescent, Camden Lock,
London NW1
T: 020 7284 7777
Helen Jones

NEVER MIND THE BUZZCOCKS
Talkback Productions
20-21 Numan St, London W12 1PG
T: 020 7861 8000
Peter Gair

PARKINSON
Rm 4100, BBC TV Centre, Wood Lane,
London W12 7RJ
T: 020 8743 8000
Sophie Newth

RICHARD & JUDY
Cactus TV, 373 Kennington Road,
London SE11 4PS
T: 020 7221 2213
Lauren Ebel
Mark Wagman

SKY MUSIC CHANNELS
Grant Way, Isleworth, Middlesex TW7 5QD
T: 020 7705 3000
Emma Usher
Ian Greaves

T4 AND POPWORLD
At It Productions, Unit 314 Westbourne Studios, 242 Acklam Road, London W10 5YG
T: 020 8964 2122
Nick Neads

THIS MORNING
2nd Floor, Granada - Dominican Ct
17 Hatfields, London SE1 8DJ
T: 020 7578 4116
Lisa Thomson
T: 020 7261 3989
Karen Moss

TOP OF THE POPS
Room 267 - Design Building, BBC Television Centre, Wood Lane, London W12 7RJ
T: 020 8743 8000
Andi Peters

TOTP2
RM 385 (Design Bldg), BBC TV Centre, Wood Lane, London W12 7RJ
T: 020 8743 8000
Mark Hagen

RADIO STATIONS

ASIAN SOUND RADIO
Globe House, Southall Street,
Manchester M3 1LG
T: 0161 288 1000 F: 0161 288 9000
Email: info@asiansoundradio.co.uk
Website: asiansoundradio.co.uk
MD/Prog Cont: Shujat Ali

107.9 BATH FM
Station House, Ashley Avenue, Lower
Weston, Bath BA1 3DS
T: 01225 471571 F: 01225 471681
Email: studio@bath.fm
Website: bath.fm
Prog Controller: Steve Collins

THE BAY
PO Box 969, St Georges Quay,
Lancaster LA1 3LD
T: 01524 848747 F: 01524 844969
Email: info@thebay.fm
Website: thebay.fm
Prog Dir/Head of Music: Tony Cookson

BBC RADIO BRISTOL
Broadcasting House, Whiteladies Rd,
Bristol BS8 2LR
T: 0117 974 1111 F: 0117 973 2549
Email: radio.bristol@bbc.co.uk
Website: bbc.co.uk/radiobristol
Station Manager: Ms Jenny Lacey

BELFAST CITY BEAT
Lamont Buildings, 46, Stranmillis
Embankment, Belfast, Co Antrim
BT9 5FN
T: 028 9020 5967 F: 028 9020 0023
Email: info@citybeat.co.uk
Website: citybeat.co.uk
Prog Dir: Owen Larkin

96.4 FM BRMB
9 Brindley Place, 4 Oozells Square,
Birmingham, West Midlands B1 2DJ
T: 0121 245 5000 F: 0121 245 5900
Email: info@brmb.co.uk
Website: brmb.co.uk
Programme Director: Adam Bridge

BROADLAND 102
St George's Plain, 47-49 Colegate,
Norwich, Norfolk NR3 1DB
T: 01603 630621 F: 01603 666252
Email: firstname.lastname@musicradio.com
Website: musicradio.com
Prog Controller: Steve Martin

95.8 CAPITAL FM
30 Leicester Square, London WC2H 7LA
T: 020 7766 6000 F: 020 7766 6100
Email: firstname.lastname@capitalradio.com
Website: capitalfm.com
Programme Dir

CAPITAL GOLD - MANCHESTER
4th Floor, Quay West, Trafford Wharf
Road, Trafford Park, Manchester M17 1FL
T: 0161 607 0420 F: 0161 607 0443
Email: info@capitalgold.co.uk
Website: capitalgold.com Network
Programme Dir: Andy Turner

CAPITAL GOLD NETWORK
30 Leicester Square, London
WC2H 7LA
T: 020 7766 6000 F: 020 7766 6393
Email: andy.turner@capitalgold.com

Website: capitalgold.com
Prog Dir: Andy Turner

CAPITAL GOLD - RED DRAGON
Radio House, Atlantic Wharf, Cardiff,
South Glamorgan CF10 4DJ
T: 029 2066 2066 F: 029 2066 2067
Email: info@capitalgold.com
Website: capitalgold.co.uk
Network Programme Dir: Andy Turner

CARILLON RADIO
Loughborough General Hospital, Baxter Gate, Loughborough, Leics LE11 1TT
T: 01509 838 671 F: 07973 987 554
Email: carillonradio@aol.com
Station Sec/Engineer: John Sketchley

97.6 CHILTERN FM
Chiltern Road, Dunstable,
Bedfordshire LU6 1HQ
T: 01582 676200 F: 01582 676201
Email: firstname.surname@musicradio.com
Website: musicradio.com
Programme Controller: Stuart Davies

CHOICE FM LONDON
291-299 Borough High Street,
London SE1 1JG
T: 020 7378 3969 F: 020 7378 3911
Email: info@choicefm.com
Website: choicefm.com
Head of Sales: Jeff Thomas

CLASSIC FM
Classic FM House, 7 Swallow Place,
Oxford Circus, London W1B 2AG
T: 020 7343 9000 F: 020 7344 2703
Email: enquiries@classicfm.com
Website: classicfm.com
MD/Prog Director: Roger Lewis

CLASSIC GOLD 774
Bridge Studios, Eastgate Centre,
Gloucester GL1 1SS
T: 01452 313200 F: 01452 529446
Email: admin@classicgolddigital.com
Website: classicgolddigital.com
Network Prog Controller: Don Douglas

CLASSIC GOLD 828
5-7 Southcote Road, Bournemouth,
Dorset BH1 3LR
T: 01202 259259 F: 01202 255244
Email: admin@classicgolddigital.com
Website: classicgolddigital.com
Network Prog Controller: Don Douglas

CLASSIC GOLD 1260
PO Box 2020, One Passage Street,
Bristol BS99 7SN
T: 0117 984 3200 F: 0117 984 3202
Email: admin@classicgolddigital.com
Website: classicgolddigital.com
Network Prog Controller: Don Douglas

CLASSIC GOLD BREEZE
Radio House, Clifftown Road,
Southend-on-Sea, Essex SS1 1SX
T: 01702 333711 F: 01702 333686
Email: admin@classicgolddigital.com
Website: classicgolddigital.com
Network Prog Controller: Don Douglas

WEST YORKSHIRE'S CLASSIC GOLD
Pennine House, Forster Square,
Bradford, West Yorkshire BD1 5NE
T: 01274 203040 F: 01274 203130
Email: westyorkshire@classicgolddigital.com
Website: classicgolddigital.com/westyorkshire
Programme Controller: Simon Walkington

CLYDE 1 FM
Clydebank Business Park, Clydebank,
Glasgow G81 2RX
T: 0141 565 2200 F: 0141 565 2301
Email: Info@RadioClyde.com
Website: RadioClyde.com
Hd of Music: Paul Saunders

CLYDE 2
Clydebank Business Park, Clydebank,
Glasgow G81 2RX
T: 0141 565 2200 F: 0141 565 2301
Email: Info@RadioClyde.com
Website: RadioClyde.com
Prog Cont-Clyde 1 & 2: Ross Macfadyen

CMRPULSE RADIO
PO Box 7218, Hook, Hampshire
RG27 8WG
T: 01252 842750 F: 01252 842279
Email: cmr@cix.co.uk
Website: cmrpulse.com
MD/Programming: Lee Williams

COAST 96.3 FM
PO Box 963, Bangor LL57 4ZR
T: 01248 673272 F: 01248 671971
Email: admin@mfm.musicradio.com
Website: musicradio.com
Programme Controller: Steve Simms

DOWNTOWN RADIO/DTR
Newtownards, Co Down BT23 4ES
T: 028 9181 5555 F: 028 9181 5252
Email: programmes@downtown.co.uk
Website: downtown.co.uk
Head of Music: Eddie West

96.4 THE EAGLE
Dolphin House, North Street, Guildford,
Surrey GU1 4AA
T: 01483 300964 F: 01483 531612
Email: onair@964eagle.co.uk
Website: 964eagle.co.uk
Prog Director: Peter Gordon

EASY RADIO LONDON 1035
43-51 Wembley Hill Road, Wembley,
London HA9 8AU
T: 020 8795 1035 F: 020 8902 9657
Email: info@easy1035.com
Website: easy1035.com
Programme Controller: Natalie King

FM 102 THE BEAR
The Guard House Studios, Banbury Rd,
Stratford upon Avon, Warwickshire
CV37 7HX
T: 01789 262636 F: 01789 263102
Email: info@thebear.co.uk
Website: thebear.co.uk
Station Director/Sales: Christine Arnold

BBC RADIO 4
Broadcasting House, Portland Place,
London W1A 1AA
T: 020 7580 4468 F: 020 7765 3421
Email: firstname.lastname@bbc.co.uk
Website: bbc.co.uk/radio4
Controller: Helen Boaden

GALAXY 102 FM
5th Floor, The Triangle, Hanging Ditch,
Manchester M4 3TR
T: 0161 279 0300 F: 0161 279 0303
Email: firstname.lastname@galaxy102.co.uk
Website: galaxy102.co.uk
Programme Director: Vaughan Hobbs

GALAXY 102.2
1 The Square, 111 Broad Street,
Birmingham B15 1AS

T: 0121 695 0000 F: 0121 696 1007
Email: firstname.lastname@galaxy1022.co.uk
Website: galaxy1022.co.uk
Prog Ctlr/Head of Music: Neil Greenslade

GALAXY 105
Joseph's Well, Hanover Walk, Leeds, West Yorkshire LS3 1AB
T: 0113 213 0105 F: 0113 213 1054
Email: mail@galaxy105.co.uk
Website: galaxy105.co.uk
Programme Director: Mike Cass

GALAXY 105-106
Kingfisher Way, Silverlink Business Park, Tyne & Wear NE28 9NX
T: 0191 206 8000 F: 0191 206 8080
Email: mail@galaxy1056.co.uk
Website: galaxy1056.co.uk
Programme Director: Matt McClure

GALWAY BAY FM
Sandy Road, Galway City, Galway, Ireland
T: +353 91 770000 F: +353 91 752689
Email: info@galwaybayfm.ie
Website: gbfm.galway.net
CEO: Keith Finnegan

GEMINI FM Hawthorn House, Exeter Business Park, Exeter, Devon EX1 3QS
T: 01392 444444 F: 01392 444433
Email: firstname.lastname@musicradio.com
Website: musicradio.com
Prog Cont/HoM: Gavin Marshall

BBC RADIO GLOUCESTERSHIRE
London Rd, Gloucester GL1 1SW
T: 01452 308585 F: 01452 306541
Email: radio.gloucestershire@bbc.co.uk
Website: bbc.co.uk/radiogloucestershire
Grams Librarian: Chris Fowler

BBC GMR (BBC GREATER MANCHESTER RADIO)
PO Box 951, New Broadcasting House, Oxford Road, Manchester M60 1SD
T: 0161 200 2020 F: 0161 236 5804
Email: manchester.online@bbc.co.uk
Website: bbc.co.uk/manchester
Managing Editor: Steve Taylor

BBC RADIO GUERNSEY
Commerce House, Les Banques, St Peter Port, Guernsey, Channel Islands GY1 2HS
T: 01481 728977 F: 01481 713557
Email: radio.guernsey@bbc.co.uk
Website: bbc.co.uk/radioguernsey
Editor: Robert Wallace

GWR FM
PO Box 2000, 1 Passage St, Bristol BS99 7SN
T: 0117 984 3200 F: 0117 984 3208
Email: firstname.lastname@musicradio.com
Website: musicradio.com
Programme Controller: Paul Andrew

GWR FM
PO Box 2000, Wootton Bassett, Swindon, Wiltshire SN4 7EX
T: 01793 842600 F: 01793 842602
Email: firstname.lastname@musicradio.com
Website: musicradio.com
Programme Controller: Sue Carter

HALLAM FM
Radio House, 900 Herries Road, Sheffield, South Yorkshire S6 1RH
T: 0114 209 1000 F: 0114 285 3159
Email: programmes@hallamfm.co.uk
Website: hallamfm.co.uk
Temp Programme Director: Paul Chantler

HEART 106.2
The Chrysalis Building, Bramley Road, London W10 6SP
T: 020 7468 1062 F: 020 7465 6196
Email: onlineenquiries@heart1062.co.uk
Website: heart1062.co.uk
Programme Director: Francis Currie

HEART FM 100.7
1 The Square, 111 Broad Street, Birmingham, West Midlands B15 1AS
T: 0121 695 0000 F: 0121 696 1007
Email: heartfm@heartfm.co.uk
Website: heartfm.co.uk
Programme Dir: Alan Carruthers

HEARTLAND FM
Lower Oakfield, Pitlochry, Perthshire PH16 5DS
T: 01796 474040 F: 01796 474007
Email: mailbox@heartlandfm.co.uk
Website: heartlandfm.co.uk
Prog Dir/Head of Music: Pete Ramsden

BBC HEREFORD & WORCESTER
Hylton Road, Worcester WR2 5WW
T: 01905 748485 F: 01905 337209
Email: worcester@bbc.co.uk
Website: bbc.co.uk/herefordandworcester
Managing Editor: James Coghill

HIGHLAND RADIO
Pine Hill, Letterkenny, Co Donegal, Ireland
T: +353 74 25000 F: +353 74 25344
Email: enquiries@highlandradio.com
Website: highlandradio.com
Head of Prog & Music: Linda McGroarty

FM 103 HORIZON
14 Vincent Ave, Crownhill, Milton Keynes, Bucks MK8 0AB
T: 01908 269111 F: 01908 591619
Email: firstname.lastname@musicradio.com
Website: musicradio.com
Prog Controller: Trevor Marshall

IMAGINE FM
Regent House, Heaton Lane, Stockport, Cheshire SK4 1BX
T: 0161 609 1400 F: 0161 609 1401
Email: firstname.lastname@imaginefm.net
Website: imaginefm.net
Station Dir: Danny Holborn

INVICTA FM
Radio House, John Wilson Business Park, Whitstable, Kent CT5 3QX
T: 01227 772004 F: 01227 774450
Email: reception@invictaradio.co.uk
Website: invictafm.com
Programme Cont/Hd of Musi: Rebecca Trbojevich

102.2 JAZZ FM
26-27 Castlereagh Street, London W1H 5DL
T: 020 7706 4100 F: 020 7723 9742
Email: music@jazzfm.com
Website: jazzfm.com
ProgCont/Head of Music: Mark Walker

BBC RADIO JERSEY
18 Parade Road, St Helier, Jersey, Channel Islands JE2 3PA
T: 01534 870000 F: 01534 631208
Email: jersey@bbc.co.uk
Website: bbc.co.uk/jersey
Asst. Editor/Programmes: Matthew Price

JUICE 107.2
170 North St, Brighton, East Sussex BN1 1EA

T: 01273 386107 F: 01273 273107
Email: info@juicebrighton.com
Website: juicebrighton.com
MD/Programme Dir/Sales: Matthew Bashford

JUICE 107.6 FM
27 Fleet St, Liverpool L1 4AR
T: 0151 707 3107 F: 0151 707 3109
Email: mail@juiceliverpool.com
Website: juice.fm
Programme Dir/Hd of Music: Grainne Landowski

KCR 106.7
Cables Retail Park, Prescot, Merseyside L34 5SW
T: 0151 290 1501 F: 0151 290 1505
Email: kcr106@btconnect.fm
Website: kcr1067.com
Prog Cont/Hd of Music: Brian Cullen

BBC RADIO KENT
The Great Hall, Mount Pleasant Rd, Royal Tunbridge Wells, Kent TN1 1QQ
T: 01892 670000 F: 01892 549118
Email: radio.kent@bbc.co.uk
Website: bbc.co.uk/kent
Head of Music/SBJ: Lynn Wallis-Eade

RADIO KERRY
Maine Street, Tralee, Kerry, Ireland
T: +353 66 712 3666
F: +353 66 712 2282
Email: john@radiokerry.ie
Website: radiokerry.ie
Programme Director: John Herlihy

KEY 103
Castle Quay, Castlefield, Manchester M15 4PR
T: 0161 288 5000 F: 0161 288 5071
Email: firstname.lastname@key103.co.uk
Website: key103.co.uk
Prog Dir/Hd of Music: Anthony Gay

KICK FM
The Studios, 42 Bone Lane, Newbury, Berks RG14 5SD
T: 01635 841600 F: 01635 841010
Email: mail@kickfm.com
Website: kickfm.com
Programme Director: Andy Green

KISS 100 FM
Emap Performance, Mappin House, 4 Winsley Street, London W1W 8HF
T: 020 7975 8100 F: 020 7975 8150
Email: firstname.lastname@kiss100.com
Website: kiss100.com
Grp Programme Director: Andy Roberts

KM-FM (THANET)
Imperial House, 2-14 High St, Margate, Kent CT9 1DH
T: 01843 220222 F: 01843 299666
Email: ajohn@kmfm.co.uk
Website: kentonline.co.uk/kmfm
Prog Mgr: Adrian John

BBC RADIO LANCASHIRE
Darwen St, Blackburn, Lancashire BB2 2EA
T: 01254 262411 F: 01254 680821
Email: radio.lancashire@bbc.co.uk
Website: bbc.co.uk/lancashire
Managing Editor: John Clayton

LBC 97.3
The Chrysalis Building, 13 Bramley Rd, London W10 6SP
T: 020 7314 7300 F: 020 7314 7317

Email: website@lbc.co.uk
Website: lbc.co.uk
MD: Mark Flanagan

BBC LEEDS
Broadcasting House, Woodhouse Lane, Leeds, West Yorkshire LS2 9PN
T: 0113 224 7300 F: 0113 242 0652
Email: radio.leeds@bbc.co.uk
Website: bbc.co.uk/leeds; bbc.co.uk/bradford
Managing Ed: Ashley Peatfield

BBC LEICESTER
Epic House, Charles Street, Leicester LE1 3SH
T: 0116 251 6688 F: 0116 251 1463
Email: radio.leicester@bbc.co.uk
Website: bbc.co.uk/radioleicester
Head of Music: Trish Dolman

LIMERICK'S LIVE 95FM
Radio House, Richmond Court, Dock Rd, Limerick, Ireland
T: +353 61 400195 F: +353 61 419595
Email: mail@live95fm.ie
Website: live95fm.ie Programme Director: Gary Connor

BBC RADIO LINCOLNSHIRE PO Box 219, Newport, Lincoln LN1 3XY
T: 01522 511411 F: 01522 511058
Email: lincolnshire@bbc.co.uk
Website: bbc.co.uk/lincolnshire
Managing Editor: Charlie Partridge

LINCS FM 102.2
Witham Park, Waterside South, Lincoln LN5 7JN
T: 01522 549900 F: 01522 549911
Email: enquiries@lincsfm.co.uk
Website: lincsfm.co.uk
Group Dir of Programming: Jane Hill

BBC LONDON
PO Box 94.9, London W1A 6FL
T: 020 7224 2424 F: 020 7208 9680
Email: yourlondon@bbc.co.uk
Website: bbc.co.uk/london
Managing Editor: David Robey

MAGIC 1152 (MANCHESTER)
Castle Quay, Castlefield, Manchester M15 4PR
T: 0161 288 5000 F: 0161 288 5151
Email: firstname.lastname@key103.co.uk
Website: key103.co.uk
Prog Dir/Head of Music: Anthony Gay

MAGIC 1161
The Boathouse, Commercial Rd, Hull, East Yorkshire HU1 2SG
T: 01482 325141 F: 0845 4580 390
Email: firstname.lastname@vikingfm.co.uk
Website: magic1161.co.uk
Prog Dir: Darrell Woodman

MAGIC 105.4
Emap Performance, Mappin House, 4 Winsley Street, London W1W 8HF
T: 020 7975 8227 F: 020 7975 8234
Email: studio@magicradio.com
Website: magiclondon.co.uk
Prog Dir/Head of Music: Trevor White

MAGIC 1170
Radio House, Yales Crescent, Thornaby, Stockton-on-Tees TS17 6AA
T: 01642 888222 F: 01642 868288
Email: tfm.reception@tfmradio.com
Programme Director: Colin Paterson

MERCIA FM
Hertford Place, Coventry, West Midlands CV1 3TT

T: 024 7686 8200 F: 024 7686 8203
Email: mercia@musicradio.com
Website: musicradio.com
Programme Director: Luis Clark

102.7 MERCURY FM
9 The Stanley Centre, Kelvin Way, Crawley, West Sussex RH10 2SE
T: 01293 519161 F: 01293 565663
Email: firstname.lastname@musicradio.com
Website: musicradio.com
Prog Cont/Head of Music: Chris Rick

BBC RADIO MERSEYSIDE
55 Paradise Street, Liverpool, Merseyside L1 3BP
T: 0151 708 5500 F: 0151 794 0988
Email: radio.merseyside@bbc.co.uk
Website: bbc.co.uk/liverpool
Head of Music: Nickie Mackay

METRO RADIO
Radio House, Longrigg, Swalwell, Newcastle upon Tyne, Tyne and Wear NE99 1BB
T: 0191 420 0971 F: 0191 488 9222
Email: enquiries@metroandmagic.com
Website: metroradio.co.uk
Programme Director: Tony McKenzie

RAIDIO NA GAELTACHTA
Casla, Conamara, County na Gaillimhe, Ireland
T: +353 91 506677 F: +353 91 506666
Email: rnag@rte.ie
Website: rnag.ie
Head of Sales: Mairin Mhic Dhonnchada

BBC NAN GAIDHEAL
52 Church Street, Stornoway, Isle of Lewis, Western Isles HS1 2LS
T: 01851 705000 F: 01851 704633
Email: rapal@bbc.co.uk
Website: bbc.co.uk/alba Music
Producer: Mairead Maclennan

BBC RADIO NEWCASTLE
Broadcasting Centre, Barrack Road, Newcastle upon Tyne, Tyne and Wear NE99 1RN
T: 0191 232 4141 F: 0191 261 8907
Email: radio.newcastle@bbc.co.uk
Website: bbc.co.uk/radionewcastle
Senior Producer: Sarah Miller

BBC RADIO NORFOLK
Norfolk Tower, Surrey Street, Norwich, Norfolk NR1 3PA
T: 01603 617411 F: 01603 633692
Email: norfolk@bbc.co.uk
Website: bbc.co.uk/radionorfolk
Editor: David Clayton

BBC RADIO NORTHAMPTON
Broadcasting House, Abington Street, Northampton NN1 2BH
T: 01604 239100 F: 01604 230709
Email: northampton@bbc.co.uk
Website: bbc.co.uk/radionorthampton
Head of Music: Anthony Isaacs

NORTHANTS 96
19-21 St Edmunds Rd, Northampton NN1 5DT
T: 01604 795600 F: 01604 795601
Email: firstname.lastname@musicradio.com
Website: musicradio.com
Programme Controller: Richard Neale

OBAN FM
132 George St, Oban, Argyll PA34 5NT
T: 01631 570057 F: 01631 570530

Email: obanfmradio@btconnect.com
Station Manager: Ian MacKay

OCEAN FM
Radio House, Whittle Avenue,
Segensworth West, Fareham,
Hampshire PO15 5SH
T: 01489 589911 F: 01489 587754
Email: info@oceanfm.com
Website: oceanfm.com
Programme Controller: Stuart Ellis

BBC RADIO 1
Yalding House, 152-156, Gt Portland
Street, London W1N 6AJ
T: 020 7580 4468 F: 020 7765 1439
Email: firstname.lastname@bbc.co.uk
Website: bbc.co.uk/radio1
Controller: Andy Parfitt

BBC RADIO OXFORD
269 Banbury Rd, Summertown,
Oxford OX2 7DW
T: 08459 311444 F: 08459 311555
Email: oxford.online@bbc.co.uk
Website: bbc.co.uk/oxford
Station Manager: Phil Ashworth

97FM PLYMOUTH SOUND
Earls Acre, Alma Road, Plymouth,
Devon PL3 4HX
T: 01752 227272 F: 01752 670730
Email: firstname.lastname@musicradio.com
Website: musicradio.com
Prog Cont/Head of Music: Dave England

103.2 POWER FM
Radio House, Whittle Avenue,
Segensworth West, Fareham,
Hampshire PO15 5SH
T: 01489 589911 F: 01489 589453
Email: info@powerfm.com
Website: powerfm.com
Programme Controller: Craig Morris

PREMIER CHRISTIAN RADIO
22 Chapter Street, London SW1P 4NP
T: 020 7316 1300 F: 020 7233 6706
Email: premier@premier.org.uk
Website: premier.org.uk
Prog Controller: Charmaine Noble-McLean

Q102
Glenageary Office Park, Glenageary,
Co. Dublin
T: +353 1 662 1022
F: +353 1 662 9974
Email: info@q102.ie
Website: q102.ie
Programme Manager: Ian Walker

Q96 FM
65 Sussex St, Glasgow G41 1DX
T: 0141 429 9430 F: 0141 429 9431
Email: firstname.lastname@q-fm.com
Website: q-fm.com
Programme Dir/Hd of Music: Mike
Richardson

READING 107FM
Radio House, Madejski Stadium,
Reading, Berkshire RG2 0FN
T: 0118 986 2555 F: 0118 945 0809
Email: studio@reading107fm.com
Website: reading107fm.com
Prog Controller: Tim Grundy

REAL RADIO FM
PO Box 101, Glasgow Business Park,
Glasgow G69 6GA
T: 0141 781 1011 F: 0141 781 1112
Email: firstname.lastname@realradiofm.com
Website: realradiofm.com
MD: Shaun Bowron

RED FM
1, UTC, Bishopstown, Cork
T: +353 21 486 5500
F: +353 21 486 5501
Email: info@redfm.ie
Website: redfm.ie
Programme Dir: Matt Dempsey

RIDINGS FM
PO Box 333, Wakefield,
West Yorkshire WF2 7YQ
T: 01924 367177 F: 01924 367133
Email: enquiries@ridingsfm.co.uk
Website: ridingsfm.co.uk
Programme Manager: Phil Butler

RTE RADIO 1
Radio Centre, Donnybrook,
Dublin 4, Ireland
T: +353 1 208 3111
F: +353 1 208 4523
Email: radio1@rte.ie
Website: rte.ie
Production Manager: Gerry Kelly

107.1 RUGBY FM
Suites 4-6, Dunsmore Business Centre,
Spring St, Rugby CV21 3HH
T: 01788 541100 F: 01788 541070
Email: mail@rugbyfm.co.uk
Website: rugbyfm.co.uk
MD/Head of Sales: Martin Mumford

SBN - STUDENT RADIO NETWORK
109A Regents Park Road,
London NW1 8UR
T: 020 7691 4777 F: 020 7691 4666
Email: information@sbn.co.uk
Website: sbn.co.uk
Station Mgr/Prog Dir: Marina Lois

BBC SCOTLAND
Queen Margaret Drive, Glasgow,
Strathclyde G12 8DG
T: 0141 338 2000 F: 0141 338 2346
Email: firstname.lastname@bbc.co.uk
Website: bbc.co.uk/scotland
Snr Prod Contemp. Music: Stewart Cruickshank

102.4 SEVERN SOUND FM
Bridge Studios, Eastgate Centre,
Gloucester GL1 1SS
T: 01452 313200 F: 01452 313213
Email: firstname.lastname@musicradio.com
Website: musicradio.com
Programme Director: Russ Wilcox

SGR COLCHESTER
Abbeygate Two, 9 Whitewell Road,
Colchester, Essex CO2 7DE
T: 01206 575859 F: 01206 216149
Email: firstname.lastname@musicradio.com
Website: musicradio.com
Programme Director: Paul Morris

BBC RADIO SHEFFIELD
54 Shoreham Street, Sheffield,
South Yorkshire S1 4RS
T: 0114 273 1177 F: 0114 267 5454
Email: radio.sheffield@bbc.co.uk
Website: bbc.co.uk/radiosheffield
Head of Music: Franca Marttella

106.9 SILK FM
Radio House, Bridge Street,
Macclesfield, Cheshire SK11 6DJ
T: 01625 268000 F: 01625 269010
Email: mail@silkfm.com
Website: silkfm.com
Brand Mgr: Andy Bailey

SOUTH EAST RADIO
Custom House Quay, Wexford, Ireland
T: +353 53 45200 F: +353 53 45295
Email: info@southeastradio.ie
Website: .southeastradio.ie
Prog Dir/Head of Music: Clive Roylance

107.8 SOUTHCITY FM
City Studios, Marsh Lane, Southampton, Hampshire SO14 3ST
T: 023 8022 0020 F: 023 8022 0060
Email: info@southcityfm.co.uk
Website: southcityfm.co.uk
Programme Controller: Stuart McGinley

SOUTHERN FM
Radio House, PO Box 2000, Brighton, East Sussex BN41 2SS
T: 01273 430111 F: 01273 430098
Email: info@southernradio.co.uk
Website: southernfm.com
Prog Contr/Head of Music: Tony Aldridge

STAR 107.2 BRISTOL
Bristol Evening Post Building, Temple Way, Bristol BS99 7HD
T: 0117 910 6600 F: 0117 925 0941
Email: firstname.lastname@star1072.co.uk
Website: star1072.co.uk
Programme Controller: Ian Downs

STAR 107.9
Radio House, Sturton Street, Cambridge CB1 2QF
T: 01223 722300 F: 01223 577686
Email: mail@star107.co.uk
Website: star107.co.uk
MD/Prog Controller: James Keen

SUNRISE RADIO
Sunrise House, Merrick Rd, Southall, Middlesex UB2 4AU
T: 020 8574 6666 F: 020 8813 9800
Email: tpatti@sunriseradio.com
Website: sunriseradio.com
Prog Dir/Head of Music: Tony Patti

TAY FM
6 North Isla St, Dundee, Tayside DD3 7JQ
T: 01382 200800 F: 01382 423252
Email: firstname.lastname@tayfm.co.uk
Website: tayfm.co.uk
Head of Music: Graeme Waggott

BBC RADIO 3
Room 4119, Broadcasting House, London W1A 1AA
T: 020 7765 2512 F: 020 7765 2511
Email: firstname.lastname@bbc.co.uk
Website: bbc.co.uk/radio3
Controller: Roger Wright

BBC THREE COUNTIES RADIO
PO Box 3CR, Luton, Beds LU1 5XL
T: 01582 637400 F: 01582 401467
Email: 3cr@bbc.co.uk
Website: bbc.co.uk/threecounties
Managing Editor: Marc Norman

100-102 TODAY FM
124 Upper Abbey St, Dublin 1, Ireland
T: +353 1 804 9000
F: +353 1 804 9099
Email: badams@todayfm.com
Website: todayfm.com
Head of Music: Brian Adams

TRAX FM
White Hart Yard, Bridge St, Worksop, Nottinghamshire S80 1HR
T: 01909 500611 F: 01909 500445
Email: enquiries@traxfm.co.uk
Website: traxfm.co.uk
Admin Manager: Paula Spencer

BBC RADIO 2
Henry Wood House, 3 and 6 Langham Place, London W1A 1AA
T: 020 7580 4468 F: 020 7725 2578
Email: firstname.lastname@bbc.co.uk
Website: bbc.co.uk/radio2
Publicity Office

UCB EUROPE
Hanchurch Christian Centre,
PO Box 255, Stoke On Trent,
Staffordshire ST4 8YY
T: 01782 642000 F: 01782 641121
Email: ucb@ucb.co.uk
Website: ucb.co.uk
Station Controller: Andrew Urquhart

BBC ULSTER
Broadcasting House, Ormeau Avenue, Belfast, Co Antrim BT2 8HQ
T: 028 9033 8000 F: 028 9033 8800
Email: firstname.lastname@bbc.co.uk
Website: bbc.co.uk/northernireland/atl
Senior Producer - Radio: Simon Taylor

VALE FM
Longmead Studios, Shaftesbury,
Dorset SP7 8QQ
T: 01747 855711 F: 01747 855722
Email: studio@valefm.co.uk
Website: valefm.co.uk
Prog Cont/Head of Music: Stewart Smith

VIRGIN RADIO
1 Golden Square, London W1F 9DJ
T: 020 7663 2000 F: 020 7434 1197
Email: reception@virginradio.co.uk
Website: virginradio.co.uk
Head of Music: James Curran

BBC WALES/CYMRU
Broadcasting House, Llantrisant Road, Llandaff, Cardiff, South Glamorgan CF5 2YQ
T: 02920 322000 F: 02920 323724
Email: radio.wales@bbc.co.uk
Website: bbc.co.uk/wales
Radio Wales Editor: Julie Barton

WAVE 102 FM
8 South Tay St, Dundee DD1 1PA
T: 01382 901000 F: 01382 900999
Email: studio@wave102.co.uk
Website: wave102.co.uk
Prog Mgr/Head of Music: Peter Mac

WAVE 105.2 FM
5 Manor Court, Barnes Wallis Rd,
Segensworth East, Fareham,
Hampshire PO15 5TH
T: 01489 481057 F: 01489 481100
Email: studio@wave105.com
Website: wave105.com
MD: Martin Ball

107.2 WIRE FM
Warrington Business Park, Long Lane,
Warrington, Cheshire WA2 8TX
T: 01925 445545 F: 01925 657705
Email: info@wirefm.com
Website: wirefm.com
Prog Mgr: Paul Holmes

WIRED FM
Mary Immaculate College, South Circular Road, Limerick, Ireland
T: +353 61 315773 F: +353 61 315776
Email: wiredfm@mic.ul.ie
Website: listen.to/wiredfm
Station Manager: Nessa McGann

XFM 104.9
30 Leicester Square, London
WC2H 7LA
T: 020 7766 6600 F: 020 7766 6601
Email: firstname.lastname@xfm.co.uk
Website: xfm.co.uk
Programme Controller: Andy Ashton

NEWSPAPERS AND MAGAZINES

AUDIENCE
Miracle Publishing Ltd, 1 York Street, London W1U 6PA
T: 020 7486 7007 F: 020 7486 2002
Email: info@audience.uk.com
Website: audience.uk.com

AUDIO MEDIA MAGAZINE
11 Station Road, St Ives, Cambridgeshire PE27 5BH
T: 01480 461555 F: 01480 461550
Email: mail@audiomedia.com
Website: audiomedia.com
Executive Editor: Paul Mac

BBC MUSIC MAGAZINE
Room A1004, Woodlands, 80 Wood Lane, London W12 0TT
T: 020 8433 3283 F: 020 8433 3293
Email: helen.wallace@bbc.co.uk
Website: bbcmusicmagazine.com
Ed: Helen Wallace

THE BIG ISSUE
1-5 Wandsworth Rd, London SW8 2LN
T: 020 7526 3201 F: 020 7526 3301
Email: matt.ford@bigissue.com
Website: bigissue.com
Ed: Matt Ford

BILLBOARD
Endeavour House, 5th floor, 189 Shaftesbury Avenue, London WC2H 8TJ
T: 020 7420 6003 F: 020 7420 6014
Email: TFerguson@eu.billboard.com
Website: billboard.com
Int Ed: Tom Ferguson

BLUES & SOUL
153 Praed Street, London W2 1RL
T: 020 7402 6869 F: 020 7224 8227
Email: editorial@bluesandsoul.demon.co.uk
Website: bluesandsoul.com
Ed: Bob Killbourn

BROADCAST
EMAP Media, 33-39 Bowling Green Lane, London EC1R 0DA
T: 020 7505 8014 F: 020 7505 8050
Email: admin@broadcastnow.co.uk
Website: broadcastnow.co.uk
Ed: Katy Elliott

CAMPAIGN
174 Hammersmith Rd, London W6 7JP
T: 020 8267 4656 F: 020 8267 4915
Email: campaign@haynet.com
Ed: Caroline Marshall

CELEBRITY SERVICE
93 Regent Street, London W1R 7TA
T: 020 7439 9840 F: 020 7494 3500
Diane Oliver

CITY LIFE
164 Deansgate, Manchester M60 2RD
T: 0161 832 7200 F: 0161 839 1488
Email: luke.bainbridge@citylife.co.uk
Website: citylife.co.uk
Editorial Director: Luke Bainbridge

CLASSIC FM MAGAZINE
Haymarket Publishing, 38-42 Hampton Road, Teddington, Middx TW11 0JE
T: 020 8267 5180 F: 020 8267 5150
Email: classicfm@haynet.com
Website: classicfm.com
Editor in Chief: John Evans

CLASSIC ROCK
99 Baker St, London W1U 6FP
T: 020 7317 2600 F: 020 7317 2686
Email: mickwall@futurenet.co.uk
Ed: Mick Wall

CLASSICAL GUITAR
Ashley Mark Publishing Co, 1 & 2 Vance Court, Trans Britannia Ent Park, Blaydon On Tyne NE21 5NH
T: 0191 414 9000 F: 0191 414 9001
Email: classicalguitar@ashleymark.co.uk
Website: ashleymark.co.uk
Ed: Colin Cooper

CLASSICAL MUSIC
Rhinegold Publishing, 241 Shaftesbury Avenue, London WC2H 8TF
T: 020 7333 1742 (Ed)
F: 020 7333 1769 (Ed)
Email: classical.music@rhinegold.co.uk
Website: rhinegold.co.uk
Ed: Keith Clarke

CMA PUBLICATIONS
Strawberry Holt, Westfield Lane, Draycott, Somerset BS27 3TN
T: 01934 740270
Email: grp@cma-publications.co.uk
Website: cma-publications.co.uk
MD: Geraldine Russell-Price

CMU: THE UPDATE
UnLimited Media, 70 Upsdell Avenue, London N13 6JN
T: 0870 744 2643 F: 070 9231 4982
Email: cmu@unlimitedmedia.co.uk
Website: cmuonline.co.uk
Publisher: Chris Cooke

COMPUTER MUSIC
Future Publishing, 30 Monmouth St, Bath BA1 2BW
T: 01225 442244
Email: ronan.macdonald@futurenet.co.uk
Website: computermusic.co.uk
Ed: Ronan Macdonald

COUNTRY MUSIC ROUND UP
PO Box 111, Waltham, Grimsby, NE Lincs DN37 0YN
T: 01472 821808 F: 01472 821808
Email: countrymusic_ru@hotmail.com
Website: cmru.co.uk
Publisher: John Emptage

THE DAILY EXPRESS
Ludgate House, 245 Blackfriars Road, London SE1 9UX
T: 020 7928 8000 F: 020 7620 1643
Email: (firstname).(surname)@express.co.uk
Website: express.co.uk
Ed: Christopher Williams

DAILY MAIL
Northcliffe House, 2 Derry Street, London W8 5TT
T: 020 7938 6000 F: 020 7937 3251
Website: dailymail.co.uk
Ed: Paul Dacre

DAILY RECORD & SUNDAY MAIL
1 Central Quay, Glasgow G3 8DA
T: 0141 309 3000 F: 0141 309 3340
Email: reporters@dailyrecord.co.uk
Website: dailyrecord.co.uk
Ed: Peter Cox

DAILY SPORT
19 Great Ancoats Street, Manchester
M60 4BT
T: 0161 236 4466 F: 0161 236 2418

DAILY STAR
Ludgate House, 245 Blackfriars Road,
London SE1 9UX
T: 020 7928 8000 F: 020 7922 7962
Ed: Peter Hill

DAILY TELEGRAPH
1 Canada Square, Canary Wharf,
London E14 5DT
T: 020 7538 5000 F: 020 7538 7650
Website: telegraph.co.uk

DAZED & CONFUSED
112 Old Street, London EC1V 9BG
T: 020 7336 0766
Email: contact@confused.co.uk
Website: confused.co.uk

DJ MAGAZINE
Highgate Studios, 53-79 Highgate
Road, London NW5 1TW
T: 020 7331 1148 F: 020 7331 1115
Email: editors@djmag.com
Website: DJmag.com
Deputy Editor: Tom Kihl

DMC UPDATE
DMC Publishing, 62 Lancaster Mews,
London W2 3QG
T: 020 7262 6777 F: 020 7706 9323
Email: info@dmcworld.com
Website: dmcworld.com
Ad & Sponsorship Mgr: John
Saunderson

DOTMUSIC
Mondial House, 90-94 Upper Thames
Street, London EC4R 3UB
T: 020 7469 2347 F: 020 7469 2251
Email: ben.drury@bt.com
Website: dotmusic.com
Head Of Music: Ben Drury

DROWNED IN SOUND
72 Palatine Rd, Stoke Newington,
London N16 8ST
T: 020 8969 2498
Email: gareth@drownedinsound.com
Website: drownedinsound.com
Editor: Gareth Dobson

EARLY MUSIC
70 Baker Street, London W1U 7DN
T: 020 7616 5902 F: 020 7616 5901
Email: jnl.early-music@oup.co.uk
Website: em.oupjournals.org
Acting Editor: Dr John Milsom

EARLY MUSIC TODAY
Rhinegold Publishing, 241 Shaftesbury
Avenue, London WC2H 8TF
T: 020 7333 1721 F: 020 7333 1769
Email: (firstname).(surname)@rhinegold.co.uk
Website: rhinegold.co.uk
Ed: Lucien Jenkins

ECHOES
Unit LFB2, The Leathermarket,
Weston Street, London SE1 3HN
T: 020 7407 5858 F: 020 7407 2929
Email: echoesmusic@aol.com
Ed: Chris Wells

ELLEGIRL
64 North Row, London W1K 7LL
T: 020 7150 7972 F: 020 7150 7572

Email: lysannecurrie@hf-uk.com
Website: hf-uk.com
Editorial Dir: Lysanne Currie

EP
Vigilante Publications, Huntingdon House, 35 Field Road, Reading, Berkshire RG1 6AP
T: 0118 958 1878 F: 07092 357238
Email: epmagazine@vigilante.co.uk
Website: vigilante.co.uk
Ed: Jon Ewing

EVENING STANDARD
Northcliffe House, 2 Derry Street, London W8 5TT
T: 020 7938 6000 F: 020 7937 7392
Website: thisislondon.co.uk
Ed: Veronica Wadley

THE FACE
Exmouth House, Pine Street, London EC1R 0JL
T: 020 7689 2225 F: 020 7689 0300
Email: kevinbraddock@theface.co.uk
Ed: Johnny Davis

FHM
40 Bernard Street, London WC1N 1LW
T: 020 7278 1452 F: 020 7278 6941
Website: fhmc.com

FINANCIAL TIMES
1 Southwark Bridge, London SE1 9HL
T: 020 7873 3000 F: 020 7873 3062
Website: ft.com
Ed: Richard Lambert

THE FLY
109X Regents Park Road, London NW1 8UR
T: 020 7691 4555 F: 020 7691 4666
Email: info@channelfly.com
Website: channelfly.com
Ed: Will Kinsman

FUSEDMAGAZINE
306f The Big Peg, 120 Vyse Street, The Jewellery Quarter, Birmingham B18 6NF
T: 0121 246 1946/7 F: 0121 246 1945
Email: fused2000@aol.com
Website: fusedmagazine.com
Editorial Director: David O'Coy

GQ
Vogue House, Hanover Square, London W1R 0AD
T: 020 7499 9080 F: 020 7495 1679
Email: gqletters@condenast.co.uk
Website: gq-magazine.co.uk
Ed: Dylan Jones

THE GRAPEVINE
45 Underwood Street, London N1 7LG
T: 020 7490 0946 F: 020 7490 1026
Email: nick@nus-ents.co.uk
Website: nusonline.co.uk
Sales Manager: Nick Woodward

THE GUARDIAN
119 Farringdon Road, London EC1R 3ER
T: 020 7278 2332 F: 020 7713 4366
Email: (name)@guardian.co.uk
Website: guardian.co.uk
Ed: Alan Rusbridger

THE GUIDE
The Guardian, 119 Farringdon Road, London EC1R 3ER
T: 020 7713 4152 F: 020 7713 4346

GUINNESS-BRITISH HIT SINGLES/ROCKOPEDIA
338 Euston Road, London NW1 3BD
T: 020 7891 4547 F: 020 7891 4501
Email: editor@15th.britishhitsingles.com
Website: britishhitsingles.com
Ed: David Roberts

GUITAR MAGAZINE
Link House, Dingwall Avenue, Croydon, Surrey CR9 2TA
T: 020 8774 0600 F: 020 8774 0934
Email: guitar@ipcmedia.com
Ed: Simon Weir

GUITARIST
Future Publishing, 30 Monmouth Street, Bath, Somerset BA1 2BW
T: 01225 442244 F: 01225 732285
Email: neville.martin@futurenet.co.uk
Ed: Neville Marten

HEAT
Endeavor House, 189 Shaftesbury Avenue, London WC2H 8JG
T: 020 7295 5000 F: 020 7859 8670
Email: heat@emap.com
Ed: Mark Frith

HELLO!
69-71 Upper Ground, London SE1 9PQ
T: 020 7667 8700 F: 020 7667 8742
Website: hello-magazine.co.uk
Publishing Dir: Sally Cartwright

THE HERALD
200 Renfield Street, Glasgow G2 3PR
T: 0141 302 7000 F: 0141 302 7171
Email: arts@theherald.co.uk
Website: theherald.co.uk
Ed: Mark Douglas-Home

HIP HOP CONNECTION
Infamous Ink Ltd, PO Box 392, Cambridge CB1 3WH
T: 01223 210536 F: 01223 210536
Email: hhc@hiphop.com
Website: hiphop.co.uk
Ed: Andy Cowan

HIT SHEET
31 The Birches, London N21 1NJ
T: 020 8360 4088 F: 020 8360 4088
Email: info@hitsheet.co.uk
Website: hitsheet.co.uk
Publisher: Paul Kramer

HOKEY POKEY
Millham Lane, Dulverton, Somerset TA22 9HQ
T: 01398 324114 F: 01398 324114
Email: hokey.pokey@bigfoot.com
Ed: Andrew Quarrie

HONK
Ty Cefn, Rectory Rd, Canton, Cardiff, South Glamorgan CF5 1QL
T: 029 2066 8127 F: 029 2034 1622
Email: honk@welshmusicfoundation.com
Website: welshmusicfoundation.com/honk
Ed: James McLaren

HOT AIR
John Brown Contract Publishing, The New Boathouse, 136-142 Bramley Road, London W10 6SR
T: 020 7565 3000
Ed: Alex Finer

HOT PRESS MAGAZINE
13 Trinity Street, Dublin 2, Ireland
T: +353 1 241 1500
F: +353 1 241 1538
Email: info@hotpress.ie

Website: hotpress.com
Ed: Niall Stokes

NERVE
Talbot Campus, Fern Barrow, Poole, Dorset BH12 5BB
T: 01202 595777 F: 01202 535990
Email: smithi@bournemouth.ac.uk
Website: subu.org.uk
Media Services Mgr: Iain Smith

A NEW DAY - THE JETHRO TULL MAGAZINE
75 Wren Way, Farnborough, Hampshire GU14 8TA
T: 01252 540270 F: 01252 372001
Email: DAVIDREES1@compuserve.com
Website: anewdayrecords.co.uk
Editor: Dave Rees

NEW MUSICAL EXPRESS
IPC Music Magazines, Kings Reach Tower, Stamford Street, London SE1 9LS
T: 020 7261 6472 F: 020 7261 5185
Email: firstname_lastname@ipcmedia.com
Website: nme.com
Ed: Conor McNicholas…x

NEW NATION NEWSPAPER
Unit 2.1, Whitechapel Technology Centre, 65 Whitechapel Road, London E1 IDU
T: 020 7650 2000 F: 020 7650 2004
Email: thepulse@newnation.co.uk
Music & Ent Ed: Justin Onyeka

NEWS OF THE WORLD
News International, 1 Virginia Street, London E1 9XR
T: 020 7782 7000 F: 020 7583 9504
Website: newsoftheworld.co.uk
Ed: Rebekah Wade

NIGHTSHIFT
Oxford Music Central, 2nd Floor, 65 George Street, Oxford OX1 2BE
T: 01865 798793 F: 01865 798793
Email: nightshift@oxfordmusic.net
Website: nightshift.oxfordmusic.net
Editor: Ronan Munro

19
IPC Magazines, Kings Reach Tower, Stamford Street, London SE1 9LS
T: 020 7261 5049 F: 020 7261 7477
Website: ipc.co.uk
Ed: Samantha Warwick

THE NOISE
Buckinghamshire College SU, Queen Alexandra Rd, High Wycombe, Bucks HP11 2JZ
T: 01494 446330 F: 01494 558195
Email: amanda.mcdowall@bcuc.ac.uk
Website: bcsu.net
Ed: Amanada McDowall

NORTHDOWN PUBLISHING LTD
PO Box 49, Bordon, Hants GU35 0AF
T: 01420 489474 F: 01420 488797
Email: enquiries@northdown.demon.co.uk
Website: northdown.demon.co.uk
Dir: Michael Heatley

THE OBSERVER
119 Farringdon Road, London EC1R 3ER
T: 020 7278 2332 F: 020 7713 4250
Email: firstname.lastname@observer.co.uk
Website: observer.co.uk
Ed in Chief: Will Hutton

OK!
Northern & Shell, Northern & Shell Tower, City Harbour, London E14 9GL
T: 020 7987 6262
Ed: Martin Townsend

ONE TO ONE
CMP Information, Ludgate House, 245 Blackfriars Road, London SE1 9UR
T: 020 7921 8376 F: 020 7921 8302
Email: tfrost@cmpinformation.com
Website: oto-online.com
Ed: Tim Frost

ONLINEPOP
PO Box 150, Chesterfield, Derbyshire S40 0YT
T: 0870 746 8478
Email: mail@onlinepopnews.com
Website: onlinepopnews.com
Editor: Tony Hedley

OPERA NOW
241 Shaftesbury Avenue, London WC2H 8EH
T: 020 7333 1733 F: 020 7333 1736
Email: opera.now@rhinegold.co.uk
Website: rhinegold.co.uk
Ed: Ashutosh Khandekar

ORIGINAL BRITISH THEATRE DIRECTORY
70-76 Bell Street, Marylebone, London NW1 6SP
T: 020 7224 9666 F: 020 7224 9688
Email: sales@rhpco.co.uk
Website: rhpco.co.uk
Manager: Spencer Block

THE PIANO
Rhinegold Publishing, 241 Shaftesbury Avenue, London WC2H 8EH
T: 020 7333 1733 F: 020 7333 1736
Website: rhinegold.co.uk
Ed: Jeremy Siepmann

POPULAR MUSIC
Cambridge University Press, The Edinburgh Building, Shaftesbury Road, Cambridge CB2 2RU
T: 01223 325757 F: 01223 315052
Eds: Lucy Green, David Laing

PRESS ASSOCIATION, ROCK LISTINGS
4th Floor, 292 Vauxhall Bridge Road, London SW1V 1AE
T: 020 7963 7749 F: 020 7963 7800
Email: gigs@pa.press.net
Rock & Pop Editor: Delia Barnard

PRO SOUND NEWS EUROPE
CMP Information Ltd., 8th Floor, Ludgate House, London SE1 9UR
T: 020 8309 7000 F: 020 7579 4011
Email: david.robinson@cmpinformation.com
Website: prosoundeurope.com
Ed: David Robinson

PROMO
CMP Information Ltd, Ludgate House, 245 Blackfriars Road, London SE1 9UR
T: 020 8309 7000 F: 020 7579 4171
Email: dknight@cmpinformation.com
Ed: David Knight

Q
EMAP Metro, Mappin House, 4 Winsley Street, London W1N 7AR
T: 020 7312 8182 F: 020 7312 8247

Email: q@ecm.emap.com
Website: qonline.co.uk
Editor: Paul Rees

Q SHEET
29-55 Gee Street, London EC1V 3RE
T: 020 7253 8888 F: 020 7253 8885
Email: info@qsheet.com
Website: qsheet.com
Music Editor: Simon Sanders

THE RADIO MAGAZINE
Goldcrest Broadcasting, Crown House, 25 High Street, Rothwell, Northamptonshire NN14 6AD
T: 01536 418558 F: 01536 418539
Email: radiomagazine-goldcrestbroadcasting@btinternet.com
Website: theradiomagazine.co.uk

RADIO TIMES
Woodlands, 80 Wood Lane, London W12 0TT
T: 020 8576 2000
Website: radiotimes.com
Ed: Sue Robinson

RECORD OF THE DAY
PO Box 37160, London E4 6XA
T: 020 8524 8151
Email: paul@recordoftheday.com
Website: recordoftheday.com
Director: Paul Scaife

RED PUBLISHING
Paulton House, 8 Shepherdess Walk, London N1 7LB
T: 020 7566 8216 F: 020 7566 8259
Email: info@redpublishing.co.uk
Website: redpublishing.co.uk
Publisher: Doug Marshall

RHYTHM
Future Publishing, 30 Monmouth St, Bath, Somerset BA1 2BW
T: 01225 442244 F: 01225 732353
Email: louise.king@futurenet.co.uk
Website: futurenet.co.uk
Editor: Louise King

ROCK SOUND
ixo Publishing UK Ltd, 50A Roseberry Avenue, London EC1R 4RP
T: 020 7278 5559 F: 020 7278 4788
Email: rsvp.rocksound@ixopub.co.uk
Website: rock-sound.net
Publisher: Patrick Napier

ROUGH GUIDES LTD
Rough Guides, 62-70 Shorts Gardens, London WC2H 9AH
T: 020 7556 5000 F: 020 7556 5050
Email: mail@roughguides.co.uk
Website: roughguides.com
Rights/Promo Ass.: Chloe Roberts

RTE GUIDE
TV Building, Donnybrook, Dublin 4, Ireland
T: +353 1 208 2919
F: +353 1 208 2092
Email: ray.walsh@rte.ie
Ed: Ray Walsh

SHOWCASE DIRECTORY
Harlequin House, 7 High St, Teddington, Middx TW11 8EL
T: 020 8943 3138 F: 020 8943 5141
Email: gillie@hollis-pr.co.uk
Website: showcase-music.com
Ed: Gillie Mayer

SLEAZENATION
1A Zetland House, 5-25 Scrutton Street, London EC2A 4HJ
T: 020 7729 3773 F: 020 7729 8312
Email: steve@sleazenation.com
Website: sleazenation.com
Publishing Dir: Rich Sutcliffe

SMASH HITS
EMAP Metro, 4th Floor, Mappin House, 4 Winsley Street, London W1N 7AR
T: 020 7436 1515 F: 020 7636 5792
Email: smash_hits@emap.com; firstname.lastname@emap.com
Website: smashhits.net
Ed: Lisa Smosarski

SONGLINK INTERNATIONAL
23 Belsize Crescent, London NW3 5QY
T: 020 7794 2540 F: 020 7794 7393
Email: david@songlink.com
Website: songlink.com
Ed/Publisher: David Stark

SONGWRITER
International Songwriters' Ass,
PO Box 46, Limerick City, Ireland
T: +353 61 228837 F: +353 61 229464
Email: jliddane@songwriter.iol.ie
Website: songwriter.co.uk
MD: James D Liddane

SONGWRITER MAGAZINE (UK)
International Songwriters Ass,
37 New Cavendish Street, London W1
T: 020 7486 5353 F: 020 7486 2094
Email: jliddane@songwriter.iol.ie
Website: songwriter.co.uk
CEO: Jim Liddane

SORTED MAGAZINE
PO Box 6804, Dublin 7, Eire
Email: editor@sortedmagazine.com
Website: sortedmagazine.com
Ed: Donnacha Delong

SOUL TRADE
PO Box 34539, London SE15 2XA
T: 020 7732 2287
Email: ash@soultrade.co.uk
Website: soultrade.co.uk
Manager: Ash Kamat

SOUND ON SOUND
Media House, Trafalgar Way, Bar Hill, Cambridgeshire CB3 8SQ
T: 01954 789888 F: 01954 789895
Email: sos@sospubs.co.uk
Website: sound-on-sound.com
Publisher: Ian Gilby

STAGE
Stage House, 47 Bermondsey Street, London SE1 3XT
T: 020 7403 1818 F: 020 7357 9287
Website: thestage.co.uk
Ed: Brian Attwood

STAGE, SCREEN & RADIO
373 -377 Clapham Rd, London SW9 9BT
T: 020 7346 0900 F: 020 7346 0901
Email: info@bectu.org.uk
Website: bectu.org.uk
Ed: Janice Turner

THE STRAD
SMG, 3 Waterhouse Square, 138-142 Holborn, London EC1N 2NY
T: 020 7882 1040 F: 020 7882 1020
Email: thestrad@orpheuspublications.com

Website: thestrad.com
Ed: Naomi Sadler

STRAIGHT NO CHASER
17D Ellingfort Rd, London E8 3PA
T: 020 8533 9999 F: 020 8985 6447
Email: info@straightnochaser.co.uk
Website: straightnochaser.co.uk
Ed: Paul Bradshaw

STUDENT OUTLOOK
17- Portobello Road, London W11 2EB
T: 020 7221 8137
Website: student.uk.com
Ian Henshall

SUGAR
64 North Row, London W1K 7LL
T: 020 7150 7972 F: 020 7150 7572
Email: lysannecurrie@hf-uk.com
Website: hf-uk.com
Editorial Dir: Lysanne Currie

THE SUN
News International, 1 Virginia Street, London E1 9BD
T: 020 7782 4000 F: 020 7782 4063
Email: talkback@the-sun.co.uk
Website: thesun.co.uk

SUNDAY MIRROR
1 Canada Square, London E14 5AD
T: 020 7510 3000 F: 020 7293 3405
Website: sundaymirror.co.uk
Ed: Colin Myler

SUNDAY PEOPLE
1 Canada Square, London E14 5AP
T: 020 7293 3000 F: 020 7293 3810
Website: people.co.uk
Ed: Neil Wallis

SUNDAY TELEGRAPH
1 Canada Square, London E14 5DT
T: 020 7538 5000
Website: telegraph.co.uk
Ed: Dominic Lawson

SUNDAY TIMES
News International, 1 Pennington Street, London E1 9XW
T: 020 7782 5000 F: 020 7782 5658
Website: timesonline.co.uk

SYPHA'S DAW BUYERS GUIDE
Gipsy Road, London SE27 9RB
T: 020 8761 1042
Email: sypha@syphaonline.com
Website: syphaonline.com
Partner: Yasmin Hashmi

TELE-TUNES
Mike Preston Music, The Glengarry, Thornton Grove, Morecambe, Lancs LA4 5PU
T: 01524 421172 F: 01524 421172
Email: mikepreston@beeb.net
Website: teletunes.co.uk
Research Ed: Mike Preston

TENSE MAGAZINE
Top Floor, 24 Porden Rd, London SW2 5RT
T: 020 7642 2030 F: 020 7274 3543
Email: editor@tensemagazine.com
Website: tensemagazine.com
Editor: Toussaint Davy

TIME OUT
Universal House, 251 Tottenham Court Road, London W1T 7AB
T: 020 7813 3000 F: 020 7813 6158
Email: music@timeout.com

Website: timeout.com/london
Music Ed: Ross Fortune

THE TIMES
1 Pennington St, London E98 1XY
T: 020 7782 5000
Website: timesonline.co.uk

THE TIMES METRO
News International, 1 Pennington Street, London E98 1TE
T: 020 7782 5000 F: 020 7782 5525
Email: metro@the-times.co.uk
Ed: Rupert Mellor

TNT MAGAZINE
14-15 Childs Place, London SW5 9RX
T: 020 7341 6685 F: 0870 752 2717
Email: arts@tntmag.co.uk
Website: tntmagazine.com
Entertainment Editor: Pierre de Villiers

TOP OF THE POPS MAGAZINE
Room A1136, 80 Wood Lane, London W12 0TT
T: 020 8433 2992 F: 020 8433 2694
Email: olivia.mclearon@bbc.co.uk
Website: bbc.co.uk/totp
PA to Editor: Olivia McLearon

TV GUIDE & DIGITAL TV GUIDE
The New Boathouse, 136-142 Bramley Rd, London W10 6SR
T: 020 7565 3000 F: 020 7565 3056
Email: skymag@bcp.co.uk

TV HITS
64 North Row, London W1K 7LL
T: 020 7150 7972 F: 020 7150 7572
Email: lysannecurrie@hf-uk.com
Website: hf-uk.com
Editorial Dir: Lysanne Currie

TV TIMES
IPC Magazines, Kings Reach Tower, Stamford Street, London SE1 9LS
T: 020 7261 7956 ad
Website: ipc.co.uk/pubs/tvtimes
Ed: Peter Genowa

TWENTY4-SEVEN MAGAZINE
After Dark Media, Grosvenor House, Belgrave Lane, Mutley, Plymouth PL4 7DA
T: 01752 294130 F: 01752 257320
Email: nigel@afterdarkmedia.net
Website: 24-7magazine.co.uk
Chief Ed: Nigel Muntz

UNCUT
IPC Music Magazines, Kings Reach Tower, Stamford Street, London SE1 9LS
T: 020 7261 6992 F: 020 7261 5573
Ed: Allan Jones

UNDERCOVER
Undercover Agents Ltd, Basement, 69 Kensington Gardens Sq, London W2 4DG
T: 020 7792 9392
Email: diagnostyx@hotmail.com
Editor In Chief: Nat Illumine

VENUE MAGAZINE
64-65 North Road, St Andrews, Bristol BS6 5AQ
T: 0117 942 8491 F: 0117 942 0369
Email: editor@venue.co.uk
Website: venue.co.uk
Music Ed: Cris Warren

VIDEO HOME ENTERTAINMENT
Video Business Entertainment,
Strandgate, 18-20 York Buildings,
London WC2N 6JU
T: 020 7839 7774 F: 020 7839 4393
Ed: John Ferguson

THE VOICE
8/9th Fl's Bluestar House, 234-244
Stockwell Road, London SW9 9UG
T: 020 7737 7377 F: 020 7501 9465
Email: advertising@the-voice.co.uk
Website: voice-online.co.uk
GM: Simbo Nuga

WHAT'S ON IN LONDON
180-182 Pentonville Rd, London N1 9LB
T: 020 7278 4393 F: 020 7837 5838
Email: whatson.advertising@virgin.net
Ed: Michael Darvell

THE WIRE
Namara House, 45-46 Poland Street,
London W1V 3DF
T: 020 7439 6422 F: 020 7287 4767
Email: the_wire@ukonline.co.uk
Website: thewire.co.uk
Ed-in-Chief/Publisher: Tony Herrington

HIGHLY RECOMMENDED MUSIC PRESS

ROCK titles (for smaller breaking indie/rock bands)

NME

New Musical Express

KERRANG

The Fly

Rocksound

MAJOR ROCK titles

MOJO

Uncut

Classic Rock

WEBSITES for unsigned breaking rock bands

drownedinsound.com

playlouder.com

URBAN

TOUCH

TENSE

LARGER TITLES

Echoes

Blues & Soul

POP titles

Smash Hits

Sneak

HIGHLY RECOMMENDED TV / RADIO / PRESS

National Radio	Company
Woolfie	Hungry Media Ltd
Brad Hunner	Anglo Plugging
Kevin Mcabe	Parlophone
Dan Drake	Polydor
Leighton Woods/Mark Murphy	BMG
Paul Kennedy	Size Nine
Marc Brown	Fore
Richard Perry	RPPR
Regional Radio	
Tom Roberts	Upshot
Jo Hart	Hart Media
Broadcast (Television)	
Tony Barker	Outside Organisation
Niki Sanderson	NonStop Promotions
National Press	
Tony Linkin	Coalition
Alan Edwards	Outside Organisation
Dave Woolf	DWL (Dave Woolf Ltd)
Terri Hall	Hall Or Nothing
Mel Brown	Impressive
Regional Press	
Gordon Duncan	APB
Mike Gourlay	Infected

HIGHLY RECOMMENDED VIDEO PRODUCTION

Black Dog

Partizan

Flynn Productions

Oil Factory

Independent Films

1
2
3
4
5
6
7
8
9
10
11
12
13
14
15

1

2

3

4

5

6

7

8

9

10

11

12

13

14

15

RETAIL

WHAT IS THE ROLE OF THE RETAILER?

IT'S TOUGH OUT THERE ...

Retail is on the front line of the music business. It is where hits are made or lost. Executives live or die by sales, and for most labels they are inextricably drifting downwards. Retail is under pressure from the Internet, a change in distribution and a hard-fought price war. It's time to take sides. The players must decide whether they are for price, or customer service and experience.

Retail has never just been about selling records. Most kids discovered music in their local music shop. It was run by older kids who were cooler than you. It was the sort of place you just hung out hoping that some of the music business would seep into your veins. But it's getting harder and harder for these places to survive unless they can offer something special.

The local record shop is in danger of going the same way as the local corner shop. The traditional record shop has faced wave after wave of competition. On price the supermarkets can sell CDs for £9.99 or £8.99, which is less than they can buy them, let alone afford to sell them. On range Amazon can beat the largest retail stock.

As if that wasn't bad enough, the iPod was the biggest-selling gizmo last Christmas, and MP3 players are now the norm, making downloading and file sharing an everyday pastime, sometimes legally and sometimes illegally.

Apple charge a flat rate of 63p a single and £6.74 for an album. Whichever way it's downloaded, it's not a retail sale, which means one more potential lost customer.

According to the BPI music sales declined by 15% in the second quarter of 2002 because of downloading, and singles crashed by 42% in the first quarter of 2003.

And that's not all: in September 2003 the world's largest label, Universal, cut prices of its CDs by a third, saying that this was their response to online piracy. In making this move Universal expected record stores to give them at least a quarter of their shelf space. But in reality the big stores will always gain more from this type of price-cutting as they can afford to take their margin down pro rata.

The pressures on the American market have led to some large casualties. Tower Records spent the first quarter of 2004 in Chapter 11 bankruptcy protection, and Wherehouse Entertainment Inc. has had to close 150 stores. So if you are thinking of leaving the rat race and setting up a record shop, think again.

HOW ARE THE BIG RETAILERS SURVIVING?

The big stores are expanding their product ranges outside traditional record sales. DVD and computer game sales are buoyant and taking up some of the slack. Virgin Megastores have gone one stage further and have teamed up with fashion brands Ben Sherman and Blue Marlin and have produced a limited line of clothing. HMV has developed its online side, and has developed special signings of books, records and DVDs into another form of live performance. In many ways it has remained more musically focused than its other large competitors.

The large supermarkets will continue to sell best-selling CDs with the same commercial determination as they sell best-selling books. They will continue to use their muscle to force other majors to follow Universal's price-cutting strategy: even at £5, an album is good business for an operation with their margin and turnover.

WHAT ABOUT THE REAL RECORD SHOPS?

Although they might not feel it, the best independent record shops are in a better position to survive the growth of online and discounting than the larger corporate shops. Admittedly they don't have the same opportunities to extend their offering to other product categories. But they do have competitive benefits that can't easily be replicated online or in a supermarket.

In many ways record shops are just like the music media: as the mainstream gets more packaged and commercial it leaves a big gap for the specialist to get closer to the customer.

Black Market Records offer a more 'streetwise' and creative 'retail experience'. They have come from a different type of record shop that originated with the development of the dance music DJ. These shops became the coolest place to hang out and either be or pretend to be a DJ.

Anyone with access to production equipment and £1,000 in cash can have a go at getting their music into shops like this, and who knows where it will end up? Try downloading that and putting it in your iPod!

WHAT'S GOING ON IN RECORD SHOPS?

- *The growth of vinyl sales:* You have probably spotted more vinyl for sale even in mainstream shops. HMV has significantly increased the amount of sales space it gives to vinyl. It's not just special editions and rereleases of old bands. The Darkness's 'I believe In A Thing Called Love' was the biggest-selling 7-inch single of 2003. The White Stripes take fourth and fifth position. The BPI say that more than 700,000 7-inch vinyl singles were sold in the year to September 2003, which was 35% up on the year before.
- *The slow death of house:* There is a noticeable decline in the number of house white labels for sale in the shops that traditionally specialised in this area. The growth of urban music has seen a shift to hip hop and R&B using the 12-inch white label format. The best shops are keeping up with this trend and getting hold of good American imports.
- *Record shops are still great ways to start off in the business:* Just make sure it is the right one. In virtually every aspect of the business an under-

standing of what's going on in the street is a real asset. In a shop like Black Market Records, you will learn more about what's happening in the scene and probably make better connections than working for a major label. That's why kids who work in this type of environment are in demand as A&R scouts and with enough experience even as A&R managers.

- *Record shops are networks:* Wherever you live you should use your record shop as a way to plug into the music business. Even shops like Fab Records that don't really specialise in white labels or customer CDs take CDs from local bands and sell them in the shop. Your local record shop is a great source of knowledge. They will know about the best venues and will be able to put you in contact with other bands. They are also places where you can raise your local profile. You should load them up with flyers and promotional materials. Even if you have never wanted to work in a shop, get a Saturday job or part-time job in your local shop; even if you are an artist, you'll make connections on the local scene that will be invaluable.

MORE ABOUT DOWNLOADING

- In 2003 EMI put 90% of its song catalogue on the Web, in the belief that the more material they put online, the less incentive there would be for piracy.
- More than one million songs were downloaded from Apple's iTunes service in its first week of operation.
- The Ministry of Sound has relaunched its website to provide more than 100,000 tracks for sale.
- Apple offers more than 200,000 tracks for downloading.
- Woolworths have tested a new way of combining online and offline sales. They put together a tie-up with Girls Aloud that enabled their customers to download their new album when they pre-ordered the physical album from one of their stores months before its official release date. Once the album was available in store, the music files expired.
- There are more than 100 million computer users worldwide registered for file-sharing services.
- OD2, Peter Gabriel's online distribution company, put together two 'Digital

Download' days in October 2002 and March 2003 to demonstrate how easy it is to download legally from the Net. Five official music sites offered downloads costing less than £5 to download an album, and in some cases for free.

TIPS FOR NEWCOMERS

- ***Business plan:*** Don't start a record shop unless you have created a detailed business plan that's been thoroughly checked by a music accountant.
- ***Start small:*** Start off small and then grow slowly.
- ***Mainstream or niche:*** HMV, Virgin, Woolworths and Tesco etc. dominate Top 40 chart music. Therefore make sure your shop is selling desired niche music which is not so easily available with big name stores.
- ***Location, location, location:*** Go for premises near or on a busy high street. Always think people are lazy, so make it easy for them to shop with you.
- ***Database and Internet:*** Everyone who walks into your shop or buys music from you should be on your database. This way you can email them about product and then eventually they can buy direct over the Internet.
- ***Promotions:*** You may be a small retailer but think like the big boys. Provide customers with incentives to shop with you. Create special packages and offers that your competition can't create.

THE VIEW FROM WITHIN

DAVE PICCONI – MD, BLACK MARKET RECORDS

Dave Picconi, MD of the legendary Black Market Records since 1990 and of Azuli Records, which puts out compilations albums, owns a publishing company and still finds time to DJ.

What do you do in your business?

It's my main job to oversee the system, making sure everyone's doing their job according to their role, fulfilling their responsibilities for the label and shop. For example, I have a shop manager who makes sure the guys get in on time and that buying product is right. It's my job to make sure the managers are happy and look at figures such as stock levels. If we have high stock levels at the end of the month then the manager may get the shit if he or she advised that those records were going to sell.

What does 'get the shit' mean? Do you hang him out of the window?

[*Laughs*] No, the systems we have in place are here to keep balances, which all the managers know and watch diligently. If he or she puts us in a position where we're facing financial risk, at first they'll get a bit of bollocking, then we'll ask why the problem happened. We then ask, 'What are you going to do to make sure it doesn't happen again?' If it does happen again then we say, you fucked up again and the third time they're fired.

Also a big headache with the business is buying, because most of the records we buy are not SOR [sale or return]. So if we buy stuff we can't sell, we're fucked. If we buy ten singles, sell seven and are left with three, we actually don't make money on the seven or cover our overheads. When we don't sell a single we know that after a week or so that record's dead. Most dance shops go bust because they're selling loads of records, then they expand, but what they're not watching is what they're not selling – this is what fucks them up. We manage at the end of the month by looking at figures. We check quantity of stock, then we go downstairs as music people and not with our business heads on and ask questions like, 'Does this record still have a buzz on it?' etc. This is why an accountant couldn't run a record shop, because it's first and foremost about music and not figures. We make decisions when buying records based on relationships with distributors, but in the end it's about making decisions on records based on their own merit. I would say we are more like Dixon's in the way we buy records. You can't do this just based on gut. We get offered around 250 new releases per week and take around seventy to eighty a week. We don't take less than ten units per artist although in some exceptional cases we'll take more.

It's all about planning and we apply that more to the label or else in the eleventh hour, you're rushing around making snap decision which could make or break your business. With this business you've always got to make a snap decision and it's your judgement that will determine if you're going to succeed. For example, we had a single out that Ministry wanted to license with a potential earning of £30,000, but it included a sample on a record from The Clash. Ministry needed a decision within two days. EMI were saying we wouldn't get it cleared, so we tried everything and everywhere and came up against a brick wall. But our philosophy at Black Market is that if one door closes we'll find another way in. That's how I encourage the team and it also sets aside those in this business who'll survive. Now we were faced with a big problem. With one day to go I made the judgement and told Ministry to license the tune. I took the risk and it was a big one, which would have destroyed the complete business if I'd got it wrong. If Ministry got sued then we would automatically have been sued by Ministry for loss of earnings to the tune of £650,000, etc. Anyway with only one day to go we had to move like thunder, so we managed to find Joe Strummer from The Clash in New York. We call his home and no answer. By now we're shitting ourselves, and try other routes until we manage to reach him.

That's what you call being on the edge.

It sure is, and we don't do things like that every day. I only made that decision because we had sat down and thought about plan A, B and C. We were not rushing around like headless chickens hoping for the best or else we might have missed a minor point that was important in going forward. Really in this business you've got to talk with your team and explore every avenue, if you want to turn things around and get the results you want. I think too many decisions in this game are made at gut level. You do need a big element of that, but you must also have tight and conservative systems in place that give you the results you want.

You seem a little bit tough and strict. Why is that?
It's not about being strict but about trusting your team. I believe in giving my employees responsibilities rather than tasks. I used to say, 'You call this guy, you do that on design,' etc. but that doesn't work or build confidence. For me it's about saying, 'I don't care how you go about achieving XYZ to achieve the objective.' It's saying, 'Nick, I want you to design a good-looking CD that people will want to buy and manufactured at the cheapest prices. How you do it is your responsibility.'

We were a bit shocked by your clocking-in machine but, to be honest, maybe that's where the music industry needs to go.
[*Laughs*] What do you mean?

We're not saying everyone in the music business must have clocking-in machines. But maybe a few in the industry need that sense of efficiency. It seems like a lot of people operate from gut and hope for the best. This is a bit odd, considering the vast sums of money they invest in projects.
I think the music industry have not adopted certain principles from normal business. They are not efficient, aggressive or looking into management strategies that build a business while at the same time stimulate innovation. Major labels don't have go-getters who want to achieve outstanding things. Too many people don't do their jobs properly. They made so much money from the past that the penny hasn't dropped on what they must do next.

It must be a nightmare for someone trying to work for you. What do you look for?
Drive and ambition, that's essential.

Yeah, but Lucian Grange said you can have someone with ambition but not necessarily good at their job.
You have to really judge what they've done with their personal life to measure their ambition – 'cause someone says I like music and they work hard does not really show you if they're go-getters and smart. I remember when I was fifteen and I couldn't get into pubs or gigs. Being from Huddersfield originally there used to be only gigs in Sheffield, Leeds and Manchester. The last bus home to Huddersfield was eleven o'clock. I rented a bus and gave out flyers outside the punk pubs in Huddersfield saying, 'Do you want to see xyz punk band?' This gave me the money for my travel and I got into the gigs. I'm looking for people who'll go the extra mile, who have that initiative, drive and ambition. If you see someone who wants to do something and they find a way around the hurdle then they're probably worth talking to.

So what do you look for in someone working in the record shop?
Knowledge of music and what will sell. We're looking for someone who's mixing with the scene, but not someone who can't get to work on time. We need people who can do the job while being able to understand what's going on and understands customer service.

This must be a great platform to get a job as an A&R person?
For dance majors it was their main source of employment.

If I'm a kid from Tottenham who's created my own record in my bedroom, can I bring in my white labels to Black Market?
Yeah, it's very important for us to take records or white labels from artists/producers who make their tunes from home. It's always been a great source for successful dance records. We do SOR so if we sell the record then we pay for them.

Do you get a lot of labels trying to get their releases into the shop?
We turn down half the stuff presented to us because there's so much product out in the market. So it's important to have a relationship with the buyers

in the shop. We know who to listen to and who we think have good taste when they recommend tunes to us. This is especially important because labels may have a record that's not an obvious hit at first, but the label or distributor will say, 'Stick with this because we think it's going to be a grower.' When we play it to DJs, if they don't get it at first we will advise them to give it time. We can only do this if we like the tune or the person tipping it to us has a good track record.

What's intriguing is how you run a business with such musical integrity, but you're also very focused on the business side. How do you balance both?
I knew when I started off there were more creative people in dance, but who didn't have the business or marketing side, so I had a head start because I do have both sides of the coin. For those who have weakness they must make sure they pick the right team who cover what they don't have.

Getting back to your team, who else do you hang out the window if they don't do the job properly?
[*Laughs*] Everyone's held responsible for what they do and are answerable if they fuck up.

Have you ever fucked up in the past?
Yes, we all have.

What's the key to your survival?
Key to survival in running a label or shop is to keep your overheads down. Dance music might be an international business, but it's still a bedroom business.

RETAIL

STEVE KNOTT – HMV

As MD of MMV Europe, Steve Knott is an incredibly busy man.

What has made HMV so successful?

We've become the UK's leading specialist music retailer, because we have kept to our ethos of giving the widest possible access to music, however people might want to acquire it. It's been like that since we opened our first shop in 1921. And now our market share in the UK is between 20% and 25% across music and DVD.

Why if HMV is so big do you still describe yourselves as 'specialist'?

Because we are a specialist retail operation, offering a comprehensive range, authoritative product knowledge and dedicated customer service. We may do this on a larger scale than most but we're still driven by the passion that we have for music and the other products that we sell.

What is your strategy versus the supermarkets?

Supermarkets have a totally different cost structure and margin requirements. It allows them to sell a limited range at lower prices, although we seek to offer value in other ways. They are prepared to use some categories as battle-grounds versus other supermarkets, whether they are clothes, records or beauty products and take the resulting profit hit. We'd go out of business if we tried to compete with them just on price. Even though they are slowly expanding their offer, they are often out of stock and don't have staff who are knowledgeable about music. It's a completely different experience.

We believe passionately that in the UK there is a real culture for buying and enjoying buying home entertainment products, especially music. Whereas in the rest of the world there is a much more functional approach. That's why downloading and CD burning is bigger in the USA.

Is it very different in the rest of Europe?

We opened up in Germany in the early 1990s. It seemed to be a huge opportunity as it is the world's fourth largest market for recorded music. We thought if you had a proper specialist music format, they would love it. We believed it would work, but we found the appetite for this type of concept just didn't exist. British consumers, on the other hand, want to enjoy the shopping experience and find it more fulfilling.

How important are small labels to HMV?

They are very important to HMV. As a specialist it's vital that our stores carry a wide and diverse range that goes well beyond chart and mainstream releases. Small and independent labels provide the British music industry with much of its creativity and dynamism, and it's crtitical they are supported.

How do you decide what to stock?

The decision about which titles to stock comes from an interaction between our buyers and the record labels, and is based on anticipated demand from our customers. We have specialist buyers in each area whether it be dance or pop. Our Oxford Street store has to retain wide appeal among the broad cross-section of our customers. We build distinctively through retail environment. We have a great dance department with the latest vinyl releases, which are promoted with insightful handwritten recommendations. The buyers and assistants in store really know their stuff. But while all this is going on, the older customers might be shopping elsewhere in the store. This approach allows HMV to appeal to different customers at the same time and it's fair to say that our brand is likely to mean different things to each of them.

How do you see the future of the record store?

For the foreseeable future I see record stores as being at the heart of the record-buying process. Of course they need to adapt to a changing culture and ensure that they continue responding to the customers' requirements. People need to aspire to own a CD, it shouldn't just be a functional purchasing decision. Take our Oxford Street store again – you wouldn't believe some of the people who have played there and signed CDs and books for fans. Even Madonna has played there.

Will the CD die as online grows?
Forty per cent of our business takes place in the run up to Christmas, and much of that is gft buying. You can't wrap up a download and give it to someone as a present, like you can a CD. Of course there are some occasions when you want to use your iPod or you may want to burn an extra copy of a CD for your car, but the real fan will want to own the real thing, as it is part of the way they define themselves. People don't often talk about it, but CDs also say a lot about you. You put them on a shelf in your flat, because you want people to know what type of music you are into.

IAN DUTT – VITAL DISTRIBUTION

The day before we met Ian Dutt, Product Director for Vital Distribution (Sales & Marketing), news was spreading around the industry about 3MV Distribution going bankrupt. This news was extremely disturbing for many labels on the 3MV roster who could also face financial disaster. It also sent a shockwave through the music industry, adding to a sense of the vulnerability of the whole business. This type of news is becoming commonplace, whether it's a record label going out of business, or thousands of employees being made redundant. However, with such fear hanging in the air, it's refreshing to speak with Ian whose musicality, success and practical approach have established him as one of the leading executives in the business.

What do you think about 3MV going under?
Not good at all. I had quite a few friends working there – and in any case it's not good for anyone in the business.

Is your phone being bombarded with labels on their roster speaking to you?
Yes, it's gone crazy. My phone hasn't stopped ringing. For indie labels we're now truly the only independent distributor within the business.

What do you look for in a label before you agree to distribute them?
It's all about the music, then we look at the team and if they have the right

focus or finance backing. If it's a small label or artist with great product but very little resource then we may provide our support depending on its potential. For example, every label was knocking back The Darkness, but we loved them and supported them. It's also easier for me to take on a label if they have a history in the business or in breaking acts. It's good for us to do a campaign that shows who's going to plug [promote] the record, the financial support behind the act, etc. It's important for them to have a team in place that can deliver the overall results.

OK, so labels have to present themselves correctly to you, but how does Vital market itself within the industry?
Retail, be it the independents to HMV, Virgin and the supermarkets, etc. We are the only label who have a sales force who do their presentations using PowerPoint on computer laptops. This enables us to present the video as well as the music at the same time. It's great for everyone because retailers don't have product being left behind they don't want and the laptop enables them to see and hear the video at the same time.

With so many records being released each week how do you compete for retail space?
The key problem for retail is that there are too many records with hype being offered to them, resulting in it being hard for them to know what to believe and what to give space to. Therefore they tend to back the projects that have a big campaign behind them because they can see the mileage behind it.

Naturally labels want their records to be racked (displayed) in prime spots in the stores. How do you go about competing for such prime spots?
Every single square foot of a record store is bought. If you want to go in front of store you have to pay. Records don't go in store for nothing. Under the right circumstances if you're a small label and you don't have the cash flow we will pay this for you upfront and recoup it from sales.

What are the main battles for distributors?

Not selling the amount of records that we anticipated. You might have expected to sell 10,000, but only shifted 4,000. Then we have to sit down and create strategies on how we shift the balance. However, we have a pretty good system in place that enables us to gauge if we are going to shift 10,000 or a million.

What happens if you don't shift the 10,000 – do you discount the record?
Again that's the problem with the industry. Big records are discounted too quickly now; resulting in the whole perception of music losing its value.

Do you think record majors have a better machine to market records on an international basis?
I think what we do on an international level is much better than a major, because a major must work with its given partner in that territory who might not like the product. We work with about five or ten different companies in each territory. Therefore we will go with whoever is into the music and provides the best deal.

What's the key difference between Vital and major record companies with their own distribution?
We can sell 500 seven inches into real specialist but can also sell two million Moby albums, so we cover the full spectrum from key tastemakers' shops to multinational retailers. One of our strengths is that we have a very big sales team on the road and also we believe in breaking records from record shops rather than just focusing on marketing media hype. The industry is having problems because it relies too much on marketing hype rather than establishing a solid audience base. They seek a quick turnaround, so they can fulfil their quarterly financial targets, when in reality a record needs at least sixteen to twenty months to break or reach its peak. Record labels market way too early with massive campaigns, fly posters, when no one's even heard about the act. They should really focus on building the base and then allowing the record to grow and then add marketing at the right time. It's about understanding the record-buying threshold which can be broken down as follows:

- There are 2,000 avid, avid music opinion formers in this country who do not care what the media or chart says; they buy records they like. To target them you have to get the records into the right specialist stores.

- Once you hit these opinion formers then they tell ten or twenty of their friends etc., who will then go out and buy it from HMV or Virgin.
- Then you've got 10,000 avid music buyers who may still need a Jo Wiley, Pete Tong or Tim Westwood to play a tune to stimulate them into actually buying a record.
- Next we have the 60,000 audience. This is when the playlist and press become important and these groups need stimulation to go out and buy.
- After that we're focusing on the 300,000, which is when you're hitting crossover and the full media machine behind the record.
- Then after that it's one million and then you're becoming a household name.

The problem with labels is that they're marketing at the wrong thresholds; you can't market to that 2,000 or 10,000 that should come from record shops. Marketing should focus on the bigger threshold, but at first it's important they get the base right. This will then mean you have real substance (a fanbase) behind your campaign and not hype.

Looking at the future how do you think downloading will affect distribution?
The way things are now I don't think there will be physical distribution in five to ten years. People are showing their record collections on iPods, not take a look at this vinyl. However, having said this, I think labels are now slowly signing better-quality acts, which have substance and something different to offer. Maybe then we will see an increase in sales as fans have more of an emotional connection with their favourite group.

1
2
3
4
5
6
7
8
9
10
11
2
3
4
5

RECORD SHOPS

AINLEYS
10-12 The Haymarket, Leicester
LE1 3GD
T: 0116 262 0618 F: 0116 262 8271
Email: orders@ainleys.com
Website: ainleys.com
Mgr: Heidi Smith

ANDY CASH MUSIC
115 High St, Harborne, Birmingham
B17 9NP
T: 0121 427 8989 F: 0121 427 9949
Owner: Andy Cash

ASDA SOUTHBANK
Great Wilson Street, Leeds, West
Yorkshire LS11 5AD
T: 0113 241 8470 F: 0113 241 8785
Email: aspoffo@asda.co.uk
Website: asda.co.uk
Entertainment Devt. Mgr.: Andy
Spofforth

ATOMIC SOUNDS
26 Brunswick Rd, Shoreham by Sea, E.
Sussex BN43 5WB
T: 01273 464211 F: 01273 464211
Email: atomic1@fastnet.co.uk
Website: atomicsounds.co.uk
Owner: Tony Grist

AUDIOSONIC
6 College St, Gloucester, Glos. GL1 2NE
T: 01452 302280 F: 01452 302202
Website: audiosonic.uk.com
Owner: Sylvia Parker

AVALANCHE RECORDS
(Head Office) 2-3 Teviot Place,
Edinburgh EH1 2QZ
T: 0131 226 7666 F: 0131 226 4002
Email: avalanche.records@virgin.net
Website: avalancherecords.co.uk
Owner: Kevin Buckle

AVID RECORDS
32-33 The Triangle, Bournemouth
BH2 5SE
T: 01202 295465 F: 01202 295465
Email: martin@avidrecords-uk.com
Website: avidrecords-uk.com
Owner: Martin Howes

BADLANDS
11 St George's Place, Cheltenham, Glos
GL50 3LA
T: 01242 227724 F: 01242 227393
Email: shop@badlands.co.uk
Website: badlands.co.uk
MD: Philip Jump

BAILEY'S RECORDS
40 Bull Ring Indoor Market, Edgbaston
Street, Birmingham, West Midlands
B5 4RQ
T: 0121 622 6899 F: 0121 622 6899
Website: birminghamindoormarket.co.uk
Manager: David Rock

BARNEYS
21A Cross Keys, Market Square, St
Neots PE19 2AR
T: 01480 406270 F: 01480 406270
Email: keith.barnes2@btinternet.com
Keith Barnes

BATH COMPACT DISCS
11 Broad St, Bath BA1 5LJ
T: 01225 464766 F: 01225 482275
Email: Bathcds@btinternet.com
Website: bathcds.btinternet.co.uk
Co-owner: Steve Macallister

BEANOS LTD
7 Middle Street, Croydon, Surrey
CR0 1RE
T: 020 8680 1202 F: 020 8680 1203
Email: enquiries@beanos.co.uk
Website: beanos.co.uk
MD: David Lashmar

BLACK MARKET RECORDS
25 D'Arblay Street, London W1F 8EJ
T: 020 7287 1932 F: 020 7494 1303
Email: shop@blackmarket.co.uk
MD: David Piccioni

BLACKWELLS MUSIC SHOP
Beaver House, Hythe Bridge Street,
Oxford OX1 2ET
T: 01865 333122 F: 01865 790937
Email: vanessa.williams@blackwellsbookshops.co.uk

BOOGIETIMES RECORDS
3 Old Mill Parade, Victoria Rd, Romford,
Essex RM1 2HU
T: 01708 727029 F: 01708 740424
Email: info@boogietimes-records.co.uk
Website: boogietimes-records.co.uk
Manager: Andy James

BORDERS BOOKS, MUSIC & VIDEO
4th Floor, 122 Charing Cross Road,
London WC2 0JR
T: 020 7379 7313 F: 020 7836 0373
Website: bordersstores.co.uk

CHANGES ONE
58 Denham Drive, Seaton Delaval,
Whitley Bay, Tyne & Wear NE25 0JY
T: 0191 237 0251 F: 0191 298 0903
Email: ian@changesone.co.uk
Website: changesone.co.uk
Owner: Ian Tunstall

CITYSOUNDS LTD
5 Kirby Street, London EC1N 8TS
T: 020 7405 5454 F: 020 7242 1863
Email: sales@city-sounds.co.uk
Website: city-sounds.co.uk
Owners: Tom & Dave

CODA MUSIC
12 Bank Street, Edinburgh EH1 2LN
T: 0131 622 7246 F: 0131 622 7245
Email: enquiries@codamusic.demon.co.uk
Website: codamusic.co.uk
Co-owner: Dougie Anderson

CONNECT RECORDS
18 Badger Road, Coventry CV3 2PU
T: 07787 553192
Email: info@connect-records.com
Website: connect-records.com
Manager: Matt Green

CRUCIAL MUSIC
Pinery Buildings, Highmoor, Wigton,
Cumbria CA7 9LW
T: 016973 45422 F: 016973 45422
Email: simon@crucialmusicuk.co.uk
Website: crucialmusicuk.co.uk
MD: Simon James

CRUISIN' RECORDS
132 Welling High St, Welling, Kent
DA16 1TJ
T: 020 8304 5853 F: 020 8304 0429

Email: john@cruisin-records.fsnet.co.uk
Website: cruisinrecords.com
Owner: John Setford

DANCE 2 RECORDS
9 Woodbridge Road, Guildford, Surrey
GU1 4PU
T: 01483 451002 F: 01483 451003
Email: info@dance2.co.uk
Website: dance2.co.uk
MD: Hans Vind

DISC-N-TAPE
17 Gloucester Road, Bishopston, Bristol
BS7 8AA
T: 0117 942 2227 F: 0117 942 2227
Email: graeme@disc-n-tape.co.uk
Website: disc-n-tape.co.uk
Owner: Graeme Cornish

DISKY.COM
3 York Street, St. Helier, Jersey, Channel
Islands JE2 3RQ
T: 01534 768860 F: 01534 729525
Email: music@disky.com
Website: disky.com
Manager: Robert Bisson

DISQUE LTD
11 Chapel Market, Islington, London
N1 9EZ
T: 020 7833 1104 F: 020 7278 4895
Email: info@disque.co.uk
Website: disque.co.uk
MD: Ed Davies

EARWAVES RECORDS
9/11 Paton St, Piccadilly, Manchester
M1 2BA
T: 0161 236 4022 F: 0161 237 5932
Email: info@earwavesrecords.co.uk
Website: earwavesrecords.co.uk
Proprietor: Alan Lacy

EASTERN BLOC RECORDS
5-6 Central Buildings, Oldham Street,
Manchester M1 1JG
T: 0161 228 6432 F: 0161 228 6728
Email: info@easternblocrecords.co.uk
Website: easternblocrecords.co.uk
Mgr: John Berry

EASY LISTENING MUSIC
224 Stratford Road, Shirley, Solihull,
Birmingham, West Midlands B90 5EH
T: 0121 733 6663 F: 0121 733 6663
John Corbett

FAB MUSIC
55 The Broadway, Crouch End, London
N8 8DT
T: 020 8347 6767 F: 020 8348 3270
Email: fab@fabmusic.co.uk
Directors: Mal Page/Kevin Payne

FAT CITY RECORDS
20 Oldham St, Manchester M1 1JN
T: 0161 237 1181 F: 0161 236 9304
Email: shop@fatcity.co.uk
Website: fatcity.co.uk
Manager: Mark Torkington

FLIP RECORDS
2 Mardol, Shrewsbury SY1 1PY
T: 01743 244469 F: 01743 260985
Email: sales@fliprecords.co.uk
Website: fliprecords.co.uk
Owner: Duncan Morris

FLYING RECORDS
94 Dean Street, London W1D 3TA
T: 020 7734 0172 F: 020 7287 0766
Email: info@flyingrecords.com
Website: flyingrecords.com
Manager: Anthony Cox

RETAIL

FOPP LTD
Head Office, 1/2 Sciennes Gardens,
Edinburgh EH9 1NR
T: 0131 668 4220
Email: info@fopp.co.uk
Website: fopp.co.uk

FOREST RECORDS
7,Earley Court, High Street, Lymington,
Hampshire SO41 9EP
T: 01590 676588 F: 01590 612162
Email: forestrec@btopenworld.com
Buyer: Neil Hutson

GATEFIELD SOUNDS
163-165 High Street, Herne Bay, Kent
CT6 5AQ
T: 01227 374759 F: 01227 374759
MD: Mike Winch

GOLDEN DISCS 3
Bow Street Mall, Lisburn, Co Antrim
BT28 1AW
T: 02892 660566 F: 02892 605711
Email: paulbdevine@hotmail.com
General Manager: Paul Devine

GOLDEN DISCS 4
29 Donegall Place, Belfast BT1 5AB
T: 02890 322653 F: 02890 439670
Email: paulbdevine@hotmail.com
General Manager: Paul Devine

HMV GROUP PLC
Shelley House, 2-4 York Road,
Maidenhead, Berkshire SL6 1SR
T: 01628 818300 F: 01628 818301
Email: firstname.lastname@hmvgroup.com
Website: hmv.co.uk
CEO: Alan Giles

HMV UK LTD
Film House, 142 Wardour Street,
London W1F 8LN
T: 020 7432 2000 F: 020 7434 1090
Email: firstname.lastname@hmv.co.uk
Website: hmv.co.uk :

J SAINSBURY
33 Holborn, London EC1N 2HT
T: 020 7695 4295 F: 020 7695 4295
Email: julian.monaghan@sainsburys.co.uk
Website: sainsbury.co.uk Music
Manager: Julian Monaghan

JIBBERING RECORDS
136 Alcester Rd, Moseley, Birmingham
B13 8EE
T: 0121 449 4551
Email: info@jibberingrecords.com
Website: jibberingrecords.com
Owner: Dan Raffety

JUNE EMERSON WIND MUSIC
Windmill Farm, Ampleforth, York
YO62 4HF
T: 01439 788324 F: 01439 788715
Email: JuneEmerson@compuserve.com
Prop: June Emerson

KEN PALK RECORDS
The Shopping Centre, Bramhall,
Stockport, Cheshire SK7 1AW
T: 0161 439 8479 F: 0161 439 0653
Email: Sales@KenPalk.co.uk
Website: KenPalk.co.uk

KINGBEE RECORDS
519 Wilbraham Road, Chorlton-Cum-
Hardy, Manchester M21 0UF
T: 0161 860 4762 F: 0161 860 4762
Les Hare

MASSIVE RECORDS
30 Stephenson St, Birmingham B2 4BH
T: 0121 633 4477 F: 0121 632 5935
Email: info@massiverecords.com
Website: massiverecords.com
Manager: Dan Gilbert

MDC CLASSIC MUSIC LTD
124 Camden High St, London NW1 0LU
T: 020 7485 4777 F: 020 7482 6888
Email: info@mdcmusic.co.uk
Website: mdcmusic.co.uk
Dir: Alan Goulden

MORNING AFTER MUSIC
Llyfnant House Shop, 22 Penrallt Street, Machynlleth, Powys SY20 8AJ
T: 01654 703767
Propietor: Malcolm Hume

PICCADILLY RECORDS
Unit G9, Smithfield Buildings, 53 Oldham Street, Manchester M1 1JR
T: 0161 834 8888 F: 0161 839 8008
Email: mail@piccadillyrecords.com
Website: piccadillyrecords.com
MD: John Kerfoot

PIED PIPER RECORDS
293 Wellingborough Rd, Northampton NN1 4EW
T: 01604 624777 F: 01604 624777
Email: piedpiperrecords@aol.com
Website: pied-piper-records.co.uk
Prop: Nick Hamlyn

PLASTIC FANTASTIC RECORDS
35 Drury Lane, Covent Garden, London WC2B 5RH
T: 020 7240 8055 F: 020 7240 7628
Email: shop@plasticfantastic.co.uk
Website: plasticfantastic.co.uk
Manager: Oliver MacGregor

PRELUDE RECORDS
25B Giles St, Norwich NR2 1JN
T: 01603 628319 F: 01603 620170
Email: admin@preluderecords.co.uk
Website: preluderecords.co.uk
Partner: Andrew Cane

RAPTURE RECORDS
37-38 St John's St, Colchester, Essex CO2 7AD
T: 01206 542541 F: 01206 542546
Email: john@rapturerecords.com
Website: rapturerecords.com
Prop: John Parkhurst

REGGAE REVIVE
26 Chamberlayne Rd, London NW10 3JD
T: 020 8968 0259 F: 020 8968 0259
Email: reggae.revive@virgin.net
Website: reggaerevive.com
Owner: Bob Brooks

SEEDS RECORDS
7 Oxton Rd, Charing Cross, Birkenhead CH41 2QQ
T: 0151 653 4224 F: 0151 653 3223
Email: lee@seedsrecords.co.uk
Website: seedsrecords.co.uk
Mgr: Lee Hessler

SLOUGH RECORD CENTRE
241-243 Farnham Rd, Slough, Berks SL2 1DE
T: 01753 528194 F: 01753 692110
Email: sloughrecords@btconnect.com
Website: sloughrecords.co.uk
Sales: Terry & Simon

TESCO STORES LTD
PO Box 44, Cirrus Building C, Shire Park, Welwyn Garden City, Herts AL7 1ZR
T: 01992 632222 F: 01707 297690
Website: tesco.com
Snr Buying Mgr, Music: Alan Hunt

TOWNSEND RECORDS
30 Queen Street, Great Harwood, Lancashire BB6 7QQ
T: 01254 887005 F: 01254 887835
Email: admin@townsend-records.co.uk
Website: townsend-records.co.uk
Owner: Steve Bamber

TOWNSEND RECORDS (2)
119 Towngate, Leyland, Lancashire PR5 1LQ
T: 01772 455265 F: 01772 455265
Email: sales@townsend-records.co.uk
Manager: Glen Melling

VIRGIN ENTERTAINMENT GROUP LTD
The School House, 50 Brook Green, London W6 7RR
T: 020 8752 9000 F: 020 8752 9001
Website: virgin.com
CEO, Virgin Ent. Group: Simon Wright

WATERSIDE MUSIC
1 Waterside House, The Plains, Totnes, Devon TQ9 5DW
T: 01803 867947
Prop: John Cooper

WHITELABEL RECORDS
4,Colomberie, St Helier, Jersey, Channel Islands JE2 4QB
T: 01534 725256 F: 01534 780956
Email: info@whitelabelrecords.co.uk
Website: whitelabelrecords.co.uk
Owner: Mal White

WOOLWORTHS PLC
Woolworth House, 242-246 Marylebone Road, London NW1 6JL
T: 020 7262 1222 F: 020 7706 5975
Email: firstname.lastname@woolworths.co.uk
Website: woolworths.co.uk

HIGHLY RECOMMENDED DISTRIBUTORS

Vital

Pinnancle Records

Amoto Distribution

Essential Exports

1

2

3

4

5

6

7

8

9

10

11

12

13

14

15

DIY

CUTTING AND RELEASING YOUR OWN RECORD

BY DOMINIC SPREADLOVE

DJ Dominic Spreadlove has been playing internationally for over fifteen years, and is now resident on London House 88.6FM. Dominic also provides a consultancy service for those who want to release their own labels.

So you've finally produced your drum n bass masterpiece. Now what do you do? Well, there's no set route to take but there are lots of things to avoid if you decide to manufacture and distribute your own record.

THE MIX-DOWN

First, make sure your track is mixed down well enough to play out in the clubs. The best way is to play or mix it in with some other tracks already on vinyl so you can compare the sound quality. Do this either on a home DJ setup or, if you can, get it played in a club. Be careful how many CDs you send out – and to whom you send them – as the more there are, the more you stand the chance of someone bootlegging it before you get it out. You'll hear straight away if the levels are wrong or the tops are too high. It may be worth spending more money in a better studio used to doing mix-downs to get the desired sound on your track. This should cost around £250 for one day. Use a local paper to find a studio or ask around the local DJs.

MASTERING

The next stage is getting your track mastered onto lacquer and then into a 12-inch vinyl single. The cut is the first of a three-stage process that you have to go through to get your track from CD to vinyl. This basically transfers the sound file from the master tape or CD by playing it through a system that sends it to the cutting head of a lathe which in turn cuts a stereo groove into the surface of a 14-inch lacquer- or acetone-covered metal disk.

There is one cut for each side of the record. You will need to ensure that the quality is as close to perfect as possible. Any more minor adjustments may then be made in the cutting room while you are there. If you intend to have more than one track on either side of the record, ensure they are in the correct order on the master: once you start to cut a groove you cannot stop to change tracks as the groove has to be cut continuously, end to end.

This will then be boxed very carefully by the engineer and sent to the plate-making stage, the second part of the process. Each lacquer is taken out of the box and coated with a silver nitrate liquid and then clipped groove side face down to a circular piece of silver nickel. It is then placed on a spindle and immersed in a bath of acid and electroplated until a ridge is formed on the metal in an exact negative copy of the groove. This is then repeated once more and the end product is a master plate from which the stampers are produced. Stampers are made every 2,000 or so runs of vinyl as they wear out, due to the heavy-duty pressure involved in the next pressing stage.

Next the stampers are placed onto a pressing machine, one for each side. Then a molten puck or biscuit of lacquer is placed on a spindle. Then the labels are placed on either side and this is then squashed in between the two stampers at over a ton per sq. inch until the whole cut surface is evenly pressed with the groove. The rough edges are then cut off and it is dropped onto another spindle to cool down while kept flat.

TEST PRESSINGS

You will always need to do at least ten to twenty test pressings (TPs) to ensure you are totally happy before the main run goes on. I learned the hard way and my first release jumped on one side due to the bass in a groove curving without enough room in between each groove. Instead of doing TPs, I was over keen to get it out and ended up with 500 jumping 12 inches. Luckily for me, I still sold out because the main mix was OK, but I learned not to rush things from then on.

My best advice is to use a broker to do your first release. There are lots of manufacturing broker companies that will take on your job from start to finish and still be cheaper because they can get very good prices due to the sheer volume of work they send to the manufacturers. You will be able to attend the actual cut for a small extra charge but it's well worth doing this to ensure you are happy with the sound quality as it is cut.

Once you have received your TPs, you will need to sit and listen to each side a couple of times end to end. Listen out for any pops or unnecessary surface noise and ensure that the 12 inch sits totally flat on the platter with no warps or uneven parts of the record. Once you are happy with it, maybe even compare the volume level with another similar-sounding 12 inch from your collection to see if the levels are nice and loud.

While this is being done you should have already made a start on having your labels designed and printed to save time so they are ready to send to the plant ready for the main run of records. Most high street printers will be able to do this but the broker will also have companies they use specially for this.

PROMOTING YOUR RECORD

Use the TPs to promote and build up a buzz of interest in your product before the release date. Depending on the style of music, the best way to do this is to use DJ friends who play on your local pirate or Internet station, and of course in the clubs. It's always better if you take the promos to each DJ by hand. Make sure you have a cover letter giving the name of the tracks, release date and any contact info to get feedback from them. Also make the DJ aware that they have a very limited exclusive before everyone else and that should ensure they play it to the maximum, which in turn should help build the interest in the track.

The other way to do this is to use a promotions company to send a copy to all the DJs on their mailing list and to radio stations who in turn have to fill out a reaction form and a chart of tracks they are currently playing. This is fairly costly due to postal costs and their administration charges, but if you are sure the track has potential then it can be well worth the extra outlay. You will get copies of all the reaction sheets and be able to see if they are playing it. It may also get some of the major labels to hear it and possibly get some interest from one to sign it and release it. This is your ultimate aim as it will help you get your name about for future releases.

DISTRIBUTION

The next stage is to find a distributor for your track. You may choose to do this yourself but although in the long run you'll earn more money, it's a lot more work running around collecting money and delivering stock to the shops. If you use a distributor they will probably take, say, 100 copies at first on sale or return. This means that after a while you will get any copies not sold given back and only pay for the ones sold. This is why it's very important to ensure the promotion is in full flow before the release of the record to the shops. Timing with this is so important if you want to make the best impact once it's reached the shops. You may be lucky enough to have a track that just sells out of the shops with no promotion at all, but that's unlikely.

If you do have some success with the first release then make sure you keep using the system you find works the best. Keep working hard on improving the quality of your music and put your money back into each release or towards new equipment.

Note: You may contact **Dominic.spreadlove@hotmail.com** for professional consultation to help you through your first releases.

MANUFACTURING (PRESSING)

HIGHLY RECOMMENDED MANUFACTURING

Many Indie labels work with a broker for their manufacturing needs. A broker handles all the stages of producing the finished product including split deliveries and communicating with their distributor to ensure release dates are met. They have an important part to play by making sure all parts of the production are correct and delivered in time for the next stage of production. Operating between the factories and the label/distributor. Artwork is checked to avoid printing problems as a lot of designers do not understand the printing process.

- **AGR MANUFACTURING**
- **IMPRESS**
- **COPS**
- **KEY PRODUCTIONS**

AGR MANUFACTURING LTD
Suite 5, Melville House, High Street, Great Dunmow, Essex CM6 1AF
T: 01371 859 393 F: 01371 859 375
Email: info@agrm.co.uk
Website: agrm.co.uk
Production Director: Ed Jones

ALL THAT DUPLICATION
59 Sutherland Place, London W2 5BY
T: 020 7229 1779
Email: info@allthat.co.uk
Website: allthat.co.uk
Mgr: Darren Tai

ARMCO
Units 1 & 2, Forest Ind Park, Forest Road, Hainault, Essex IG6 3HL
T: 020 8500 1981 F: 020 8501 1319
Email: armco@globalnet.co.uk
Website: armco.co.uk
MD: Jan Fonseca

AUDIO SERVICES LTD (ASL)
6 Orsman Road, London N1 5JQ
T: 020 7739 9672 F: 020 7739 4070
Email: asl@audio-services.co.uk
Website: audio-services.co.uk
General Manager: Mel Gale

BLUECREST INTERNATIONAL LTD
272 Field End Rd, Eastcote, Ruislip, Middx HA4 9NA
T: 020 8582 0230 F: 020 8582 0232
Email: info@bluecrest.com
Website: bluecrest.com

CD AND CASSETTE DUPLICATION LTD
77 Barlow Road, Stannington, Sheffield, South Yorkshire S6 5HR
T: 0114 233 0033 F: 0114 233 0033
MD: Ian Stead

CD CENTRAL LTD
3 Grange Yard, London SE1 3AG
T: 020 7231 4805 F: 020 7237 0633
Email: sales@riverproaudio.co.uk
Website: cdcentral.ltd.co.uk
Joel Monger

CHAMELEON DEVELOPMENTS LTD
1 North Terrace, Sawston, Cambridge CB2 4EJ
T: 01223 832536 F: 01223 832537
Email: chameleon-d@btconnect.com
Website: chameleon-developments.com
MD: Tash Cox

CINE WESSEX
Westway House, St Thomas Street, Winchester, Hampshire SO23 9HJ
T: 01962 865454 F: 01962 842017
Email: info@cinewessex.co.uk
Website: cinewessex.co.uk
Duplication Manager: Ema Branton

COPS
The Studio, Kent House Station Approach, Barnmead Road, Beckenham, Kent BR3 1JD
T: 020 8778 8556 F: 020 8676 9716
Email: info@cops.co.uk
Website: cops.co.uk
Managing Director: Jeremy Dahdi

CUTGROOVE LTD (VINYL PRESSING AGENCY)
101 Bashley Rd, Park Royal, London NW10 6TE
T: 020 8838 8270 F: 020 8838 2012
Email: nikki@cutgroove.com
Website: intergroove.co.uk
Manager: Nikki Howarth

CVB DUPLICATION
179A Bilton Road, Perivale, Middlesex
UB6 7HQ
T: 020 8991 2610 F: 020 8997 0180
Email: sales@cvbduplication.co.uk
Website: cvbduplication.co.uk
Sales & Marketing: Phil Stringer

DELUXE GLOBAL MEDIA SERVICES LTD
Southwater Southwater Business Park,
Worthing Road, Southwater, West
Sussex RH13 9YT
T: 01403 739600 F: 01403 739601
Email: sales@disctronics.com
Website: disctronics.com; bydeluxe.com

DOCDATA UK LTD
Halesfield 14, Telford, Shropshire
TF7 4QR
T: 01952 680131 F: 01952 583501
Email: uksales@docdata.com
Website: docdata.co.uk
Sales Director: Martine Tatman

EURODISC MANUFACTURING LTD
1st floor, Howard House, The Runway,
South Ruslip, Middlessex, HA4 6SE,
T:0208.839.0060 F: 020 8845 6679
Email: info@eurodisc w euro-disc.co.uk

FILTERBOND LTD
19 Sadlers Way, Hertford, Hertfordshire
SG14 2DZ
T: 01992 500101 F: 01992 500101
Email: jbsrecords.filterbondltd@virgin.net
MD: John B Schefel

HEATHMANS
7 Heathmans Road, London SW6 4TJ
T: 020 7371 0978 F: 020 7371 9360
Website: heathmans.co.uk
MD: Ronnie Garrity

ICC DUPLICATION
Unit 27, Hawthorn Road Industrial Est,
Eastbourne, East Sussex BN23 6QA
T: 01323 647880 F: 01323 643095
Email: info@iccduplication.co.uk
Website: iccduplication.co.uk
Operations Dir: Andy Thorpe

ICON MARKETING LTD
Park House, 27 South Avenue, Thorpe
St Andrew, Norwich NR7 0EZ
T: 01603 708050 F: 01603 708005
Email: Icon@dircon.co.uk
Website: icon-marketing.co.uk
Production Manager: Sarah Neve

IMPRESS MUSIC LTD
Unit 5C, Northfield Industrial Estate,
Beresford Avenue, Wembley, Middx
HA0 1NW
T: 020 8795 0101 F: 020 8795 0303
Email: info@impressmusic-uk.com
Website: impressmusic-uk.com
Chairman: Alastair Bloom

ISIS DUPLICATING CO
Unit 11 Shaftesbury Ind Centre, The
Runnings, Cheltenham, Gloucestershire
GL51 9NH
T: 01242 571818 F: 01242 571315
Sales Mgr: Glyn Ellis Evans

JTS
73 Digby Road, London E9 6HX
T: 020 8985 3000 F: 020 8986 7688
Email: sales@jts-uk.com
Website: jts-uk.com
Studio Mgr: Keith Jeffrey

KEY PRODUCTION
8 Jeffreys Place, London NW1 9PP
T: 020 7284 8800 F: 020 7284 8844
Email: mail@keyproduction.co.uk
Website: keyproduction.co.uk
Sales & Marketing: Melodie Greenwell

KEYNOTE AUDIO SERVICES LTD
Smoke Tree House, Tilford Rd, Farnham, Surrey GU10 2EN
T: 01252 794253 F: 01252 792642
Email: admin@keynoteaudio.co.uk
Website: keynoteaudio.co.uk
MD: Tim Wheatley

KMS
79 Fortess Road, Kentish Town, London NW5 1AG
T: 020 7482 4555 F: 020 7482 4551
Email: kms@kudosrecords.co.uk
Director: Danny Ryan

LOGICOM SOUND AND VISION
Portland House, 1 Portland Drive, Willen, Milton Keynes, Buckinghamshire MK15 9JW
T: 01908 663848 F: 01908 666654
Email: grayham.amos@luk.net
Website: luk.net
Bus Dev Mgr: Grayham Amos

LYNIC GROUP PLC
645 Ajax Avenue, Slough, Berkshire SL1 4BG
T: 01753 786200 F: 01753 786201
Email: trevors@lynic.com
Website: lynic.com
Business Developement Mgr: Trevor Southam

MAP MUSIC LTD
46 Grafton Road, London NW5 3DU
T: 020 7916 0545 F: 020 7284 4232
Email: info@mapmusic.net
Website: mapmusic.net
MD: Chris Townsend

METRO BROADCAST LTD
53 Great Suffolk Street, London SE1 0DB
T: 020 7928 2088 F: 020 7202 2001
Email: info@metrobroadcast.co.uk
Website: metrobroadcast.co.uk
Mktg Exec: Joanna Heaviside

MPO UK LTD
Unit 3-4, Nucleus Central Way, Park Royal, London NW10 7XT
T: 020 8963 6888 F: 020 8963 6841
Email: info@MPO.co.uk
Website: MPO.co.uk
Audio Sales Manager: Lisa Dickenson

MUSIC MEDIA MANUFACTURERS LTD
Unit F11D, 1st Floor, Parkhall Road Trading Estate, 40 Martell Road, London SE21 8EN
T: 020 8265 6364 F: 020 8265 6423
Email: mail@musicmedia-uk.com
Website: musicmedia-uk.com
GM: Mike Spenser

OFFSIDE MANAGEMENT
Unit A, 16-24 Brewery Road, London N7 9NH
T: 020 7700 2662 F: 020 7700 2882
Email: info@bsimerch.com
Website: bsimerch.com
Sales Director: Richard Cassar

OPEN EAR PRODUCTIONS LTD
Kinarva, Co. Galway, Ireland
T: +353 91 635810
F: +353 87 58575588
Email: info@openear.ie
Website: openear.ie
MD: Bruno Staehelin

REPEAT PERFORMANCE RPM
Unit 6, Grand Union Centre, West Row, London W10 5AS
T: 020 8960 7222 F: 020 8968 1378
Email: info@rpmuk.com
Website: rpmuk.com
MD: Robin Springall

RMS STUDIOS
43-45 Clifton Road, London SE25 6PX
T: 020 8653 4965 F: 020 8653 4965
Duplicating Mgr: Alan Jones

RTS ONESTOP
Unit M2, Albany Road, Prescot, Merseyside L34 2UP
T: 0151 430 9001 F: 0151 430 7441
Email: rts.onestop@virgin.net
MD: John Fairclough

SDC GB LTD
Fairview Business Cent., 29-31 Clayton Rd, Hayes, Middx UB3 1AN
T: 020 8581 9200 F: 020 8581 9249
Email: sales@sdcuk.com
Website: sdc-group.com
Sales Mgr: Colin Rye

SONOPRESS (UK)
Wednesbury One Business Park, Black Country New Rd, Wednesbury, West Midlands WS10 7NY
T: 0121 502 7800 F: 0121 502 7811
Email: sales@sonopress.co.uk
Website: sonopress.co.uk
Audio Business Dev't Mgr: Anthony Daly

SOUND DISCS LTD
5 Barley Shotts Business Park, 246 Acklam Road, (off St Ervans Rd), London W10 5YG
T: 020 8968 7080 F: 020 8968 7475
Email: sound.discs@virgin.net
Website: sound-discs.co.uk
Production Director: Peter Bullick

SOUNDS GOOD LTD
12 Chiltern Enterprise Centre, Station Rd, Theale, Berks RG7 4AA
T: 0118 930 1700 F: 0118 930 1709
Email: sales-info@sounds-good.co.uk
Website: sounds-good.co.uk
Dir: Martin Maynard

SPONGE MULTIMEDIA LTD
Sponge Studios, Cross Chancellor Street, Leeds, West Yorkshire LS6 2TG
T: 0113 234 0004 F: 0113 242 4296
Email: damian@spongestudios.demon.co.uk
Website: spongestudios.demon.co.uk
Director: Damian McLean-Brown

TECHNICOLOR
Llantarnam Park, Cwmbran, Gwent NP44 3AB
T: 01633 465259 F: 01633 867799
Email: technicolor.europe@thomson.net
Website: technicolor.com
Dir, Optical Disc: Emil Dudek

TELECINE LTD
Video House, 48 Charlotte St, London W1T 2NS
T: 020 7208 2200 F: 020 7208 2252

Email: shortform@telecine.co.uk
Website: telecine.co.uk
Head of Shortform: Claire Booth

TRIBAL MANUFACTURING
11 Hillgate Place, Balham Hill, London
SW12 9ER
T: 020 8673 0610 F: 020 8675 8562
Email: sales@tribal.co.uk
Website: tribal.co.uk
Directors: Alison Wilson, Terry Woolner

UNIMAGNETIC EUROPE
3 King Edward Drive, Chessington,
Surrey KT9 1DW
T: 020 8391 9406 F: 020 8391 8924
Email: tony@meltones.com
Website: meltones.com
Sales/Mkt Dir: Tony Fernandez

VDC GROUP
VDC House, South Way, Wembley,
Middlesex HA9 0HB
T: 020 8903 3345 F: 020 8900 1427
Email: enquiries@vdcgroup.com
Website: vdcgroup.com
Sales Executive: Aaron Williamson

WARNER MUSIC MANUFACTURING EUROPE
77 Oxford Street, London W1D 2ES
T: 020 7659 2530 F: 020 7659 2100
Email: sam.menezes@warnermusic.com
Website: wmme.co.uk
UK Sales & Marketing Mgr: Sam Menezes

1
2
3
4
5
6
7
8
9
10
11
12
13
14
15

1

2

3

4

5

6

7

8

9

10

1

2

3

4

5

SETTING UP A RECORD LABEL

FROM A FINANCIAL POINT OF VIEW

BY GERAINT HOWELLS

Geraint joined Willott Kingston Smith in November 1997 as a partner responsible for a portfolio of clients in the music and entertainment industries. He fulfils the role of financial adviser to his client base who consult him on commercial, taxation and general business issues. Geraint also lectures to a variety of audiences on raising finance, copyright issues, intellectual property and other aspects of the music industry.

Setting up and running a new record label is not just about finding the right artists and doing the right promotion. Planning and good administration can be the difference between success and failure.

SETTING UP A LABEL

TO INCORPORATE OR NOT TO INCORPORATE

First you need to think about what type of entity you are going to use to conduct the business. There are two main options: operating as a sole trader/partnership or running everything through a limited company.

If you operate as a sole trader you are the business and the business is you. This means that it is very easy to take any money you make out of the business. You will be taxed under Schedule D case I as a self-employed individual and will have to file accounts and a tax return with the Inland Revenue. The onus of reporting is minimised and you will have the least amount of legal requirements in the way you administer your business. As long as you file your tax return on time and keep enough money aside to pay whatever income tax bill arises, you should be fine.

Or will you be? A significant number of record labels that are formed follow a simple life cycle: they are formed, they lose a lot of money and are closed down. However, as a sole trader you are the business. So if it owes a lot of money, you owe a lot of money. You cannot just close it down. You will still owe the money. This means that creditors of the business could claim payment of their debt from your other assets or income streams, even your house!

Granted there are some other benefits: being able to offset those inevitable early business losses against any other income you may have had in up to the last three years, resulting in a repayment of income tax is one for instance. However, the risk of putting your personal assets and income streams at risk in my opinion is not worth it.

A partnership is very similar to a sole trader except with more than one person involved. It has all the same pros and cons as detailed above: low reporting, access to profits, risk, etc. There are a couple of further considerations, however. You will have to file a partnership tax return as well as one for each of the partners. Again, however, the reporting is far less onerous than it would be for a company. However, because of the nature of a partnership, there are a number of other considerations. In a partnership all partners are jointly and separately liable. This means that the risks are the same as detailed above for a sole trader. You might think that if there were five partners, for example, and the business folded owing a large amount of money, you would owe a fifth of the amount owed. Unfortunately that is not the case. Each partner is potentially liable for all of the debts. Each partner would pay his or her share of the liability but if one partner could not meet their share, you might be responsible for that too. For this and many other reasons, in a partnership you will always be reliant on the integrity of your partners.

The solution to this is to have a partnership agreement drawn up and signed by all parties. By entering into a legally binding contract, which sets out what each partner can and cannot do, you may be able to mitigate some but not all of the risk.

The other choice is to form a limited company. A limited company is a separate legal entity. This means that shareholders and directors will not be held accountable for the debt of the company,* thus providing the ultimate protection against any personal financial exposure.

If you operate through a limited company, there are certain tax advantages. First, the company is charged corporation tax on the profits rather than paying income tax on the profits. Currently, corporation tax is at a much lower rate than the income tax and National Insurance would be on similar profits for a sole trader or partnership. The company pays corporation tax and then you pay nothing further unless you actually take money out of the company. If you do this by virtue of a dividend (once the company is making profits) you will find that in the vast majority of cases, the total tax paid will still be significantly less than the income tax and NI would have been were you a sole trader. Obviously the tax planning involved can be complex and you would be advised to seek advice from a tax adviser in any case. The point is that you have many more options for tax planning when you have a limited company than when you operate as a sole trader/partnership and hence there is more scope for dramatically reducing your tax bills. This will also be especially true when you come to sell the business at the end of its life. In these cases, the limited company will provide an enormous benefit in terms of tax savings.

A limited company has other more esoteric advantages too. Simply by being a limited company, there is created a perception of greater size and scale. You may find that it will be easier to get credit with suppliers and gain contacts through corporate memberships of trade bodies and other organisations.

**This assumes that the directors have acted in a lawful manner and are not found guilty of deliberately running the company while it is insolvent.*

The real downside is administration and cost. There is a cost in having the company formed. Further costs will be incurred due to your corporate status, as we explain below.

There is no doubt that there is a greater burden of reporting upon a company to bodies such as Companies House as well as the Inland Revenue. A company has to file a company tax return and statutory accounts must be filed at Companies House. The directors of the company will also have to file their own personal tax returns. In addition, any changes in directors, company secretary, shareholdings, registered office and accounting date, among other things, must be approved at a meeting of shareholders/directors and minuted by company law. Some of these changes then have to be formalised and submitted to Companies House. This additional administration leads to greater cost as well. Usually you would need an accountant to review the accounts to ensure they comply with the requirements of the Companies Act and accounting standards; to prepare the corporation tax computations and returns; and to deal with the various company secretarial matters including reporting to Companies House. The additional cost compared to being a sole trader can be significant. If the turnover of the company is greater than £5.6 million and the gross assets are more than £2.8 million the statutory accounts will also need to be audited (thresholds as at 1 April 2004).

Having looked at the arguments for and against, in most cases I would advise anyone serious about starting a record label to do it through a company. Record labels are notoriously risky enterprises and therefore you need that extra protection. However, where perhaps it is something that is going to begin part time and slowly grow in size, it may be worth beginning as self-employed and then incorporating later once the business starts to grow. In this way, you could make use of the tax benefits associated with early years losses that I mentioned above. Most importantly, however, do not take my word for it. Talk to a professional because every situation is different and they will be able to give you specific advice for you and your business needs.

THE SHAREHOLDERS' AGREEMENT

Assuming that the decision has been made to opt for a limited company as the vehicle through which to run the label, what is the next step?

Before the company starts signing artists and recording anything there are still some further administrative hurdles that need to be dealt with. The first is the shareholders' agreement. The section above talked about the partnership agreement and there are many similarities in the purpose and principles of a partnership agreement and the shareholders' agreement. The fundamental concept of both documents is to set out what is expected and required of those who have chosen to invest together and to ensure that no one party can act in a manner detrimental to other investors or partners or the business entity as a whole.

When drafting a partnership agreement, however, there is not so much regulation and strict organisation to contend with. Company law requires far more reporting and since the company is a separate legal entity, provisions need to be made to ensure that all shareholders' rights will be maintained, especially those with minority holdings.

For example, X Limited is a company owned by three shareholders. Mr Smith is a director and holds 55% of the shares. He is the principal driving force in the business with all of the contacts in the industry and the expertise. He needed financial backing, however, and this was provided by Mr Jones who received 25% of the issued shares and Mr Richards who received 20% of the shares. Now let us assume that there is no agreement in place. Mr Smith as the director and holder of the majority of the shares could do whatever he liked with the company, outvoting the others at any shareholder's meeting. He could for instance decide to increase his salary, leaving very little or no funds left to pay dividends to his financial backers. The opportunities for him to benefit personally from his dominant position are enormous.

What is put in the agreement are clauses that state that certain issues must be voted on or agreed by all shareholders rather than a majority, such as issues regarding winding up, sale of shares, remuneration for the director, dividend policy, etc. This puts in a layer of protection so that all of the rights of the shareholders are protected.

Obviously, all parties should get independent legal advice before undertaking any such agreement.

VALUE ADDED TAX (VAT) REGISTRATION

Once the company is formed, it can apply at any point thereafter to be registered for VAT. When should you register? Do you have to register at all?

It is compulsory to be registered for VAT when the company's turnover in the previous twelve months or any shorter period has exceeded the VAT registration limit. At the time of writing (2003/4 tax year), that limit is £56,000. You are also obliged to register for VAT if you believe that your turnover for the next thirty days will exceed this limit. However, you may avoid registration even though you have exceeded the thirty-day limit, provided that you can demonstrate that your turnover will be less than the deregistration limit (currently £53,000), for the following twelve months.

Once you have registered, you will have to charge VAT on all of your taxable supplies (in the case of the record industry this will usually be on all supplies except where you are exporting goods or services to other countries, though specific advice should be obtained as the rules are complex). Generally, you will be able to reclaim the VAT suffered on all business expenses except for certain costs especially those deemed to be entertaining.

So, should you register straight away even though you almost certainly will not be immediately over the registration limit?

The advantage is that you can reclaim any VAT suffered on expenses. This will probably be a significant amount of money (17.5% of the cost of VAT-able expenses). Some of the expenses that would have a VAT element that can be reclaimed are: telephone, professional fees, studio costs, equipment and production costs. If the label is short of funds at the start of its life a refund cheque from HM Customs may well come in handy!

Probably the most important factor to consider when deciding whether you should register is who will you be invoicing when you sell your product. If you invoice and receive money from another business that is also VAT registered, be it another record label, a collection society or a retail outlet, then they will not mind being invoiced for £x + 17.5% VAT because they can claim the VAT back like you do with your expenses. Since you receive up front from the customer the extra amount, which needs to be paid to HM Customs, you will never lose out and indeed will gain from being registered by whatever the amounts of VAT you can reclaim for your expenses. However, if you sell a large amount direct to the public, you will have a problem. They cannot reclaim the VAT you charge them on top of your usual price. To them it is simply another expense. This could influence the amount you sell.

The other problem with being registered is the additional reporting requirements. Every quarter you will have to send a form to HM Customs, which details turnover, expenses and VAT to be reclaimed or paid. Frequent late submission of these returns or any resulting payments will result in substantial fines.

A decision will have to be made if the extra administrative headache is worth it for the potential financial rewards.

PAYROLL

Even when the record company is first set up, it will have employees: the directors. As you set up the systems you will probably also have a PA/secretary and perhaps an in-house accountant, someone to handle A&R, marketing or recording. As soon as you have even one employee, you will need to register the company as an employer with the Inland Revenue and start operating a PAYE system.

It is relatively easy to register and can normally be done over the telephone with a call to the local tax office who will guide you through the procedures. The Revenue then issue a pack which fully explains how to operate the payroll and how and when to account to them for the income tax and National Insurance deducted.

Of course, because you have to deduct tax before paying your employees and since you will also be liable for employer's National Insurance on the payments as well, it is a temptation to try and class all those working for you as self-employed. This would be unwise because companies are regularly inspected to ensure they are operating their payroll correctly, and on all relevant payments made to employees or company officers. The rules on what is classed as employment and what is self-employment are not straightforward and you should assume that anyone who works for you is employed unless you have reason to believe otherwise. Even then, it would be advisable to talk to your accountant before making the decision to treat them as self-employed.

Please note that any payments to the directors which are not dividends will almost certainly fall within the payroll system and you would have an extremely difficult job indeed convincing the Revenue that a director was a self-employed individual. It is for this reason that you should ensure a payroll system is put in place even if the only people who work for the record label are the directors. In any case, it is a good idea to pay the directors a salary and dividends rather than exclusively all dividends as the directors will not be paying any National Insurance contributions and this may then have an impact on their benefit entitlements.

Once the system is in place, the company is required to pay the tax and NI deducted to the Inland Revenue on a monthly basis. Similarly it is a legal requirement that the company provides its employees with a monthly (or weekly if relevant) payslip. At the end of the tax year, a P60 must be given to each employee detailing the total amounts paid and deducted in the year. A copy of the P60s, called the P14s, and a summary for the company (P35) must be submitted to the Revenue. Finally on a yearly basis, you must also submit P11d's for all employees earning over £8,500 and for all of the directors, which detail any benefits in kind received. Generally anything that the company pays for and the individual benefits from will be classified as a benefit.

You will probably find it useful to talk to an accountant, be it your own in-house or an outside professional, to get some advice on your payroll, or with a view to getting an outside payroll bureau to handle the whole function for you. These external bureaus are usually relatively inexpensive and will save you a great deal of time.

AGREEMENTS WITH ARTISTS: CUTTING THE FIRST DEAL

If the company is ready to begin trading as a record label, the first step is to sign an artist. The terms of the contract are crucial since there is no such thing as a standard record contract. We will try to explain the different possible financial arrangements. An example of a typical deal is as follows:

The record company will pay the artist an advance. This could be a substantial sum of money. However, it is not simply paid and forgotten about. The payment is a prepayment against the artist's future royalties. As the company sells records, the artist's share is calculated but this will not be paid over until all of the advances paid out have been recouped. It is worth remembering, however, that recoupable is not repayable. If the artist sells no records and there are no royalties, the advance is still not repayable.

There are certain other expenses that the record company will pay for which can be recouped against the artist's share of future royalties. These are typically expenses such as recording costs, video production costs and producer's royalties. In turn the record company pays some costs that it will not recoup from the artist such as promotional and marketing costs. Some further costs are usually negotiable. An example of this is where the band goes on tour to promote a record. The record company may pay 'tour support' to cover the loss the tour will almost invariably make. But is this recoupable against the artist's royalties? Some deals might say yes, others no, while others may say only 50% is recoupable.

It will be up to you to fight your corner to get the best deal you can. The artist will probably prefer to get as big an advance as possible since this guarantees that whether or not the record sells well, they will get some money for the time, effort and creativity they will be putting in. Likewise, with the company being new and cash flow a serious issue, you will want to avoid paying a higher advance than you have to, preferably no advance at all in fact. This can be achieved by offering a higher royalty rate as part of the deal. It will always be a delicate balancing act of course because you want to get the best deal you can but without losing the artist or damaging the relationship.

There are certain other types of deals you could consider doing. There are profit share deals for example where the company pays for all of the expenditure and then as the records are sold and the money rolls in, the artist and record label simply share the profit after all relevant expenses are paid off. This type of deal will often be very attractive for both the artist and the label where both are new to the business. You will probably not pay any advance to the artist but the share that the artist gets will be far more in the long term if the record is successful.

A new appraoch in recent times has been to tie in the artist to bigger deals where the record label will earn out of the artist's touring and merchandising income as well as the recording. Historically, it has been the case that these income streams were the sole preserve of the artist, but some of the current thinking is that the record company deserves a share because it is they who have spent all the money on marketing and promoting the artist to the point where they can sell out gigs and sell lots of merchandise. This type of deal is not for a new label, however, as the label would be expected to pay a larger advance and give very favourable royalty rates to the artists to convince them to give up these income streams.

The only other issue to remember concerns the way the artist royalty is calculated. A reasonable royalty percentage for a new artist would be 10–12%. But 10–12% of what? The price on which this percentage is calculated and the various adjustments that can be made to arrive at the final royalty figure is negotiable. Next we look at how the artist royalty is calculated.

RUNNING A LABEL

You have set up all the systems necessary to ensure that the company is prepared for the future. You've signed a couple of acts and have cut a few singles and maybe even an album. Everything seems to be going well. But there are still some issues that you will encounter that could prove to be potential banana skins if you do not know how to deal with them.

ACCOUNTING TO THE ARTISTS

In the recording contract there will be a requirement for the record company to account to the artist at regular intervals throughout the term of the contract. In most cases this will be twice a year, with each year split into two periods: January to June and July to December. The record company will have to account for all income received from record sales, etc., during this period within a stipulated deadline. The usual time frame is 90 days, meaning that royalty statements have to be delivered and any relevant royalty payments made, for example, by 30 September in respect of the period ended 30 June.

Although six monthly periods are usual, it is quite acceptable for the periods to be quarterly or even monthly. It is also perfectly acceptable for the time to account after the period's end to be 30 or 60 days instead of 90 days. These are all part of the terms to be negotiated in the record contract.

The agreed contract will detail the percentage royalty rate to be calculated on a particular 'base price'. The calculation of this base price, however, can be complicated. At present the 'base price' in the UK will be either a notional retail price arrived at after applying a percentage mark-up to the published dealer price or the dealer price itself. The reason for this is that it would be too unwieldy to try to use an actual retail price since the retail outlets will be selling the records at differing prices.

After arriving at a 'base price', you must then apply any deductions and rate reductions mentioned in the record contract. Commonly, packaging deduction would be one of these. The packaging deduction represents the cost of the packaging in which the record is sold and can be a substantial deduction, usually 25% for CDs. The reason for this deduction is for the record company to be able to recover the cost of the packaging including design and artwork that could have been quite expensive to create.

Other common adjustments before arriving at the final royalty due are:

- *white labels/ promotional copies* – there would generally not be a royalty to pay as they are viewed as a marketing tool;
- *12-inch singles* – there may well be a different royalty rate altogether on these;
- *reserves allowance* – this is a percentage of the royalties due which are held back to offset any faulty or broken product returned by retailers. The reserve deduction could be high if there are sales made on a 'sale or return' basis. Obviously these reserves are temporary and should be released to the artist within a couple of royalty periods.

Let's take a simple example:

- CDs sold to wholesalers at published dealer price during the period totalled £10,000.

- There is a deduction for packaging of 20% thus leaving £10,000 x 80% = £8,000.
- The artist's contracted royalty rate is 11%. £8,000 x 11%= £880.

So the amount of £880 is posted to the artist's account. If the artist has recouped their advance already, then this amount will be paid to the artist.

LICENSING TRACKS OR ALBUMS OVERSEAS

Licensing can take several forms. Basically it is allowing others to exploit a track or album master owned by your record company. In its simplest form, it will be a licence for tracks or albums to be released overseas in the format already produced by your record company. This obviously has huge benefits. Your fledgling label is unlikely to have the contacts or resources to release the tracks/albums in other territories and even if it did, it would almost certainly not have the market knowledge to be able to market and promote the release properly. It is appropriate in these circumstances therefore to come to an agreement with a foreign label for them to release the tracks/albums within their territory. Obviously for a very popular release this could mean doing several deals so that the track gets sold in all the major territories.

The licensing deal will be similar to the deal you have with your artist in that you will usually negotiate an advance and then you will receive royalties on the income the foreign label makes on the release. The promotional and marketing costs the other label incurs should not be recouped against any advance you receive, but if other costs are required, e.g. artwork on the packaging or further production costs, these may be recouped by the other label against your future royalties.

It is not uncommon for the label you license your tracks to, to sub-license them further, unless you specifically forbid it in the deal you do with them. For example you might license a track to a French label for Europe (excluding the UK), and they may sub-license the rights in Germany to a German label, etc.

You should bear in mind that for every extra label involved, the time it takes to receive your royalties would increase. For example, you will probably receive the income on UK sales on a quarterly or half yearly basis in arrears.

For example on sales of your track that a French label made in January, you will not receive a royalty until September, since their royalty period may be January to June and they have to account within 90 days of the end of that period. Obviously, if they were to sub-license it, you would probably have to wait a further six months to receive your share of that income.

It is very likely that someone will license a track for use on a compilation. Obviously be careful how this might affect sales of your own releases, but generally there is money to be made from this type of licensing. Again, it works in a similar way to other licensing in that you will receive an advance and then royalties on sales of the compilation.

The kind of deal you do is up to you, but you may decide to stipulate a limit on who or what they can sub-license.

VAT – CHANGE OF BASIS OF ACCOUNTING

The normal way of accounting for VAT to HM Customs & Excise is to calculate the total amount of VAT on sales you have invoiced and deduct the total amount of VAT you have suffered on expense invoices received to arrive at an amount payable/repayable to/from HM Customs.

However, there is an obvious problem with this. With this system, you may have to account to HM Customs for VAT on sales where you have not actually been paid the money yet. In the record industry there are circumstances where you may have to send a VAT invoice before you receive the VAT portion of the gross sales. HM Customs in this case will still insist that you pay the VAT over to them even though you have not received it.

However, there is a way around this for smaller businesses. HM Customs have a cash accounting scheme you may choose to join. The scheme allows you to account only on what you receive or pay, i.e. you must account on the basis of sales received and payments made. Obviously this will help the cash flow of the business considerably.

The scheme will be available until you believe turnover for the next twelve months will exceed £600,000 or the preceding twelve-month period has exceeded £750,000. Be careful, you will find that once you reach the threshold, the following quarter's VAT liability could be significant as effectively you have to pay over the VAT on all of your trade debtors immediately (offset of course by all of the VAT on trade creditors).

REPORTING REQUIREMENTS

Here's a checklist of documents you may need to submit.

- *VAT*: Quarterly filing of VAT returns, 30 days after the end of the quarterly period. The penalties for late filing rises for each late return and can be as much as 15% of the amount due.
- *PAYE*:
  - PAYE/NIC payable for each month is due by the 19th of the following month.
  - The P35 end of year return and the accompanying P14s are due by 19 May following the end of the 5 April tax year.
  - P11D forms are due in by 6 July following the end of the 5 April tax year.
- *Income tax*:
  - Self-assessment tax returns are due on 31 January following the end of the previous 5 April tax year. There is a £100 penalty for late submission, and if not submitted by the end of February, a 5% surcharge on amounts due.
  - Payments on account for each tax year are due on 31 January during that tax year and 31 July following the end of the tax year.
- *Corporation tax*:
  - Payment of outstanding amount is due by 9 months and 1 day after the end of the company's accounting period.
  - The Corporation tax return is due 12 months following the company's accounting year-end. There is a £100 penalty for late submission of the return.
- *Companies House*:
  - For private limited companies, the accounts must be filed by 10 months following the year-end. There is a £100 fine for late submission, rising periodically thereafter.
  - Annual returns must be submitted within 28 days of the return date.

It should be noted that all amounts payable will also attract interest if unpaid, and that some of the fines mentioned can be significantly higher if non-payment or non-submission continues or is repeated.

WITHHOLDING TAX

When you have musical artists flying all around the world performing, and labels receiving royalties from all over the world, the Inland Revenue and their equivalents in other territories feel it is imperative they ensure that no income will go untaxed. The way this is done is through withholding tax.

Whenever you make royalty payments to an overseas artist or record label, you should withhold UK income tax on it. The idea is that this is income gained from activities in the UK and so UK tax is chargeable. The amount to be withheld will be at the UK basic rate of tax. Therefore you pay the artist or label an amount net of the tax and then at the end of each quarter pay over to the Inland Revenue the tax amount along with a return form CT61. This can be avoided on payments to overseas labels if the overseas entity sends you a certification of their status as taxpayers, which has been authorised by the tax authorities of both countries. You can then pay them the full 100% of their royalties. This is because of the double taxation treaties in existence between the UK and various overseas territories.

If you are receiving money from overseas, the situation is reversed, with the overseas label withholding tax from any payments made. The percentage withheld will differ from territory to territory. Again, these amounts can often be mitigated by supplying the overseas entity with certification from the UK Revenue.

Even if you have suffered the withheld tax, all is not lost. You may still effectively be able to reclaim that money. The double taxation treaties between the various territories is there to ensure that tax is paid somewhere but they also exist so that if you have had tax withheld on your income you hopefully will not be taxed on it twice. If the company has made profits and is due to pay corporation tax, it may be able to offset any tax withheld against the corporation tax bill. This is subject to a few conditions:

- You must have a valid withholding tax certificate from the territory where the tax was withheld.
- You must have 'attributable' profits that relate to the income upon which tax was withheld. In layman's terms, you may have made £20k profits in the year, but if the Revenue can show that that £20k was attributable to UK income, for example, rather than the overseas income on which tax was withheld and on which they can show little profit was made, they may refuse to allow offset of any of the withholding tax or only a reduced amount.
- It must be a territory with which the UK has a double taxation treaty.

Even if you find that you cannot offset the withholding tax, you should remember it would still count as an allowable expense for tax purposes.

THE NEW MARKETS: INTERNET DISTRIBUTION

There is a continuing trend at present for more and more music to be distributed via the Internet. Unfortunately a lot of this distribution is not paid for and the record labels and artists get no money. There is, however, a growing number of players in the market who are providing legal downloading services to the general public. Some of these services follow a classical record company sales format such as Apple's service that offers downloads at 99 cents a track. Many in the industry, however, still feel that this is too expensive when for very little extra effort an individual can use Peer to Peer (P2P) software to get the same track for free.

There are other providers offering Internet distribution of tracks to the public on a subscription basis, say $30 or $50 a year. The problem of course with this idea is that it does not conform to the standard royalty model for record sales because there is no consistent base price per unit sold. Royalties are paid from a pot gleaned from advertising as well as subscriptions. A total pot each period is calculated and then distributed by apportioning it according to the tracks downloaded. Of course this means that in one period you could 'sell' 20 'units' and receive less than for another period when 10 units are 'sold', because the payment is reliant on how big the pot is and how many tracks other people are selling as well.

SELLING THE LABEL

If you decide to sell the label you will need to know how much the business is worth so that you can be prepared for any offers you might receive. It may also be that once the label has become successful, a major label offers you a deal whereby they purchase an interest in the business and possibly fund further development in return for an option to purchase the remaining shares at a later date, often five years, for a price based on an agreed formula. These types of deals are not by any means uncommon.

SALE OR LICENSING DEAL WITH A MAJOR

For some years now the major record companies have been cutting their A&R departments and budgets dramatically. They have decided that it is too risky to take on a large number of new acts, many of which will not sell many records and will lose money. Instead, they have been driven to spending their cash on marketing formulaic pop and their older established artists.

The question which then arises is where will the future 'established artists' come from? This is precisely where the small independent record labels come in. Independents are more flexible and closer to the ground and so invariably will be better at finding new talent. They can locate it, develop it and nurture it, releasing tracks and albums and helping the band build up a fan base.

At this point, the major could step in and sign the artist. Either the label is paid off for its contract with the artist or, unfortunately, the label has no contract with the artist and just gets cut out. Hopefully, the label may be able to strike a deal on the back catalogue they funded and helped record.

The other option, however, and one that will be especially true if the major has noticed a particular skill for finding talent, is to 'sign' the label itself. This operates by the major record company funding the label to go out, find and develop new artists. The deals vary. It may be that things carry on much as before but the major has a right to buy the contract of any artist on the books of the independent, or it may be that the major simply shares in the profits of the independent.

Besides the obvious financial rewards for the independents' founders of selling pieces of their company for a profit, there are other bigger potential rewards. Often the label will be left to its own (creative) devices and the major simply has the independent report to it on a regular basis as to its profit, activities and cash flow position. Their greater expertise in running a business could prove helpful. Furthermore, acts may be licensed to the major for overseas territories. The major will have good representation in all of the major territories and will be able to market the artists there in a way that the independent cannot.

Once the licensing deal has gone on for some time and been a success, the major may want to buy out the rest of the company, thus providing the original founders with a final exit strategy.

VALUING THE COMPANY AND ACCOUNTING FOR MASTERS

Normally when you attempt to value a company for a potential sale of shares, you would use one of two methods, depending on the most appropriate.

Less often the balance sheet method is used, where the valuation is based purely on the value of the assets. The balance sheet will show a value for items such as stock; fixed assets and debtor as well as the cash the business holds. By netting this off against any liabilities the company also has, you can arrive at a 'value' for what the company is worth. This method has a significant weakness, namely the value of the recording masters is, if internally generated, not shown as an asset on the balance sheet, but is likely to be one of the company's biggest assets. Furthermore no value is placed on the artist roster.

As mentioned, when valuing a record label there is one fairly unique problem. The masters and its royalty stream do not appear as assets in the company's balance sheet. The accounting standards by which company accounts must comply state that intangible assets (i.e. assets that are not physical such as intellectual property) cannot be capitalised in the balance sheet unless they have been acquired from a third party, or, internally generated, are part of a homogenous population and there is a reasonably active market for them. This unfortunately is not currently the case.

The only way that we can value masters therefore is by looking at the value using a profit basis. We have to investigate historically the amounts received in relation to this master, being careful to look only at the label's share of any such receipts, as a proportion will of course always be due to the artist. We need to make a reasoned judgement on what we believe the average yearly future income will be from the master and apply the relevant multiple to come to a value.

WHAT KILLS A COMPANY?

Even though we have gone through most of the issues you will face from the starting of the company through to your exit strategy, there are still other danger areas you need to be most aware of. These are the things that in my experience are the downfall of aspiring record labels:

- *Cash*. Forget everything else. This is the most important factor for any small business, if not any business. Your fledgling label will live or die by how it copes with its cash flows. It is inherent in the industry that you will have major problems at the outset with cash because of the long lead time before the costs you spend out bring in the income.

  Imagine this. You sign a band in January for £x,xxx. How long do you think it will be before you get the first piece of income that will go towards paying back that outlay?

  Well, after further recording costs and the release of a single perhaps and some white labels, the album is probably released six months later (and that's optimistic). So you release the album in July, having spent even more money on promotion. The first amount of money you will get in will not be until August and then you will probably start seeing bigger cash flows in September. Now obviously you won't just have one act. So how much money do you think you will have spent out before you even see a penny come back in?

  Therefore it's really important to keep a very close eye on how much cash you have (or more likely have not) got. And remember that on paper you could be making a profit, but you can easily still be facing liquidation because you don't have the cash to meet liabilities as they fall due. If you take away nothing else from reading this chapter, then remember at least this: *watch your cash!*

- The next biggest culprit for a young label going under is really linked to the above: *bad or non-existent forecasting*. When you're running a small business that has just started up, you really cannot just fly by the seat of your pants. It is vital before you start, to have a clear idea of where you're going and then translate that idea into a financial plan. Every detail should be considered and you should add sensitivity into the plan so that you'll be able to update it easily and see how any difference in what you envisaged and what actually happens will affect the future of the label. This means researching how much everything is going to cost and most importantly being realistic about how many record sales you will make. After all, if your plan assumes you are going to sell a million albums of your first release, then of course everything is going to look rosy. But your plan needs to show the worst-case scenario, and not just the best. You need to plan contingencies for both.

  This is really important for your financing arrangements. Assuming you're borrowing a reasonably large percentage of the capital to start the label, the financers will want to see a plan. But more crucially, they will be less than impressed if three months into the life of the business, you are going back to them cap in hand to ask for more funds because you didn't foresee this expense or that blip in the income.
- Another big failing of many record industry entrepreneurs is a lack of understanding of the costs of putting a record out. They understand precisely how much the recording will cost. They know all the ins and outs of production. But, then they go to release it and either one of two things happens: (a) the record just doesn't sell at all and a vast amount of money is lost; or (b) you realise that you have to promote the release hard but are amazed by exactly how much that costs. (Oh, so you don't just send a copy to some DJs and hope for the best?) Promoting a record is very expensive and you must be aware of just what kind of costs you will incur to push those releases:

- *Video costs*: You can easily spend £5,000 on a basic promo video. Carefully consider your cashflow position before you commit yourself to shooting a video early in the life of the label.
- *Plugging costs*: There are specialists who you hire to plug a song to the radio and TV stations. You will not get very far trying to ring them yourself unless you already have the contacts.
- *Promotion*: Promotion for the press and regional promotion is money well spent: without it you will find it hard to get the band mentioned in even the local papers. Without that buzz, it will be hard to sell records.
- *Touring costs*: This is the easiest one to forget about. Most laymen believe that when a band does a gig they actually make money out of it. This is simply not true for a great deal of touring. The bigger bands that can sell out 1,000+ seater venues and the small bands that don't record and just do pubs/clubs can make money from touring. For up and coming newly signed bands it is a promotional/marketing tool to help sell records and will nearly always make a loss that the record label is usually expected to cover! As you might imagine this could be substantial sums of money. Again budgeting the costs and forecasting the level of tour support required are very important.

- Money is going to be tight in the early days. Be organised. Get VAT returns in on time and do the accounts. Fines and penalties mount up and generally government agencies are quicker to prosecute you for non-payment of outstanding amounts than private suppliers.

1
2
3
4
5
6
7
8
9
10
11
12
13
14
15

ACCOUNTANTS

WILLOTT KINGSTON SMITH & ASSOCIATES
2nd Floor, Quadrant House, (Air Street Entrance), 80-82 Regent Street, London W1B 5RP
T: 020 7304 4646 F: 020 7304 4647
Email: ghowells@kingstonsmith.co.uk
Website: kingstonsmith.co.uk
Partner: Geraint Howells

BAKER TILLY
2 Bloomsbury Street, London WC1B 3ST
T: 020 7413 5100 F: 020 7413 5101
emedia@bakertilly.co.uk
Contact: Tim Berg

BBO STOY HAYWARD
8 Baker St, London W1 U 3LL
Website: bdo.co.uk
Partner: Michael Haan

CONROY & COMPANY
Suite 231, Kinetic Business Centre, Borehamwood, Herts WD6 4PJ
T: 020 8387 4121 F: 020 8387 4124
Email: conroyandcompany@aol.com
Snr Partner: A Conroy FCA, FSCA

DBM LTD
8 The Glasshouse, 49A Goldhawk Road, London W12 8QP
T: 020 8222 6628 F: 020 8222 6629
Email: david@dbmltd.co.uk
MD: David Hitchcock

DE LA HAYE ROYALTY SERVICES
76 High Street, Stony Stratford, Bucks MK11 1AH
T: 01908 568800 F: 01908 568890
Email: delahaye@btinternet.com
Website: delahaye.co.uk
MD: Roger La Haye

DELOITTE & TOUCHE
180 Strand, London WC2R 1BL
T: 020 7007 6023 F: 020 7007 0177
Email: cbradbrook@deloitte.co.uk
Website: deloitte.co.uk
Tax Partner, Music/ Media: Charles Bradbrook

DPC MEDIA
The Barn, Stisted Cottage Farm, Hollies Road, Bradwell, Braintree, Essex CM7 8DZ
T: 01376 551426 F: 01376 551787
Email: info@dpcmedia.demon.co.uk
Business Mgr: Dave Clark

EMTACS-ENTERTAINERS & MUSICIANS TAX & ACCOUNTANCY
61 Loughborough Road, West Bridgford, Nottingham NG2 7LA
T: 0115 981 5001 F: 0115 981 5005
Email: info@emtacs.com
Website: emtacs.com
Partner: Geoff Challinger

ERNST & YOUNG
Becket House, 1 Lambeth Palace Road, London SE1 7EU
T: 020 7951 2000 F: 020 7951 1345
Email: aflitcroft@uk.ey.com
Website: ey.com
Partner: Alan Flitcroft

1
2
3
4
5
6
7
8
9
10
11
12
13
14
15

HW FISHER & COMPANY
Acre House, 11-15 William Road,
London NW1 3ER
T: 020 7388 7000 F: 020 7380 4900
Email: info@hwfisher.co.uk
Website: hwfisher.co.uk
Partner: Martin Taylor

GELFAND RENNERT FELDMAN & BROWN
Langham House, 1b Portland Place,
London W1B 1GR
T: 020 7636 1776 F: 020 7636 6331
Email: info@grfb-uk.com
Stephen Marks, Robert Perez

HARRIS & TROTTER
65 New Cavendish Street, London
W1G 7LS
T: 020 7467 6300 F: 020 7467 6363
Email: mail@harrisandtrotter.co.uk

HARWICK & MORRIS
4 New Burlington Street, London
W1S 2JG
T: 020 7287 9940 F: 020 7434 9817
Email: stephanie@hardwickandmorris.co.uk
Website: hardwickandmorris.co.uk
Partner: Stephanie Hardwick

GEORGE HAY & CO
83 Cambridge Street, London
SW1V 4PS
T: 020 7630 0582 F: 020 7630 1502
Email: george.hay@virgin.net
The Snr Partner

HORWATH CLARK WHITEHILL
25 New Street Square, London
EC4A 3LN
T: 020 7353 1577 F: 020 7583 1720
Email: norkettt@horwathcw.co.uk
Website: horwathcw.com
Partner: Tim Norkett

JOHNSONS CHARTERED ACCOUNTANTS
Lancashire House, 217 Uxbridge Road,
London W13 9AA
T: 020 8567 3451 F: 020 8840 6823
Email: mail@johnsonsca.com
Website: johnsonsca.com
Partner: Shaukat Murad

OJ KILKENNY & COMPANY
6 Lansdowne Mews, London W11 3BH
T: 020 7792 9494 F: 020 7792 1722
Email: dmoss@ojkilkenny.co.uk
David Moss

KPMG LLP
Aquis Court, 31 Fishpool St, St Albans
AL3 4RF
T: 01727 733063 F: 01727 733001
Email: charles.lestrangemeakin@kpmg.co.uk
Website: kpmg.com
Dir: Charles Le Strange Meakin

LEWIS-SIMLER
4 Prince Albert Road, London NW1 7SN
T: 020 7482 4424 F: 020 7482 4623
Email: advice@eles.co.uk
Partner: GJ Simler

MARTIN GREENE RAVDEN
55 Loudoun Road, St John's Wood,
London NW8 0DL
T: 020 7625 4545 F: 020 7625 5265
Email: mgr@mgr.co.uk
Website: mgr.co.uk

MAZARS NEVILLE RUSSELL – CHARTERED ACCOUNATNTS
24 Bevis Marks, London EC3A 7NR
T: 020 7377 1000 F: 020 7377 8931
Website: mazars-nr.co.uk
Head of IP Services

MUSIC ROYALTIES LTD
18 Cavendish Close, Hayes, Middlesex UB4 8AJ
T: 020 8569 3936
Email: david@musicroyalties.co.uk
Dir: David Rayment

LLOYD PIGGOTT
Blackfriars House, Parsonage, Manchester M3 2JA
T: 0161 833 0346 F: 0161 832 0045
Email: info@lloydpiggott.co.uk
Website: lloydpiggott.co.uk
Tax Associate: Paula Abbott

PORTMAN MUSIC SERVICES LTD
38 Osnaburgh Street, London NW1 3ND
T: 01962 732033 F: 01962 732032
Email: maria@portmanmusicservices.com
Royalty & Copyright Mgr: Maria Comiskey

PRAGER AND FENTON
Midway House, 27-29 Cursitor Street, London EC4A 1LT
T: 020 7831 4200 F: 020 7831 5080
Email: mgoldberg@pragerfenton.co.uk
Website: pragerfenton.com
Partners: Martin Goldberg

PRICEWATERHOUSECOOPERS
1 Embankment Place, London WC2N 6RH
T: 020 7583 5000 F: 020 7822 4652
Email: firstname.lastname@uk.pwcglobal.com
Website: pwcglobal.co.uk
Head of UK E&M: Murray Legg

RCO - ROYALTY COMPLIANCE ORGANISATION
4 Crescent Stables, 139 Upper Richmond Rd, London SW15 2TN
T: 020 8789 6444 F: 020 8785 1960
Email: ask@TheRcO.co.uk
Website: rcoonline.com
Partners: Mike Skeet, Gill Sharp

GUY RIPPON ORGANIZATION
24 Pepper Street, London SE1 0EB
T: 020 7928 9777 F: 020 7928 9222
Email: guy@guyrippon.org
Website: guyrippon.org
MD: Guy Rippon

RSM ROBSON RHODES
186 City Road, London EC1V 2NU
T: 020 7251 1644 F: 020 7250 0801
Email: marketing@rsmi.co.uk
Website: rsmi.co.uk
Dir of Communications

RYAN & CO
4F, Shirland Mews, London W9 3DY
T: 020 8960 0961 F: 020 8960 0963
Email: ryan@ryanandco.com
Website: ryanandco.com
Chartered Accountant: Cliff Ryan

SAFFERY CHAMPNESS
Lion House, Red Lion Street, London WC1R 4GB
T: 020 7841 4000 F: 020 7841 4100
Email: nkelsey@saffery.com
Website: saffery.com
Partners: Nick Kelsey, Nick Gaskell

SLOANE & CO
36-38 Westbourne Grove, Newton Road, London W2 5SH
T: 020 7221 3292 F: 020 7229 4810
Email: mail@sloane.co.uk
Website: sloane.co.uk
David Sloane

TENON GODFREY ALLAN
66 Chiltern St, London W1U 4JT
T: 020 7535 1400 F: 020 7535 1401
Email: julian.hedley@tenongroup.com
Website: tenongroup.com
MD: Julian Hedley

WYNDHAMS
177 High Street, Harlesden, London NW10 4TE
T: 020 8961 3889 F: 020 8961 4620
Email: right@supanet.com
Partner: David Landau

HIGHLY RECOMMENDED ACCOUNTANTS

Willott Kingston Smith & Associates

Hardwick & Morris

Baker Tilly

Deloitte & Touche

BBO Stoy Hayward

APPENDIX

PRODUCTION CHECKLIST

1. MAKING THE SINGLE/ALBUM

Process from pre-production, recording, and mastering.

- *Writing*
- *Demoing:* sometimes useful for development of the track
- *Pre-production*: preparation for recording, including finalising arrangement/ instrumentation and rehearsal
- *Recording*
- *Editing:* including 'comping' the vocals if necessary; may be carried out during recording
- *Mixing*
- *Mastering*

2. PEOPLE INVOLVED IN CREATING THE SINGLE/ALBUM

IN THE STUDIO:

- *Writer(s)* – could include the artist and/or producer
- *Artist:* solo or band
- *Producer* – oversees whole process and uses knowledge, experience and skill to transform rough sketch of song into well-arranged, professional

recording; different producers will be more hands on than others; some set up, record and mix the whole record themselves, physically arranging the equipment and doing the 'knob-twiddling'; others employ engineers or specialist mixers to do parts of the process and will have an overseeing role, directing those involved; generally has big creative input to song, instrumentation, arrangement, sound and mixing of the record; role is similar to that of film or theatre director

- *Programmer*: creates backing tracks, beats and loops using samples, synths and computers. Programming can be an integral part of the writing process, or programmers can be brought in at a later stage to improve or add to the basic instrumentation. Often writers or producers do their own programming
- *Session musicians* (if required): could include artist's regular band, or musicians recruited specially for the session and/or string sections/orchestras
- *Recording engineer*: sets up equipment necessary for recording and operates it during recording; highly technical; often producer will carry out this role himself rather than bringing someone else in specially
- *Mix engineer/mixer*: mixes track, balancing different instruments and elements, applying equalisation, compression and effects; also sets up equipment necessary for mixing and operates it; can be quite a creative role, often transforming the song
- *Pro-Tools editor*: it's common to have an assistant carry out editing and other tasks within Pro-Tools or other digital recording software being used; may well be carried out by programmer or assistant engineer
- *Assistant engineer/tape op*: provides basic assistance with setting up, wiring and operating equipment – and makes tea
- *Arranger/conductor*: necessary if strings or orchestra involved
- *Mastering engineer*: masters stereo mix; the mix created by the mixer is supplied to the mastering studio; during mastering process, engineer will make very fine adjustments to sound of mix by applying equalisation and compression, giving mix professional sound and quality necessary for it to be released on a record or broadcast on radio/TV; producer usually attends mastering

- *Studio manager*: liases with record companies and management companies, organises booking of studio and oversees sessions in studio to make sure everything runs smoothly

AT THE RECORD COMPANY:

- *A&R person*: initially responsible for signing the artist; should have strong involvement in recording process providing artistic input/feedback and monitoring progress of the tracks to ensure they meet the record company's desires and that they are commercially suitable; will often have input into choice of producer, mixer, studio, musicians, etc.; usually negotiates key terms for engaging producer or mixer and approve the budget; obviously involved in a lot of other tasks outside recording process, e.g. promotion, live performances, record releases, etc.
- *Production co-ordinator*: oversees logistical side of the process, liaising between all parties and ensuring that everything is organised and runs smoothly; may also create/manage budget; role may be carried out by producer management company
- *Business affairs person*: deals with negotiation of contract between record company and artists/producers/mixers, sometimes in conjunction with external lawyer
- *Finance/accounts*: process all payments

AT MANAGEMENT COMPANIES:

- *Artist manager*: organises everything on artist's side of things and represents artist's interests in the whole process; liaises with all other parties; will usually approve recording budget, choice of producer/mixer, terms for engaging producer/mixer. May be involved in recording process to ensure that artist is satisfied with outcome as well as record company, as artist's and record company's interests can often differ
- *Producer manager/project manager*: will actively seek work for producers and manage development of their career; will liaise with all other parties and negotiate producer's/mixer's terms of engagement; will often oversee organisation of project

- *Production co-ordinators*: often production co-ordination is partly or wholly carried out by producer's management company rather than record company
- *Finance/accounts*: invoice record company for fees due and look after finances for artist/producer

OTHER EXTERNAL PEOPLE

- *Artist's lawyer*: negotiates contracts for artist
- *Record company's lawyer*: sometimes record company uses external lawyer to negotiate contracts on its behalf
- *Producer's lawyer:* negotiates contracts for producer
- *Session fixer*: will supply and organise session musicians/string sections/orchestras
- *Accountants (artist's/producer's*: sometimes artist/producer or their management company use external lawyer to oversee their finances

3. PRODUCTION SAFETY NETS

The following are the precautions Stephen Budd Management establish around the producer and project for the single/album to be delivered on time and on budget.

Typically budget management and time-frame are down to the producer, with assistance from their management company and the record company. If circumstances change during the project so that the budget or delivery date are affected the producer (or their management company) will need to liaise with the record company to get approval for the new budget/timescale. Key factors to ensuring a project is delivered on time and on budget are:

- creating a realistic budget and timescale from the start;
- closely monitoring progress and costs during the project; and
- making changes where necessary and working quickly.

We normally incorporate a 10% safety margin or contingency into our budgets to cover unforeseen costs.

MUSIC INDUSTRY ORGANISATIONS

AIM (THE ASSOCIATION OF INDEPENDENT MUSIC)
Lamb House, Church Street,
Chiswick, London W4 2PD
T: 020 8994 5599 F: 020 8994 5222
Email: info@musicindie.com
Website: musicindie.org
Chief Executive: Alison Wenham

ASCAP (AMERICAN SOC. OF COMPOSERS, AUTHORS & PUBL)
8 Cork Street, London W1S 3LJ
T: 020 7439 0909 F: 020 7434 0073
Email: initial+lastname@ascap.com
Website: ascap.com
Karen Hewson

ASSOCIATION OF BRITISH JAZZ MUSICIANS
First Floor, 132 Southwark
St, London SE1 0SW
T: 020 7928 9089 F: 020 7401 6870
Email: admin@jazzservices.org.uk
Website: jazzservices.org.uk
Hon Sec: Chris Hodgkins

BAND REGISTER (BANDREG.COM)
PO Box 594, Richmond,
Surrey TW10 6YT
T: 07973 297011
Email: peter@bandreg.com
Website: bandreg.com
MD: Peter Whitehead

BARD (BRITISH ASSOCIATION OF RECORD DEALERS)
1st Floor, Colonnade House, 2 Westover
Road, Bournemouth, Dorset BH1 2BY
T: 01202 292063 F: 01202 292067
Email: admin@bardltd.org
Website: bardltd.org
Dir Gen: Bob Lewis

BMI (BROADCAST MUSIC INCORPORATED)
84 Harley House, Marylebone Road,
London NW1 5HN
T: 020 7486 2036 F: 020 7224 1046
Email: London@bmi.com
Website: bmi.com

BPI (BRITISH PHONOGRAPHIC INDUSTRY)
Riverside Building, County Hall,
Westminster Bridge Rd,
London SE1 7JA
T: 020 7803 1300 F: 020 7803 1310
Email: general@bpi.co.uk
Website: bpi.co.uk
Dir Gen: Andrew Yeates

GUILD OF INTERNATIONAL SONGWRITERS & COMPOSERS
Sovereign House, 12 Trewartha Road,
Praa Sands, Penzance, Cornwall
TR20 9ST
T: 01736 762826 F: 01736 763328
Email: songmag@aol.com
Website: songwriters-guild.co.uk
Membership Sec: Carole A Jones

IFPI (INT FEDERATION OF THE PHONOGRAPHIC INDUSTRY)
IFPI Secretariat, 54-62 Regent Street,
London W1B 5RE
T: 020 7878 7900 F: 020 7878 7950

Email: info@ifpi.org
Website: ifpi.org
Dir of Comms: Adrian Strain

INTERNATIONAL MUSIC MANAGERS FORUM (IMMF)
1 York St, London W1U 6PA
T: 020 7935 2446 F: 020 7486 6045
Email: nicka@immf.net
Website: immf.net
Exec Dir: Nick Ashton-Hart

IRMA
IRMA House, 1 Corrig Avenue,
Dun Laoghaire, Co Dublin, Ireland
T: +353 1 280 6571
F: +353 1 280 6579
Email: info@irma.ie
Website: irma.ie
Dir Gen: Dick Doyle

MCPS (MECHANICAL COPYRIGHT PROTECTION SOCIETY LTD)
Copyright House, 29-33 Berners Street,
London W1T 3AB
T: 020 7580 5544 F: 020 7306 4455
Email: info@mcps.co.uk
Website: mcps.co.uk
Exec Officer: Terri Anderson

MERCURY MUSIC PRIZE
3 Grand Union Centre,
London W10 5AS
T: 020 8964 9964 F: 020 8969 7249
Email: (firstname)@mercuryprize.co.uk
Website: mercurymusicprize.com
Dir: Kevin Milburn

MILLWARD BROWN UK
Olympus Avenue, Tachbrook Park,
Warwick CV34 6RJ
T: 01926 826610 F: 01926 826209
Email: bob.barnes@uk.millwardbrown.com
Website: millwardbrown.com
Charts Dir: Bob Barnes

MMF (MUSIC MANAGERS FORUM)
1 York Street, London W1U 6PA
T: 0870 8507 800 F: 0870 8507 801
Email: office@ukmmf.net
Website: ukmmf.net
Gen Sec: James Sellar

MMF
North Fourways House,
57 Hilton Street, Manchester M1 2EJ
T: 0161 228 3993 F: 0161 228 3773
Email: north@ukmmf.net
Website: ukmmf.net
Project Manager: Stuart Worthington

MOBO AWARDS
22 Stephenson Way, London NW1 2HD
T: 020 7419 1800 F: 020 7419 1600
Email: info@mobo.com
Website: mobo.com
Founder: Kanya King MBE

NORDOFF-ROBBINS MUSIC THERAPY
Studio A2, 1927 Building,
2 Michael Road, London SW6 2AD
T: 020 7371 8404 F: 020 7371 8206
Email: lindamac@nrfr.co.uk
Website: silverclef.com
Appeals Manager: Linda McLean

THE OFFICIAL UK CHARTS COMPANY LTD
4th Floor, 58/59 Great Marlborough St,
London W1F 7JY
T: 020 7478 8500 F: 020 7478 8519